LOSING HEARTS AND MINDS

STANFORD BRITISH HISTORIES

Edited by Priya Satia

Losing Hearts and Minds

RACE, WAR, AND EMPIRE IN SINGAPORE AND MALAYA, 1915–1960

Kate Imy

STANFORD UNIVERSITY PRESS
Stanford, California

Stanford University Press
Stanford, California

This book has been partially underwritten by the Peter Stansky Publication Fund in British Studies. For more information on the fund, please see www.sup.org/stanskyfund.

Printed in the United States of America on acid-free, archival-quality paper.

Library of Congress Cataloging-in-Publication Data

Names: Imy, Kate, 1987- author.
Title: Losing hearts and minds : race, war, and empire in Singapore and
    Malaya, 1915-1960 / Kate Imy.
Other titles: Race, war, and empire in Singapore and Malaya, 1915-1960 |
    Stanford British histories.
Description: Stanford, California : Stanford University Press, [2024] |
    Series: Stanford British histories | Includes bibliographical references
    and index.
Identifiers: LCCN 2023044745 (print) | LCCN 2023044746 (ebook) | ISBN
    9781503634626 (cloth) | ISBN 9781503639850 (paperback) | ISBN
    9781503639867 (ebook)
Subjects: LCSH: Anti-imperialist movements—Southeast Asia—History—20th
    century. | Singapore—History—1867-1942. | Singapore—History—Japanese
    occupation, 1942-1945. | Singapore—History—1945-1963. |
    Malaya—History—British rule, 1867-1942. | Malaya—History—Japanese
    occupation, 1942-1945. | Malaya—History—Malayan Emergency, 1948-1960.
    | Great Britain—Colonies—Asia—Race relations—History—20th century.
Classification: LCC DS610.5 .I49 2024 (print) | LCC DS610.5 (ebook) | DDC
    959.5/03—dc23/eng/20231220
LC record available at https://lccn.loc.gov/2023044745
LC ebook record available at https://lccn.loc.gov/2023044746

Cover design: Michele Wetherbee
Cover photograph: White women recreating the vigorous physical labor they per-
formed while interned by the Japanese military in the Second World War. Argus
(Melbourne, Vic.) Australia. Department of Information. Courtesy of State Library
Victoria, www.slv.vic.gov.au
Typeset by Newgen in Adobe Caslon Pro Regular 9.75/14

For Tinny

CONTENTS

ACKNOWLEDGMENTS

I wrote this book when my own faith in and love for certain institutions evaporated. Doing so meant relying heavily on a network of care and support to which I owe my life. I owe deep gratitude to Michelle Moyd, Melissa Shaw, Sue Grayzel, and Tammy Proctor, who were a lifeline during the COVID-19 pandemic. They not only provided invaluable feedback on most of the chapters but always lent a helping hand when things got tough. They are a shining model of what intellectual collaboration can and should look like. Most institutions would improve by following their model of genuine leadership and mutual support.

Teresa Segura-Garcia, Erica Wald, and Elena Valdemari have been incredible collaborators for many years, enabling this project to develop from its earliest seeds. Their intellectual community and friendship took us to London, Zürich, Barcelona, and beyond and is something that I will always treasure. Selections from chapters 4 and 5 will be published in our forthcoming edited volume with Leiden University Press, *Bodies Beyond Binaries in Colonial and Postcolonial Asia*. Sections from chapter 4 have also been published as "Dream Mother: Race, Gender, and Intimacy in Japanese-Occupied Singapore," *Journal of Southeast Asian Studies* 52, 3 (2021): 464–491.

I am also grateful to the many brilliant, empathetic scholars, including Sara Black, Chris Bischof, King James, Courtney Doucette, Audrey Thorstad, Allison Abra, Amy Milne-Smith, and Nancy Stockdale, who provided a sympathetic ear on the road to publishing this book. Seth Koven, Bonnie Smith, Lynn Hollen Lees, Tan Tai Yong, and Sue Thompson were invaluable mentors who helped me secure the research funding necessary for this international project. David

Baillargeon and Jeremy Taylor have done excellent work renewing interest in the Malayan Emergency and included me in many productive conversations.

Some institutions take seriously their role as leaders and community builders that enable and support research, collaboration, and intellectual growth. The North American Conference of British Studies has been an invaluable ally to scholars and made it possible for me to attend their national conference, present research, and maintain my networks with brilliant scholars. I am also grateful to the audiences and organizers of conferences and events that provided generous intellectual forums to refine the ideas of this work, including: the Society for Military History; the International Society for Cultural History; the Annual Conference on South Asia; Universitat Pompeu Fabra's Research Group on Empires, Metropolises, and Extra-European Societies (GRIMSE); the University of Texas at Arlington; the International Society for First World War Studies; and Monash University Malaysia's Malayan Emergency in Film and Literature Workshop. The American Historical Association kindly supported this project with a Bernadotte E. Schmitt Grant for Research in European, African, or Asian History. This funding enabled me to complete the remaining research required for this project despite the travel limitations necessitated by a global pandemic.

The Lee Kong Chian NUS-Stanford Fellowship on Southeast Asia made it possible for me to spend seven months researching at the National University of Singapore and Stanford University. These intellectual communities, including the Asia-Pacific Research Center supported by Donald K. Emmerson, Kristen Lee, and Lisa Lee, were invaluable resources for collaboration and intellectual exchange. While in Singapore, I benefited immensely from the guidance and support of Chang Zhi'An Andrew and enjoyed many fruitful conversations with Maitrii Aung-Thwin, Enze Han, Tapsi Mathur, Jess Hinchy, and Faizah Zakaria, among others. At Stanford, meeting Priya Satia, after many years of admiration, not only sated my inner fangirl over her enviable breadth and depth of research but also started the conversations that would lead to the publication of this book.

My first book, *Faithful Fighters*, benefited from the support, professionalism, and clarity offered by Stanford University Press, so I eagerly returned with this manuscript. While researching at Stanford, I was fortunate to meet Margo Irvin to enjoy a fruitful conversation about the exciting direction of British History at Stanford University Press. In this, Priya Satia has continued to be an invaluable ally and mentor. Her guidance for revising the manuscript, together with that of the anonymous reviewers, provided detailed and encouraging notes that improved the manuscript. Peter Stansky's support of Stanford University Press, and his kind words after *Faithful Fighters* won the prize named in his honor, have been a guiding light for how senior scholars can support fellow scholars and the profession.

I also owe a major debt to the staff at numerous archives. Dolores Ho not only provided me with amazing resources at the National Army Museum in Waiouru but also shared her life story of living through the Emergency. Fiona Tan at the National University of Singapore provided me with immensely valuable assistance prior to my arrival in Singapore to make my research as efficient and rewarding as possible. Doug Henderson at the Gurkha Museum in Winchester ensured that I made the most of their rich personal and published collections. Additionally, I owe considerable debt to archivists and staff at the Imperial War Museum, Australian War Memorial, National Archives of Australia, National Library of Australia, British Library, National Army Museum, Wrexham Archives, Bodleian Library, the Hoover Institution, the UK National Archives (Kew), the National Library of New Zealand, the Liddell Hart Centre for Military Archives, and the Cambridge University Libraries. Without their tireless efforts, scholarly work could not exist.

The University of North Texas provided financial support for this project through the Scholarly and Creative Award (SCA), College of Liberal Arts and Social Sciences (CLASS), UNT History Department, Creative and Research and Enhancement Activity Time for Engagement (CREATE) Grant, and a Junior Research Fellowship.

In the past several years, most people, including academics, authors, and intellectuals, found themselves subject to varying degrees of institutional horror as a result of the COVID-19 pandemic. When things got bad, we realized very quickly which bonds were real and which were merely smoke screens for overwork and coercion. Institutional corruption, and the money required for research, occasionally means that institutions can provide financial assistance while also enabling abuse, overwork, and inequitable pay, pushing "beneficiaries" to the point of exhaustion and mental collapse. As a result, I have come to value other connections so deeply.

I am grateful to a burgeoning network of screenwriters and teachers who have reignited my joy and passion for writing. The Outfest Screenwriting Lab, Cinestory, and Stowe Lab, as well as teachers and writers at UCLA Extension, Writing Pad, Script Anatomy, and Sundance Collab, provided excellent forums for artists to workshop and collaborate. Michael Barlow and Geraldine Inoa got me to think about my writing differently while providing invaluable mentorship. I take immense inspiration from the Writer's Guilds of America (East and West), which show with actions as well as words how important it is to protect not only the craft of writing but also the writers who tell the stories that keep us alive.

I am most grateful to my family—Collins, Imys, Polings, and beyond. I lost many in the years it took to complete this project and have a deeper and richer love for them and for those still with us. Megan, Nick, and Kitty Elizarraraz; Tara, Jason, and Remi Collins-L'Heureux; and Charlie, Benji, Cody, my parents, David, Brenda, Katherine, Danny, Taylor, Dylan, and Kamryn have reminded me many times that I am not alone. I hold in my heart those dear to us whom we lost, including Aunt Phyllis, Uncle Mike, "Gumball," Tinny, and Dr. Bart. Most of all, I am grateful to Kenneth for weathering the impossible storm of the past years. Together we built a life capable of sustaining six cats and dogs while I endeavored to reimagine my career as a writer without falling into the familiar traps of overwork and underpay. I hope that I can pay it forward for our family and for other writers without the same support. Many thanks to Pinky, Tars, Jack, Ladybird, Liza, Little Miss, and Princess for many reassuring snuggles and smiles.

This work was a labor of love and anguish completed, against the odds, without the security of an academic salary. Finishing it is an investment in the belief that we can put people, and their stories, before institutional indifference. I hope that one day we can build a world in which power does not bring death. The people cited in these acknowledgements give me hope that we have the ingredients to build a better world. We just need more institutions with the courage to enable rather than thwart creativity, passion, and mutual care.

ABBREVIATIONS

AWM—Australian War Memorial
BL—British Library
CPM—Communist Party of Malaya (alternative to MCP)
CT—Communist Terrorist
EIC—East India Company
INA—Indian National Army
IOR—India Office Records, British Library
IWM—Imperial War Museum
KMT—Kuomintang (Chinese Nationalist Party)
MCP—Malayan Communist Party
MPAJA—Malayan People's Anti-Japanese Army
NAI—National Archives of India
NAM—National Army Museum
NAS—National Archives of Singapore
NML—Nehru Memorial Library
RIMC—Royal Indian Military College
RJR—Rani of Jhansi Regiment
TGM—The Gurkha Museum (Winchester)

Introduction

When Dolores Ho was a young girl in the military station of Taiping, she worried that celebrating Chinese holidays by hanging red cloth might flag her family as communists. This could have been a deadly declaration during Britain's prolonged anti-communist campaign, known as the "Malayan Emergency" (1948–1960). Tamil rubber tappers frequently told her about Chinese civilians who "disappeared." Her brother considered joining the military to protect their family from violence. Living through the "Emergency," they found, extended the trauma of the Second World War into the "postwar" period. During that prior conflict, Ho's family felt "abandoned" when British leaders surrendered Singapore to the Japanese military in February 1942.[1] Over the next three years, they lived in chicken coops and searched for food along storm drains to avoid Japanese soldiers, who targeted Chinese civilians for violence. British forces' similar tendency to single out Chinese civilians after reoccupying Malaya and Singapore felt like another betrayal. For soldiers and civilians living under colonialism, war often provided continuity, rather than change, for the racialized traumas of military occupation.

Losing Hearts and Minds analyzes soldier and civilian experiences of war and anti-colonialism in Singapore and Malaya from the First World War to the Malayan Emergency. In so doing, it examines the colonial roots of military claims to win civilian "hearts and minds" in war. Many associate this phrase with U.S. military strategies during the Cold War, after Presidents John F. Kennedy and Lyndon B. Johnson used it in this context. It gained renewed relevance when President George W. Bush said it to justify the military invasion of Iraq. It then appeared in the U.S. Army and Marine Corps' revised "Counterinsurgency Field Manual" in 2006, citing the Malayan Emergency as a successful counterinsurgency campaign.[2] However, the phrase gained its martial popularity due to British, rather than American, militarism. Director of Operations and High Commissioner of Malaya Sir Gerald Templer (1951–1954) famously claimed that the key to success in the Malayan Emergency "lies not in pouring more troops into the jungle but in the hearts and minds of the people."[3] Still, the Malayan Emergency demanded an extensive military presence in the jungle, including soldiers from Nepal, Australia, New Zealand, East Africa, and Fiji. *Losing Hearts and Minds*, therefore, asks how colonial subjects' experiences of imperialism and war shaped Britain's stated emphasis on fostering positive soldier-civilian relations. It shows that the "hearts and minds" approach remade and replicated colonial racial and gender hierarchies, increasing rather than reducing violence against civilians.

Across multiple conflicts, British leaders tried to claim soldier and civilian loyalties despite the challenges of anti-colonial rebellion, military occupation, and the rise of communism. As a result, Singapore and Malaya became sites of some of the most impactful military and anti-colonial conflicts of the twentieth century. A 1915 mutiny of Indian troops in Singapore revealed Indian soldiers' immersion in global anti-colonial networks and their ease in finding supporters among European, Malay, and Chinese civilians.[4] The 1942 "fall" of Singapore represented a lasting blow to British imperial and military power as some colonial subjects aided the Japanese invasion and occupation.[5] The Malayan Emergency (1948–1960) laid the groundwork for global wars of decolonization and anti-communism, bringing soldiers around the globe into contact with civilians weary from endless war.[6] These recurring conflicts forced European, Indigenous, Chinese, Malay, and Indian civilians to resist or collaborate with British and Commonwealth soldiers, rebellious Indian troops (1915 and 1942), invading Japanese combatants (1941–1945), and communists (1948–1960). British military leaders tried—but largely failed—to win the "hearts and minds" of colonial subjects many times before Templer popularized this famous phrase. As a result, *Losing Hearts and Minds* examines the fraught history of war and empire that made British leaders like Templer believe that "winning hearts and minds" was innovative, necessary, and possible.

One major impediment to earning and maintaining civilian confidence was that British rule in Asia hinged on racial hierarchy. Farish Noor and Peter Carey have argued that "theories of racial difference and white supremacy were at the very heart of the empire-building process in the nineteenth century." As a result, nineteenth-century conflicts in Southeast Asia were "*race* wars" that "were conceived, rationalized, fought or justified at times on the basis of racial ideas and understandings."[7] Yet "race" is a complex term that deserves further analysis. As many scholars have argued, race is not a fixed biological reality but rather a shifting and relational category of power, similar to and intersecting with gender, class, and sexuality.[8] This was especially true in colonial Asia, where diverse colonial populations vied for opportunity despite limits on their upward mobility. According to Kristy Walker, "race became the primary category of social analysis in Southeast Asia, governing employment opportunities and public space."[9] Yet racial stratification was also gendered. For Evelyn Brooks Higginbotham, in "societies where racial demarcation is endemic to their sociocultural fabric and heritage, gender identity is inextricably linked to and even determined by racial identity."[10] British leaders in Singapore and Malaya heavily relied on gender-segregated military and labor recruitment, as well as racial stratification, to define people's value and limit their access to power.

For Ann Laura Stoler, racial categorization is also complicated by the fact that terms like "colonizer" and "colonized" were not fixed and self-evident, but rather "an historically shifting pair of social categories."[11] Many white settlers brought their own ideas of Britishness or Europeanness but also adopted norms and styles that would amplify their difference from the colonized. In turn, definitions of "British" or "European" identity proved complex. Some understood "British" to be an inclusive term that forged unity across the empire. This included colonial subjects and soldiers from Asia, Africa, and the Caribbean with no direct family ties to, or experiences in, Britain but who still understood themselves as "British" because of their inclusion within the empire.[12] This was especially common in the military, where the idea of the imperial, and later Commonwealth, family helped secure personnel and material support from colonies in wartime.[13] At the same time, white settlers and their descendants in Canada, Australia, New Zealand, and South Africa increasingly embraced the term "British" to distinguish themselves from racialized Indigenous and migrant populations, as well as those living in predominantly Black or Asian colonies.[14] Whiteness, in these contexts, became a precondition of "British" belonging, making anyone not white implicitly not British. "European," similarly, was a malleable rather than fixed term.[15] Entering elite clubs, cinemas, and cafés often meant an ability to pass as white. As a result, many British and Asian soldiers and civilians used "British" and "European" to mark the white colonial population as separate and distinct from Asian colonial subjects. They often extended these terms to white Americans, Australians, and New Zealanders, further emphasizing Britishness and Europeanness as whiteness. Given that not all Britons or Europeans were white, this work often contextualizes the terms European or British by adding "white" before them, to signify people benefiting from the status of whiteness. "European," "white," and "British" were all contested terms that had multiple meanings. Yet whiteness, in this period, carried currency for those who claimed it.

Another difficulty of early-twentieth-century racial categorization is that it often existed as a binary between Black and white. "Native" became shorthand for colonial leaders to cast all racialized subjects as possessing similar traits, flattening their identities and making them easier to rule. As a result, the complex meanings of "Asian" often get left out of the conversation. Anne Anlin Cheng has argued for reclaiming the term "yellow" to discuss racialization of Asian people in the present.[16] In the period discussed, however, "yellow" was a common slur used against Asian migrants.[17] Many in Southeast Asia understood it as a pejorative term that denied them connections to a specific homeland or claims to Britishness.[18] It signified them as "colonial others," betraying promises of inclusive Britishness that transcended racial differences. It also flagged the "otherness" of people with both European and Asian ("Eurasian") heritage, underlining their tenuous connections to Britishness, Europeanness, and whiteness. As a result, when discussing racial bars or racial exclusion along a color line, I use the term "Asian" while recognizing that the term has limitations. Writing during the Emergency, Eurasian doctor and author Han Suyin explained that:

> Asians now spoke of themselves as *we-Asians*, as if Asia were an entity, when really it was a huge agglomeration of continents and cultures and races and religions and governments further apart from each other than any European country could be from any other European country. And yet *we-Asians* gripped the imagination . . . It meant something. There was a feeling of akinness, from Egypt to Japan . . . and all these countries were changing, changing, running the centuries into days, hurrying and scrambling forward, at a breathless speed which left European prejudices and platitudes about them as far behind as the buggy horse was left panting after a jet plane. Somehow Europe appeared so staid, stay-behind and unimaginative beside this surging exaltation of Asia.[19]

As Han Suyin suggests, "Asian" was an important concept for how people self-identified to create transnational solidarities that transcended imperial identity. The complexity and imprecision of racial categorization, alongside its very real consequences, is exactly why race and militarism are essential to understanding British colonial rule in Asia. Racial identities enabled the implementation of, and resistance to, colonial violence in times both of formal war and colonial "peace."

While this study focuses on the twentieth century, ideas about race in Southeast Asia were central to Britain's earliest colonial and trade settlements in the nineteenth century. One of Singapore's most influential governors, Stamford Raffles, was also a member of the English East India Company and hoped to divide Singapore into racially segregated districts. As a result, Lt. Philip Jackson mapped a (never executed) plan of the city in this light in 1828.[20] As British demands for trade increased, Company leaders emphasized racialized labor recruitment to encourage and coerce Chinese and Indian migrants to come to the region for work. On arrival, they often faced plantation-style discipline and severe racial hierarchy.[21] As Lynn Lees has explained, "If sugar planted a harsh, hierarchical empire in rural Malaya, plantation rubber cultivated its growth by identifying colonial rule with unfree labour, endemic violence, and racial separation."[22] At the same time, British leaders relied on the heavy recruitment of men from India to maintain and defend the region's profitable trade. After a major rebellion against the East India Company started with a mutiny of troops in India in 1857, British suspicions toward colonial subjects intensified.[23] Military investment increased across Asia, including building Fort Canning in Singapore. While this ostensibly protected the colony from external attack, defenses towered over Chinese residential districts. Military power was as much, if not more, about protecting colonial investments from colonial subjects as it was about defending against external threats.

When the British Colonial Office took control of the Straits Settlements (Singapore, Malacca, Penang) in 1867, they integrated the region more formally into networks of British military power.[24] This included a recurring reliance on colonial troops and police to curb Indigenous resistance, such as the heavy use of Sikh police during the Pahang Civil War (1891–1895).[25] A series of treaties in the early twentieth century expanded British rule even further, bringing previously independent regions under the umbrella of British kingship as "Unfederated" Malay states with protectorate status. These states retained previous rulers as figureheads to legitimize unpopular imperial policies.[26] As war and anti-colonial activity intensified in the twentieth century, British leaders hoped that policing the population with Indian men would retain colonial control.[27] Instead, Singapore and Malaya became fertile sites of revolt that undermined British assumptions about governance and rebellion because soldiers and civilians constantly found commonalities. Long before Singapore gained its reputation as an "impregnable fortress," and Malaya became a test case for winning "hearts and minds," soldiers and civilians alike dreamed of freedom from military occupation.

British leaders' reliance on Indian soldiers also influenced racial assumptions about martial prowess in Singapore and Malaya. In particular, the Indian Army prioritized the recruitment of men who belonged to the so-called "martial races." This proved to be a malleable set of ideals that defined men's martial potential through their faith, region of origin, ethnicity, and physical stature.[28] Gajendra

Singh has applied Ann Laura Stoler's phrase about "colonial negatives" to Indian Army martial race concepts. Just as photograph negatives are colorless shadows that can be cropped, redeveloped, or discarded, martial race ideas are adjustable, "half formed images" that do as much to distort as portray the living breathing men they represent.[29] Gender, as much as race, was central to these formulations, as "martial race" status granted some men claims to robust, powerful masculinity, while relegating others to the marginal status of "effeminacy."[30] This was also dehumanizing. Michelle Moyd has argued that the idealized image of East African askari, which echoed Indian "martial race" thinking, allowed real men to become "a beautiful object—a myth—floating above history."[31] For Moyd, martial race theories shaped how young men understood themselves in relation to colonial regimes. Tim Parsons also notes that "martial race" categorization was rooted in the political economies of different colonial contexts and involved inventing or hardening existing identities. Officers encouraged "martial race" soldiers to think of the army as their tribe, family, or community, isolating them from civilian experiences of colonialism and collective identity.[32] Simeon Man suggests that diverse recruitment enabled empires to claim "antiracism and anticolonialism" without actually ending "imperial violence."[33] In Singapore and Malaya, the reliance on international imperial soldiers, and selective racialized recruiting in local police and volunteer forces, ensured pervasive tensions around race and militarism. These echoed and duplicated the problems of British rule in India rather than laying the groundwork for a "successful" model of imperial war.

British militarism in India cast such a large shadow over Malaya and Singapore that it also shaped the "hearts and minds" approach to war. In 1891, Sir Robert Groves Sandeman, working for the governor-general in Baluchistan on the Indian borderlands, wrote to a friend that "to be successful on this frontier a man has to deal with the hearts and minds of the people and not only with their fears."[34] This made Sandeman, rather than Templer, the originator of perhaps the most famous phrase in military history. The "Sandeman system" emphasized the recruitment of local personnel into militias to become a "civilizing" influence that could maintain colonial order. As Nivi Manchanda has argued, the perceived unpredictability of the region created an "emergency episteme" in which experts were born overnight to create "practical" knowledge recycled through an "academic-military complex" that served "overwhelmingly . . . military purposes."[35] Of course, this approach did not bring stability to the Indo-Afghan border region, which remained a space of colonial militarization and brutality up to and through the partition of India and Pakistan in 1947. Still, the Sandeman system influenced colonial leaders beyond India. Harold Briggs, who preceded Templer as high commissioner in Malaya, had served in Baluchistan with the son of one of Sandeman's assistants. Briggs would introduce the mass internment and resettlement of predominantly Chinese civilians, renamed "New Villages" by Templer, in Malaya during the Emergency. The phrase that made Templer famous in military circles, and profoundly influenced U.S. militarism, had clear roots in the "high tide" of British colonialism in India. Yet Templer did not understand himself as part of this imperial history. Years later, he referred to "winning hearts and minds" as "that nauseating phrase I think I invented."[36] Ignoring or forgetting the imperial past enabled leaders to suggest that winning "hearts and minds" offered something other than a repackaged rationale for continued violence.

Rather than tracking if Templer introduced a "successful" model of counterinsurgency, *Losing Hearts and Minds* interrogates how wartime experiences made, remade, destroyed, or fortified imperial identities. While the title speaks to a famous military phrase, it does not center the voices of leaders and policy makers who inspired, defined, or took inspiration from it.[37] Instead, it prioritizes the people whose hearts and minds British leaders claimed to win. It does so by using a wide range of diaries, letters, oral histories, and memoirs of people who identified with or served British power. This includes Indian soldiers who longed for respect back home, Eurasian nurses who identified as British without ever setting foot in Britain, and Chinese businessmen who rushed to defend white Britons from rebelling Indian soldiers. It also examines white soldiers and civilians who saw themselves as challenging, rather than reinforcing, colonial racial hierarchies. Some white women doctors claimed to "understand" Malays. Many Australian internees lived beside Asian and Eurasian civilians in internment camps. A few British soldiers felt that their service was about cross-cultural collaboration. Many colonial subjects believed or hoped that serving the empire could facilitate egalitarian, interracial unity. Yet these testimonies—whether by white, Asian, or Eurasian authors—more often reveal the limitations of forging inclusivity in wartime. Most felt betrayed, in one way or another, by the racial biases embedded in colonial law, policing, and militarism, which limited their ability to secure the power promised to them. As a result, this work seeks to understand how people emotionally processed such betrayals. As Tiffany Florvil has argued, emotions could help a "community cohere" by serving as tools for "refashioning of new transnational, diasporic, identities and kinships."[38] Similarly, *Losing Hearts and Minds* respects people's emotions as legitimate ways of processing war and rejecting the dehumanization of colonial violence that treated them like disposable pawns.

The source base for this project includes archival resources originally produced in English, Chinese, Hindi, Urdu, and Malay from Britain, Australia, New

Zealand, India, Nepal, Malaysia, and Singapore. Yet the focus on those serving or proximate to British power means that many sources were translated into English either by colonial officials or archivists and scholars. Many of the Indian, Malay, and Chinese actors documented in this story left testimonies in English through either oral histories or memoirs. As Gauri Viswanathan has explored, English education in colonial spaces often inculcated Christian values that shaped how colonial subjects understood the world.[39] Ashis Nandy, Homi Bhaba, and Gayatri Chakravorty Spivak similarly warn scholars that such cultural "mimicry" reinforces colonial power, limiting self-formation and colonized people's ability to "speak" or even know their own voices.[40] However, throughout this study, I follow Gajendra Singh in seeing these sources as contested rather than compromised. For Singh, even court testimonies were a "process" rather than a fixed text.[41] In this, Singh goes beyond James C. Scott's notion that sources contain "hidden transcripts" of resistance because colonial subjects' intentions often went beyond simple colonial binaries of either compliance or resistance.[42] Instead, this analysis takes all forms of collaboration, resistance, self-preservation, uncertainty, and fear as contingent responses rooted in immediate needs to survive warfare and colonial rule. Where my own language skills are inadequate, I rely on scholars such as Francis Loh Kok Wah, Mahani Musa, Agnes Khoo, and Tan Teng Phee, who provide invaluable insight into how Chinese and Malay language actors understood these events.[43]

This study also relies on oral history interviews to understand the perspectives of those who lacked the power to write detailed reports or memoirs about their experiences. The National Archives of Singapore provides useful translations of interviews with Malay, Indian, and Chinese eyewitnesses. Translations, of course, hold many limitations, particularly when discussing emotional histories of war steeped in nationalist or anti-colonial narratives. As Sandra Taylor recalled of her research on Vietnamese communist women, she was American and her translator was a communist. As a result, she never got "their true feelings" but rather "a dramatized account of their heroism." Since memories, like translations, are "reconstructions" rather than factual records of the past, they often justify certain actions or inactions that may not conform to present social, cultural, or political norms, particularly in a context of collaboration or resistance. Yet for Taylor, like Singh, these stories are not "falsifications" but rather "paeans to the glories of a particular ideology, testaments to the righteousness of their cause, testimonies to the need to persist against what these women saw as the cruelties of a foreign imperialist and its local supporters."[44] Similarly, *Losing Hearts and Minds* closely tracks the stories people tell about war and colonialism to understand the long-term limitations of Britain's perceived "success" at winning hearts and minds. If people's memories of war involved discrimination, hatred, isolation, and racial persecution, then their hearts were never won.

In colonial Singapore and Malaya, people used their personal histories of war to process their experiences and forge a place for themselves within or beyond colonial society. Interpreting these diverse sources benefits from Joan Scott's understanding of "the evidence of experience," which she calls the "evidence for the fact of difference." In her analysis, people use specific memories to understand and define their identities—such as framing early erotic encounters as integral to "coming out" stories. Instead of naturalizing identity categories, she encourages "exploring how difference is established, how it operates, how and in what ways it constitutes subjects who see and act in the world."[45] Similarly, *Losing Hearts and Minds* recognizes that no individual account stands in as a "typical" British, Malay, Chinese, Australian, or Indian perspective. Instead, these sources show how people in wartime experienced similar emotional responses to the conflicts in which they were immersed but had unequal methods of coping with and acting upon these traumas. As Tan Teng Phee has argued, this makes it possible for "elites and 'small people' alike" to "become the keepers and makers of the past."[46] By examining deeply emotional personal stories of militarization and military service from the high tide of imperial power to decolonization, *Losing Hearts and Minds* shows that military leaders rarely understood the varied human consequences of war and empire. This was especially true when they claimed to "win" civilian favor.

This work builds on rich "war and society" and post-colonial scholarship that explores the violent consequences of imperialism, war, and racism. Many scholars have examined the role of colonial soldiers in Asia during the world wars.[47] Others have considered the cosmopolitan and multilingual nature of cultural, economic, and political life in colonial Singapore and Malaya.[48] Some have shown how colonial subjects used vast interconnected anti-colonial networks across Asia-Pacific to challenge imperial rule.[49] Many more have demonstrated that British colonialism depended on everyday and exceptional violence to maintain colonial control.[50] As Caroline Elkins has recently argued, "violence was not just the British Empire's midwife, it was endemic to the structures and systems of British rule."[51] *Losing Hearts and Minds* builds on this impressive work by comparing soldier and civilian experiences to tell a global story of various colonial and anti-colonial actors living, working, and fighting across multiple conflicts in a single colonial space. Singapore and Malaya's populations—soldier or civilian, revolutionary or cautiously "loyal"—were highly mobile, with connections across the colonial world. Yet war came, again and again, to this place. As a result,

Losing Hearts and Minds understands these mobile experiences of war as essential to the fabric of colonial society. It seeks to reconstruct the social and racial worlds of British Malaya and how this shaped the perceived success, and overlooked failures, of the hearts-and-minds strategy. As people lived, migrated, or served in Malaya and Singapore, they brought assumptions about difference that trembled or solidified in the face of conflict. By emphasizing the many faces of war from the perspective of those who experienced it, this book tells the story of living in a place constantly made and remade by war and empire.

Seven chapters analyze soldier and civilian experiences across conflicts. The first two chapters consider the role of colonial racism in shaping soldier-civilian relations before, during, and after the First World War. The first chapter, "Race War in Singapore," examines events leading up to and including the 1915 mutiny of Indian troops in Singapore. This rebellion revealed the ease with which mutinous and non-mutinous Indian soldiers found support among civilians. This made British leaders see whiteness as a source of isolation rather than power. In response, leaders deepened racial hierarchies and systemic violence to crush Indian resistance, undermining broader civilian confidence. The second chapter, "Making Enemies between the Wars," examines the impact of the 1915 rebellion on interwar politics and race relations. Many civilians who had supported, or not explicitly resisted, British efforts during the mutiny were not included in British visions of "peace." Many Chinese civilians felt that their sacrifices and contributions to restoring British rule went unnoticed. Japanese civilians, who aided the British against Indian rebels, received no support against Chinese-led boycotts that protested Japanese imperialism. Instead, British leaders militarized police forces to undermine anti-colonial activities. Militarization after the 1915 "mutiny" encouraged colonial subjects and leaders to seek new solidarities or find new enemies.

The middle three chapters consider the breakdown and reassertion of British racial hierarchies during the Second World War and Japanese occupation. British leaders had long claimed that their military presence was necessary to "defend" their subjects from foreign invasion. In reality, they escaped and surrendered when facing it. Chapter three, "The Pride and the Fall," shows that many white soldiers arriving in Singapore from 1939 to 1941 felt like they were stepping into a paradise. Films, movie theaters, rickshaws, and cabarets delighted the new arrivals, who felt a world away from the European conflict. Once the Japanese bombing and invasion began in December 1941, however, existing tensions of colonial militarism came to the surface. Many white Europeans departed in the dead of night, claiming that they would bear the brunt of violence from the Japanese. This left Asian friends, allies, and servants to fend for themselves, culminating in the deaths of between 30,000 and 50,000 Chinese civilians at the hands of the Japanese military.[52] Remaining white Europeans demanded the continued labor and loyalty of Asian civilians. While imperial troops fought hopelessly against a well-organized opponent, some civilians aided the Japanese or rejected British mandates as a way to cope with the realities of war and abandonment.

The fourth chapter, "Labored Intimacies," tracks the centrality of labor for dictating value, survival, and intimacy during the Japanese occupation, from internment camps to paramilitary units, from Chinese households in Singapore to Eurasian resettlement villages in Malaya. Some experiences of internment crossed lines of class, race, and faith and had the potential to challenge colonial hierarchies. White Australian nurse Veronica Clancy felt that after doing hard labor, white women could no longer "retain their former prestige." Sheila Allan, who had a white Australian father and an Asian mother, believed that hard work would endear her to white internees and ensure her survival. For colonial subjects, serving British needs through hard work temporarily transcended the racial and gender segregation of the Japanese occupation while also reinforcing British hierarchies.

The fifth chapter, "Making and Unmaking 'Martial Races,'" explores how soldiers fought in vain to fulfil their assigned status as "martial" communities after the "fall" of Singapore in 1942. Troops from Britain, India, and Australia, long categorized as paragons of martial masculinity, endured the humiliation of surrender. Their wartime hardships challenged their ability to claim military masculinity and "racial" supremacy. Some Indian men sought to rekindle or challenge the martial race ethos through service to the Indian National Army, an anti-colonial force that allied with the Japanese in the hopes of "liberating" India. Chinese and Eurasian civilians stepped in to claim the venerated status of being martial allies to British power while protecting their homes and resisting the Japanese occupation. At a moment when the "martial race" ethos of imperial military service crumbled, British leaders doubled down on the racial exclusion that underpinned colonial rule.

The final two chapters explore the recalibration of British power during the anti-communist Malayan Emergency. The sixth chapter, "Forging the Commonwealth," focuses on British leaders' efforts to recast Britain's police and military presence in Malaya and Singapore, euphemistically referred to as "security forces," as an interracial brotherhood of arms supporting an imperial family.[53] Following the independence and partition of India and Pakistan in 1947, British leaders lost the immense power of the colonial Indian Army. The exception was that some "Gurkha" soldiers, from the independent nation of Nepal, were part of the British Army under the Brigade of Gurkhas. These men became some of the first soldiers on the ground when the anti-communist Malayan Emergency broke out in 1948. Many civilians in Malaya and Singapore continued to support communists, as they had during the Japanese occupation. British leaders also relied on soldiers from Nepal, Australia, New Zealand, Fiji, and East Africa to carry out the campaign. The result was that British leaders emphasized the inclusivity and diversity of the British Empire and Commonwealth while portraying communists as "Chinese outsiders." Like their Indian predecessors, these soldiers ultimately found more in common with the communities they were meant to control than with the British leaders demanding their loyalty.

The final chapter, "Pregnant in the Jungle," focuses on how gender, sexuality, and reproduction were primary avenues through which British leaders hoped—and claimed—to win civilian "hearts and minds." Chinese-language British propaganda cartoons warned women about becoming communists because of the danger of giving birth in the jungle. By contrast, they portrayed white women as "civilizing" forces that transcended racial differences by promoting military domesticity, nursing, and welfare. They contrasted this to frequent reports of babies "abandoned" by communist mothers, eliding the culpability of British-led security forces who likely killed them. While Commonwealth armies emphasized the military as an interracial brotherhood of arms, British leaders hoped that the idea of a supportive military family could outlast military occupation, ignoring the realities of gendered violence and racist extermination. This chapter shows that, despite Templer's reputation for remaking war, and American leaders' efforts to replicate his model of "success," colonial militarism in Singapore and Malaya only won the "hearts and minds" of those who experienced war from a safe distance. The endemic gender and racial violence of colonial militarism was anything but a "success."

Losing Hearts and Minds is a story about people who fought to survive deadly institutions. Militaries exist for lethality and create profound consequences for the societies that sustain them. Some institutions, particularly with colonial origins, kill through extraction, privileging economic profit over the people whose labor and health ensure that profitability. In other instances, institutional death is about neglect, and killing people by ignoring problems. Dealing with problems requires potentially life-saving labor from the powerful—who rarely face the dangers that they create. Letting people die out of sight requires nothing. Writing this book during a global pandemic brought clarity and frustration, as those who put themselves forward to serve did so without fair or equitable compensation and protection, amplifying race, gender, disability, and class stratification. All human presents live in the shadow of colonial extraction and death. Our bodies are meant to serve until they have no purpose, and then quietly die. This is a story about the people who lived and died in defiance of the institutions that sought to destroy them.

ONE

Race War in Singapore

On February 20, 1915, British administrative cadet Frank Kershaw Wilson wrote home from Singapore that he felt "an unpleasant consciousness of being a white man."[1] The origins of his "unpleasant consciousness," as he perceived it, was an outbreak of violence—later referred to as the "Singapore Mutiny"—among Indian soldiers of the 5th Light Infantry. Five days earlier, on February 15, 1915, some Indian soldiers, hired to fight for the British Empire, raided an armory and opened fire on their officers. This occurred the day before their planned relocation to Hong Kong. Fighting spread across Singapore island but British leaders regained control within days after Russian, French, and Japanese intervention. Over one hundred people, including soldiers and civilians of all ethnicities, died in the struggle. Over subsequent months, official British accounts of the rebellion focused on jealousies between Indian soldiers about promotion, infiltration by "outside agitators" (especially Germans and Indian revolutionaries), Indian Muslim soldiers' supposed "religious" motivations, and inefficiencies among British officers.[2] However, Wilson's specific anxiety about what it felt like to be a "white man" suggests that these events laid bare the vulnerability of colonial racial hierarchies and the military state meant to support them. His "unpleasant consciousness" represented a deeply-rooted fear that this system would no longer protect and serve him. This perceived vulnerability of whiteness would enable British leaders to carry out a *de facto* race war for "peace."[3]

As Wilson's fears suggest, ideas about racial difference underpinned British rule in colonial Asia. This was due, in part, to the mobilization of identity to create unequal access to wealth and power. By the twentieth century, under half of Malaya's total population were Malay. Chinese people comprised just under 40 percent, Indians 14 percent, and less than 1 percent were European or Eurasian. This reflected regional migration patterns and colonial labor demands. Malaya became one of Britain's most profitable colonies through Indian convict and indentured labor that supported lucrative tin mining and rubber trades.[4] Malaya's relative isolation from the main action of the First World War, and access to raw materials vital for the war effort, meant that Malaya produced over half of the world's rubber by 1930.[5] This facilitated the rapid growth and prosperity of the port city and island of Singapore. Chinese civilians held prominent social and economic positions, both numerically as laborers and as leaders in trade and commerce. European and Chinese plantations in Malaya were predominantly staffed by Chinese and Indian laborers who faced coercion and long, factory-like hours and segregated working conditions. British leaders often played groups against one another to maintain power and profit. For example, if Chinese laborers went on strike, plantation managers undercut them with Indian Tamil workers. Indian Bengalis could work as watchmen and monitor Chinese estate workers, while Malay police coerced strikers to return to work.[6] Government jobs also maintained racial bars, enabling upwardly mobile white Europeans, like Wilson, to isolate themselves from Asian civilians in bungalows, golf courses, and clubs with ample servants. Differences of class, rank, language, faith, and ethnicity shaped identities, intersecting and diverting according to personal relationships of kinship, sex, friendship, employment, or convenience.[7] These dynamics largely escaped the grasp of British leaders, but had profound influence on colonial subjects living and working within and beyond Singapore.

British rule also depended on a large presence of colonial soldiers to defend the colonies' profitable resources. British conquest in the region began under the East India Company, which relied on the recruitment of Indian men for overseas service. Increasingly, British leaders emphasized the recruitment of Indian men according to the principle of so-called "martial races," which regarded some Indian men as natural warriors based on region of origin, faith group, ethnicity, and physical stature. It led to the disproportionate representation in the army of communities such as Sikhs, Punjabi Muslims, and Pashtuns (Pathans) from the Indo-Afghan border region.[8] Compared to India, Indian soldiers in Singapore struggled with the high cost of living while losing the exalted status that they enjoyed back home. They experienced isolation from both the civilian population and their commanding officers due to language barriers and unstable racial and labor hierarchies. Compared to the rotating cast of white colonial officers and administrators who took the place of their predecessors in clubs, sporting arenas, or dance halls, Indian soldiers lacked a clearly defined social position. In some ways, this granted them the possibility of adapting or "blending in," especially in a multi-ethnic place like Singapore with a large Indian population. However, this betrayed their presumed isolation and "otherness," which British leaders saw as necessary for them to impose the violent power of the colonial state. It also brought them into contact with food vendors, barbers, tailors, religious allies, and other local contacts of all ethnicities who helped them adapt. These encounters profoundly shaped the colonial and anti-colonial milieu of Singapore life well beyond 1915.

Indian soldiers also found themselves at the intersection of anti-colonial movements and mounting British fears of their colonial subjects. Several wars and rebellions challenged British economic and political power in South Asia in the eighteenth and nineteenth centuries. Most famously, the rebellion of 1857 started with a military mutiny and spread across north India. By the early twentieth century, Indian revolutionaries and nationalists found allies or inspiration around the world, including from the so-called Boxer Rebellion in China (1899–1901) and Japan's victory in the Russo-Japanese War (1904–1905), both of which challenged European power in Asia. In India, agrarian resistance to colonial extraction also intensified anti-colonial and nationalist agendas. On the eve of the First World War, the Ghadar (Ghadr)—or Mutiny—movement combined these goals by appealing directly to active servicemen, veterans, and their families across Asia, North America, and Europe to encourage them to use their military experience against colonial powers. Some of the soldiers who rebelled in 1915 took inspiration from these growing networks of anti-colonial revolt and believed that they could undermine or even end British power in Asia. As a result, scholars have turned increasingly to the Singapore Mutiny to better understand Indian anti-colonialism and global anti-colonial networks in Asia. However, none have analyzed the Singapore Mutiny as a reflection of the racial politics of British military rule in Singapore and Malaya.[9] In reality, Indian, Chinese, and Malay soldiers and civilians were equally important players in the future of Britain's empire in Southeast Asia.

This chapter explores how Indian experiences of soldiering in the multi-ethnic space of colonial Singapore shaped how and why they rebelled in this particular place and time. Despite colonial leaders' fears, diversity was not an inevitable precursor of social ill. Rather, the strict prejudices and racial hierarchies engendered by militarism, global anti-colonial networks, unequal labor migration, and imperial rule created the conditions under which colonial and military leaders mobilized difference to implement power and control. In order to reconstruct Indian soldiers' experiences, this chapter relies on Indian testimonies provided in the aftermath of the 1915 rebellion. These testimonies—taken under duress and often with faulty translations—are nonetheless valuable for providing a window into the everyday fears and anxieties—sometimes shared with civilians, sometimes disparate—of living and working under colonialism.[10] Colonial administrators used these testimonies to ascribe innocence and guilt. By contrast, this chapter reads soldiers' accounts, alongside memoirs, oral histories, and colonial reports, along the "bias grain" to understand how soldiers conveyed the emotional experience of laboring under colonialism.[11] These suggest that while British soldiers feared uprisings from Indian troops under their command, Indian soldiers lived in constant fear of racialized violence from British leaders. Bad leadership, poor decision-making, or even bland indifference had dire consequences for these men's quality of life—and death.

A WARRING PEACE IN SINGAPORE AND MALAYA

In the months leading up to the 1915 rebellion, few colonial leaders anticipated serious trouble among Indian soldiers, even as they worried about maintaining control over a multi-ethnic empire. Singapore and Malaya felt a world away from the European conflict, and Britain, with its military alliances with Japan and the United States, and imperial ties with India, Australia, and New Zealand, held a relatively confident military position in Asia-Pacific. As part of the Straits Settlements (Singapore, Penang, and Malacca), British leaders governed Singapore separately from mainland Malaya. Still, regional military decisions were centralized through the Governor and Officer Commanding the Straits Settlements. As early as December 1914, Governor Young confidently asserted that the experienced General Officer Commanding the Straits Settlements, General Reade, could be sent elsewhere for the war effort. Going one step further, he argued that "a reduction in the Military Staff could be made."[12] This led to the planned, but never executed, departure of the 5th Light Infantry for Hong Kong on February 16, 1915. While Governor Young felt confident that Singapore was safe, soldiers saw danger all around them.

In the days before the 5th Light Infantry planned to set sail for Hong Kong, many soldiers expressed fears of being killed at sea. Lance Naik Maksud of D Company recalled hearing that "if we went into a ship we should be sunk by the Government." News of German victories convinced some that the British would lose the war and "have no use for them [Indian soldiers] and would send them away in a ship and sink them." Whether or not soldiers believed these rumors, they found receptive ears. In the C Company cookhouse, according to Maksud, soldiers urged one another to "eat your food and enjoy your pipe for in a few days we shall all be drowned."[13] Some soldiers believed that British leaders saw them as disposable. Several seaborne disasters contributed to their fears. Early in the war, the German cruiser *Emden* wreaked havoc on British and allied vessels around South and Southeast Asia. German Captain Karl von Müller took the ship from Tsingtao, China, to inflict as much damage on British shipping, trade, and travel as possible, ultimately sinking or possessing twenty-three ships. The *Emden* made it as far as Madras, India, where it attacked and destroyed oil supplies in September 1914. By October, the ship sailed into Penang Harbor, which was, like Singapore, part of the Straits Settlements. There the *Emden* sank two cruisers— one Russian and one French—before escaping.[14] This seemingly invincible vessel, therefore, made it all the way to Indian soldiers' home country and then haunted the shores near Singapore.

When Australians finally sank the *Emden* in November 1914, it did little to calm Indian soldiers' minds. By November, soldiers knew about the realities of service on the Western Front, despite the glowing praise for Britain's war effort in the local press. This, along with rumors and reports of the *Emden* crew escaping, led many soldiers to doubt reports of *Emden*'s demise. Colour Havildar Rahmat Khan of D Company claimed that men "heard from Malays round about" that the *Emden* never sank and that their Captain lied by saying that it had.[15] Making matters worse, many of the *Emden*'s crew were held at Tanglin Barracks in Singapore. Their guards included the locally-raised Indian force of the Malay States Guides and the 5th Light Infantry. Several soldiers reported conversations with Germans and seeing Germans praying to Mecca or uttering Muslim prayers. The *Emden*'s successes made Germans seem invincible. Guarding them revealed their humanity, and possible affinity. Both proved unsettling for soldiers hired to see the British as friends and the Germans as enemies.

Further injuring soldiers' confidence boarding vessels to serve Britain was the debacle over the *Komagata Maru*. During its journey, the *Komagata Maru* passed through Singapore, apparently leaving "a bad effect" in the minds of some Indian soldiers.[16] The matter began when Gurdit Singh, an Indian émigré who had lived in Singapore, commissioned the ship to leave Hong Kong and enter Vancouver full of Punjabi—predominantly Sikh—migrants. The goal was to undermine the British Empire's discriminatory migration policies with communities connected to soldiering.[17] Ultimately, officials in Vancouver refused the ship entry and sent it to India, forcing passengers to remain on the ship for months in unsanitary conditions. When passengers arrived in India in September 1914, they protested and rebelled, which British leaders crushed with violent force. Taken together, the *Emden* and the *Komagata Maru* deepened soldiers' fears of setting sail in the service of the British Empire. Months before boarding a ship for war, they heard about Germans sinking British vessels and Indian migrants powerlessly confined at sea before enduring brutal violence in India. In the minds of colonial officials, however, these threats were contained. Soldiers' feelings went unassuaged.

These incidents suggest that civilian leaders felt overconfident about the war's (lack of) impact in Asia. This was often at odds with soldiers' feelings of impending doom. Soon enough, Indian soldiers lost their ability to perform devotion to British rule. Lt. Morrison of the Indian Medical Service observed that soldiers became "very casual in their attitude to British Officers."[18] He heard men complaining about their low wages and minimal compensation for death in battle, which felt likely due to German victories. Quartermaster Lt. E. M. Malone noted that men were slack with saluting during an inspection in October 1914. Sub-Assistant Surgeon Bell observed that in plainclothes, "half the men I saw never took the trouble to salute me."[19] The 5th Light Infantry's commanding officer, Colonel Martin, denied such assertions, insisting that "even civilians remarked the men always saluted Europeans."[20] For British leaders, normalcy in colonial Singapore was for Indian troops to have such devotion to racial hierarchy that they saluted white civilians and non-uniformed officers. Soldiers' failure to maintain racial hierarchy, they reasoned, became a sign of the violence to come. However, most of these men recorded their impressions only *after* February 1915. At the end of 1914, most assumed that the 5th Light Infantry—but not all Indian men-of-arms—was devoted to the empire.

By the end of 1914, the locally-recruited Malay States Guides, rather than the 5th Light Infantry, appeared ready for a fight. While the 5th was a Muslim-majority unit of the Indian Army stationed in Singapore, the Malay States Guides (MSG) were a locally-raised unit of Indians comprised mostly of Sikhs and Indian Muslims.[21] Their experiences reveal much about British leaders' indifference toward soldiers' concerns. When the war first broke out, the MSG expressed a willingness to serve in Europe and arrived in Singapore in August anticipating active duty. After months of delays and unanswered requests, the men received an offer to serve in East Africa, rather than Europe. By December 1914, the bulk of the MSG left Singapore, not for East Africa—but to return to Taiping in disgrace, having refused service. Over the course of their four months in Singapore, soldiers' enthusiasm for the war had waned. British officials suspected that "a certain amount of sedition" had played a role.[22]

FIGURE I.   Mountain Battery of the Malay States Guides, 1915.
Courtesy of National Archives of Singapore.

Colonial racism influenced the decision to offer the Malay States Guides service in East Africa, instead of Europe. British leaders held long-standing concerns about sending Indian soldiers to fight white Europeans. In the latter years of the war, most Indian service personnel went to non-European theaters, such as Mesopotamia and Egypt. Yet the offer for the MSG to serve in East Africa went further, enticing them with anti-Black racism. Soldiers learned that in East Africa "[t]here are not many Germans," but rather they had "raised the Negroes, and it is to guard against trouble from these that His Majesty requires our services." This encouraged Indian soldiers to see themselves as active participants in and beneficiaries of empire, who were separate and distinct from Black colonial subjects "raised" by Germans. Further, British leaders encouraged Indian men to think of themselves as settlers: "German East Africa is a very fine country" where "grants of land" could be secured "for Soldiers who have done well in this small campaign."[23] Despite promises of a higher position in colonial racial hierarchy, the Malay States Guides remained unmoved. According to the General Officer Commanding in January, soldiers refused to go on service due to "fear of losses and defeat," which was "spread by Enemy Agents."[24] Soldiers had their own reasons.

An anonymous address from the "Men of the Guides" in December 1914 outlined soldiers' concerns about serving in East Africa. They pointed out that their service agreements only required them to serve in the Malay Peninsula and the Straits Settlements. The address also claimed that their highest-ranking Indian officer, the Subedar Major, offered their services without consulting other Indian officers and men. As a result, the men were "quite unprepared" to go to Africa. If they were forced to go, "it will bring a very disastrous result." The anonymous letter also indicated that soldiers feared colonial violence. It mentioned that "our brethren who have been shot in the Komagatamaru [sic] case" has "troubled and grieved us" because "some of us have lost dear brothers and other blood-relations." They condemned "the Indian Government (British) for shooting and slaughtering the dead" only to cast their victims as "seditious people," echoing common arguments of the Ghadr movement. The soldiers wondered: "When we have no right to walk freely on our own land then what do you want from us in other countries? As we are butchered in our own country we cannot expect better treatment from other countries."[25] The author suggested that if Indian soldiers could no longer feel safe in British-ruled India, or believe that their grievances would be addressed without accusations of "sedition," how could they trust the British to send them overseas?

British leaders acted quickly in response to the petition. Captain G. Badham Thornhill told the MSG's commanding officer, Lt. Col. C.H.B. Lees: "It rests for you to shew that no grounds existed for such a grievance."[26] He emphasized *showing* that the grievance was groundless, rather than understanding if this was the case. Lees went fast to work. He argued that problems started when officers received an anonymous letter from a Punjabi Muslim soldier serving on the small island of Blakan Mati. In response to the letter, one soldier, Jemadar Sher Zaman, apparently stated that if "the Sahib tells me to go [to Africa] I will hand him over my sword." Lees met with Sher Zaman, who, by Lees's account, became defensive about an accusation that could have cost him his job or life, before avowing his loyalty. Based only on this brief and tense encounter, Lees concluded that "that was the man to watch and that he was thoroughly guilty of all that had been written to me."[27] Tasked with proving that the Malay States Guides' petition was groundless, Lees offered a scapegoat. This contrasted Zaman's previous distinguished record of service, which included leadership positions and praise from other officers.[28]

Unacknowledged by Lees was that service on Blakan Mati may have contributed to soldiers' anguish. A 1914 Report of the Malay States Guides noted that malaria "was very prevalent" in this "unhealthy place."[29] British leaders never mentioned how service conditions influenced soldiers' reluctance to fight wherever the British commanded, even though soldiers mentioned this in their petition. Yet Blakan Mati continued to cast a shadow. Lees suspected Subedar Elim Din, commanding troops at Blakan Mati, of being the "prime mover in the whole affair." He alleged that the Subedar "rules the Punjabi Mahomedans by terror," but provided no examples. He also alleged that his other suspected ringleader, Zaman, was "under Subadar Elim Din's thumb." He still lacked evidence but said, "I hope to have got fairly good proof of the complicity of both of them." Here, Lees admits to having no evidence but "hopes" to find "good proof" of their "complicity." Lacking that, he undermined the Subedar's character, suggesting that he had received a dubious promotion and was "a shoe maker by caste."[30] Ultimately, these features—ethnicity, circumstances of promotion, and perceived personality flaws—brought Elim Din under suspicion of being a "prime mover" of dissent. Once British leaders decided that men were guilty, reports *became* the evidence to support the accusation.[31]

Despite his preoccupation with ringleaders, Lees suggested that service in Singapore contributed to soldiers' discontent. He argued that "a great change has come over the Corps since its arrival in Singapore." Some soldiers, like Jemadar Samund Singh, believed that "meeting people in the bazaar" dissuaded soldiers from overseas service, as they learned information about the reality of the war. Having lost confidence in their British leaders, Indian soldiers looked for information elsewhere. As a result, just four months of service in Singapore turned an apparently enthusiastic unit into a disgruntled one that refused service and became more vocal about their concerns. Listening to civilians in Singapore, apparently, made them feel empowered to speak. Lees also speculated (without evidence) that German and Turkish agents were to blame. Slightly more convincing was his belief that "the German prisoners here, whom my men were guarding," spoke to them "in Malay" and swayed their loyalties. This only worked because, in his view, Indians were "credulous people." He dismissed the possibility that Indian soldiers had their own grievances. Lees feared that it would take a massive German disaster to convince Indian soldiers that the British could "come through victorious." In the meantime, he proposed sending as many men away from Singapore as possible.[32]

Despite Lees's suggestion that the MSG had seditious encounters in Singapore, he also portrayed dissent as inevitable: "There is of course here, as in every Indian Regt. a certain amount of sedition, but their refusal to go on service now proceeds from fear, and not from any seditious wish to embarras [*sic*] the Govt." Despite this belief in perennial sedition, he discredited the anonymous letter, suggesting that it was written "by someone outside the Regt." Once again, he provided no evidence. He ultimately recommended "immediate disbandment" of the MSG upon "peace in Europe," with pensions, gratuities, and compensation "settled according to individual cases."[33] Due to British men's inability to understand their soldiers' needs and fears, soldiers were at risk of losing their livelihoods.

The MSG's refusal to serve inspired British leaders to hire two secret agents to keep an eye on Indian troops in mosques and other public spaces.[34] Their unwillingness to understand their soldiers led them to intrude upon sacred spaces and mobilize racialized subjects to undermine networks of support, solidarity, and comfort. Equally important, the Malay States Guides lived in the same barracks as the 5th Light Infantry. This meant that the men of the 5th saw and heard the MSG's feelings of betrayal. They witnessed how an offer of service in one place (Europe) resulted in the near compulsion to serve elsewhere (East Africa). They saw the MSG *successfully* resist being sent overseas. While the nature of Indian Army and MSG service was different, this event suggested to some Indian soldiers that they could have a say in shaping their service. Major Cotton of the 5th Light Infantry later claimed that the Malay States Guides' actions were the chief contribution to the mutiny. In his words, "It had a very bad effect on the men and made their minds ripe for joining in any outbreak."[35] The more British officials dug, the more "any outbreak" became a real possibility.

Concerns about the MSG led Lees to investigate the Northern Indian community in Malaya more broadly in January 1915—one month prior to the rebellion of the 5th Light Infantry. While the focus of the report was on the Federated Malay States (FMS), his conclusions reflected many issues that resonated for soldiers in Singapore. He identified "[s]editious activity from outside," the *Komagata Maru* incident, war against the Ottoman Empire, German activities, and the "attitude of the M.S.G." as key reasons for wider Indian "unrest." However, he also listed one striking and telling dynamic: "Peculiar perverse feeling of hostility for which no special reason can be assigned."[36] In the minds of colonial leaders, Indians were hostile for no reason. They refused to understand how and why Indian soldiers and civilians carried a pervasive feeling of discontent rooted in the inequities of empire.

For British leaders, Lees's report provided some disquieting revelations. The first was that British rule was defenseless against a general Indian rising. Part of the problem was that Indian men dominated forces such as the Malay States Guides and the police. Leaders assumed that if Indian civilians rose up, about half of the Sikhs and Punjabi Muslims in these forces "would openly resist," while the remaining Indian population "would not actively assist us against their own countrymen." Loyalty and common struggle, in the eyes of British officials, inevitably followed ethnic lines. Despite this grim prognostication, they regarded a rebellion as a "very remote" possibility because Northern Indians had too many economic interests in Malaya. They similarly assumed that Chinese civilians were unlikely to rebel, unless tin prices changed or Indians rose up first, in which case they would "seize the opportunity to loot & rob throughout the country."[37] The War Office was less certain, worrying about the "large Chinese population, whose disposition might not always remain favourable."[38] Despite this difference of opinion about which colonial subjects they had to fear, British leaders agreed that all communities were always on the verge of rebellion. However, as long as the war kept the tin and rubber trades healthy, they assumed, soldiers and civilians would remain compliant.

This rationale underpinned Young's belief that the garrison at Singapore could be reduced—a decision setting the 5th Light Infantry on a course for Hong Kong.[39] Major General Reade, Commanding the Troops, Straits Settlements echoed the committee's conclusions that a general rising of Northern Indians "seemed very unlikely." He acknowledged that he had insufficient forces "to deal with a general rising of Northern Indians" but reiterated that its probability was "very remote."[40] Governor Young agreed that they could not defend against a general Indian rising but the "occurrence of any such disturbance is not anticipated by me." He suggested reducing the garrison because "even if there is a small risk, I hold that that risk ought to be taken."[41] British confidence was so high that when General Ridout, the new Officer Commanding the Straits Settlements, arrived in Singapore one week before the mutiny, he did not receive a copy of Lees's report. They did take other precautions, such as confiscating ammunition to prevent it "falling into the hands of possible enemies."[42] This once again sent a message to Indian soldiers that they may become victims rather than perpetuators of colonial violence. Ironically, this only added to the challenge of the volunteer forces later called to suppress the rebellion, because Indian rebels started their uprising with a raid on an armory.[43]

Hindsight makes British leaders' overconfidence grimly ironic. British observers such as Edwin Brown, who helped put down the 1915 rebellion, subsequently criticized the "ineptitude" of British leadership. However, the wider view shows that British leaders' inability to deal with soldiers' feelings of being misunderstood and racially antagonized, and mobilizing their own fears to monitor and alienate soldiers, was much more to blame. Despite—or perhaps, because of—investigations, reports, and monitoring, Indian troops rebelled in Singapore after months of expressing unresolved grievances. Even after the rising, British officials comforted themselves with the belief that rebellion was inevitable. One official note in 1916 suggested, "There has been, and always will be, a certain amount of sedition amongst Indians," echoing Lees's language from December 1914.[44] This provided a parallel to the suspicion of a "[p]eculiar perverse feeling of hostility for which no special reason can be assigned."[45] This sense of inevitability—that Indians would always rebel if not carefully controlled—reflected the mindset of colonial leaders in 1915. Nothing they did to improve the lives, conditions, or treatment of Indian soldiers—or colonial subjects more broadly—mattered. They did not care that they were losing soldiers' "hearts and minds." This only increased Indian soldiers' fears that violence was inevitable—and that they could be the targets.

DEADLY CONFUSION

Soldier and civilian anxieties culminated in a violent clash on February 15, 1915, when members of the 5th Light Infantry—a regiment of 818 men—rebelled at Alexandra Barracks.[46] While preparing for their departure, a detail of Indian soldiers moved small arms, ammo, and oil drums to a lorry, when someone opened fire from the direction of the Quarter Guard. Some soldiers raided the magazine, while others fled in fear. Some men went to the POW camp at Tanglin and released crew of the *Emden*. Others went to the center of Singapore. Another group of soldiers went to the barracks of the Malay States Guides artillery unit and attempted to storm Colonel Martin's house. Thirty-one people died within the first hours of the rebellion. In response, British leaders mobilized reinforcements from British, Japanese, French, and Russian ships as well as soldiers from Johore. They raised volunteers, including Japanese civilians, Chinese Volunteer units, Malay policemen, and European special constables.[47] Many of these forces later noted that Indian soldiers appeared unfocused and disorganized compared to the British. In reality, soldiers' lack of clear goals reflected their disordered experience of the rebellion specifically and colonial service more broadly. Confusion, deception, and resentment were normal features of military service, made worse by colonial inequities, racial exclusion, and language barriers. Various accounts of these events revealed that everyone—from Indian soldiers to British officers—responded to the rebellion with confusion. This left networks of rumor, hearsay, and preexisting assumptions to fill in the gaps. Yet Indian soldiers' uncertainty predated the outbreak. On the morning of the rebellion, many already dreaded their fates. The "mutiny," and the British response, only deepened their terror.

One of the earliest events on February 15 indicated the severe gap in trust between British leaders and Indian soldiers. On that morning, General Ridout inspected the men at a parade. He offered ambiguous information about their departure which Colonel Martin translated poorly, leaving men uncertain that they were being sent to Hong Kong. In his address, Ridout mentioned Europe *twice* but did not say "Hong Kong" once.[48] This fed existing rumors that soldiers were not being sent to Hong Kong, as promised, but rather to the horrific battlefields of Europe, or to Egypt to kill other Muslims.[49] A Brahmin shopkeeper, Sambhudat, who kept a grocery store on Alexandra Barracks across from regimental quarters, noted that men shared these fears whenever they came to his shop for food. According to the Subedar Major, the Friday before the mutiny "all the syces [horse-groomers] bolted" because "the regiment was not for Hong Kong but for the front."[50] Well before the morning of February 15, many soldiers knew that the Malay States Guides put themselves forward for service in Europe, only to be "offered" a place in East Africa instead. They were not the only ones. The King's Own Yorkshire Light Infantry left Singapore not knowing their destination and ended up on service in Europe.[51] Similarly, the 36th Sikhs believed they would go to Hong Kong before rerouting to France instead.[52] Even L. A. Thomas, the Assistant Superintendent of the Police, misremembered that the 5th were assigned to service in East Africa, perhaps confusing them with the Malay States Guides.[53] This makes it unsurprising that men doubted their destination. Many soldiers, including Jemadar Rahmat Khan of A Company, recalled everyone saying they were going on active service rather than Hong Kong. A few men even put forward their (unsuccessful) requests for discharges as a result.[54] The possibility of serving somewhere other than where was promised felt very real. Considering all they had heard and experienced about the war and military service, this uncertainty felt like imminent death.

Soldiers' testimonies indicate that the most common response to the rebellion was fear and confusion, even among those who may have wanted the rebellion to occur. Many soldiers claimed ignorance about what was going on—and hid for days fearing reprisals. It did not help that their officers gave ambiguous orders. Pay Havildar Sikhdar of E Company remembered that despite Lieutenant Elliott's warnings, "Everybody rather lost their heads. Men were rushing about."[55] Drummer Abdul Hamid Khan of F Company recalled Elliott telling them "You had better save your lives," so many men ran into the jungle.[56] It is unclear whether fleeing into the jungle was an official order. Sepoy Momin of E Company remembered three hospital assistants telling patients: "Those who can, run away and save yourselves."[57] Edwin Brown suggested that running into the jungle was an official order, with Hall instructing his men to disperse and "get into the jungle nearby, and lie 'doggo' [hidden] for the present."[58]

Hiding was not unique to Indian soldiers. Most British officers hid in Colonel Martin's residence, while some rebelling soldiers laid siege to the building. British officers' inability to organize their men or fight back led to subsequent criticism from observers and volunteers. It also contributed to soldiers' terror. Sepoy Yasin Mahomed, of G Company, who worked as Captain Hall's orderly, remembered that men felt abandoned. He was cleaning Hall's bicycle when the firing broke out. He assisted officers by dropping provisions—such as Major Cotton's bedding—at the Colonel's bungalow. However, that night, "all the Sahibs, including the Volunteers, went up above and we were left down below." Uncertain of what to do, he went "into jungle."[59] Even Sepoy Hakim Ali, working as the *colonel's* orderly, stayed in the jungle for twenty-two days. Sub-Assistant Surgeon Bell hid in the servants' quarters and refused to return to the hospital until the next day "because I was afraid," before seeking refuge in a Chinese woman's house.[60] Hospital orderly Alla Dir had a similar response, hiding near the hospital before escaping to a "hedge" on a pineapple plantation.[61] Fear and hiding, of course, produced very different consequences for British and Indian men.

With the collapse in British leadership, many men followed their Indian non-commissioned officers (NCOs), often implicating themselves in violence. Camp followers felt especially vulnerable, as some Indian soldiers used their superior status to pressure them to join the rebellion.[62] Shoemaker Kian Khan suggested that Indian NCOs "sent a lot of men to our camp who threatened us and fired on us. I ran away in native clothes."[63] Fatteh Mohammed Khan of C Company similarly remembered that "Lance Naik Feroze told us to go with him and that he would take us to safety." Instead, he apparently took them to Tanglin, where German prisoners were interned.[64] Sepoy Ali Nawaz of C Company also claimed ignorance when he followed a group of men going toward Tanglin. There, he saw two Indian soldiers shaking hands with the Germans. Despite being present at one of the most brutal sites of the rebellion, he avoided punishment by identifying several men, some of whom were subsequently executed.[65] These testimonies indicate the difficulty of classifying men as mutineers, including if they were part of the three mutinous "groups" who led the rebellion. Many men were in the wrong place at the wrong time.

Soldiers' experiences of running into the jungle or following the wrong person, rather than staying and fighting, hint at a larger problem of the rebellion. Both British leaders and Indian soldiers had difficulty distinguishing friends from enemies. Sikh Jat Driver Jawala Singh of the Malay States Guides insisted that he was "afraid of being shot either by the 5th Light Infantry or the white people," so he hid in the jungle and laid "low until things were quiet."[66] One Subedar told Jemadar Hans Raj that if "we go out now we will be shot, because the white soldiers cannot discriminate between the loyal and the disloyal."[67] Havildar Abdul Ghani apparently told Lance Havildar Niaz Mahomed of C Company that there was "firing going on and all the sepoys are being killed."[68] Jemadar Rahmat Khan, who communicated with British officers by phone, instructed soldiers: "If you are fired on by black men then you must save your lives, the best you can. If you are fired on by white men throw down your arms and put your hands up."[69] Gunner Ahmed Din of the Malay States Guides did not know who to trust, so he hid near the Kampong Java mosque—a poor choice, given that British leaders considered it a place of sedition. Driver Corporal Ghulam Din, also of the MSG, claimed that he found a Malay civilian and tried to surrender but they told him not to because Indians were "being shot on sight."[70]

As these accounts suggest, many soldiers heard—and believed—that simply being Indian put them in danger of retaliatory violence, whether they had mutinied or not. This also made them uncertain if they should carry or discard their arms. Admiral Jerram apparently told the British men of *Cadmus* to go to Pasir Panjang and "shoot to kill any Indian who they met with a rifle in his hands."[71] Colour Havildar Mahboob of C Company, 5th Light Infantry, noted that officers would think "that if I had a rifle in my hands I was an enemy," so he handed his rifle off to another man.[72] Lance Naik Feroze of C Company recalled his fear of being "shot by either mutineers or soldiers," so he hid his rifle near a Chinese temple, where he found other rifles. He took off his uniform, found "a Malay cap," and met a Malay policeman who directed him to the police thana. En route, he met a Sikh man who told him "that if any of us went near a thana we would be killed." In response, he went to the notorious Kampong Java mosque, where he bought food, prayed, and slept.[73] Sepoy Ibrahim of C Company ran to the jungle on hearing the alarm before heading to the police station. Before arriving, he learned that if someone found him with arms "we would die." This only contributed to his existential fear, and he remained hidden for two weeks. While some men feared being caught with rifles, others were afraid of being caught without them. Lance Naik Ghaffur Khan of C Company stated that some men ran into the barracks, grabbed weapons, and yelled that those without weapons and ammo would be shot.[74] Fear and confusion reigned supreme in the hours and days after the rebellion. Whether they rebelled or wandered in confusion, Indian soldiers fought against the odds to survive.

REFUGE AND SURRENDER

In this tense climate of mistrust and fear, many Indian soldiers fled military spaces and searched for safety. To the surprise of colonial leaders, they often found it from civilians. Within three days of the outbreak, Governor Young asserted confidently that "[t]he Malays are hostile to the mutineers."[75] It is unclear how he ascertained this feeling, given the intensity and confusion of the previous days. In reality, many Indian soldiers mentioned receiving aid from Malay civilians. Sepoy Maksud stayed in a Malay house all night.[76] Bugler Khuda Baksh first hid "in a urine tub" before running "to a Malay's house in the direction of Pasir Panjang and hid there for the rest of the day."[77] Sepoy Zafar Mohamed of H Company was on guard duty and leaving the latrines when shots were fired. Like others, he initially hid in the jungle. He then proceeded to a "Malay Mosque" where he stayed two days. Zahur Ali of B Company came in from jungle without arms or ammo, dressed in Malay clothes. One man was "disguised as a Malay" when arrested and "had shaved off his beard."[78] Mohamed Ishaq of H Company "met a native who talked Hindustani" who helped him find the police station.[79] Colonial leaders found it incomprehensible that non-Indian civilians would assist Indian soldiers. The collapse in British leadership made Asian civilians a source of much-needed help and support.

While Governor Young (incorrectly) asserted that Malay civilians were hostile to Indian soldiers, he did not mention the Chinese population at all. He might have noted that many Chinese civilians aided the British. Edwin Brown believed that the men of his Chinese Company were among the only men to appear organized, in uniform, and with military training when the crisis began. As a result, he prioritized them for operations over untrained and filthy European men in ill-fitting uniforms. When Brown marched captured Indian men to jail, he used his Chinese Company "as they, and they only, of the men at the Drill Hall had any knowledge of the meaning of discipline." These men marched, surrounding the prisoners with fixed bayonets, which Brown believed "did a good deal to calm the fears of the natives in the streets."[80] Sng Choon Yee had a slightly different view. He was a cadet at Raffles school and was posted "on sentry" at a reservoir near the government house during in 1915. When he saw Chinese Volunteers near the jail, he realized that the British "depend very much" on them.[81] Governor Young may have declined to mention the Chinese community because their participation revealed the inadequacy of British militarism.

Another reason for the oversight may have been that some Chinese men faced punishment for trying to help. Bean Lai Hing and Bean Joo Jean—two Chinese men working in European households with "long records of good service"—gave evidence that they were assaulted by "Bengali soldiers."[82] When police investigated, they found a military jacket and evidence of an assault. Since no soldiers were present, though, both men faced sentences of two months' imprisonment for providing "false information."[83] After appeal, they had to pay a fine. Still, British officials defended the initial sentencing, noting that "wild stories" sent troops "on wild goose chases."[84] Despite enduring violence for serving in a European household, and providing evidence of their assault, these men were liars in British leaders' eyes. The courts even extracted money from them because they reported the crime to the proper authorities, as was mandatory under martial law. This further underlined how British legal racism made it impossible for even a "loyal" Chinese civilian to avoid punishment.

While some Chinese civilians aided the British, others appeared as important aids in Indian soldiers' accounts. Havildar Mahboob fled being shot by a Frenchmen by staying in the hut of a Chinese shopkeeper for two nights while wounded. Chaudri Khuda Baksh Khan found refuge in a Chinese hut until nightfall and then asked a Chinese civilian for directions to Singapore center.[85] Some soldiers sought out Chinese civilians because they believed that they were neutral observers to the violence of the rebellion. Bahadur Khan spent the night with Hall in the Colonel's Bungalow and sent messages via a "Chinese boy" because, they believed, "the mutineers were not killing Chinese."[86] Sng Choon Yee confirmed that an Indian soldier went to his cousin's house but didn't "meddle" because they were Chinese. Their family realized that "only Europeans are concerned so we all don't care. None of our business."[87]

Many European and Asian civilians shared the perception that Chinese civilians were immune to the violence of the rebellion. Chin Sian, a Chinese accountant who lived on Pasir Panjang Road, at about 3:30 p.m. "saw about 50 Indian soldiers armed with rifles marching along the road from the west. Three entered his house but did not molest anyone."[88] Captain Ball apparently took refuge at a Chinese civilian's home, believing that this would spare him from violence. A Mr. and Mrs. Reeder "and some ladies" similarly stopped a car and "went to a Chinese house and stayed the night there."[89] A Japanese barber to the German POWs recalled seeing soldiers "firing on the Englishmen who were hiding in a Chinese house."[90] To these observers, some colonial communities could escape violence directed toward another.

Other accounts implied that Indian soldiers collaborated with Chinese civilians. According to Mr. Herbert Smith, a Chinese man named Boey Ah Fook spoke with Indian men about meetings held by a civilian, Mansur, who was later executed for being an anti-colonial revolutionary and planning the rebellion.[91] F. Brooke Hunt, writing on behalf of a Dr. Middleton at Tanglin Hill, witnessed a group of Indian soldiers heading straight for the Chinese kampong (village) after the firing broke out. Staff Sergeant Farrer and Royal Engineers grass cutter Ramoo also noted that Indian soldiers fleeing Tanglin went straight toward the "Chinese village."[92] According to the *Straits Times*, Sapper T. Gough, 41st Company, Royal Engineers, saw Indian soldiers hide together in "a Chinese Kampong near Sepoy Lines."[93] A Mrs. Howell came upon "one soldier talking English to the Chinaman" about how there were "[n]o more officers."[94] Despite what appeared, to some observers, as collaboration between Indian soldiers and Chinese civilians, very few officials or administrators commented upon these encounters. Yet as Sho Kuwajima argues, it is impossible to conclude that Asian civilians were "indifferent" to these events, as so many British leaders claimed, because they were under martial law and feared retribution.[95]

Asian civilians' willingness to aid Indian soldiers reveals much about everyday life in colonial Singapore. Indian soldiers had to perceive Malay and Chinese civilians as a source of comfort and safety to take shelter with them. Civilians, in turn, needed to have sufficient empathy for soldiers to see them as frightened men instead of deadly rebels. Soldiers transgressed ethnic boundaries by putting on and taking off markers of identity that enabled them to assimilate into communities where they sought comfort. Many captured men were "dressed as a Chinaman" or "in Malay clothing." One man remained disguised as a Chinese civilian more than two months after the rebellion.[96] Such disguises were more likely to fool British leaders than the Malay or Chinese civilians who helped in the charade.[97] Still, it reflects Tim Harper's understanding of Singapore as a space where people could constantly reinvent themselves by shedding or gaining class, ethnic, and religious identities so that even "a Punjabi sepoy could become a Malay."[98] British leaders' lack of understanding about soldier-civilian relations suggests that, despite pervasive colonial categorizations, ethnic and racial designations were poor indicators of "loyalty" or "disloyalty," rebellion or support, including among Indian soldiers.

Indian soldiers' feelings of safety among other Asian subjects led them to surrender more readily to Asian police and volunteers than their white counterparts.[99] For some, language barriers played a role. Jemadar Hoshiar Ali saw a British officer coming and believed that "now everything would be all right," however "the officer I could see did not understand our language."[100] The possibility of being misunderstood amplified the tension of surrender. Colour Havildar

Mahboob of C Company noted that when a car carrying armed Europeans approached his party, most of the men laid down their weapons and put up their hands. Two ran away as French soldiers fired on them.[101] Edwin Brown similarly recounted that one "man was seen running away and was shot."[102] Running away created a presumption of guilt. Yet surrendering was an act of trust—and trust between British officers and Indian soldiers had already been broken. By contrast, Asian policemen used their perceived trustworthiness and commonality to capture Indian soldiers. A Malay Lance Corporal, Ibrahim, and an unnamed Bengali policeman successfully captured a group of about fifteen men. The Bengali police constable apparently found the soldiers while he was in uniform, and disguised himself in mufti (plainclothes) to approach them. When they asked why he was armed, he suggested that he was a plantation watchman "and that his rifle was to frighten any wicked Chinese who might be about the plantation." He persuaded them to come to a nearby "Chinese house"—which was actually the police station. When they glimpsed the lock-up, he assured them that it was for "wicked Chinese." He promised food and protection, while also playing into their fears. He suggested that if they got into the lock-up "they would not be seen by soldiers who might shoot them." Once they realized that he was a policeman, and that they were in a police station, one soldier protested: "It is not fair. You are a Mohammedan and you have cheated us."[103] By this account, soldiers felt betrayed by someone they assumed had been trying to help them—amplified by a sense of ethnic and faith-based kinship.

These accounts indicate that there is more at play than "cowardice" or complicity when assessing Indian soldiers' behavior and the responses of Asian civilians. Soldiers repeatedly expressed fears of unjust reprisal—of being killed not in battle, but simply for being perceived as a threat by those they were paid to serve. They lived with the assumption that government officials viewed their lives as disposable, and sought comfort and safety from other colonial subjects. Being murdered without cause was something that *felt* possible. This may have given some a genuine desire to support Ghadar or other revolutionary causes, or to see the rebellion as an opportunity to escape death. Despite this reality, soldiers' fears of being killed by the British was not mentioned in the official report as a reason for the rebellion, or for the delay in "rounding up" men. Instead, persistent *British* fears, such as religious "fanaticism" or "outside instigators," became the primary "causes," erasing soldiers' feelings of powerlessness. Colonial leaders' silence about soldier-civilian relations also complicated any single narrative of white vs. "Black" or Asian. Nonetheless, racism became a primary means through which British officials and white civilians understood the rebellion.

CONSTRUCTING A RACE WAR

During and after the rebellion, most white civilians cast events in Singapore as a pseudo race war—where Indian soldiers were hell-bent on attacking white people. Their evidence usually was secondhand information from Asian civilians rather than direct encounters with soldiers. For example, Mr. Herbert Smith heard from a "boy" that "soldiers had been searching for 'orang putehs'"—white people.[104] European residents at Pasir Panjang learned from a Mandor (supervisor) that the soldiers were "killing Europeans." Mr. E. F. Boode found a "Malay" who told him that "the Indian soldiers were killing all the Europeans." Barrister-at-Law W. Frank Zehnder saw "a Bengali boy" who asked if he was German, and after he responded in the negative, the boy said to him in Malay, "Go at once if you value your life; these Sepoys are shooting all the English." Sikh civilian Narain Singh claimed that Pathans of the Malay States Guides told him that "we are going to shoot the white man."[105] It is unclear if wishful thinking or a desire to redirect violence to soldiers instead of civilians inspired so many to tell white Europeans that they were singularly under attack. The prevalence of rumor and hearsay in both Indian and European accounts suggests that everyone was operating under fear and uncertainty. However, this "race war" idea of the rebellion dominated the colonial response.

Very early in the rebellion, many white Europeans embraced violently racist rhetoric—and actions—against Indian soldiers and Asian civilians. When Indian soldiers left Tanglin, a Tanglin prisoner, Mr. Hanke, heard a Red Cross man distributing ammunition say "When those n------ come back you will have something to shoot with."[106] By rebelling, these soldiers apparently lost their ability to see themselves as superior to Black colonial subjects, betraying a longstanding colonial hierarchy integral to South Asian martial race status. Instead, they became racialized Black "others" in need of violent reprisal. This also made it easier for white observers to justify the deaths of Asian civilians. Eighteen-year-old Marjorie Binnie recalled a rumor that some naval men from the British ship *Cadmus* found the body of a woman killed and "went on their way shooting at all kinds of dark-skinned but quite innocent people—milk and food vendors plying their trade in the streets. I do not know if this rumour was contradicted, but everyone was rather agitated and uncertain at the time, and accidents may easily have happened."[107] British leaders and civilians cast Indian soldiers as "murderous" and indiscriminate "Black" killers. By contrast, Binnie suggests that deliberate, retaliatory killings of "quite innocent" but "dark-skinned" people were just "accidents."

Even missionaries participated in the violent crackdown. White American missionary Preston L. Peach was part of the Civil Guard in 1914 and an honorary Captain in the British army. After the outbreak of violence in 1915, he became an integral part of a "missionary company," under English engineer W. G. Shellabear, tasked "to shoot mutineers."[108] At no point did this religious man question the righteousness of shooting Indian men without trials—though apparently his company was never compelled to do so. Similarly, the rebellion interrupted an annual Methodist conference. While Methodist women boarded ships in the harbor with other white women and children, men appeared at Drill Hall and offered themselves for service. The *Singapore Free Press* reported that it was "very unusual for a body of peaceful Methodist missionaries to adjourn their annual conference in order that they may shoulder rifles."[109] This deployment of "peaceful" Europeans was less surprising for Indian soldiers.

The desire to mobilize as many white people as possible benefited Britain's official wartime enemy: Germans. Mr. Hagemann, a prisoner in Tanglin, recalled a German saying that "all the English dogs ought to be shot."[110] Another Tanglin prisoner, Mr. Hanke, observed Germans destroying bicycles, robbing abandoned bungalows, and decommissioning cars, with the sentiment that they "belong to dead English pig-dogs (*Schweinhund*)." He felt Germans "were quite hostile to any one sympathising with the English."[111] Despite these sentiments, and Britain's active war against Germany, many British men saw Germans as *allies* against Indian troops. This reflected colonial trends that enabled "European" identity to unite white settlers in opposition to Asian and Eurasian "others." As a result, many Britons in Malaya faced accusations of pro-German feeling during the war, including Governor Arthur Young's wife, Lady Evelyn.[112] During the rebellion, a Dr. Fowlie sympathized with Germans for being "frightened—for their own safety" and helpful toward the British. He praised the fact that Germans "helped to search for and attend the wounded."[113] L. A. Thomas recalled that an Indian soldier shot his friend R. L. D. Wodehouse six or seven times while he guarded German internees, but the "German internees came to his rescue."[114] Edwin A. Brown, who fought with a Chinese Company of the Singapore Volunteer Rifles, similarly praised Germans. When offered the chance to escape, he claimed, "To the credit of the Germans let it be said here that they refused as a body."[115] In truth, about seventeen Germans escaped. One of these, Julius Lauterbach, still pointed out that Germans assisted in capturing mutineers.[116] Sergeant C. Keeble of the Royal Garrison Artillery went one step further. He "armed the prisoners as best I could."[117] A rebellion of colonial soldiers led many Britons to cling to white supremacy, with colonial order holding greater importance than the war against Germany.

Compared to widespread white mobilization against Indians, many Indian soldiers protected white soldiers and civilians. Jemadar Hoshiar Ali apparently "restrained Captain Ball thinking that if he moved closer to firing he would be shot."[118] Some Indian soldiers, like their Chinese and Malay counterparts, may have hoped that by aiding the British they could gain protection from rebels and avoid retribution. This was not always successful. Many soldiers later executed as "ringleaders" were at the Indian officers' quarters with British officers Major Cotton, Captain Ball, and Captain Boyce well after the firing had started.[119] Rather than using this opportunity to kill British men, which European accounts portrayed as inevitable, Indian officers Subedar Mohamed Yunnas, Subedar Dunde Khan, Jemadar Chiste Khan, Jemadar Abdul Ali, and Jemadar Hoshiar Ali restrained the British officers from proceeding to their respective Double Company lines because "their lives would be endangered."[120] If these men were "ringleaders," hell-bent on indiscriminately killing British officers, why were they spending the first minutes of the rebellion warning them? Was it a rouse to prevent successful mobilization? Or a genuine attempt to protect them?

White civilians also noted that they were warned or saved by Indian soldiers. Barrister Zehnder heard from a Mr. and Mrs. Finley that they had been "advised by a Native officer of the 5th Light Infantry to get away as the trouble was serious."[121] Other Indian soldiers, by Bell's account, told rebels not to shoot him because "this is our doctor."[122] One soldier warned European residents of Pasir Panjang that "orang puteh" (white people) had been killed. Mr. Mansfield also found fifteen soldiers of the 5th Light Infantry in an office who tried to persuade him to remain there to avoid violence.[123] Mr. Herbert Smith "met a good many soldiers both armed and unarmed" who "did not molest me in any way."[124] Sunder Singh, working as a watchman at Pasir Panjang Rubber Works, noted that Subedar Wahid Ali approached the building to warn and protect the Dutchmen inside.[125] Rebelling Indian soldiers made careful decisions about who was targeted for violence and who should be spared. Many soldiers did what they could to protect civilians. Whiteness was not a death sentence.

Strikingly, soldiers were most consistent in avoiding violence against white women. This contrasted a wider colonial perception that white women embodied imperial victimhood and vulnerability.[126] The most famous example was the notorious massacre of white women and children in Cawnpore (Kanpur) during a major rebellion of Indian soldiers in 1857. Such events received far more commemoration and public attention than British leaders' brutality against Indian soldiers and civilians during the same conflict. Still, such events weighed on the minds of British officials in 1915, and they quickly evacuated white women and children living in Singapore by putting them on ships in the harbor. While many women remained behind, the only confirmed death of a white woman was Mrs. Woollcombe, who died after attempting to save her husband.[127] The far more common experience was for soldiers to spare them. Two women survived an attack during which their husbands were shot.[128] One European woman in Pasir Panjang telephoned her husband because "there were so many soldiers in our garden."[129] A Mrs. Gertrude Marshall was in a car when soldiers opened fire, striking both men but neither of the women or a baby.[130] A Mrs. Robinson encountered "a Sepoy without a turban" in uniform who had "a rifle and a bag full of ammunition." He claimed responsibility for killing European men, but did not threaten her.[131] She had another encounter with "10 or 12 Sepoys in uniform with turbans, all with rifles and bayonets fixed," but they "motioned with their hands that they did not want to hurt them."[132]

As these accounts suggest, many Indian soldiers spent the uncertain days of the rebellion sparing or saving white people. Despite this reality, the "race war" narrative endured, emphasizing white vulnerability. American missionary Peach's memoirs claimed that the "whole European population narrowly excaped [*sic*] a tragic end" in 1915.[133] Assistant Police Superintendent Thomas suggested that rebel soldiers "shot any Europeans they believed to be British."[134] The *Straits Times* in 1928 described soldiers' intentions in 1915 as "to murder every white man in Singapore."[135] A 2021 display at the National Museum of Singapore still claimed that "850 soldiers from the 5th Light Infantry" killed "47 officers and civilians, mostly British."[136] Similarly, the Singapore National Gallery described the 1915 rebellion as follows: "Around 800 Indian mutineers roam Singapore's streets, killing British officers they encounter."[137] By these accounts, all eight hundred Indian soldiers were rebels, and only the deaths of (white) British people counted. Yet the real race war was against Indian men.

CRIMINALIZING INDIANS

Once white soldiers and civilians internalized the fear of the rising, they responded by doubling down on existing patterns of racial violence. All Indian soldiers—and many civilians—became "mutineers" in the eyes of Europeans.[138] By February 20, a formal "Proclamation under Martial Law" required "all Indians of whatever race to report" at police stations, where they "were required to satisfy the authorities that they were not soldiers."[139] Indian men were guilty until they could prove their innocence. This forced men over eighteen to make themselves vulnerable by leaving safe cover and approaching police stations. There, or en route, they might encounter armed British volunteers with minimal military training—or French, Russian, Malay, or Japanese troops instructed to view all Indian men as mutineers. Some civilians, including Kasim Ismail Mansur and Pir Nur Alam Shah, were arrested and hanged due to alleged links to anticolonial networks.[140] In 1915 Singapore, the people most likely to experience violence were Indian.

Soon after the rebellion, British leaders used a variety of assumptions to define Indian disloyalty. Just three days after the initial firing, Governor Arthur Young suggested that the "mutineers are the Right Wing of the 5th Light Infantry, Rajput Moslems," even though many men were still missing at the time. By contrast, he found that on the left wing "many men are offering assistance and surrendering."[141] As with military recruitment, unit organization followed ethnic lines: The right wing of the 5th Light Infantry was predominantly filled with Ranghars, Muslim Rajputs from Punjab, as well as Jats and Lohias (blacksmiths). The left wing was staffed by Hindustani Pathans. British leaders perceived differences of rank, caste, and faith to be major issues in the regiment prior to the outbreak and therefore searched for culpability using the same parameters.[142] In reality, identity did not predict which men were guilty as much as it determined who British leaders condemned.

Despite confidence in distinguishing the "loyal" from the "mutinous," many British leaders' initial assumptions were quickly debunked. On the day of the rising, Governor Young wrote to the Governor of Hong Kong alleging the complicity of the 36th Sikhs.[143] By the next day, he confidently asserted that "the detachment of 36th Sikhs is not implicated in the outbreak, as formerly held."[144] The earlier report was, according to General Ridout, a case of mistaken identity. Ridout stated that "the persons reporting it had applied the term Sikhs to all natives."[145] Embarrassingly, this "person" may have been Ridout's own wife. Lt W. N. Sneesby suggested that Mrs. Ridout came to the bungalow and informed his wife that the Sikh guard had mutinied.[146] She was not the only one. Several European observers suspected Sikhs or pointed out their suspicious behavior.[147] Private Robertson of the Singapore Volunteer Rifles "noticed the Sikhs were rather excited: a number of them were rushing about in their barrack room in mufti," although "I did not see them shooting." When members of the court of inquiry asked him about their behavior toward volunteers, he said, "They appeared to be very 'sombong,' high and haughty and insolent. They rather looked down on us. It was generally noticed by our men that they looked upon us very contemptuously."[148] General Ridout also believed that there was "a good deal of sedition talked by the men of the Sikh watchmen class, but little or no constructive sedition."[149] It is unclear what he meant by "constructive sedition." What is clear is that British leaders perceived Muslim soldiers as guilty, so they ignored or excused Sikh men's behavior.

Many civilians also struggled to comprehend soldiers' identities. Sng Choon Yee referred to the events as the "Kabul revolution" and referred to soldiers as "the Kabuls." This may have been a reference to men's recruitment from the Afghan border area or their presumed inclusion in anti-colonial plots linking Indian activists with revolutionaries in Afghanistan.[150] Other misidentification happened because of the unit name: the 5th Bengal Light Infantry. Many people, from Indian grass cutters to police, Japanese barbers to European civilians, reported seeing a "lot of Bengalis."[151] Mr. Hanke in Tanglin claimed to see "Bengali Sepoys" shaking hands with German prisoners. He also referred to the troops as "natives."[152] Even though Indian troops were not Indigenous or permanent residents of Singapore, their distance from whiteness in colonial categorization made them "natives," collapsing their identities into an incomprehensible jumble.

These dynamics made the identification of suspects challenging. The official report suggested that due to the "alarming" and "rapidly passing events," it was difficult to attain positive "recognition of the offenders."[153] The report suggested that this was gendered, because among "those who were in a position to have identified the murderers were civilians, some of them ladies who were not accustomed to dealing with Indians." Yet several women had vivid memories of men they encountered. Mary Robinson remembered soldiers who "were perfectly polite and respectful to us" when they approached "to be taken to the Police Station."[154] She also recalled meeting a "thin and palish" Malay "boy" with "a very clear complexion for a native" who was "good looking."[155] Others indicated that Sikh men received rides in cars from European women during the rebellion, providing opportunities for close contact.[156] Mrs. Gertrude M. Marshall vividly described an Indian soldier who was "quite young, smooth faced. He had a white turban with something red in his hat, conical shape. He had rather a clean fair skin, was a few inches over 5 feet high, and particularly handsome."[157] These thorough descriptions indicate that women remembered Indian soldiers very well. The problem may not have been that women could not identify soldiers. Some may have been reluctant to do so given their positive encounters, the hasty nature of retribution, or underlying eroticism.

The desire to differentiate loyal/disloyal soldiers as quickly as possible benefited men of the Malay States Guides. According to the official report, when Captain Maclean died, "the great majority appear to have dispersed into the jungle."[158] In other words, they took almost identical actions to the men of the 5th

Light Infantry. Despite official disdain for the MSG in December 1914, officials in February 1915 portrayed them as well-intentioned rubes manipulated by the scheming 5th Light Infantry. One British leader rationalized the MSG's fearful response to flee into the jungle: "[T]hey had few arms and but little ammunition, their conduct, though lacking in initiative, was perhaps justifiable." Such rationale was not offered for the men of the 5th who made the same choice.[159] Another officer reasoned that the MSG were "drivers who were not trained to arms," so the 5th Light Infantry must have forced them to join. These soldiers' agency was erased beneath colonial assumptions about which types of men could be instigators of rebellion, and which were passive and coerced. Preexisting assumptions about which soldiers were culpable, and which were in the wrong place at the wrong time, enabled some men to escape punishment while others came under suspicion.

Efforts to portray the MSG as hapless victims contrasted reports that some of their men were instigators and leaders in the rebellion. Narain Singh, a Sikh civilian, saw five men of the Malay States Guides declare their intention to kill Mr. Herbert Smith.[160] Colour Havildar Mohamed Din of B Company "noticed some of the Malay States Guides amongst the attackers." He was "quite certain that I saw them," including "a tall fair Sikh, with a little hair on his face" who was wounded and bleeding. He claimed to see this man "bending down and taking ammunition out of a box near the lorry" but was unable—or unwilling—to identify him when given the opportunity.[161] Shopkeeper Sambhudat witnessed soldiers trying to break into the magazine with pickaxes and singled out a man named Nutha Singh, a Sikh, who apparently "had friends in the Battery (Malay States Guides)" and "was a drunkard and frequently talked angrily to sepoys."[162] Despite a variety of men implicated in these events—including Sikhs and members of the Malay States Guides—earlier assumptions guided the court proceedings. When a group of seven soldiers was found hiding in a Chinese kampong, the defense, Mr. da Silva, noted that "they were also Sikhs, not men of the religion of the people who, they knew as a fact, were the mutineers."[163] The fact that these men were armed was irrelevant. Also unacknowledged was that Sikhs—long prized as ideal "martial races"—had connections to the anti-colonial Ghadar—or Mutiny—movement that spanned from India, across Southeast Asia, to the Pacific Northwest.[164] However, they did not fit into British understandings of supposed Muslim violence, so they evaded punishment.

These perceptions had a profound influence on Singapore's Muslim community. Sng Choon Yee observed that one civilian, Mansur, had been "highly respected by the government" until he was killed for contributing to the mutiny.

Sng associated this decision with his faith more than his actions because "he's a Muslim" and the rebels, he believed, were "all Muslims."[165] Meanwhile, according to prominent Singapore Muslim Syed Omer Alsagoff, "there was great excitement in the town over recent occurrences."[166] This included prevalent rumors that the Muslim men of the 5th Light Infantry were killed because they had refused to fight, rather than because they had mutinied.[167] This led Governor Arthur Young to suggest holding "a meeting" to "explain as widely as possible the action the Government had taken."[168] As a result, on March 6, 1915, Victoria Memorial Hall hosted three thousand members of Singapore's Muslim community. The *Malaya Tribune* described the event as a chance for Muslims to avow their loyalty.[169] Official correspondence suggests that the meeting was about giving the government the chance to explain its actions. Instead, it became a vehicle for surveillance. Young enlisted "[a] secret agent" from India who already provided information to the General Officer Commanding that led to several arrests. The agent attended the meeting and concluded that he did "not question the sincere loyalty of the leading Mohammedans in Singapore, although he did hear the expression of disloyal sentiments in the crowd."[170] An event organized to give the government the chance to explain its actions and calm the Muslim community resulted in further criminalization and monitoring. This revealed that the extreme violence of the rebellion had contributed to, rather than curbed, "disloyal sentiments."

For most white volunteers, who knew little of the differences between the 5th and the MSG, or Muslims and Sikhs, all Indian men were culpable because their *existence* contributed to white men's fears. Missionary Preston Peach recalled that while patrolling for Indian soldiers, "We saw none but I fully believe they saw us."[171] Even more experienced men, like Brown, echoed this view: "[Y]ou may imagine what it felt like to know that somewhere, certainly not more than a mile off, behind that line of mangrove swamp and bits of scrub, seven hundred men well trained in the use of arms were concentrating."[172] The fact that soldiers existed temporarily outside the strict boundaries of military discipline and racial hierarchy made them inherently threatening. His mention of "seven hundred men" hiding in the jungle dismissed their possible innocence. This helped to romanticize the plucky and outnumbered, if ill-trained, Europeans who violently crushed the rebellion. Ultimately, for many Europeans, distinctions between the loyal and the disloyal did not matter.[173] Brown oversaw the relocation of surrendered Indian soldiers from the barracks to the prison. While doing so, he forced Indian soldiers to tend to a herd of donkeys and carry up to twelve boltless rifles each. This understandably irritated the men—many of whom had, by Brown's own account, "taken refuge with the Colonel."[174] Even men who helped the British and stayed with them all night could not avoid punishment. This revealed how whiteness functioned in colonial Singapore in 1915. White fears of racial persecution created the conditions for the imprisonment of and violence against racialized colonial subjects, regardless of "guilt" or "innocence."

RETRIBUTION

The uncertainty and contradiction evident throughout many testimonies and reports contrasts the speed and certainty with which British officials meted out heavy punishments. British courts tried more than two hundred Indian soldiers—a quarter of the 5th Light Infantry—by court-martial. They convicted more than two hundred. Sentences included over forty executions, over sixty transportations for life, dozens of prison terms between ten and twenty years, and over twenty shorter prison terms between six weeks and seven years. Fifty-two soldiers died fighting or trying to escape. The total death toll of soldiers and civilians was at least 124. Executions continued until April 18, with courts-martial until September 1915 as men continued to come out of hiding.[175] However, British officials admitted that they made these decisions with limited evidence. The official report noted that "[i]t is much to be regretted that practically no evidence to connect the individuals responsible for these outrages has been adduced."[176] Despite "practically no evidence," they sentenced more than forty men to death. This echoed the behavior of MSG commander Lees, who accused men of the Malay States Guides in December 1914 while "hoping" to find evidence. Margaret Binnie, who was eighteen in Singapore, recalled years later: "Of the trial and execution of several of these soldiers it suffices to say that it was a chapter unworthy of British decency and fit, perhaps, to be associated with the savage punishment of Indian soldiers fifty years or more earlier when they were blown from guns after the Indian Mutiny."[177] As a white woman—the paragon of imagined British vulnerability—Binnie's parallel to the more famous 1857 rebellion did not emphasize British helplessness, but brutality. British racial violence proved to be far more all-encompassing than anything carried out by Indian soldiers.

Even sympathetic accounts of Indian men hint at how colonial racism facilitated violence. Binnie worked during the trials as a secretary for a group of barristers and attended the trial of civilian Kasi Ismail Mansur. She recalled that it "remains in my memory as the most solemn and dignified tragedy I have ever witnessed." She had "doubts as to the justice of the sentence."[178] British leaders even admitted that they lacked evidence in this case, with General Ridout expressing that "I have no doubt that Mansur did try to alienate the loyalty of the

5th Light Infantry, although no direct proof can be obtained."[179] As with Lees, Ridout supported harsh sentences and punishments—including death—despite "no direct proof." However, even Binnie was swayed by the appeal of colonial victimhood. The barrister, her "best beloved friend, Clad Terrell," dispelled her anxieties by suggesting that Mansur "lived as a British subject within the benevolence of the British nation and he sought to betray that nation and bring untold sufferings to its people here."[180] The tendency to regard British rule as "benevolent" and to see colonial subjects as deserving of violent reprisals for threatening "the British nation" and "its people" hints at the larger stakes of the rebellion. The perceived credibility and viability of British imperialism were on the line. As a result, many leaders, witnesses, and officials erased the realities of the rebellion and the complexities of Indian soldiers' experiences to emphasize white victimhood.

Despite minimal evidence, public executions became a way to perform and reassert colonial power. A particularly noteworthy example occurred on March 22, 1915, when twenty-one Indian soldiers received sentences before a crowd of six thousand civilians.[181] The British-led court found all of the court-martialed men guilty. Sixteen received sentences of transportation or imprisonment, and five—Subedar Dunde Khan, Jemadar Chisti Khan, Havildar Rahmat Ali, Sepoy Hakim Ali, and Havildar Abdul Ghani—were sentenced to summary execution by firing squad. One *Malaya Tribune* article suggested the desired outcome of such proceedings. Men left the prison "punctually," accompanied by a "strong guard." Those convicted of being absent for three days with arms received prison sentences of one and half or two years. Men alleged to have "joined a mutiny" and "absented themselves for several days" received sentences ranging from transportation (banishment to a prison island) for fifteen years, to transportation for life. Five men accused of "stirring up and joining in a Mutiny" were sentenced to death. The article explained that "these men of the Indian Army have broken their oaths as soldiers of His Majesty the King. *Thus justice is done*."[182] "Justice" included tying men to posts so they could "pay the price for their traitorous deed." A party of Royal Garrison Artillery and Royal Engineers "were speedily facing them." Sentences of death were read in all four languages, before giving the order of "Ready," "Present," "Fire." According to the article, "the traitors met their well-deserved doom. The firing was splendidly timed and the whole affair quickly over." The medical examiner inspected the men's bodies. The crowd then "quickly left the scene after justice had been done and which most undoubtedly have left a salutary impression on the minds of the spectators."[183] By this account, the entire event was logical, disciplined, and justified.

In reality, public executions inspired a range of reactions. A common response was horror at the ineptitude and brutality of British power. On one occasion, according to Assistant Superintendent of Police Thomas, a firing squad shot a convicted man and took him to the mortuary. There, they found that he was not dead and amputated his leg instead. He was subsequently "shot sitting in a chair."[184] Another early firing party commanded by Lt. Malcolm Bond Shelley of the Malay States Volunteers had problems when two of the ten men were unable to load their clips and then missed their targets when they fired.[185] On March 25, just three days after the apparently "splendidly timed" and "punctual" events described above, an execution underlined military inefficiency by mishandling the simultaneous execution of twenty-two men. As detailed above, the men were tied against the stakes in front of the firing party, consisting of 110 men of the Singapore Volunteers Corps, under Captain Tongue, S.V.A. There were five soldiers in the firing party per one convicted man. The order to fire came at 5:30 p.m. and "all the men fell." However, Captain Fraser of the RAMC examined the bodies and found that "in some cases . . . life did not appear extinct" so "the men were despatched by revolver shots." An even larger crowd than before was present, amounting to approximately 15,000. Officials found that the "proceedings passed off quietly and the crowd dispersed as soon as the bodies were removed."[186] Silence, to the British, meant that the crowd left with the intended respect for justice. However, many among them had encountered and even sheltered Indian soldiers, and they now witnessed Indian soldiers executed in a haphazard way without evidence. Eventually, Chinese Volunteers replaced Europeans because their superior training enabled them to carry out executions with greater precision. If anything, public executions revealed British inadequacy.

Death was not the only fate facing Indian soldiers in 1915. All men of the 5th Light Infantry suffered from the rebellion, whether they were executed, imprisoned, or under no suspicion whatsoever. The outbreak forced them to live in unsanitary, packed conditions or wander in the jungle without supplies, clean clothes, sanitation, or food. Numerous European military and police personnel commented on Indian men being "dirty and wet" and "very emaciated and fatigued" when captured.[187] Those fearing unjust retribution only gave themselves up after days or weeks of privation, and then invariably faced death or years in prison. General Officer Commanding Ridout was unsympathetic, portraying soldiers as beasts: "The enemy are very scattered, they hide by day in dense jungle and come out to feed at night."[188] Here, all Indian soldiers were "enemies" if they remained outside of British custody. The *Singapore Free Press* similarly emphasized the men's sad state to reassure the public: "The men who have been lately captured show great exhaustion from exposure and want of food."[189] Few accounts wrestled with the reality of soldiers' privation, and the fear and desperation that motivated them to stay in the jungle for days—if not weeks or months—in such conditions.

After capture or surrender, Indian soldiers' hardships continued. They had to live in a variety of locations—Drill Hall, prison, or a prison ship, where they were almost uniformly treated like criminals. Many remained on the prison ship for months.[190] During that time, many, like Lance Naik Ghaffur Khan of C Company, were unable to offer testimony because the "sergeant in charge of the ship does not understand Hindustani."[191] Eventually, those considered "loyal" relocated to St. John's Island, a former quarantine station. By April 27, 1915, more than two months after the rebellion, over 400 men remained on St. John's.[192] Over 150 remained on the prison ship. For months, Straits Settlements, War Office, and Government of India officials debated what to do with the remainder of the regiment. Surviving men of the 5th Light Infantry ultimately remained in Singapore, unsure of their fates, until July. At that point, the "depressed" convicted men went to India to face imprisonment, while the non-convicted men went to West Africa to continue their service.

The best-case scenario for the surviving men of the 5th Light Infantry was some combination of a few terrible days in the jungle, months on a prison ship or remote island, followed by the rigors of war. R.C.D. Bradley, British Advisor to Johore State in 1933, delighted in their universal suffering. He referred to the non-convicted men, many of whom surrendered immediately, aided civilians, and even protected British officers, as "the remnant of that mutinous Hindustani crowd." He appreciated that they were referred to as "Snake Charmers" by other units serving with them in Africa and "had a strenuous and anything but rosy time." Colonial racism enabled him to assert (incorrectly) that they were "Hindustani Mohammedans" and therefore "birds of an entirely different species" from the more widely recruited communities like Punjabi Muslims. This made them "the same breed exactly that was the worst for cruelties to our women and children during the great mutiny of 1857."[193] It did not matter that the 5th was a "loyal" unit in 1857, or that soldiers in 1915 spared and even saved women. Through Bradley's (deeply inaccurate) lens, the rebellion was an inevitable and unbroken line of ethnic disloyalty, and Indian men could only be controlled through racism and violence.

RACE WAR RESUMED

Brigadier General Frederick Aubrey Hoghton, who authored the Court of Inquiry and summary report of the 1915 rebellion, concluded that the events of February 1915 could have been prevented if Europeans had remained unified.[194] He believed that a few bad officers, alongside Indian "fanatics," were to blame, absolving the army and colonial leadership of greater scrutiny. A *Singapore Free Press* author claimed similarly in June 1915 that the mutiny happened because British leaders failed to maintain racial hierarchy. The author explained that when he came to Singapore years before, he noticed "the laxity on the part of natives of India in showing any respect to Europeans." He lamented that "Asiatics generally pushed past and jostled Europeans," which contrasted "the relations existing in India between the European and the native." He speculated that Indians perceived "*Tuans* [masters] on the Malay standard, but precious few *Sahibs* [sirs] of the Indian standard." In his view, this led Indian soldiers to believe "that there are no Sahibs here. With all the regrettable political results that must follow from that quite inevitable impression."[195] Stable governance, in his view, hinged on colonial subjects knowing their place. Yet white Europeans proved to be more unified than anyone else. Racism and racial violence had unsettled soldiers long before 1915. British leaders used the same to reinstate colonial rule. The wrong lessons had been learned.

British leaders imagined the 1915 rebellion as a race war—targeting white Europeans indiscriminately. They, and many subsequent scholars, marveled at rebels' seeming lack of leadership and coherence, given their numeric advantage. However, this only makes sense under the assumption that all soldiers were motivated by a principle of racial annihilation. Undoubtedly, the British response became a race war. All Indian soldiers caught with rifles endured the fate of mutineers. Nearly one hundred soldiers died—over forty from executions and at least fifty while fighting. The latter were not counted in the tallies of victims, whether they fought for or against the British, turning them into mutineers by default. All Indians faced criminalization. Asian civilians tried to harbor scared men—white and Indian—while evading violence. Indian soldiers failed to indiscriminately murder Europeans because it was never their intention. Some fought for revolution. Others fought for their lives. Many were caught in the cross fire. The rebellion "failed" precisely because it did not follow a pattern of indiscriminate colonial violence.

When British officials feared an Indian rebellion, they commissioned reports, discharged dissenters, identified "ringleaders," and reassessed troop movements. When they feared for their lives, they used force of arms to impose what was implicit in their previous actions: a belief that Indians were violent and brutal subjects who needed to be tamed by force. When Indian soldiers feared their officers, they sought comfort—by sharing news with one another or by seeking alternative information in the bazaar, barracks, or mosques. When they feared for their lives, they rebelled. Both leaders and subjects sought information and control before turning to violence. The difference was their ability to access and implement both. British leaders retained far greater power over both information and violence—attempting to control what soldiers learned, who they talked to, and what they could think. They could—and did—inflict violence against soldiers and civilians on a much larger scale in the name of preserving "peace." Meanwhile, Indian soldiers' pre-rebellion visions of being indiscriminately killed by the British, getting trapped on a ship like the *Komagata Maru*, or not going to Hong Kong, all came true.

The seemingly swift end to the rebellion did little to end British fears of Indian men, as anti-colonial activities continued during and after the war. In the months after the 1915 rebellion, Governor Young worried that "a section of Sikhs here have seditious sympathies," indicating the continued influence of Ghadar and other anti-colonial networks on some Sikh men. Nonetheless, by August 1916, he supported the formation of a Sikh Volunteer Company, believing that it "would be a centre of loyalty."[196] General Officer Commanding Ridout agreed, believing that Sikhs were "earnest of their loyalty to the Crown."[197] It did not take long for colonial leaders to return to the belief that through careful recruitment and ethnic hierarchy, loyalty could be pruned—hand-picked from uncontrollable masses of racialized "others." By contrast, the white civilian population clung to the (equally) racist narratives of fear during the revolt used to justify brutal, relentless violence and retribution. If Indians had carried out a race war against Europeans, and needed to be violently crushed to end it, how could Indians— they reasoned—ever be trusted to bear arms in Singapore again? The rebellion laid bare the fault lines of racial militarism in colonial Singapore. These only magnified the feelings of racial terror underpinning the everyday experience of colonialism for Asian soldiers and civilians. Meanwhile, the Malay and Chinese civilians who aided Indian soldiers fleeing for their lives witnessed British leaders, allies, and volunteers haphazardly and indiscriminately kill Indian soldiers, while criminalizing civilians. By failing to acknowledge that such soldier-civilian sympathies even existed, British leaders similarly ignored how these events might have unsettled colonial subjects more broadly.

The 1915 rebellion led many white civilians, officers, and volunteers to fear or experience violence, which they cast as feelings of racial persecution. Yet Indian soldiers carried real and persistent fears of death, of dishonor, of racism, and of war before, during, and after 1915. This lingering and sinking anxiety often connected them to other Asian civilians living under colonialism. Even though many of Singapore's Chinese, Malay, and Indian residents had not yet embraced a united front of explicit anti-colonialism, they nonetheless aided soldiers commissioned to fight *for*—rather than against—Britain and its empire. British leaders observed and responded to these nascent anti-colonial allegiances by mobilizing racism to justify violent reprisals. Doing so during a global war revealed how anti-colonial aims could—and could not—be attained in wartime, setting the stage for future upheavals.

TWO

Making Enemies between the Wars

Amid global war, a Japanese journalist, Koji Tsukuda, recalled the rise of Japanese power in Singapore: "All races without exception, gave way to the Japanese on the footpath . . . we were in military possession of a Portion of the British territory." He wondered about the significance of "the flag of the Rising Sun" being "set up in the centre of Singapore?"[1] This patriotic depiction of Japanese triumph was not in response to the Japanese conquest of Singapore in 1942. Rather, Tsukuda wrote about the 1915 rebellion, when Japanese military personnel and civilians aided the British against a revolt of Indian troops. For Tsukuda, Britain's dependence on Japanese aid during the First World War revealed British fragility in Asia and Japan's own triumphant rise to power. He recalled that the Japanese in Singapore had been "slighted both by the British and the native," but now it "devolved upon us to protect the feeble and pitiable British." He insisted that when the Japanese arrived on the scene against Indian forces, they "at once broke up the main strength of the enemy," succeeding militarily where the British had failed.[2] Even an assistant superintendent of police recalled that the Japanese "seemed to be better organised than any other community."[3] Tsukuda viewed the 1915 rebellion as a display of Britain's dependence on, and inferiority to, its Asian allies. This, he suggested, forced both British leaders and Asian civilians in Singapore to recognize the value of the Japanese. The racial politics of the British Empire, he suggested, could never be the same.

British leaders disagreed. The General Staff in 1917 denied that the British owed their success to the Japanese, noting that "the Japanese did not do much."[4]

This response contrasted Britain's outpouring of gratitude to the landing parties of Japanese warships and the Japanese Consul at Singapore in 1915.[5] Ultimately, the 1917 response more accurately reflected the length of British gratitude to their Asian allies. Japan's unsuccessful petition for racial equality at the 1919 Versailles conference indicated just how fleeting wartime "equality" had been.[6] Yet this exclusion obscures the fact that Japanese volunteers, like Tsukuda, brought their own assumptions of racial difference to Singapore. Tsukuda reinforced British narratives of the revolt by suggesting that Indian troops were "savages" who exhibited "the greatest violence." He echoed colonial racialization by suggesting that Indians were "easily managed" and "like little children" when "in a good temper" but "as fearful as fierce tigers or demons" when angry. Staking a claim for Japanese preeminence over Indians, he believed, was a precondition of claiming equality to the British. He delighted in the once "so arrogant" British coming to "greatly value us."[7] He even noted that a condition of Japanese aid was that Japanese men were "treated in exactly the same way as the British volunteers" and remained under "the command of their own officers." Britain's vulnerable position forced them to accept these conditions. Once they regained control, overtures for equal treatment ended.

This chapter examines how British leaders' unresolved racial animosity, laid bare in the 1915 rebellion, deepened in the interwar period as nations and empires vied for primacy on the world stage. Many historians have discussed how the period was one of vast cosmopolitan revolutionary activism emanating from the First World War. This, they argue, compelled colonial leaders to grudgingly give greater rights and privileges to colonial subjects, particularly in the military, making possible the slow but inevitable transition to decolonization.[8] However, this chapter looks at the collision of anti-colonial activism and waning European power through the lens of white racial resentment toward rising Asian powers. This often manifested as racism against colonial subjects who might find affinity with nations such as Japan or China and question the rule of white leaders. As Tsukuda's testimony indicates, Japan's colonial and martial growth included cultivation of Japan's own racial colonial identity. Meanwhile, Chinese nationalists increasingly positioned themselves through resistance to Japanese domination. This was especially true after the First World War, when the Treaty of Versailles conceded Chinese territory to the Japanese with British assent. Since both Japan and China had aided the British, it seemed inexplicable that China should lose territory with British support. This resulted in backlash and resentment among many of Singapore and Malaya's residents whose homes or family origins were in China, spurring further support for Chinese nationalist politics.[9] Rather than addressing their subjects' concerns, British leaders regarded Asian subjects as nascent problems fomenting "racial" antagonisms. As Britain anticipated another global war, British leaders made many enemies in the name of preserving a fragile colonial "peace."

LOSING "LOYALTY"

Before the end of the First World War, many colonial subjects wondered what "peace" could mean for them. While Tsukuda revealed British leaders' short-lived gratitude to Japanese volunteers, many colonial subjects who aided the British in 1915 faced punishment or slander, rather than rewards, for doing so. One striking case involved Towkay (Boss) Yeo Bian Chuan, who by all accounts sheltered at least seventeen Europeans in his home on Pasir Panjang in 1915. As a result, he faced years of slander and harassment despite British leaders considering him loyal. This was not a foregone conclusion. In 1916, some of those he sheltered offered a letter citing their "sincere appreciation" for his "congeniality and unfailing kindness" in allowing them to "shelter in your house."[10] After the war, a few British officials believed that he deserved official government recognition—perhaps even a medal. Events then took an unexpected turn. European officials and civilians ultimately disparaged Yeo's personality and character. Yeo, in turn, sought legal and press support to get what he was promised. All of this occurred even though no one ever disputed that Yeo sheltered Europeans on February 15, 1915. However, accounts varied widely about events of that night. British leaders enacted a "hierarchy of credibility" that privileged European testimonies over that of a Chinese man who fulfilled British standards of heroism.[11] For Yeo, inconsistencies and half-truths became evidence of his—but not Europeans'—duplicity. His case shows that even when civilians endured personal risk to aid British power, British martial racism discarded them.

According to Yeo, the night of February 15, 1915, started with a party at his home in celebration of the Chinese New Year. Soon, "English ladies and their husbands" came to his home "terribly upset" about the rebellion. He understood the risk but "never hesitated," opening his home to them and escorting them to the top level. He continued with his party to avoid suspicion and instructed his servants to act normally. He claimed that on two occasions, Indian soldiers came to his home. Once, they even threatened him with bayonets. He apparently bluffed by telling them they were free to search the house and that he would accept death if they found any Europeans inside. He then "comforted the European Party, especially the ladies and said that in the morning undoubtedly the

English soldiers would come and rescue them." His immediate reward was to have his home wrecked—not by mutineers—but by a drunk European man who recklessly shot off a pistol, destroyed property, and had to be restrained by others. Yeo felt powerless because the man responsible was the son of longtime friend and neighbor. The next morning, the Europeans went away. Yeo rewarded his servants and comforted his family.[12]

Throughout his testimony, Yeo Bian Chuan evoked narratives of heroism that would resonate with British leaders. He admitted to being scared but nonetheless portrayed himself heroically: "seeming very brave, but my knees knocking together." He cast Indian soldiers as violent and fearsome—"fully armed with rolling eyes and I could see murder in their faces." He emphasized the "blackness" of the soldiers and their intention to kill "white people" indiscriminately—echoing British narratives. He cast himself as a hapless if well-intentioned victim, enduring the violence of a drunk European man, who carelessly destroyed Yeo's possessions. He reassured white women—ever the embodiment of British imperial victimhood—that they would be safe, while fulfilling his duty to protect his own family. Whether true, false, or embellished, these details are largely irrelevant to the larger story—that Yeo sheltered Europeans in his home. However, the smaller details became British leaders' primary focus to undermine his claims to heroism.

Initially, British leaders agreed that Yeo deserved recognition. In October 1920, one colonial official recalled that "Towkay Yeo Bian Chuan behaved very well indeed" and found his account "substantially correct."[13] Several officials debated what reward to offer.[14] By December, H. Allen of the Chinese Protectorate's office offered Yeo the choice of either "a Gold Medal from Government" or $5,000 cash. Yeo chose the medal. In February 1921, he gained naturalization as a British subject, free of charge, solidifying his path to officially-recognized heroism.[15] However, things changed with the involvement of Dudley Ridout, the General Officer Commanding the Straits Settlements during the 1915 rebellion. In late January 1921, Ridout suggested that Yeo had received sufficient gratitude from those he sheltered. He believed that Yeo's assistance "in critical times" was "not a solitary" example and mentioned the "dozens of cases of fine self sacrificing [*sic*] help given by Asiatics that day." Rather than encouraging British leaders to recognize Britain's debt to Asian civilians in Singapore more widely, Ridout insisted that celebrating Yeo would only "raise the question of others among the Asiatic communities." As a result, Ridout opposed providing either "money or medal."[16]

Ridout's suggestions were enough for other colonial administrators to change course. Instead of issuing Yeo a medal, they sent copies of his testimony to multiple European men with connections to the events of that night. Those who replied all confirmed that Yeo took them in. However, they disagreed widely—with him and with one another—about what else transpired. One of the first Europeans to analyze the testimony was Mr. D. D. Mackie Sr.—who was not present at Yeo's residence on the night in question. Rather, he was the father of the man accused of getting drunk and shooting off a pistol. Mackie Sr. admitted that it was "true" that Yeo "gave them shelter" but insisted that his "story is a far exaggeration." Mindful of his son's reputation, Mackie Sr. dismantled Yeo's credibility. He fixated on small inaccuracies and depicted British men as the real heroes of the moment, protecting the women while "armed with guns or rifles." Mackie explained away his son's drunkenness by suggesting that they "were plied with drink," which led to "a violent argument during the night" between Mackie Jr. and a Mr. F. Keller.[17] What might have been a gesture of hospitality—offering drinks during a Chinese holiday party—Mackie cast as coercively "plying" men with alcohol, creating the conditions for the "violent argument."

Mackie's testimony heavily influenced subsequent government action. The Colonial Secretary's office reached out to four men present that night—Mr. Gibson, Mr. Keller, Mr. Callwood, and Mr. Knott—requesting them to assess Yeo's testimony. Mackie Sr. provided the addresses of Gibson, Keller, and Knott and accompanied Knott to the Colonial Secretary's office to record his testimony. He even submitted an additional letter, in which he refers to the "Chinaman's Letter" and "the Chinaman's house," reducing a longtime acquaintance and neighbor who sheltered his son to just another anonymous Asian subject.[18] Knott, who was accompanied by Mackie Sr., provided the most critical, and least specific, account of these events. He found Yeo's statement "greatly exaggerated and untrue" and considered it "very avaricious and unloyal to the country which has sheltered him to send in such a statement." He stated that "if renumeration is asked then it is not hospitality but the act of a very mercenary person."[19] This was a strange statement, since Yeo's testimony made no demand for money or an award. Even when offered cash, he chose a medal. Despite these facts, Knott labeled Yeo "avaricious," "unloyal," and "mercenary" after sheltering Europeans in 1915.

Other European accounts only added further ambiguity. One witness, F. Keller, clearly had his own agenda. He suggested that the "groundwork of the Towkay's statement is more or less accurate, but there are several details evidently drawn from his imagination."[20] Keller emphasized his own heroism by suggesting that he invited European women and children "to my bungalow" and did not relocate to Yeo's home until dusk. He then stated that it took "much persuasion" for

Yeo to allow them to enter. Yeo, by his account, was passive while European men "took charge of all arrangements for the defence of the house, and the Towkay had nothing to do but to obey orders." By Keller's account, Yeo also lacked masculinity by failing to reassure and comfort women, unlike European men.[21] Keller also disputed that mutineers came to the house while European women were there. However, he did suggest that "a party of about 60 armed Sepoys" passed by after the women left, providing another opportunity for Indian soldiers to have threatened Yeo.[22] Tellingly, no women were among those interviewed.

While Keller opened his statement by suggesting that Yeo's testimony was "more or less accurate," he quickly changed his mind. He concluded that Yeo's testimony was "greatly exaggerated in all essential details and quite unreliable as a report of actualities."[23] Keller emphasized his credibility by noting that he gave military evidence in 1915. Yet he made a few omissions of his own. He did not address Mackie's allegation that he, rather than Mackie Jr., was the drunk of the evening. Instead, Keller downplayed the devastation caused by European drunkenness. He noted that some "glasses were accidentally knocked off a small side table, but this was evidently an accident, as the house was in darkness. No mirrors or Furniture was broken by any European, neither was any Revolver fired from the house or the grounds of same."[24] While Mackie blamed Yeo for "plying" the Europeans with alcohol, Keller cast drunken disorder as an accident exaggerated by Yeo.

Not all Europeans undermined Yeo's testimony. Unlike Keller and Mackie, A. Callwood was not implicated in the drunken violence. And unlike Knott, he was not accompanied by Mackie to give his testimony. Having the least outside influence, Callwood struck a delicate balance between defending Europeans and praising Yeo. He stated that Yeo provided "shelter . . . to over 30 people (Europeans)."[25] He found Yeo's testimony "in the main quite correct."[26] He even admitted that a "revolver was certainly fired off in the compound and afterwards forcibly removed from the [European] man." Like Keller, Callwood minimized the property damage and portrayed the European drunk as heroic: "In justice to him, however, I must [sic] say that he 'ran the gauntlet' through a crowd of the mutiners [sic] to dispatch the telephone message that ultimately brought relief." Still, Callwood believed that Yeo should not have included the incident of drunkenness in his statement because it betrayed a code of honor and decency.[27] Yet having a drunken European in his home revealed Yeo's precarious position. According to Yeo, the European was "waving a revolver at the same time and shouting that he didn't care for all the Mutineers in Singapore." He had to worry not only about Indian soldiers but also about Europeans, who admitted to ordering him around in his own home. Their hostile written responses convey the entitlement, resentment, and recklessness that Yeo likely faced. Aiding Europeans resulted in personal financial loss and a greater risk of danger than those who clearly felt no mutual obligation.[28]

Despite many contradictions and motives within European testimonies, these became evidence of Yeo's duplicity. One relatively sympathetic official acknowledged that Yeo took "grave personal risk" by "giving shelter to Europeans." He even noted the contradictions in European statements. Still, he fell back on racism, suggesting that "all Asiatics" were prone to "exaggerate details." He did not say the same about Europeans who also exaggerated. Instead, he supported the view that Yeo deserved no further compensation.[29] By February 5, 1921, this became the official perspective, with L. N. Guillemard writing to the Colonial Office that he conducted "exhaustive enquiries" and found that Yeo "has greatly exaggerated both the actual occurrences and his personal share in what took place at his house," echoing Mackie and Knott's language almost entirely. Guillemard also confirmed Ridout, Mackie, and Keller's characterization of Yeo as passive and unremarkable. While Ridout was apprehensive about setting a precedent for rewarding other Asian civilians, Guillemard worried that it would negatively reflect on "my predecessor" if he gave "any public recognition" after "so long an interval."[30] It was more important for British officials to avoid setting precedents, or slighting one another, than to acknowledge their dependence on Asian civilians. Unfortunately, no one told Yeo Bian Chuan. Between February and November 1921, he heard nothing about the status of the medal that he was promised. When he inquired, he received a letter reminding him of the free naturalization and stating that there would be no further action.[31]

While British leaders worried about precedents, Yeo Bian Chuan became a minor cause célèbre among Singapore's Chinese population. In 1925, the editor of the leading newspaper, the *Straits Times*, wrote to the Acting Colonial Secretary that "Certain Chinese have been worrying me to take up the grievance of one Towkay Yeo Bian Chuan, who believes that he has been very unfairly treated by the Government of the Colony."[32] The editor acknowledged that Yeo's "action exposed him and his property to grave danger, the object of the mutineers being to slay all Europeans, and punish all who aided them." The emphasis in Yeo's story was his own personal risk and the (false) British narrative of indiscriminate violence against white Europeans, showing the unintended consequences of the "race war" narrative. If the entire white population faced indiscriminate murder from Indian soldiers, as press and military leaders repeatedly claimed, then Yeo undeniably saved many lives. Still, Yeo focused on the facts. He retained documents, which he regarded "as an official communication," from Mr. Allen of the Chinese Protectorate promising a medal or $5,000. The *Straits Times* editor understood that Yeo chose the medal "to obtain a memento which he could hand down to his family." He worried that "the credit and honour of the Government is involved" and felt that it would be better to extend the medal privately "instead of the grievance being made public, or allowed to become a theme of comment among our Chinese friends."[33]

Ultimately, the possibility of alienating the Chinese community mattered less than British leaders saving face. The editor received a prompt reply, which reiterated earlier conclusions. The official suggested that Yeo had "much exaggerated" his account according to "all" of the Europeans interviewed.[34] This was enough to convince the editor to drop the issue. Still, Yeo persisted.[35] In 1926, a solicitor contacted the Acting Colonial Secretary, indicating Yeo's intention to draft a petition for his medal.[36] The Acting Colonial Secretary reiterated that the Colonial Office's extension of free naturalization was a suitable reward and lamented that "the man labours under an impression that he has been shabbily treated, but the trouble is that his account of what he did at the Mutiny is by no means borne out by the 10 or a dozen Europeans that he sheltered." He found Yeo "suffering under delusions in this matter." The Acting Colonial Secretary not only undermined Yeo by calling him delusional but also lied about securing testimonies from "10 or a dozen Europeans" who were all in agreement with one another.[37] The loss of respectability among Singapore's Chinese community was less important than slandering a man to justify inaction.

By 1928, Yeo's story appeared in the *Straits Times*, despite the editor's previous agreement with officials. The article hinted at problems with broader race-class tensions by explaining that Yeo in 1915 felt isolated as virtually "the only influential Asiatic living in the district."[38] This added pressure for him to provide a safe haven for Europeans. The article debunked the "reward" of free naturalization by stating that government officials had actually required Yeo to get this to receive his medal. The *Straits Times* suggested that the government's "failure to respond" to Yeo was "the basis of much disagreeably honest criticism among the Chinese."[39] After this article, the *Times of Malaya* reported on Yeo in an even more scathing piece entitled "Good Work Unappreciated." It presented a sympathetic portrait of a man wronged by the government. It reiterated the threat to whiteness that the events of 1915 represented, with "European civilians of Singapore" left "to fend for themselves."[40] Yeo was, by their account, a "Chinese gentleman" who "knew the risk that he was running in taking in the refugees." Still, he "opened his house to them" and "did all he could to make them comfortable." For the *Times of Malaya*,

Yeo took "no small risk in sheltering those 17 Europeans who had sought refuge at his house." Despite his "courageous" efforts, he "made no 'song' about what he had done."[41] To the press, Yeo was brave, humble, and wronged. Despite this support, Yeo passed away in 1929 without receiving his medal. The last attempt happened after his death, with a member of Parliament raising his case as a "subject of enquiry" in the House of Commons. Colonial leaders responded with a copy of Guillemard's dismissive letter, closing the matter.

Yeo's case showed that the 1915 rebellion went far beyond British and Indian memories and fears. Many colonial subjects came to Britain's aid in a time of need. Some embraced and replicated European narratives of the rebellion, emphasizing the deadly threat to white people. For this they expected only what British leaders promised. Instead, British officials launched an investigation to disparage a colonial subject who, without dispute, had aided Europeans. In turn, white men cast him as everything from a well-intentioned man to a disloyal mercenary. The press found it indicative of larger dynamics, forcing an Asian resident of a predominantly European area to open his home to Europeans without compensation or gratitude. British officials and European civilians dismissed Yeo's claims because they did not want to compensate other Asian civilians or discredit their predecessors. Many fell back on racist assumptions about Asian greed or exaggeration to justify their actions. Even colonial subjects who exemplified British definitions of heroism could not escape colonial racism and violence. This did not go unnoticed.

BOYCOTTS AND "BANDITRY"

Yeo Bian Chuan's inability to claim heroism from the British, while earning the support of the Chinese community, hints at British leaders' fears about failing to control Singapore and Malaya's Chinese population. Prior to the First World War, a primary concern was the prevalence of Chinese secret societies. Colonial administrator Wilfred Blythe noted that many of these had their origins in China and existed for "self-protection and spiritual satisfaction."[42] In some cases, societies participated in criminal activity and exercised power and control over Chinese civilians. This not only threatened British authority, but also forced civilians to face financial extraction and violent intimidation from multiple sources. While colonial leaders could dismantle societies that they found "incompatible with the peace or good order of the Colony," they retained an impression that "the Chinese population contained unruly elements which were insufficiently restrained." The rise of political societies and organizations after the Chinese Revolution of 1911, including the formation of a leading nationalist organization, the Kuomintang (KMT), in 1912, added greater resentment to British fears of "unruly" subjects. These fortified a sense of Chinese nationhood and nationalism that increasingly replaced regional, secret society, or linguistic ties. Blythe found this problematic because it caused "a process of reorientation for Chinese everywhere." He believed that Straits Chinese, largely born in Malaya and Singapore, previously declared "themselves to be loyal subjects of Her Majesty the Queen of England" but increasingly identified with Chinese interests.[43] Throughout the interwar period, British leaders worried how nationalist sentiment among "unruly" subjects would function in a diverse colonial state.

After the First World War, some Chinese nationalists became more militant to counter Japanese attacks on China. In response, Chinese-led boycotts of Japanese goods became common in Singapore and Malaya by April 1915, just a few months after the Singapore Mutiny, when Japan presented China with its Twenty-One Demands. British leaders took the opportunity to banish many KMT leaders from 1915 until 1919.[44] Against this crackdown, KMT supporters in British territory increased recruitment of new members and sought influence in Chinese schools. While one Political Intelligence officer blamed "Japanese political activities in North China" for such developments, another characterized it as "natural racial antipathy." None considered British leaders' role in exacerbating conflicts. Instead, some observed gleefully that anti-Japanese boycotts were a boon to British trade.[45] Apparently, "natural racial antipathy" was forgivable if it was economically beneficial.

British leaders' mixed responses to rising Chinese nationalist activism reflected the importance of the community in Singapore and Malaya. Sir Leopold Gammans claimed that "European enterprise" combined with "Chinese industry" was responsible for making "Malaya what it is."[46] Several Chinese characters in Han Suyin's novel . . . *And the Rain My Drink* similarly believed that if one removed "the Chinese of Malaya," then "there would not be any Malaya."[47] While there was already a large Chinese population in Malaya prior to the twentieth century, labor migration became even more important after 1905 when rubber emerged as the main crop. In China, difficult economic, political, and environmental circumstances brought a seemingly limitless supply of Chinese laborers, giving British colonial administrators the confidence to use banishment as a punishment with greater frequency.[48] Yet the war disrupted immigration, bringing the lowest on record in 1918.[49] Trade disruption cause a shortage of goods and a higher cost of living. This increased strikes and demands for higher wages across various professions. The Protector of the Chinese reasoned that this was inevitable: "It would be strange indeed if the mingled influences of high prices, food shortage, anti-Japanese propaganda and Labour agitation, backed wherever they can obtain an entry by Bolshevik agents, had not produced unrest." "Anti-Japanese propaganda" and "Labour agitation," to many leaders, were nothing more than the meddling of "Bolshevik agents." This echoed the perception that Indian soldiers in 1915 were only upset because of manipulation by German agents, reflecting a common tendency for conspiratorial thinking among British leaders of the era.[50] As a result, British leaders reasoned that "[c]heap food" would ensure "a contented people," once again dismissing colonial subjects' true concerns.[51]

The tendency to see civilian unrest as motivated by outside "Bolshevik" influence resulted in further militarization and surveillance of a population that British leaders already viewed as "unruly." In 1919 Penang, British leaders declared martial law, including the mobilization of the Penang Volunteers.[52] The Federated Malay States (FMS) then witnessed a massive slump in both the tin and rubber industries at the end of 1920, bringing "gloom and depression." The following year was "black all through."[53] While immigration reached its prewar levels by 1921, the tin and rubber industries still stagnated, reducing the wage gains earned in 1919.[54] Migration rates decreased the following year. In both 1921 and 1922, the Protector of the Chinese noted "an unusual amount of fighting," but he failed to connect this to economic conditions.[55] Despite these trends, he was confident that there was no "communistic or anarchistic" feeling in "the consciousness of the people."[56] Nonetheless, he encouraged monitoring Chinese newspapers. Other British leaders blamed "the influence of unsettled conditions in China and of COMMUNIST ideas brought in from China."[57] Immigration, therefore, was both necessary to fund the empire and threatening to colonial stability.

As trade, migration, and crime rates rebounded by 1924, British leaders believed that militarization and policing were the reasons. One official ascribed the drop in crime to "the increased preventive work due to an enlargement of the patrol and beat systems" rather than improved economic conditions.[58] As a result, British leaders increased the recruitment of military and police personnel. This included further European Inspectors, "Asiatic Inspectors," and an "Armed Police Reserve" recruited from India.[59] Recruitment of Indian police no doubt perplexed Asian and European civilians still clinging to the narratives of Indian criminality from 1915. Yet British leaders found this necessary because they had difficulty finding "suitable" men locally. In fact, recruitment of Chinese police had not existed in the colony for many years owing to fears of secret society infiltration.[60] Still, one police official complained that the recruitment of Chinese police was difficult because only men "of a poor coolie type with low morality" applied.

Following the ingratitude of British leaders to Chinese civilians and volunteers in 1915, the only men who wanted to serve in policing were those who could gain economic upward mobility from their service. As a result, they relied on "young untrained and inexperienced officers," placing "a great strain on all concerned."[61] An economic boom that benefited other industries opened the door to "untrained and inexperienced officers" charged with imposing Britain's racial militarism.

Despite an increase in policing, police struggled to understand the motives of those challenging British power. On January 23, 1925, a woman, referred to as Wong Sang or Wong So Ying,[62] launched a bomb attack against the Chinese Protectorate.[63] Newspapers reported her to be "well-dressed" in clothing of "the new style" with a "skirt and jacket" and "bobbed hair." Some interpreted her modern styling as evidence of her being an outsider from Hong Kong. However, she spoke "Malay quite fluently," leading to speculation that she was from Penang.[64] In many ways she evoked the fear of the "modern girl" who was hyper modern, independent, and masculine, with dangerous proximity to anarchism and nihilism.[65] None mentioned that Penang endured martial law for anti-Japanese violence a few years earlier, during which time Wong Sang had lived with Mak Peng Chho, her lover and a known anarchist. Police even raided their home and found anarchist pamphlets. While Mak escaped, British leaders later banished him to China in July 1923, where he was shot on orders of a Chinese district magistrate in 1924.[66] For many journalists, however, it was more important to emphasize that Wong Sang had a "singularly masculine appearance," a "peculiarly masculine appearance," or a "distinctly mannish demeanour."[67] Dismissing a woman for mannishness took precedence over addressing the police violence that preceded her actions.

Very few journalists attempted to explain why Wong Sang targeted the Chinese Protectorate—the central office for the Chinese community under British rule—specifically. Some speculated that she was motivated by "anarchistic ideas" after being "self-educated . . . in opposition to the wishes of her parents." To them she was "obsessed with an idea of grievance against the world in general."[68] None mentioned that the Chinese Protectorate had played a leading role in monitoring the Chinese population since the nineteenth century, often furnishing police with the information necessary to make arrests.[69] Instead, British officials characterized her as "a Cantonese woman" who was a "member of a band of anarchists" who wanted to strike "a blow against organised Govt." They believed that she chose the Protectorate because it had "the easiest and most accessible victims."[70] In reality, she had tried to assassinate Governor Guillemard, the same man who dismissed Yeo Bian Chuan's complaints, for representing a "system which hinders the progress of the world."[71] She appealed for leniency, citing a "bad temper," but still received ten years' rigorous imprisonment.[72] Those who assisted her were banished.[73] Yet police continued to track Wong Sang and her associates for global anarchist activities throughout the decade.[74] The emphasis on her modern styling, masculinity, vague "anarchistic ideas" and general "grievance against the world" prevented the wider colonial public from knowing or understanding her motives. This maintained the fiction that martial law and policing curbed all forms of sedition, revolution, and anarchism, rather than added to the motivations of those perpetuating it.

Ultimately, policing failed to eliminate Chinese nationalism, communism, or broader British fears of their Chinese subjects.[75] In 1926, the largest Chinese migration ever took place, bringing in well over 300,000 Chinese migrants during a period of continued tin and rubber productivity.[76] By 1927, Perak officials noted the existence of numerous "unlawful workers' societies" with connections to "Left Wing, or Communist" Chinese nationalists.[77] This proved a departure from earlier in the decade, when many Chinese businessmen felt alienated by the KMT because of their acceptance of communists.[78] However, by the mid-1920s, nationalist organizations found success recruiting through Chinese schools. In response, police targeted schools that they believed "spread their propaganda" throughout Malaya. They banished more leaders in 1926.[79] This, along with the decision of the KMT in China to banish communist members in 1927, made the KMT in Malaya more right-wing. The same year, communists who previously supported the KMT attempted to assassinate Chinese political leaders in Singapore.[80] When another economic slump came in 1928, high unemployment and communist activity enabled the police to become more selective in their recruiting.[81] More than 150 men in Singapore and Penang were dismissed. A "higher standard of intelligence" was expected from new recruits. Difficult economic times, in other words, enabled the police to deprive many men of their employment, despite their prior willingness to serve on behalf of British interests. This, they believed, helped check the "considerable activity amongst the so-called Communists" in Negri Sembilan in April 1929. In response, police visited "all known Communist centres throughout the State," culminating in confiscations of documents and arrests. They believed that as a result of these activities, "Communist activity was fitful, and at the end of the year almost non-existent."[82]

In 1929, police felt confident that they controlled the colony and had gained the upper hand on "RED activity, calculated to disturb the peace of the Settlement."[83] As Tim Harper has argued, there was a feeling that "the government honed its formidable powers to arrest and banish 'undesirables,'" collapsing the distance between colonial subject and criminal. While "a façade of order was restored," it was "buttressed by the armoury of emergency or 'exorbitant' powers that colonial regimes had accumulated during the crisis years and now retained in perpetuity."[84] Yet many white Europeans at the time focused instead on the fact that Malaya had the comfortable, and profitable, position of producing more than half of the world's rubber. This one commodity commanded over half of the country's cultivated land and employed roughly 30 percent of agricultural workers. The GDP in Malaya, relative to population, was greater than in Japan.[85] For a fleeting moment, British martial capitalism felt invincible. These illusions shattered with the global economic depression.

DEPRESSED POLICING

The start of the Great Depression brought economic and political turmoil that revealed colonial leaders' swiftness in discarding those on whose labor they depended. During the 1920s, Britain made enemies of left-leaning nationalist and anti-colonial leaders with increased policing, and lost the imperial loyalty of some former allies now looking to China. The 1930s, however, amplified the bitterness of laborers who already failed to share in imperial prosperity. Many continued to hold their jobs and sustain the empire at lower wages. This did not prevent them from being discarded and policed for their economic precarity. In this environment, the police forces bolstered in the 1920s set their attention to a colonial population struggling to survive. Feeling abandoned and vulnerable, some turned to communists to seek a better future and to challenge a colonial power unwilling to protect them from economic death.

The most immediate impact of the Great Depression in colonial Malaya and Singapore was the swift dismissal of large swaths of the workforce. In the Straits Settlements, Chinese male laborers were restricted to a quota of roughly 6,000 migrants per month, and, consequently, there were "more labour troubles than usual." Rubber factories were hit hard in Singapore, and in the summer of 1930, over 1,000 rubber workers lost employment. Sawmills, timber yards, and pineapple factories dismissed entire workforces or lowered wages. Over 10,000 "Destitute Chinese" were repatriated in 1930.[86] By 1932, 12,000 more faced repatriation.[87] Ultimately, government funding supported the departure of more than 75,000 Chinese and 190,000 Indian people between 1930 and 1932.[88] In the FMS, according the Chief Secretary, "Large numbers of mining coolies and rubber tappers were thrown out of employment."[89] The "wholesale discharge of coolie labour from rubber estates and tin mines" continued in 1931, and with it the "mass repatriation of South Indian coolies."[90] However, administrators praised the Chinese workforce for handling this uncertainty with grace: "[T]he attitude of the heavily hit Chinese cooly [*sic*] class has been praiseworthy. Where work was to be found they accepted it gladly even on greatly reduced wages." British leaders found few "outbreaks of any kind and their general attitude has been extremely law-abiding."[91] Another official praised the"labouring class" for adapting "to the new conditions with stoical philosophy and with a patient fortitude that has been the envy of other races."[92] One FMS administrator expressed that one "can only hope that the Chinese labourer will reap his full reward when conditions improve, for his behaviour in these times of stress."[93] Unsurprisingly, this admiration for Asian laborers' steadfastness did not result in material support.

During the depression, police used periods of relatively low crime to crack down on political organizations. They gained support from the newest Straits Settlements Governor, Cecil Clementi, who arrived in 1930 from Hong Kong, where the KMT was illegal. By 1931, officials limited the power of political parties that had links to China, weakening the KMT and preventing it from becoming a unified party in Malaya. In 1930, the Malayan Communist Party (MCP) established itself under the guidance of the Comintern in Shanghai. However, it faced immediate setbacks with the arrest of Nguyen Ai Quoc—also known as Ho Chi Minh—in Hong Kong in 1931. Neither the MCP nor the KMT received official recognition from British leaders until they needed their assistance defending the colonies against the Japanese invasion in 1941. For British administrator Wilfred Blythe, such organizations only recovered with the revival of anti-Japanese boycotts. These provided "an excellent patriotic theme for propaganda" especially after 1937, when "National Salvation" became a slogan for Chinese patriotism.[94]

While political organizations struggled, police used racial profiling to tackle crime. Chief of Police C. H. Sansom had a shorthand for the types of crimes allegedly committed by each community. He held that Southern Indians committed violent crime "prompted generally by sexual jealousy." Sikhs and Northern Indians apparently "do not figure extensively in reports of serious crime" but "exhibit more ingenuity and preparation than the general run of Asiatic races." Malays purportedly indulged in violent crime because of "sexual intrigue" or ridding themselves of "inconvenient creditors." Japanese people allegedly dealt with criminal "traffic in women or drugs." He maintained that Hailam Chinese had "an inferiority complex" that led them to political trouble "but their communistic tendencies have been tightly curbed."[95] Such racial profiling convinced some civilians that police arbitrarily chose victims for imprisonment. Malay guerilla Ropiah Binti Mat Yatin, alias Mak Chu, recalled that her father was imprisoned

during these years even though he had not "done anything wrong." She speculated that "the British would arrest the first people they got their hands on." They
kept him in custody for a year, forcing him to work as a rubber tapper.[96] This sense
of seemingly arbitrary racial injustice during already hard times pushed her to
embrace the communist cause.

Despite racial profiling, some British officials believed the police were a bas-
tion of interracial solidarity. William Arthur Campion Haines served with the
Kedah Police and insisted that "I made friends among the Malay, Chinese and
Indian communities." One of his "best Indian friends" was an assistant surgeon at
the hospital, with whom he often played tennis (and lost).[97] This was possible because the police consisted of Malays, Sikhs, and Pathans, reflecting the influence
of military "martial race" recruiting biases.[98] It also showed a not-uncommon
dynamic of white military men in the 1930s who saw interracial recruitment, and
the opening of officer ranks to Asian men, as an opportunity for unambiguous
"friendship."[99] In many cases, this outlook went hand in hand with celebrations
of imperial brotherhood that dismissed anti-colonial activity, occasionally man-
ifesting as fascist sympathies.[100] Asian men rarely found these relationships genuine, given the racialized disparity in their access to power and their own need
to navigate multiple loyalties simultaneously. Still, for Haines, even though the
Criminal Investigation Department was "armed and para-military," he celebrated
that it represented "almost every nationality." Participation in policing further
required knowledge of Malay and either a Chinese or Indian language.[101] For
Haines, this facilitated conversation and connection. John Davis was less optimistic. He gained notoriety during the Second World War but started his career
in policing, where he found the interracial composition a source of frustration.
Language differences meant that Malay and Sikh police rarely understood each
other.[102] He found that Sikhs thought that Malays were like children, while
Malays found Sikhs stupid and clumsy.[103] He believed that Indian police were
poorly trained and had spent "several years in a sleepy kampong out in the jungle
somewhere where they have nothing to do but get fat."[104]

While Haines and Davis disagreed about interracial unity, they agreed that
they depended on Asian men's martial prowess. Davis appreciated having colonial police around when visiting camps for unemployed Chinese laborers, whom
he regarded as "tough coolies." He was relieved to have a "nice fat revolver" and
"20 Sikhs and Malays to protect me."[105] Haines, meanwhile, admired the men he
was supposed to imprison. He recalled that his job was "to capture the villains,"
specifically "Malay gangs." Still, he found them "such delightful people; they
were Nature's gentlemen: courteous, hospitable and generally a charming race."

Violence made them "a picturesque collection" as some were "armed with spears and parangs, others with Dutch swords." He essentialized robberies as part of their everyday life and cast them as "courageous and accept hardship stoically."[106] Romanticizing friendship often went hand in hand with racialized generalizations that enabled violent police work.

Despite his insistence about policing enabling "friendship," Haines revealed that his racialized colleagues had to take subservient roles to fight communism. He relayed one story of a Frenchman from Saigon, possibly Serge Lefranc or an associate of global communist organizer Joseph Ducroux, opening an office in Raffles Place.[107] A Malay police constable under Haines's command took a job as a peon, or "office boy," to the Frenchman. A Chinese officer of the Special Branch became his servant. After eighteen months, the Chinese and Malay officers collected enough evidence to make an arrest.[108] The policing of communism, therefore, required Asian police to become subservient to a European communist for over a year. Still, communism did not disappear. In Johore in 1935, Haines found communists "fomenting dissatisfaction amongst labour forces on the rubber estates." He helped combat a riot at Batu Pahat that led to the banishment of 190 Chinese workers, despite acknowledging that these men's lives were "exceedingly precarious."[109] By 1940, Haines worked in Seremban and faced "a violent attack on the police by a very large number of Communist inspired Chinese at Bahau" that resulted in numerous casualties. Rubber estates continued to face incidents "promoted by agitators in the Malayan Communist Party."[110] Haines had been optimistic that policing created an interracial community. In reality, policing reinforced Asian men's subservience to Europeans and facilitated violence against them.

By the mid-1930s, some British leaders recognized that police repression failed to end communism, necessitating a softer approach. Chief of Police Sansom, who created an ethnic roadmap for crime, reported that George V's Jubilee in 1935 led to "spontaneity and unanimity of the rejoicings" in Singapore and Malaya. He found this "a far more effective counter to communist ambitions than the usual measures of repression to which police forces have to resort."[111] Still, as colonial prosperity rebounded, Malay and Chinese laborers "in almost all types of employment" demanded wage increases. The Secretary for Chinese Affairs blamed this on global labor activism and "agitation by communists."[112] Unacknowledged was the FMS administrator's hope in 1930 that "the Chinese labourer will reap his full reward when conditions improve."[113] The good behavior of Chinese laborers remained unrewarded as police repression continued. Soon, the FMS noted that despite economic recovery, there was also growing "interest in communism" among "Hailams, Hakkas and Hokkiens."[114] While some noted that communists in Singapore and Malaya had developed networks with revolutionaries in China, Siam, French Indochina, and the Netherlands East Indies, British officials still comforted themselves with the belief that the communist party in Singapore and Malaya was "rudderless" in 1936.[115] In declaring a temporary victory against communism, British leaders continued to disregard colonial subjects' demands for shared prosperity, and instead perpetuated violence against them.

By 1937, many British leaders' interwar fears collided. Sino-Japanese relations worsened with the Japanese invasion of China. This caused "considerable anxiety in Malaya." Some Chinese civilians declared another boycott of Japanese goods and forcefully increased subscriptions to Chinese patriotic and Red Cross funds.[116] Police observed nervously that communists in Malaya and Singapore increasingly followed "in conformity with the policy of the China Communist Party," which included resisting the Japanese alongside non-communist Chinese nationalists.[117] Singapore became an undisputed epicenter of activity for resisting the Japanese war in China, often under the umbrella of the Chinese National Salvation Associations against Japanese aggression. The Communist Party of Malaya also gained power by appealing to Chinese nationalism.[118] Militarization intensified, as groups like "Hot Blooded Corps," "Traitors Elimination Corps," and "Dare to Die Corps" merged into larger groups with reported memberships of 30,000. Officials believed that this was "a very real danger" because of "assaults and other acts of violence." Police in the FMS found "bullying and extortion" the norm. British officials worried that this was often done in "subservience to the Communist Party."[119] While various political groups were active by 1939, officials lauded "the restraint of the large Chinese population in Malaya" for resisting "hysteria" despite being "all bitterly anti-Jap[anese]."[120]

Yet anti-Japanese activity was not the source of activism, as a growing number of labor movements also intensified. In 1937, the Malayan General Labour Union organized strikes in Singapore, Johore, Malacca, Negri Sembilan, and Selangor. Rubber estates laborers in Selangor and Negri Sembilan protested their employers' failure to raise wages. The Secretary of Chinese Affairs remained uncertain if communists "caused the strike or fomented a strike that had already begun."[121] However, the scale was concerning.[122] Ten thousand Chinese rubber estate employees assembled and clashed with police.[123] Some officials blamed interethnic jealousy, with Chinese laborers resenting Malay laborers gaining better wages.[124] As a result, strike action continued in 1938 and 1939, particularly among Chinese laborers.[125] This forced police to acknowledge that industrial unrest was due in large part to the delay in letting "labour participate in returning prosperity."[126]

The Secretary for Chinese Affairs agreed, noting that "Malaya's labour troubles" were the result of Chinese laborers expecting "to share in the benefits of returning prosperity to Malaya's main industries."[127] Despite this recognition, colonial officials continued to respond with militarization rather than shared prosperity. The FMS called in the military "in aid of the civil power" for the first time in twenty-five years. At the Batu Arang coal mines, roughly 5,000 workers went on strike, prompting companies of the Malay Regiment "to protect the property and personnel" and prevent sabotage.[128] Meanwhile, 250 armed police raided the mine headquarters. Two companies of the Punjab Regiment from Taiping moved to Kuala Lumpur to occupy a police depot and assist the Malay Regiment. British leaders found this necessary "to restore confidence among the population."[129] While massive strike action finally forced colonial leaders to consider that workers might have valid arguments, police and military action remained their primary method of control.

For some civilians, the collision of anti-Japanese activity, labor activism, and anti-communist policing was a consequence of British ambivalence. Tan Chong Tee was a civilian who returned to Singapore in the 1930s after attending school in China. He planned to run the Kheng Cheng Private School, which his mother founded.[130] He immediately introduced military training in the school, organized anti-Japanese propaganda, and joined the St. John's Ambulance Brigade. This gave him a front seat to British political ambivalence. He noted that on "the surface, the British was [*sic*] afraid of opposition from the Japanese so they seemed to oppress the Kuomintang and the Communist Party. But in actuality, they turned a blind eye in dealing with these anti-Japanese war efforts." Rather than trying to build peace between communities, British leaders sat on the sidelines because they "wanted to curry favour with the Japanese but at the same time suppress activities conducted by the Chinese by disallowing the Chinese from attending military activities. Then how could they protect Singapore?" Feeling repressed by British inaction, he and his friends "decided to help China defeat the Japanese so as to protect the safety of Singapore. Otherwise, we would only be sacrificed needlessly in Singapore if the Japanese invaded us in the future."[131] While young Chinese men journeyed to China to fight against an active war and potential fight for Malaya, British leaders policed the local population and enabled in-fighting.

Throughout the interwar period, British leaders saw everything—from anti-Japanese boycotts to labor activism—as signs of the need to control their "unruly" population. In response, they increased policing, despite existing class and racial biases that made it difficult to find "suitable" men for government employment. Meanwhile, they found nationalist activism unremarkable if it was directed against Asian, rather than white, people. British leaders repeatedly dismissed Asian colonial subjects' concerns about Japanese colonization in Asia, loss of jobs and wages, and greater surveillance as seeds for communist revolution that needed to be stamped out. In turn, they kept declaring victory against communism only to see it constantly reemerge. Eventually, they had no choice but to start blaming "employers" for workers' problems, rather than workers or vague racial antagonisms. In the face of overwhelming pressure from colonial subjects—including but not exclusively anti-colonial activists—British leaders finally acknowledged that colonial trade and economic policies, including hierarchical and extractive labor practices, discontented the population. Unfortunately, investing so much time, energy, and resources in targeting and surveilling colonial subjects did not address these underlying problems. Instead, it showed colonial subjects that British leaders cared more about controlling internal threats than protecting the colony or its people.

POLICING SOCIETY

While some colonial leaders gradually acknowledged subjects' grievances, they did not change their methods of control. Instead, many government welfare initiatives, such as improved minimum wage, maximum hours, and improved health standards on estates, disappeared during the depression.[132] As a result, the 1930s witnessed many flocking to Singapore and Malaya promising to bring egalitarian social reforms that government officials failed to provide. Increasingly, teachers, missionaries, and medical professionals all hoped to fill the gaps of colonial administrators buckling under the pressure of global economic collapse. Yet the vast majority of white people outside of Southeast Asia knew little about the tensions and fractures within colonial and anti-colonial politics. Many white Britons came of age believing that the empire was just and benevolent, and trained in schools that encouraged service to the empire. In many cases, they became overwhelmed and frustrated by the level of ill-health and poverty that they encountered, even critiquing British policies. At the same time, if colonial subjects did not accept welfare with humility and gratitude, and instead continued their activism, then it became evidence that they were to blame for the problems of the colony. As a result, many humanitarian efforts descended into racist apologias of imperial governance. This further widened the gap in perception between colonial subjects who hoped that British leaders would make good on their promises of shared interracial prosperity and white civilians who believed that paradise had been won.

Some white working professionals genuinely believed that they were promoting interracial unity even as they reinforced racist tropes about colonial subjects. American missionary Preston Peach worked in Malayan schools for decades and was optimistic about the influence of Christianity for cultivating loyal and devoted colonial subjects. He ignored the protests of a "very faithful Presbyterian" who worried that Peach's school was "becoming a 'hot bed' of democracy."[133] Peach retorted that "if any young man or woman Chinese, Indian or Malay" decided to convert to Christianity then "we must allow that person freedom." Freedom, for Peach, was dependent on conversion. Not uncommon among missionaries of the era, Peach believed that Christian teachings eliminated racial barriers. He celebrated that in Malaya, "the three great races of Asia mingle together in busines [*sic*] on the playground in school rooms, on the trains, boats and tram cars." Ironically, he did not include Europeans as part of this interracial paradise, so he clarified "indeed I should say the four races." He felt this interracial harmony was a result of the "the Christian religion" bringing "closely together all the races except the Malay, who is a Mohammedan." Religion, more than race, he insisted, was the greatest impediment to inclusivity. While he acknowledged that "there were separate clubs for the Europeans," he suggested that there "was never any Segregation except what would necessarily exist because of language." Sporting events were "happily carried on by all." He believed that race riots, common in the United States, never happened in Malaya, unless they were sparked by Chinese secret societies. Instead, organizations like Rotary "cut across racial lines throughout Malaya" to enable "Malays, Chinese and Indian people" to live "so happily together."[134]

Peach's optimism that Malaya was an interracial paradise related, in part, to the class positions of those he encountered. He marveled that Hindus, Buddhists, Muslims, and Confucianists all attended Christian schools with "practically no criticism or opposition."[135] Parents, he found, prioritized their children having a good education "that fitted them for becoming wage earners" and gave them "strong character." It was this feature—upwardly-mobile parents wanting good jobs for their children—that sent them to Christian schools, rather than an unwavering trust in British rule or Christian teachings.[136] For this reason, enrollment in English schools exploded between 1913 and 1929, with a staggering increase of 226 percent.[137] Still, Peach took pride in the fact that Chinese banks sought graduates from Christian schools and local rulers often donated funds. He contrasted this with "Chinese schools" that were "infiltrated by communism" to the extent that "the term 'hot bed' could rightly be applied." At one Chinese school in Kuala Lumpur the headmaster was even "removed by Government order." By contrast,

Peach felt that he never saw communist influence in Christian schools because such an "ideology could not grow in a Christian environment."[138] In reality, most English-language schools shared an emphasis on cultivating imperial loyalty and multilingual partnership to build ties that would outlast independence.[139] Yet for Peach, Christianity instilled valuable, democratic ideals that would protect against communism. It did not occur to him that the parents and children who found upwardly-mobile value in missionary schools might not be the most open to communist ideas, or express them to him openly. Still, British officials shared his optimism about the preventative merits of education. Administrator Wilfred Blythe believed that if "English school education" was provided to "the whole of the Chinese child population" from the nineteenth century, it would have inculcated loyalty and prevented the influence of secret societies, political organizations, and communists.[140]

As Peach implied, Rotary was another important force for promising interracial unity. Leonard David Gammans of the Rotary noted that the Chinese population in Malaya was excluded from political rights, so a primary goal of Rotary was "fostering good feeling and understanding between the many races which inhabit the country." It did so by allowing club membership to "all races."[141] Civilian institutions attempted to provide the inclusivity that the government did not. However, Gammans specified that it was important to counter a different threat from communism: "The repercussions of Gandyism [*sic*] and all that it means will be felt in every part of the Empire." Like Peach, he found the "genuine feeling of Nationalism" to be "both understandable and commendable." However, he worried about "the whole basis of British rule" coming into question with prominent leaders like Mohandas Gandhi leading the charge for independence. Much like the administrators who regretted Chinese laborers' inability to share in returned prosperity, Peach recognized that "we are charged with having neglected the the [*sic*] economic welfare of the subject races for whose future we have assumed responsibility."[142] This was especially important because of Malaya's role as a producer of half the world's rubber and tin and a growing dependency on "American prosperity."[143] Inclusivity, for this American missionary, was a prerequisite of continued British rule and profitable trade.

For other civilians, interracial unity was only possible by improving the health and well-being of colonial subjects, rather than converting them to Christianity or including them in interracial organizations. As many scholars have noted, mandates about health and medicine often led to greater colonial control over colonized people and frequent condemnation of their bodily practices.[144] However, by the twentieth century, some colonial leaders prioritized welfare reform as a paternalistic antidote to the more negligent model of nineteenth century governance. This resulted in opening a medical school in Singapore and the Institute for Medical Research in Kuala Lumpur in 1901, which specialized in tropical medicine. Between 1908 and 1937, death rates dropped by 50 percent for adults and 40 percent for infants.[145] Still, such efforts often hinged on racist notions of uplift. Improving civilians' lives often included harsh criticisms of urban spaces that were prone to overcrowding. Singapore's reputation for sexual laxity, meanwhile, came under scrutiny for causing high infant mortality and "rife" cases of venereal diseases.[146] By the 1920s, the League of Nations and the British Social Hygiene Council pressured colonial governments to become, according to historian Lenore Manderson, the "moral guardian and surveyor of public health," which included the suppression of prostitution. By the 1930s, the end of prostitution brought dance halls, cafés, and teahouses that offered healthier entertainment for white patrons and alternative employment for Asian women. However, the global economic depression, and a severe drop in rubber prices, halted many welfare efforts.[147] Many estates closed their hospitals, while funding for malaria research and mitigation ceased. Mortality rates increased once again, reversing much of the progress from earlier in the century.[148] Without profitable global trade, welfare initiatives and care for colonized bodies disappeared.

Facing these challenges, many medical professionals oscillated between blaming colonial officials and colonial subjects for laborers' ill-health. Some focused on planters' reliance on rural migrant populations because many migrants were unfamiliar with city life and sanitation. In response, according to Public Health Matron Ida M. M. Simmons, "a campaign of health work" started "among the kampong folk in the rural areas of Singapore" by about 1927.[149] Some recognized that the boom-and-bust economy also contributed to poor health. A large population of "squatters," likely exceeding 150,000, developed because of the massive layoffs in the tin and rubber mining industries in the 1930s.[150] This was not exclusive to one community. In rural areas, Simmons believed, "squatters, made up of Malays, Tamils, Sikhs, Chinese, Arabs, Eurasians and some Japanese," faced dire infant mortality rates, totaling at least 300 per 1,000.[151] Colonial labor and trade practices, therefore, had deleterious effects on the health of all people. Among children, virtually "every child over one year was infested with worms, and consequently were victims of coughs, fever, anaemia and general debility." Those families who lived and worked in Malaya for employment paid for economic instability with their bodies. Initially, Simmons found that most people living in kampongs "made no use of the facilities provided for the sick in Singapore" because "they were too afraid to go to them." By contrast, once they set up welfare centers, clinics became frequent and well-attended. In ten years, the infant mortality rate in rural areas decreased from 263 in 1927 to 86.36 per 1,000 in 1938.[152] Yet in some rural areas, infant mortality remained four times as high as it was in the United Kingdom.[153]

For Dr. Cicely Williams, infant mortality was a result of impoverishment. She lamented the existence of "dark, ill-ventilated cubicles in the town" where babies lacked access to essential "air and light" to stimulate health and growth.[154] As a result, infant mortality rates had a clear "class prejudice." Among the European and Asian colonial and commercial elite, death rates among babies were not exceptional.[155] For small shopkeepers and the middle class, however, "the death rate is distinctly higher." The most striking demographic was "among the coolie population, the really poor people of China town [sic] and the kampongs" where babies had very high death rates. She believed that the culprit was "overwork and unsuitable food," which had "an adverse effect on the ability of the mother to produce milk." Class position, as much as medical practice, dictated life or death. Williams suggested that many babies died because of "bad economic conditions" that left mothers weak and tired, living in poor conditions, and unable to stay with children or ensure sanitary conditions. She explained that "the coolie baby in the slums of Singapore" often contracts "the Singapore Disease, that is malnutrition with rickets, anaemia, boils, it may be blindness and finally diarrhoea and pneumonia." Thus, she reasoned, "a baby is murdered by a community that permits the mother to live under such conditions and to discontinue breast feeding."[156] In this, Williams revealed her view that community, rather than colonialism, murdered children.

Many medical professionals like Williams walked a fine line between blaming colonial subjects and leaders for ill-health. For example, Williams blamed "the well-to-do classes" of Chinese women for abandoning "breastfeeding because she wishes to be free to go out and play mahjong or because she considers it beneath her dignity to feed her own baby."[157] At the same time, she pressured men attending her lectures to "insist on decent housing conditions. Make certain that your own domestics and dependents are decently housed. See that slum areas are dealt with as they should be." She pressed "employers of female labour" to "insist that maternity benefits are obtained so that all women workers, clerks and coolies, teachers, doctors and domestic servants alike should have adequate time off after confinement in order to feed their own babies." Yet the lecture took a carceral tone. Williams suggested that infant mortality should be "regarded as murder" and "be punished as the most criminal form of sedition."[158] Impoverished mothers who lost their children due to dire economic conditions, she reasoned, deserved to be prosecuted with equal severity as communists and anti-colonial activists.

Despite her disciplinary tone, Williams's medical work sometimes challenged imperial clichés. She questioned the notion of the "survival of the fittest" and the prevalent idea that hardship made people stronger.[159] She dismissed "long resident Malayophiles" who insisted that Malays "are a very happy people."[160] She found the reason for this perception was that Malays will "engage in conversation and laugh with Europeans" and appear "happy—at that time." In reality, most were "both sick and sorry" because of "[d]irt and ignorance, poverty and prejudices" that "produce a most unnecessarily large mortality and morbidity." Many Malay people, including children, dealt constantly with "yaws and ulcers externally, and worms and dysenteries internally," which made them "indolent and conservative, largely as a result of their diseases." She explained that they were "cheerful as long as they have no anxieties."[161] While she again condemned Malay people as "indolent and conservative" and their customs as "prejudice," she also recognized that prevalent British perceptions of inherent Malay cheerfulness and pro-British loyalty were rooted in suffering.

Medicalization also extended the reach of colonial leaders into civilians' everyday lives, exposing them to colonial and medical racism. For example, when Australian Staff Nurse V. A. Clancy arrived in Malacca to work with sisters of 2/10th Australian General Hospital, she noted that Singapore had a reputation for being "the land of 'stinks and [Chinese slur] and drinks.'"[162] She noted that few nurses "had ever encountered coloured people before" and marveled at laborers with "abnormal knotty muscled legs!"[163] Her exposure to Asian bodies at their most vulnerable only deepened her sense of racial superiority. While working at a mental hospital, she condemned patients for chewing beetle nuts, which she saw as "a filthy custom so prevalent in the East." She noted that while patients suffered from malaria, typhus, and skin diseases, "it was not physical illness that made them so discontented It [*sic*] was frustration and bitterness at their lot."[164] Medical professionals' access to Asian people in colonial hospitals often led to resentment rather than empathy.

White women's medical work also threatened the livelihoods of Asian women. Chinese Christian Elizabeth Choy recalled Indigenous women's medical work as essential and life-saving in the absence of formally trained doctors.[165] Dr. Williams noted that that her policy was "not to try and supersede the old village handy woman or 'bidan,' but to try and teach her some very simple rules of conduct." Medical practitioners only interfered with "local customs," she insisted, when they were harmful to mother or child.[166] Since the majority of bidan women were well over sixty, she found it important to get them education but noted, "Some are too old and decrepit to learn, a few are persistently hostile." By contrast, she found younger bidans "easier to teach" and willing to work in hospitals or visit nurses and welfare centers to learn. Some even took apprenticeships for 40 cents a day, which attracted a wider labor pool: "Bidans from the kampongs as well as from the town are coming in for this training."[167] Women who had worked for years and even decades delivering and caring for children had to submit to the medical authority of white men and women to retain their livelihoods. What Williams failed to note was that this could threaten their credibility in the community, especially if women had political reasons for refusing the new training. Former guerilla Chen Xiu Zhu recalled that her mother acted as "a kind of barefoot doctor" with skills so exceptional that even "capitalists came to ask her for help." However, her mother "ignored them. She only treated the poor people for free."[168] Controlling medicine meant controlling who women served.

While some Asian women faced threats to their livelihoods, others faced accusations of being dangerous to colonial society.[169] S. E. Nicoll-Jones went to Singapore to investigate prostitution and suggested that the "amah has been looked upon in Singapore as a harmless nonentity."[170] While most amahs worked as women's servants, Nicoll-Jones insisted that many became "gaolers" by procuring women and forcing them into sex work. Yet Nicoll-Jones was aware that this was a classed as well as gendered issue. She explained that many Asian girls and young women went to Singapore as cabaret dancers but had to pay for English and dancing lessons. Most took up sex work by accompanying dance partners to their flats, because their pay at the cabarets was not enough to cover their debts. Sex work existed, she maintained, "in everything that allows loop-holes for money making without being detected." She pointed to "amusements [*sic*] parks" and "liquor bars" as primary culprits because "no opportunity is lost where a new focus can be created to obtain indirect control over the young people who can be exploited."[171] This reflected the ban on procuring and brothel-keeping in 1930, making such spaces important avenues for sexual trade.[172] Meanwhile, workers in entertainment facilities often earned no salaries and had no standard contracts. For Nicoll-Jones, prostitution, like high infant mortality, was the result of poverty and bad housing. Unlike many medical professionals, she did not blame vulnerable migrant populations, instead reasoning that they possessed "the legitimate desire for adventure and expression of a fuller life." In making her recommendations, she suggested that "nothing should be done to emphasize the need for penitence." Instead, she encouraged women leaving the profession to be given "a fair wage" so that she can "live happily."[173] In other words, social "vices" were also a consequence of poverty. Better wages would help women find better employment.

Despite Nicoll-Jones's desire to avoid punishing women, police monitored working women in the name of limiting prostitution. Sex trafficking between Malaya and China was, according to the police, "an old and well-organised trade." It could only be stopped, they reasoned, when "the source of the supply in China is closed."[174] This racialized the problem of prostitution as specifically Chinese even though women working in prostitution hailed from all over the globe. Many worked in Singapore's racially segregated sexual labor market, which included diverse European women.[175] Yet Asian women had a difficult time avoiding police surveillance. For example, police suspected waitresses in coffee shops of being at the center of "minor fights and numerous society quarrels." As a result, "great care has been exercised . . . in granting permission to individual women to be employed in such places." Some police speculated that it might become necessary "to refuse permission altogether for women to be employed as waitresses."[176] In Selangor, the "ineffective enforcement of the prohibition against the employment of waitresses in coffee shops and amusement parks" led to "society bullies" collecting "'protection' money." They believed that "[l]axity in control of women and hawkers leads directly to the encouragement of society bullies."[177] Due to British concerns about lawlessness, crime, and vice, women faced roadblocks to earning a living without scrutiny and surveillance during a depression.

Efforts to improve the conditions of colonial subjects' lives through social welfare struggled due to prevalent gender and racial biases. Many leaders fell back on the assumption that colonial subjects were unable to care for and manage themselves and needed to be supervised by white Europeans. Meanwhile, attacks on Asian women's work suggested that controlling them was necessary for social stability. While many British civilians and officials believed that they went to Singapore and Malaya to create a more equitable colonial society, they often deepened existing hierarchies. Singapore's reputation for sexual laxity contributed to sexual exploitation, high infant mortality, and restrictions on women's labor. The boom-and-bust economy created a large population of "squatters" and destitute laborers who struggled to maintain their health. The more welfare and missionary workers looked, the more evidence they found of colonial neglect. These everyday realities influenced the extreme political and labor activism of the period. Unfortunately, few British leaders saw the connection.

CHANGE AND CONTINUITY

When visitors came to Singapore and Malaya in the 1930s, many noted how much things had changed. English engineer and surveyor Arthur John Moore Bennett enjoyed his retirement from government service in Canada, Australia, and China by taking a trip around the world in his yacht. Along the way, he stopped in Singapore, noting that it had "changed out of all knowledge." He observed that "the two rubber booms had made of a quiet, rather smug English settlement, a roaring, snorting, semi-Americanized place, of roaring traffic, ugly 'MODERN' buildings." Older buildings, and memories, had been "swept away."[178] The "resplendent show place" of Orchard Road "had now lost its shine" despite the presence of brands like Dodge, Buick, Ford, Chevrolet, Morris, Standard, Rover, Sunbeam, and Vauxhall.[179] As Moore Bennett suggests, interwar Singapore was noteworthy for its difference from the prewar period. To a casual visitor it appeared "roaring," "smug," and "modern." Two tumultuous decades of booms and busts, increased policing, rising communism, and American investment left visitors with the impression of a bloated capitalist metropolis. Yet his panoramic reflections on the eve of war revealed what had, and had not, changed in the previous decades.

Moore Bennett followed other travelers and administrators in romanticizing Malaya as a tropical paradise. He could think of no "more beautiful country, than this of Malaya with its myriad of islands, straits, Malay and other peoples living peaceful lives in such a land of plenty."[180] He imagined that before colonialism "the natives must have had a wonderful time." On later reflection, he acknowledged the impact of British rule, explaining that the "beautiful country" of wooded hills, peaks, white sand beaches, mangroves, and great rivers was ruined by "the infernal white man, with his licenses, taxes in and on every possible thing and occupation." He resented "the coming of the pedatory [*sic*] races from the West, Arab, Portuguese, Spanish, Dutch, French and now English."[181] Here, Moore Bennett critiques British imperialism as an exploitative endeavor ruining a "beautiful country." Yet by characterizing British people as one among many "predatory races," he places equal blame on other colonizing powers while racializing Britons as possessing inherent martial supremacy.[182]

Despite his critiques of empire, racism was a common feature of Moore Bennett's analysis. Like other visitors, he regarded "the diversity of the races" as one of Singapore's remarkable features, noting several specific groups and "a score of others and breeds between the races by the hundreds."[183] Despite his fetishization of diversity, he chafed against its particularities. He described meeting a "disconsolate, friendless and discontented 'English' halfcaste [*sic*] of British nationality and presumably half Chinese-half Malay." He found the woman with him a "lump of discontented foolishness." His feeling was that the man "had been had" by yet another "Eurasian mama" with "doubtful daughters" trying to catch a husband. At a time when race and gender limited opportunities for employment, Moore Bennett saw a racialized woman with a child as nothing more than an opportunist. Yet he was even less empathetic to Black and Indigenous men who worked hard to be upwardly mobile. He recalled a governor in the Dutch East Indies making "a chap as black as your hat" a ship captain. When the captain arrived in Sydney, the white boarding officer "collared him and shoving him over with the blackgang, from below stairs, told him that all n------ were to be together." Moore Bennett delighted in the story because the "Australians however have their own ideas of fitness." He admired that Australians preserved the racial hierarchy of the British Empire by refusing to extend dignity and respect to Black men who earned positions of power. For Moore Bennett, the Australians' actions were necessary to prevent racialized "others" from gaining "the rights, status and calling of another race."[184]

Moore Bennett's racism also led him to condemn the migration that was so essential to the profitability of the colony. He explained that once it "was discovered by Kew and the Ceylon Rubber fraternity" that rubber grew well in Malaya, it "spelt the ruin of the country."[185] This ruin was not the result of colonial extraction or environmental destruction, but "[h]undreds of thousands of the lowest type of Hindu natives, Tamils and Southern Indian people, all aliens were introduced into the country holus bolus to provide 'cheap labour.'" He felt that this would result in "the total elimination of the Malays, the Sakais [Orang Asli] and every other race there and the substitution of low cast [*sic*] Southern Indians and South western Chinese tribes folk." Those coming in could "be forced to work long hours, accept any form of government given and not to criticise." Rather than sympathize with this exploited workforce, he resented the influx of Chinese migrants and "low caste Indian of a most depraved type." He saw welfare efforts to improve their lives as socialism. He blamed "vote-snatchers in Westminster" for allowing "coolies and coolie contractors" to "sit back and call the price of labour themselves." As a result, many of the once grand rubber plantations near Singapore, in his view, were "either being felled or allowed to go back to the jungle" in part because "the cost of labour had been artificially raised so much by the extravagance of government and its contractors." The chief problem of Singapore, he believed, was that "the commercial crowd" fought "to wring every possible farthing out of the territory" through exploited labor. Moore Bennett's

resentment toward migrants made him welcome racial violence. He claimed
that prior to British rule, the already-large Chinese population was "carefully
decimated from time to time, by the Malay Chiefs, whenever these interlopers
became too numerous or too cheeky."[186] They apparently "wiped out a few thousand" people at a time to prevent Chinese numbers from rising to their present
level. He lamented that by the 1930s, the Chinese population far outnumbered
the roughly one million Malays.[187] Moore Bennett felt the greatest sin of British
colonialism was bringing a large migrant population to Malaya without having
the will to kill those who caused problems.

Despite their power to command people and resources across vast distances,
British leaders, according to Moore Bennett, did not enjoy the trade monopoly
or geopolitical power that they imagined. This, he felt, was a result of both local
enterprise and Japanese success. He explained that locally, "white men and the
big plantations no longer had things all their own way."[188] Rather, "[t]ens of thousands of natives" now had access to rubber trees and sold their product in bazaars.
He also estimated that by 1931 the Japanese controlled 53 percent of total export
trade and 57 percent of the import trade from the Dutch East Indies and looked
on the Dutch East Indies as "Japanese preserves." While he suspected that all
fish sold by Chinese vendors were from Japanese importers, he also noted that
the Dutch appeared "very scared of the Japanese." This was because they had
"their so called 'fishing-boats' all around the Dutch Island." He implied that the
British should have feared the Japanese as the Dutch did, given their prominence in trade throughout the region. Instead, British leaders failed to grasp that
"all Western powers were being overswept, by Japan, who had already learnt the
powerlessness of the west." Despite his occasional criticism of "predatory races,"
Moore Bennett admired the Japanese. He respected them "more than ever" because they achieved a level of "domination" that other colonial powers "dreamt
of, but never succeeded in doing to Asia." At the same time, he felt "the British
and Germans have taught Japan all they both know, in getting slavery fastened on
weaker races."[189] In condemning migrants as "weaker races" deserving of death,
and portraying colonizers as "predatory races," Moore Bennett felt that Japan was
the perfect empire.

Moore Bennett's praise of Japan hinged on a growing disdain for fellow Britons. He insisted that Englishmen should be "bitterly ashamed of the cruelty,
crookedness, lust and greed" of the government of Malaya.[190] He found British
people in Malaya absent-minded and frivolous. He described meeting the Bing-
hams, whose main interests were jealousies, sex scandals, and battles for honor.
In Moore Bennett's eyes they were a "simple minded English pair" who prayed

"for a move back again to England—to a land and a people they loved, away, from what seemed to them, nothing but an hollow bluff full of pretense and makebelief."[191] Europeans in Malaya, he felt, had become so disconnected from reality that they lived in an imaginary world. This flight into fantasy enabled the government to become "nothing if not socialistic in all its tendencies." He loathed taxation and forcing estates to "erect and run schools, hospitals." He resented that "long nosed-government [sic] inspectors" visited "coolie lines" and "sympathise always with them, never with the management." For this reason, he felt he could never live in the country despite its beauty. He decided that "all beautiful things have some inherent defect," and in the case of Malaya, "the defect we saw, was the one-sidedness of the administration."[192] In his view, the welfare that addressed the conditions of Malaya's laborers was ruining the country, and British people were to blame.

Moore Bennett reveals a fascistic mentality not uncommon among current and former imperial administrators and military officers who came to admire Japan and Germany in the 1930s.[193] He resented the "socialistic" intentions to improve the lives of civilians. He condemned "the crafty folk in London" and "long nosed" government officials, evoking prevalent antisemitic tropes.[194] He regarded migrant populations, which had contributed to British prosperity, as inconvenient outsiders disturbing the tranquility of "peaceful" Malays. He went even further, believing that things were better when Malay chiefs "carefully decimated" inconvenient populations. He also suggested that "we 'Christians' have indeed taken a wrong turning somewhere" because "I have always preferred the savages." He added that "I firmly believe that all governments are just the same kind of ravening wolves as the old feudal lords." Most governments, he found, were "just plain robbers of the credulous—just as all medecine [sic] men, witch-doctors, clergymen, rabbis, bishops, archbishops, cardinals popes [sic]" that "pray on the superstitions of fools, so do governments on their material beliefs."[195] Such impressions were the culmination of a life supported by government service and a comfortable retirement on a personal yacht.

Ultimately, Moore Bennett's trip was a farewell to the world he had known: "Truly my world was falling about my ears."[196] He longed for the days when white people could live how they wanted "during boom years, bungalow, club, good cigars, liquer [sic] of known brands, the best of clothes, imported foods and many servants." Unfortunately, for him, "those days were as dead as the dodo." Over the course of "much instructive conversation, with many races," he recognized that the "coveted position of the whiteman [sic] was being challenged, more and more." He believed that Europeans became frivolous and distracted while trade union strikes destroyed "patriotism" and left "governments increasingly menac-ing." As a result, "the machine began to show signs of wearing out." Despite all of this, he believed that "the easterner is a freer man" than the European. His reasoning was that "he works less hours, is less held by laws, licenses, taxes, con-ventions, religious beliefs and superstitions." Having never worked on a rubber plantation, he claimed that "the crushing burdens of factories, timeclocks, rail-ways train timings—have not yet eaten the soul right out of him."[197] Using stan-dard orientalist and fascist tropes, Moore Bennett imagined those living under colonialism as free, and those enforcing it as doomed.

DANGEROUS DIVISIONS

The 1920s and 1930s exposed the pervasive racism at the heart of British rule in Singapore and Malaya in times of so-called "peace." Frequent booms and busts devastated the lives and livelihoods of Asian civilian laborers as British travelers, planters, and administrators mourned the loss of a prosperous colonial space. The result was a colony that invested massive resources in trade and militarism, train-ing each of its military and civilian leaders to prioritize these at all costs. British prejudices made it impossible to address civilian laborers' needs without repli-cating racism, bringing further humiliation to colonial subjects. Those who re-fused European aid or fought to claim wealth, heroism, or equality for themselves faced the condemnation of the colonial state. Colonial subjects were meant to be pawns to imperial power—tools in the trades of tin and rubber, which fueled the empire's prosperity and war machine. Despite these realities, British civilians repeatedly stated their intentions to build an inclusive empire while working to undermine it. Racism was baked into every assumption about "uplift"—from the medicalization of the "coolie" body to the need for more Chinese police. The intention was to control the colonial population so that they would not disrupt the trade and profitability of the empire. Welfare projects were reactionary to the boom-and-bust model of economic prosperity. The same refusal to recognize Yeo Bian Chuan after 1915 inspired the refusal to share prosperity with Asian la-borers on the front lines of combating economic turmoil. Financial and military resources were about preserving European illusions of stability and squashing anyone who threatened their fantasies of peace.

By the 1930s, many Britons realized that their illusions of stability were crum-bling. Missionaries, military leaders, Rotary men, medical professionals, and casual travelers all noted with apprehension that the conditions of laborers were dismal. They understood that this made the British Empire look bad, and, in some cases, worked to address it. Yet as war raged in Europe, Sir Robert Brooke-Popham, the commander-in-chief of the Far East Command, warned of the dangerous divisions within Malaya and Singapore. He noted that the "colour bar" in Malaya was more pronounced than in the region's other European colonies. This made it difficult to gain a "sympathetic understanding of their outlook on life." As a result, colonial leaders struggled "to improve the conditions of the non-British races in Malaya, especially hospital and medical facilities, anti-malarial measures and education."[198] He reported that racism was a major impediment to understanding between ruler and ruled. Unfortunately, his report would not receive a reply until after the war. Before then, as will be discussed in the next chapter, white civilians retreated in mass numbers during the Japanese invasion. This was not only a reflection of civilian fear, a lack of military preparedness, or colonial decadence. It also exposed what was already there: a militarized state that ascribed value and protection based on race, ethnicity, and class. White Europeans knew that these prosperous colonies had unequal foundations. They tried to leave these problems behind as they evacuated. As a result, the Second World War forestalled the tentative self-awareness of inequity that crept into interwar European accounts. Instead, narratives of heroic European wartime suffering would overshadow the everyday hardships of colonial subjects. The unresolved racialization, militarization, and inequity of the interwar period would return to colonial Malaya with full force after the Japanese occupation.

THREE

The Pride and the Fall

When the Japanese military invaded Singapore and Malaya from December 8, 1941, to February 15, 1945, interwar illusions about imperial inclusivity crumbled against the reality of war. Before the war, Policeman William Arthur Campion Haines felt that interracial police forces represented friendship and inclusivity.[1] Facing the Japanese invasion, he commanded his men to return to their homes and integrate with the civil population. This proved difficult, as some of the "Sikh and Pathan police" were recruited directly from India. Still, Haines rationalized that they "would nevertheless be absorbed into their respective communities without difficulties."[2] Inclusion, for Haines, fell along racial lines. Instead of trusting Indian men to fight the Japanese, Haines and his forces soon "were training and arming the Chinese members of the M.C.P. [Malayan Communist Party]," even though he had spent decades fighting them.[3] As Chinese communists transformed from enemies to allies, Japanese civilians became enemies. S. E. Nicoll-Jones spent the interwar years trying to improve the conditions of women sexual laborers but soon accompanied five hundred Japanese civilians to internment. This took her to St. John's Island, once used to shelter the "loyal" men of the 5th Light Infantry in 1915. There, she became commandant of the women's and children's camp. When Japanese internees were transferred to India in January 1942, Nicoll-Jones left on the *SS Gian Bee*. Unfortunately, the Japanese Navy sunk the vessel "with heavy loss of life of women and children," according to her obituary.[4] Power over life and death no longer rested in British hands.

While it is tempting to say that the Japanese invasion reversed the gains of the interwar period, it is more instructive to understand how the British response to the invasion reflected the colonial racial and military politics of the interwar era. A leveling of racial, class, disability, gender, military, and ethnic identities only came with a relentless onslaught of privation and trauma. This, in many ways, embodied the story of the Japanese invasion and British evacuation. British leaders concentrated on evacuating those they perceived as vulnerable and deserving, leaving a tremendous gap for those left behind.[5] To C. A. Bayly and Tim Harper, Britain's flight from Singapore laid bare the "complacency and racial arrogance" of colonial masters.[6] This chapter examines not only the racial arrogance of colonial leaders, but how this saturated everyday life for soldiers and civilians working in the colony prior to and during the invasion. As this chapter shows, Asian civilians possessed the same fears of invasion as their white counterparts but possessed less support in their efforts to survive. This contrasted the hundreds of thousands of British and Australian troops flooding into the region in 1940 and 1941 who found Singapore and Malaya safe and fun. British officer F. Spencer Chapman arrived in Singapore in 1941 to work with the Special Training School (STS 101) and prepare British forces for jungle warfare. He recalled "a comfortable feeling of security" from seeing uniforms "of all kinds" and "aeroplanes" droning "incessantly overhead."[7] At night, "the sky was streaked with the pale beams of searchlights." He knew that the naval base, completed during the depression, and "fifteen-inch guns" would be formidable opponents to anyone who tried to attack the island.[8] Like Chapman, many white military personnel believed that interwar efforts created a strong, unified colony. In reality, interwar racial inequity was not just a reflection of colonial leaders' arrogant overconfidence, but a call to arms for change among colonial subjects.

This chapter analyzes white British military and service personnel's impressions of colonial Singapore and Malaya prior to and during the Japanese invasion. It places these in conversation with Asian soldiers' and civilians' testimonies to show a pervasive pattern of white entitlement to Asian labor. By cutting across multiple sources and perspectives under an umbrella of whiteness—from young Australian soldiers newly arrived for war to civilian British women with years of experience in Malaya—it shows how shared assumptions about racial labor shaped everyday colonial encounters. In so doing, this chapter transforms authors of letters, reports, and memoirs from viewer to viewed, or from "objective" author to object of study, "reversing the gaze" of colonial encounters.[9] This shows that Singapore's early "war" years from 1939 to the "fall" in February 1942 embodied the inequities of colonial militarism, facilitating Britain's ultimate surrender. The creation of sanitized commercial spaces for white servicepeople to enjoy and Asian labor to support created severe gaps between who received—or felt entitled—to care and comfort and whose labor provided it. These unresolved inequities, as much as the material failures to prepare for war, accelerated Singapore's notoriously swift and humiliating fall.

A FOOL'S PARADISE

In the early years of the Second World War, soldiers from across the British Empire arrived in Singapore believing that they had found paradise. While some lamented their inability to participate in action in Europe or the Middle East, others saw Singapore as a pleasure palace offering freedom from racial hierarchies so firmly entrenched in other locales. The Governor of the Straits Settlements, Sir Shenton Thomas, noted that soldiers received duty-free cigarettes, tobacco, beer, and spirits, and discounts at cinemas.[10] Officers enjoyed honorary memberships at the primary social club, Tanglin Club, and access to golf and swimming clubs. Men, according to the Governor, "were lavishly catered for with canteens and dances."[11] As a result, these new arrivals enjoyed films, movie theaters, rickshaws, and cabarets packed with diverse clientele. White Australian Jack Turner of the Reserve Motor Transport Coy arrived in February 1941 and recalled being "enthusiastically welcomed by natives of all nationalities."[12] On a bus to Seremban, he met Amar Singh, a Sikh merchant, who took "a great fancy to me," treated him to dinner, gave him a ring and cigarettes, and exchanged letters over several months.[13] He also attended cabarets and played mahjong with Chinese police and civilians.[14] These interracial encounters helped him see Singapore as a "[l]ovely place" offering a "[m]arvelous time."[15] For Turner, and many other white soldiers, Singapore offered a mirage of privilege and pleasure.

Like Turner, former English bank clerk A. J. S. Holman emphasized Singapore's interracial social scene and extravagant amenities as inclusive recreation. He attended artistic exhibits featuring many Chinese artists.[16] At rugby games, "our Indian and Malay supporters . . . would cheer like mad!" He even had "really good fun" playing hockey on "mixed teams with the Indians." He appreciated the relative luxury of the mess, which was a "high airy room" with tables covered in white linen and luxurious food offerings such as iced lime juice and iced milkshakes. Within the garrison, soldiers amused themselves with a billiard table, table tennis, wicker chairs on verandas, a garrison cinema, and music from the radiogram. In Singapore city, they enjoyed playing rugby, as well as attending dances and other events at Victoria Memorial Hall and Raffles Hotel, concerts sponsored by the Singapore Gramophone and Music Society, and visits to the botanical gardens in Tanglin. Such luxuries made Holman feel that "maybe soldiering in Singapore wasn't too bad at all." In fact, "soldiering in Singapore was a good thing."[17] Service in Singapore gave white soldiers a life of luxury whether they were elite officers or low-ranking working-class men.

As a civilian by trade newly arrived in Malaya rather than career soldier or administrator, Holman's testimony shows the tension between simultaneously learning about and benefiting from British military and colonial racism. He embodies the attempt, not uncommon among Second World War soldiers, to pursue interracial "friendship" while constantly experiencing and benefiting from colonial hierarchy. In this, he shows continuity with interwar civilians who offered medical and educational support in the name of interracial solidarity, only to give in to the pressure to rule in a colonial space. Alongside his tales of extravagance, Holman indicated that soldiers' comfort depended on the availability of Asian labor. He noted that in the Navy, Army, and Air Force Institutes, his access to comfortable chairs, a gramophone, cigarettes, and tea were made possible through the labor of "Chinese boys."[18] At the mess, one "Chinese boy" brought them their cutlery and silver, while another brought their tiffin. In the garrison, "Chinese boys" provided "beer, minerals, cigarettes, chocolate, sandwiches and various cooked dishes." Describing laborers of undetermined age as "boys" reflected the hierarchical paternalism that made ethnicity and status, as well as domesticated labor, a marker of inferiority and a denial of manhood. Yet Holman believed that Asian personnel were so ready and willing to serve white soldiers that they fought for the privilege. On one occasion a group of Chinese "boys" asked to shine his shoes and badges, but an Indian man with a military pass insisted that he should do it. By Holman's account the Indian man "was certainly keen; he even scrubbed our topees!" The Indian and Chinese personnel then had an argument and "started a game of you-push-me-and-I'll-push-you."[19] Holman expressed amusement at Chinese and Indian competition for employment. Regardless of the outcome of the fight, he would emerge as the salary-granting patriarch and beneficiary.

Such experiences make it unsurprising that Holman found ethnic diversity an added allure of his posting. When he went to the Straits Cabaret, a "low waterfront dive," he felt like he had stepped "into a Hollywood film set."[20] He delighted in the "polyglot conversations" and the diversity of the patrons on the seafront, which included seamen ranging from "British Mercantile Marine to American negroes." Even among those speaking English he could find "the Scots accent, and Chinese, and American, and Danish and Swedish, and English with the Eurasians' lisp, and American with the Negroes' accent, and certainly many more." This diversity also reflected racial and gender commodification. Holman described the Pavilion cinema having a balcony occupied by "mainly Europeans and the higher classes of Chinese." The implication was that all "Europeans" deserved such spaces, while only "higher classes" of Chinese people did.[21] This reflected the Chief Police Officer of Perak's impression that "Singapore was a wealthy and expensive place, and wealth was not the monopoly of the whites. There was a rich and cultured Asiatic community."[22] Still, whiteness was almost a guarantee of access to elite spaces and pleasure. At dance halls, Holman described when he "chose" (danced with) "a slender Chinese girl." Together they danced to "the rhythm of the coloured band" while fighting the "crowded state of the floor sufficiently to dance." Black musicians and Asian dancers were exotic window-dressing for his colonial adventures.

As Holman implies, entertainment facilities often encouraged servicemen to view women as commodities. Holman complained that "the standard of the girls' dancing" at one dance hall was superior to that of another. Asian women's dancing skills were available for purchase—products to be consumed by white soldiers.[23] While this echoed the "good-time-girl" clichés in Britain, which portrayed lower class women as sexually available, the racial politics of colonial Singapore prevented most white women from gaining such a reputation.[24] By contrast, when Holman danced with white women they were "young wives and daughters" who "came along to do their duty and dance with the Navy, the Army and the Air Force." While Asian women worked jobs by dancing with white men, it was a "duty" of white women in wartime to do so for free. For Holman, however, white women's affections represented a wartime breakdown of class lines. Prior to the war, army men in Singapore often felt "snubbed" by white European women, making wartime dancing a rare delight. Part of the problem, he reasoned, was "among the troops there was a lot of unorthodox dancing which seemed to go a little hard on young ladies who had received their experience in the more select academies and ballrooms of England." One "unfortunate girl" was even "caught by an outrageous jitterbug from the Navy."[25] He did not add such reflection on his own dancing skills and whether his Asian dancing partners enjoyed "hard" dances. The combination of racial and gender privilege spared Holman from considering whether he was good company. As a British soldier in Singapore, it felt like everyone lived to serve him.

Australian Private Alfred Lyal Lever was more explicit—and critical—than other soldiers about the racialized labor that facilitated his access to pleasure. In his letters home, he noted frequent visits to the cinema and cabaret where he found "the dancing girls are all Chinese & pretty good dancers too."[26] However, such spectacles only made him miss the girls and dances back home because there were "cabarets over here but I am damned if I would dance with a c----girl."[27] He attempted to visit a village but "didn't stay long" in part because of the "mob of dirty c----s."[28] He loathed being around Chinese civilians and "not being able to understand what the Chinese & other occupants of this country are talking about." It made him worry about the possibility of Asian migration to Australia, suggesting that if a Chinese person "comes near me when I get back to 'Aussie' I'll sure crown him."[29] Such racist language and threats of violence appeared in letters to both his mother and father, indicating that racism against Asian people linked a white soldier in Malaya to civilians in the white settler colony of Australia.[30] The experience of colonial war did not give him an appreciation for Singapore's diversity. Rather, it deepened his existing prejudices.

Even Holman, who was more positive about his experiences, demonstrated a marked tendency to cast Asian women as either decorative objects lacking agency or pathetic and desperate. He discussed the Q-Cat, a Chinese owned café managed by a Eurasian woman called Kathy. He regarded her as "intensely jealous" of the "lovely young girls" working there, even though he often visited the café, chatted, smoked, and drank tea with Kathy and a "rather pretty little Chinese" woman named Lucy.[31] Holman saw nothing but Kathy's perceived "jealousy" toward young women, ignoring the complex class, gender, and racial politics of these spaces. Like dances, such encounters were deeply commodified around his patronage of the café and his desire to talk with young women. Such entitlement to women's affections even extended to Holman's driver, a "Pathan" (Pashtun) man named Shuja-ud-din. While driving home, Holman apparently stared at a European girl walking alone. Shuja-ud-din slammed on the brakes of the car and said he would proposition her on Holman's behalf, which Holman apparently declined.[32] Dancing, drinking, and driving enabled colonial subjects to work in the service of white men's comfort, often at the expense of women. This deepened the unequal raced and gendered access to public space.

When not delighting in Singapore's cafés and cabarets, Holman treated his coworkers as ethnographic objects. Part of his duties included working in an office with Chinese, Eurasian, Filipino, and Indian colleagues, whom he described in detail.[33] He believed that some men enjoyed being objectified, with "jagirs, the Sikh Guards" of "fine physique" asking him to take their photos with his camera. Despite this eager ethnography, Holman also believed that diversity made his job more difficult. While working in the Singapore Fortress Supply Depot with Chinese, Indian, and Eurasian personnel, he noted that he had to manage "separate ration scales for British troops, Australian troops, Malays, Malay followers, Chinese soldiers, Chinese followers, Enrolled Chinese, Indian rice-eaters, Indian atta-eaters, Indian non-meat-eaters, Indian meat-eaters, Indian live-meat-eaters and even more!" He cited a common colonial rationale that it was important to defer to "religious scruples but also to taste and custom, all of which were carefully observed to avoid trouble." By indicating that respect for the beliefs and customs of colonial subjects was merely to "avoid trouble," Holman followed countless colonial officials in regarding Asian people as a burden and inconvenience.[34] Despite the clichéd perception of Asian "scruples," Holman acknowledged that trouble was rare: "[C]ontrary to what one had been led to believe, they lived together in something like peaceful amity, a feast day for one group was considered good enough to make an excuse for everyone to feast."[35] He even benefited from having Hindu, Muslim, and Sikh colleagues because of the culinary diversity they offered. Still, Holman complained frequently about the logistical burden— and noise—of diverse food management, including keeping live sheep, goats, and chickens ready for fresh slaughter.[36] For Holman, Singapore's religious and ethnic plurality made colonial service exciting, delicious, and cinematic. It also added to his labor, increasing his sense of entitlement to pleasure.

Compared to Holman, who delighted in interracial recreation, other soldiers noticed the cracks in the façade. After being admitted to a hospital with a foot injury, Australian soldier Turner saw a man admitted to hospital "who killed a Chinaman in K.L. Got drunk & ran over him."[37] He did not indicate that the man was likely to be held accountable for this death.[38] Turner even admitted going to a cabaret and then getting "tipped out of Rick-shaw by a drunk. Got mixed up in a fight. Landed a few good ones & received a few."[39] Holman similarly observed that the "regular soldier seems always to be ready to adopt any fight as his own, it being, apparently, one of his few 'pleasures.'" As a result, knife fights at dances were not uncommon.[40] While many servicemen delighted in cabarets, films, and rickshaws, Asian civilians navigated the drunken disorder of living and working in a soldiers' paradise.

Not all violence against Asian people was a result of white soldiers' drunkenness. Australian private Lever's bitterness toward Asian people in Singapore increased his desires to inflict violence against potential Asian foes. He expressed, "I wish the Jap[ane]s[e] would start some thing [*sic*]" because "the boys are just rearing to have a smack at some one."[41] He condemned the Japanese as "little yellow devils" who should "either fight or else back down altogether." Instead, he felt that they just "sit on the fence," which prevented "us chaps in Malaya" from moving "from the country as much as we would like to." When he received news of his brother's death in the Middle East, he resented being "over in this damn dump while our mates are getting blown to hell."[42] This reflected a wider pattern of frustration. Turner suggested that Australians felt "fed up" and kept "wishing we were either sent home or to the Middle East." Being sent to Southeast Asia was "always a sore point."[43] Occupying colonial Asia, rather than fighting in Europe or the Middle East, increased many servicepeople's frustrations. Rather than protesting up the military hierarchy, they directed this hostility toward Asian civilians. When the Japanese invasion finally started, Lever looked forward to "get[ting] a smack at the dirty little yellow cows."[44] Servicepeople's frustrations about the war, distance from home, and feelings of dislocation in a foreign place led them eagerly await the start of the war. This let them exercise their racial hatred through the permissible violence of war.

While Holman believed that Asian men eagerly served British needs, Asian men frequently expressed their frustrations with expected subservience. Singapore resident Mehervan Singh believed that Indians worked for the British "strictly for renumeration." They wanted to do their work and make a living because going to prison or "getting hot headed against the British would be of no use." Eagerness to work was more about avoiding incarceration and violence than dedication to serving British needs. In fact, working for the British did not prevent many from feeling, in Singh's words, "anti British."[45] Even more telling, Indian soldiers shared similar sentiments. Indian officer Naranjan Singh Gill recalled that "if India was under the Imperial rule, Malaya was more so. The local people were even worse off."[46] He observed that the "Indians had very little respect" in Malaya because most were there "to make money or they were engaged in menial work." This pervasive disrespect led many Indian soldiers and officers to receive a warm reception from the Indian community in Singapore. Indian Army Officer Mohan Singh recalled that Indians in Ipoh "welcomed us with open arms."[47] Gill insisted similarly that "the local Indians rose to their feet and entertained us grandly because that raised the prestige of India as a whole."[48] Their arrival signaled to the local population that it was possible to find "Indian commissioned officers coming in who were equal to the Britishers."[49] This enthusiastic acceptance contrasted Indian soldiers' and officers' feelings of being constantly disrespected compared to white men. S. P. P. Thorat remembered that officers trained in India were "disgruntled" because they were paid less than those trained in England.[50] Gill noted that the Simla Club remained "exclusively for the British. Even the princes were not admitted." When he did find opportunities to dance, he shocked a white British girl who remarked: "You people dance!"[51] Local Indians' delight in the novelty of seeing uniformed Asian men with equal rank as British leaders was something worth celebrating. To them, it was the fruition of long-held promises of imperial racial inclusivity. It was remarkable because it was so rare. To soldiers, however, this equality was just a smoke screen for other forms of exclusion and inequity.

Indian officers also were keenly aware of the anti-Asian tone in military circles and increasingly sought pan-Asian solidarities to address it. Officer Mohan Singh, who later formed the pro-Japanese Indian National Army, recognized an affinity with other colonial subjects in Malaya. He described, "The natives, the real Malays were mere serfs, while the masters were the British, who ruled them. They were like us."[52] He couldn't help but notice being "in one of the most beautiful and rich lands of the world" that nonetheless exhibited "the worst picture of exploited humanity." He resented that:

> The Britishers in Malaya were far more arrogant and snobbish than those in India. They were rolling in wealth. Every planter considered himself to be a mini king, madly rushing through life. Wine and women, dancing, gambling and racing appeared to be their only serious occupation of life. Unmindful of poverty, illiteracy, ignorance, disease and dirt, which was the lot of the common man, the rich drove along the highways of sensual pleasures, accumulating more and more wealth by bleeding white the already impoverished humanity.[53]

Compared to the luxurious lives of white soldiers and civilians, Singh and other Indian soldiers had to construct defense works "in the marshy and malaria-infested lands of Northern Malaya." They lived more like laborers than warriors in the wooden huts of a rubber plantation.[54] While Mohan Singh did not discuss his relative privilege as an officer compared to lower-paid soldiers or Asian laborers, he shows that the racist experience of military service in Malaya and Singapore was central to his eventual decision to align with the Japanese against the British.

For many white soldiers, access to Asian labor created a pleasure palace that enabled them to assert their place in an empire built and sustained by inequity. The sense that Asian civilians were, at best, annoying and commodifiable made some white servicepeople crave wartime violence. Holman's ethnographic encounters with Singapore and Malaya, compared to Lever's hostility, show how access to recreation and pleasure was intended to mitigate such frustrations. For Lever, being constantly exposed to Asian people while far from home, experiencing personal losses, or longing to fight, fomented hostility toward his colonial posting and the people residing there. Even Holman's more positive experiences revealed a pervasive pattern of objectifying and commodifying Asian civilians at work and play. Both experiences—of racial hatred toward those in subservient positions, and of an expectation of labor for pleasure—underlined the realities of being colonial occupiers. White soldiers' bitter entitlement alienated many Asian soldiers and civilians on the eve of war. For Indian soldiers, however, everyday racism amplified the desire for something new.

INVASION AND INVERSION

When K. P. Kesava Menon learned about the Japanese landing at Kota Bharu in Malaya on December 8, 1941, from "a Chinese clerk" in Ipoh, he immediately registered it as a challenge to white supremacy. By Menon's account, the clerk exclaimed, "The bloody British and the boasts of their might!" Menon apparently responded, "We may be able to see what happens to the 'White man's superiority.'"[55] Soon, "members of the Asiatic staff" debated the risks or value of the invasion despite a manager's encouragement to keep working. While many Chinese employees worried about the Japanese due to the Sino-Japanese war, others felt "there would be room for a lot of adventure."[56] As Japanese forces made their way down the Malay peninsula toward Singapore from December 1941 until February 1942, the everyday realities of racial hierarchy, long accepted by white service-people, intensified. Colonial leaders prioritized the protection and evacuation of white people, often leaving Asian civilians to fend for themselves. One civilian official even insisted that "the majority of the population has been evacuated" from Malaya in December 1941.[57] In his mind, only white people counted. This caused considerable hardship, confusion, and frustration for those left behind. Any illusion that Asian colonial subjects were eager to serve British interests at all costs quickly faded against the realities and traumas of war.

For Menon, the Japanese invasion not only destroyed imperial leaders' claims to racial supremacy, but also exposed how hard many fought to keep it intact. He recalled that when evacuees arrived by train in Ipoh from Kedah and Penang, "there were only Europeans and a few Eurasians. Not a single Chinese, Malay or Indian was inside the train." Observers asked about the stark demographics and learned that "there was no accommodation and transport facilities to bring all those who wanted to leave and naturally, preference was given to Europeans and Eurasians." The explanation was that Europeans and Eurasians "would suffer more than the other nationalities from the Japanese in case the latter succeeded in occupying Penang."[58] This provided cool comfort to many Indians waiting anxiously for their families in Penang without reliable telephone and telegraph service between Penang and Ipoh. The European press, however, played up the success of the evacuation without mentioning "the discrimination shown against the local population." According to Menon, a protest in Penang prompted the governor to make "an apologetic statement" and give "clear assurance that in future, in the matter of evacuation, no discrimination will be shown against Indians, Chinese or Malays."[59]

The racism of evacuation amplified colonial subjects' hardships and engendered greater hostility. Jernail Singh, a Sikh watchman, relayed to Menon that he saw many Punjabi soldiers arriving via hospital train from the Siamese (Thai) border who "lost their arms, many others had lost their legs, a lot of them were having bullet wounds and many of them were suffering from burns." Many of them were "shivering and howling" while "bitterly cursing the British Sirkar [government] and the Orang Puteh (white man)."[60] Menon noted that his first reaction was to blame the Japanese, even though soldiers lamented devastating defeats in British service. This made Menon reconsider: "If the British want to keep this country let them fight it out alone with the Japanese. Why should they make use of our brothers to keep this country for their advantage?" He feared Japanese rule less than "the Orang Putehs who are keeping Malaya for their benefit. So if white men are driven out from Malaya we are not the losers."[61] Seeing so many colonial subjects abandoned, put on the front, or left to die shook whatever confidence remained in British leadership. The invasion and evacuation shattered dreams of inclusivity.

English soldier Holman also noted that the invasion immediately changed the dynamics between ruler and ruled, though he interpreted this change more positively. His "last great feast with the Indians" was "hurriedly terminated by an air-raid," but the tone of this encounter separated it from previous shared meals. Holman was just twenty-two years old and remembered that instead of British officers treating Indian soldiers as a "father" would treat his child, as was common previously, British officers and men finally started "to relax with them and enjoy their company and their different culture."[62] In noting how things changed, he admitted that racial hierarchy and performances of supremacy were the previous norm. By contrast, during the invasion, he shared tea with Santok Singh, his bearer, enjoyed a Madrasi meal with Madhaven, listened to Rawel Singh sing and play Punjabi instruments, and engaged in conversations about Sikh, Hindu, and Christian customs.[63] Holman's account indicates that the uncertainty of the invasion enabled white soldiers to make good on the interracial paradise that they imagined already existed. The uncertainties of war freed white men from the expectation to enforce colonial and military hierarchies.

Despite Holman's belief that the invasion broke down inequities, he still admitted that rank and hierarchy enabled his survival. During a period of daily Japanese bombings, Holman worked in a chemical store in an old dhobi (washerman's) hut that got bombed. Indians surrounded him and were "trying to support me and to brush me down, and perhaps for the first time I realised how very much they were attached to me."[64] He described similarly how the Indian men followed him "close around like a bodyguard" and obeyed without question when he ordered them to collect typewriters and other important materials. Protection and obedience, for Holman, meant camaraderie and "attachment." He never considered that these soldiers cared as much if not more about their own fears and need for protection—made easier by aiding a white man. While Holman noted that Indian soldiers appeared steadfast, he had a harder time securing laborers. He found "Chinese coolies" difficult to find, which left "faithful Indians" to do much of the desired work. Yet ethnicity proved to be a poor marker of "loyalty." As Japanese troops closed in on Johor Bahru, Holman could not keep Indian clerks working in the office with shells overhead and explosions nearby. He saw this as a reflection of British soldiers' need to lead by example, because "if they saw just one British soldier dive for a slit trench they all disappeared in a flash like magic."[65] Colonial subjects could only earn praise for exposing themselves to danger with unquestioning devotion to British leaders.

Despite continued inequity, Holman's invasion experience brought a newfound appreciation for Asian soldiers. When a battalion of Nepali "Gurkhas" arrived at Chickabu after the Japanese crossed the Johor Strait into Singapore island, Holman was relieved because he felt unprepared with just "half-a-dozen of us armed and about eighty or more non-combatant Indians—quite a responsibility. Needless to say, I made sure that the Gurkhas had everything they wanted."[66] As non-colonial subjects serving in the colonial Indian Army, Nepali men had an ambiguous position in colonial order.[67] Yet Holman's deference suggests that he became an eager server, while Asian military personnel became the served, reversing his earlier experiences. At the same time, he evoked common tropes of British adoration for Gurkhas, describing them as "short fierce men" and "terrific and fearless fighters," reducing them to ethnographic objects worthy of praise for supposedly natural qualities. Nonetheless, these soldiers enabled Holman to escape. He admitted, "I have a great deal to thank the Gurkhas for and it is no wonder that I have great feeling for them, and I believe I always shall."[68] Unfortunately, perceptions of Nepali loyalty became a liability. Holman heard from Indian soldiers "that because of their intense pro-British loyalty the

FIGURE 2.   White women and children preparing to evacuate Singapore, c.
1941. Courtesy of State Library Victoria, www.slv.vic.gov.au

Gurkhas have been much persecuted by the Japanese."[69] Nepali rewards for protecting British interests were racialized declarations of gratitude and enduring
greater hardships.

The Japanese invasion quickly revealed the fragility of an interracial paradise
built for white servicemen. Men who once enjoyed lavish cafés, ample servants,
and plentiful recreation came face-to-face with the danger and vulnerability of
poor leadership that no longer benefited them. At one point, Holman learned
that he was all but abandoned with no troops between him and Japanese forces.
Beyond this existential fear, his inability to communicate with superior officers
or the command at Fort Canning made him worry about being named a deserter.
Other men he encountered also had no contact with Command and had no idea
what was happening. Holman nearly opened fire on a group of Englishmen.[70]
This powerlessness and confusion completely upended Holman's previous feeling that Singapore was a nice place to serve and that soldiering was a desirable
profession. When they came upon a private bungalow and former Officers' Mess
with white linen, regimental silver, and silver candlesticks still laid out, which

Holman previously adored, Holman instead felt that the "whole setting looked like something from another world, completely irrelevant."[71]

LABORED EVACUATION

While servicemen confronted fear and uncertainty, servicewomen received priority evacuations that underlined colonial ideas about racial and gender vulnerability. Dr. Cicely Williams's professional status and age, and ability to benefit from the exalted status of white womanhood, gave her a unique experience of the invasion. She was not one among many white women to evacuate as quickly as possible. Rather, as a rural doctor working in a genuinely multi-ethnic space, she felt a sense of duty to Asian civilians rather than just British interests. Prior to the invasion, Williams had a long career in child and infant care and "was well over forty-five." She was "not allowed to retire" because "I was both too valuable to be spared and too valueless to get any sort of promotion," a dynamic not uncommon among women professionals.[72] By early 1941, she disliked Singapore for its "apathies and antipathies" and accepted a position in rural Trengganu in eastern Malaya to do a health survey and advise on welfare work. After months of dedicated service, she anticipated leaving Trengganu for India in December 1941. Instead, she heard on the radio news of the landing at Kota Bharu—about 100 miles from her "undefended" location. News broadcasts and planes overhead contributed to her unease. By December 9, she realized that "we should get less bombing, for which we were prepared, than troops advancing on us, for which we were not."[73] Williams's tale of fleeing Trengganu to escape an invading army exposed her feelings of guilt and anxiety about shirking her duty while continuing to depend on racialized labor.

Immediately, Williams noted how the invasion prompted greater racial exclusion. Police arrested and interned roughly sixty Japanese civilians who previously worked in iron mines.[74] Williams initially remained behind to help patients unable to leave the hospital but soon faced pressure to depart. She reasoned that the evacuation of predominantly white people was for the protection of Asian civilians: "We could be of little use to the local population once the Japanese had arrived, in fact our presence might make things harder for them." The only certainty, in the eyes of white people in Malaya, was that their evacuation would make life better for colonial subjects. However, remaining behind was not a choice for one Asian nurse because of the ableism among evacuees. This woman was "only recently arrived from Singapore" and had no nearby relatives. Williams "knew she was a bad walker and I thought that on the whole it would be better

to risk allowing her to stay in the kampongs with the other nurses than to attempt taking her back through the jungle."[75] Race and disability, therefore, left
an Asian nurse far from home without support, depriving her of the professional
status offered by nursing. The underlying assumption was that Japanese military
personnel represented no threat to Asian civilians, and white people could do
nothing to help.

Europeans' assumptions about Asian civilians' inherent safety contrasted the
overwhelming evidence of panic. Williams noted that when they drove into town
to pick up supplies, they found "shops were being shuttered, there were no women
in the streets and the men and boys seemed to be poised for flight. A great many
people had left the town already and taken their women and put valuables to the
kampongs." All along their journey, they found people "racing away from the
town and cars overturned."[76] A young Eurasian woman, Sheila Allan, recalled in
Ipoh that people were no "longer carefree—the people had a nervous, scared look
on their faces."[77] F. Spencer Chapman remarked similarly that it was "astonish-
ing, as we passed by, to see kampong after kampong of attractive Malay houses
surrounded by their coconut groves, fruit trees, hibiscus bushes, and vegetable
gardens, all completely deserted."[78] Asian civilians, unsurprisingly, were just as
scared as their white counterparts. Still, white people assumed that being Asian
offered protection. Williams recalled one bank manager whose escape involved
"excitements that included being disguised for some days as a Malay."[79] While
Williams described this racial drag as excitement, those participating likely
lacked sufficient linguistic or local knowledge to convince any Asian person of
their charade.[80] Still, in the minds of many white people during the invasion, race
dictated safety or danger, making white people the most vulnerable. This will-
fully ignored the fact that Asian civilians had identical fears of facing an invading
army. Instead, many white leaders operated under the belief that Asian civilians'
experiences only mattered if it impacted them.

While declining to help Asian subjects, British leaders also refused to give
them the power to protect themselves. Williams was frustrated that British leaders refused to "hand over to the Malays such things as control of police, prisons,
etc." The consequence, in Williams's eyes, was "they were all disbanded, police
and volunteers, and there was a stampede and general looting and disorder." The
sixty Japanese internees sent to Kuala Trengganu "were released when we ran
away."[81] Such hasty disbandment was not uncommon. While Haines disbanded
Indian police, Major I. A. McDonald regretted having to leave "my Chinese."
Feeling he had no choice, he told them to go home and throw their weapons into
the sea.[82] General Officer Commanding Percival, who ultimately surrendered,

later suggested that men in the FMS Volunteer Force "were given the option, as fighting passed into their States, of continuing to serve or of handing in their arms and equipment and going home." He felt that most of the men "chose the latter course."[83] The hasty evacuation of white Europeans resulted in greater chaos and a loss of livelihood for the Asian people who previously served them.

Asian people also faced greater risk during the invasion because destruction was a key feature of the British retreat. Williams noted that one Australian, MacVilly, put extensive effort into "'denying' [the Japanese] as much as he could, sinking barges, sabotaging machinery, blowing up railway, etc. They said he did a very good job of work."[84] Nona Baker, who hid in the jungle with her mine manager brother, recalled flooding the mine, forcing her brother to come "face to face with the disintegration of his life's work." She said nothing about the impact on his employees.[85] British policeman Haines also noted rubber "was burnt on the estates throughout the State and anything else that might have been useful to the enemy was destroyed."[86] These actions made sense strategically, but denying resources to the Japanese also meant destroying much-needed material for Asian civilians.

Even when British and Australian leaders built rather than destroyed, they reinforced their entitlement to Asian labor and material resources. Major I. A. McDonald worked on roads outside Kluang and employed rubber estate workers to build roads that would help Australians evacuate. When the work was completed, "all the coolies lined up for their reward" and "were amazed to hear the C.O. (a planter) announce that one dollar should be given to every three coolies." McDonald noted that a "dollar a head would have been more to the point." He found this "a complete lack of understanding and foresight" given that this was one of the last encounters they would have with the civilian population.[87] Meanwhile, basic sanitary services for Asian civilians stopped almost immediately. Eurasian doctor Sybil Kathigasu recalled that the sanitation in the town of Papan depended on "a handful of Indian coolies, supervised by a sanitary inspector." However, the disappearance of British leaders meant that these laborers received no pay, so "all work ceased."[88] The result was that roads and drains were filthy, no one collected excrement, and the reservoir almost ran dry. Even while desperate for aid and assistance to evacuate, British leaders underpaid those on whose labor they depended and destroyed or abandoned the resources necessary to survive another imperial occupation.

Despite these realities, Williams noted that several Asian people expressed care and concern about her. After several Asian doctors and dressers took their wives up-country or into the kampongs, the head dresser, Gomez, asked

Williams to stay in the kampong with his wife. She asked Gomez "if he realised that sheltering Europeans might get him into trouble, but he and several of the others tried to persuade me, and it was a tempting offer."[89] It is unclear, in her telling, if Gomez offered this because of Williams's perceived vulnerability as a woman and the gendered care that other women could provide, or the hopes of gaining favors from the British for helping a white woman, long considered the height of imperial vulnerability. Sometimes Williams embraced her perceived limitations to influence others. She insisted to her colleague Leslie Sheild that "as a man, he would be more use than I would be in the defence of Malaya, and that I, as a woman would probably receive better treatment from the Nip[pone]s[e] if I stayed behind to work at the Hospital."[90] Williams also made a point of being the one who "called the halts" while evacuating. She found "if one of the men had to call a halt he immediately became furiously irritable, but if I did then everybody was pleased."[91] Most of the men in the party were too proud to admit weakness, making Williams's presence an asset rather than a burden.

Despite her value to white evacuees, Williams remained dependent on Asian laborers during her evacuation. She stopped at a Chinese house for shelter, finding everyone "very friendly and sympathetic and could not do enough for us."[92] They also stayed at Jonka Batu, a kampong near the mine of "a Malay, Hadji, Ali (Ali Pilot)," who "cooked rice for us and curry." Still, Williams noted the difficulty of finding laborers to support her journey. While Holman lamented the lack of "Chinese coolies," Williams racialized her lack of support as a reflection of the "upcountry Malays" who "are a small, wiry, but often sick and unenterprising lot." This apparent lack of "enterprise" forced Williams and her party to carry their own packs. However, she did receive other aid. The same Malay police who British leaders did not trust to remain mobilized accompanied Williams and her party on their evacuation. Williams noted that "Che Yup Osman, and the other Malay policeman [*sic*]" were "ordered to come with us: it was extremely decent of them to obey. They had to leave their wives and families behind and they were accordingly grim with anxiety." These men "carried the food and the haversack of medical stores."[93] British leaders prioritized the evacuation of white people, disbanded the police, left Asian civilians to fend for themselves, and forced Malay policemen to aid Europeans in their flight. This left them "grim with anxiety" about the families they left behind. Their reward was to become laborers carrying heavy loads to facilitate European departures.

Sometimes, Williams praised those who aided her. In particular, she admired Ah Yong, an amah "of about fifty, small, neat, always sweet, hard-working and invariably cheerful."[94] Williams admired Ah Yong's ability to carry large quantities of goods on a pole "up rivers, through jungle, over mountains where I was crawling on all fours, she never flagged." Ah Yong even retained her femininity, with Williams admiring her "always trotting along with a little smile" and being "gentle and demure," with hair "always shining and neat." Most often, Williams emphasized Ah Yong's hard work, which included carrying Williams's possessions as well as her own. Ah Yong even guarded Williams while bathing, acting "as a sort of chaperone." When Williams returned from a bath, she often found Ah Yong "crouching over the fire with the carriers drying my scanties in sections." She even "snuggled up to me" when Williams shivered in the night.[95] Ah Yong, therefore, did much of the heavy labor of carrying Williams's belongings, washing her clothes, and keeping her warm and clean. They existed in a tenuous form of intimacy, which granted Ah Yong access to Williams's underwear and body. This hard work enabled her to evacuate with Europeans.

Despite Williams's enthusiasm for Ah Yong, their encounters remained structured around racial labor. When they stayed in a hospital, Williams enjoyed the luxury of a bath. On her return, she found her satin nightgown laid out for her because "Ah Yong had collected and transported them packed in my attache case" enabling her to "return to civilisation."[96] Ah Yong maintained her value by holding the line as a dutiful Asian laborer, preserving Williams's access to "civilization." While Williams noted that Ah Yong's gesture was "deeply touching," Williams still spent "ten minutes hard work next morning in persuading her to take money."[97] Insistently paying Ah Yong translated their encounter into an exchange of labor for wages, as opposed to a mutual economy of care. Money was a crucial resource for survival but also a way for Williams to effectively end her contract with Ah Yong. As a result, Ah Yong joined a party with her former employers, John and Norah Chambers.

Parting ways with Ah Yong, Williams arrived in Singapore still dependent on Asian women. While working in hospitals, she delighted in meeting "Mrs. Pereira, her sister and daughters, who also stuck to me and my tribe right through the whole show."[98] Williams also praised Bertha Wong, a nurse at St. Andrews in charge of the orthopedic children, who "never failed to come on duty and to do her work magnificently."[99] She even reconnected with Ah Yong after her previous employer, Norah Chambers, evacuated and left her behind without a job. As white women evacuated and British leadership collapsed, Asian women's labors proved essential—and life-saving.

Compared to Ah Yong, Dr. Williams loathed a woman named Ah Moy. Williams described her as "the attachee" [*sic*], rather than wife, of eleven years of Barnett Smith, a customs officer. She found Smith a "handsome burly fellow with a beard" and "a tiger for work." However, he became a "crawling worm in the presence of Ah Moy."[100] Ah Moy was a burden because of her impact on a white man's work ethic. Further, Williams found Ah Moy "plump and oppressive and eternally complaining." Williams had "no objection" to Ah Moy traveling with their party as long as "she would try and make the best of things." Unfortunately, Williams speculated that Smith had spoiled her so much that Ah Moy "had made no effort to be in the least useful." Ultimately, this cost Smith and Ah Moy their spot in the party. For Williams, it was Ah Moy's "everlasting complaints, greed and laziness," rather than Smith's indulgence, that cost them assistance while evacuating.[101] Smith and Ah Moy only rejoined the group when Ah Moy proved that she was "more used to the exigencies of life."[102] Ah Moy's treatment showed that Asian women faced concrete, potentially life-threatening consequences for failing to perform productive labor with and for white Europeans.

White men did not face such consequences even when they were a constant source of annoyance. Williams described one man, Rees, who was the superintending inspector of schools and an officer in the Local Defence Corps. When things got tense, "he appeared to have gone off and disbanded his men—entirely on his own initiative—and led the van of the escape with unseemly enthusiasm."[103] This "unseemly enthusiasm" no doubt irritated Williams, who wanted to stay behind to care for her patients. She also criticized a Mr. Bailey as "an eternal nuisance" for hoarding equipment and supplies. He made a point of getting "the first and last and biggest share of food." He also "had a horrid way of going about improperly dressed." She would often refuse him breakfast "till he puts his trousers on."[104] Any inherent respect that men like Mr. Bailey might have commanded in colonial Malaya prior to the war was now brushed away with his embarrassing behavior. Men who found Malaya and Singapore nice, relaxing stations with endless amenities and servants were not prepared to handle the rigors of war. This brought into sharp relief their inadequacy as the colony's former ruling elite. Yet none of them lost their place in the party, unlike Ah Moy.

Being surrounded by white Europeans so ready to abandon their posts amplified Williams's sense of humiliation. When she failed to convince Leslie Sheild to evacuate, Sheild's "boy Saleh" insisted that "'Kiita tuan ta'mou lari.' (Our tuan will not run away), [*sic*] which made me feel rather worse."[105] Embarrassment also influenced how they evacuated because they realized they would "look damn silly" if, "within a few days, the Jap[ane]s[e] were driven out." They made movement plans to avoid "looking foolish." They assuaged their guilt by pressing on to Singapore to help in "defending Malaya" and avoid becoming "captives in Japanese hands." Yet such decisions did not eliminate Williams's guilt. She reiterated that the "feeling of dereliction of duty was uppermost." They "were suffering from acute shock, we had lost most of our possessions and our self-respect. We had no idea of what we were running away from, or into." Her hopelessness led her to imagine affinity with colonized subjects. On reaching a bombed railway station, Williams found that "[t]housands of refugees from Kelantan, Trengganu and Pahang had already passed through the place. There was that curious atmosphere of tenseness, patience, fatalism and indifference which mean war. Chinese, Malays, Tamils, Europeans were all the same."[106] Even though Williams's ability to evacuate with a guard of Malay police underlined her unique position and ability to survive, the feeling of hopelessness and fear felt universal.

Reaching Singapore on December 20, 1941 deepened rather than alleviated Williams's powerlessness. Due to the rapid evacuation of Europeans, there were "too many doctors in Singapore—they were all coming down from upcountry." A Dr. MacGregor expressed his frustration to Williams that he "did not know what to do with them all." Williams asked to be sent to Calcutta, where a job waited for her, but instead she found work caring for "War Orphans," including unhoused and disabled children across various hospitals.[107] Despite her fears and anxieties about leaving her post and patients in Trengganu, Singapore brought ample opportunity to help those in need. This proved no easy task in early 1942 given labor shortages and disappearing leadership. Williams lamented that many of the women running hospitals were "determined to stay" but "in fact were not determined. The staff was constantly evaporating." As bombing and shelling intensified, much of the staff disappeared, and food became harder to secure for either patients or employees. She repeatedly lamented the lack of "proper domestic staff."[108]

Williams felt frustrated by the lack of personnel to aid Singapore in a time of crisis. At one point, she was the sole carer for thirty babies during intense shelling, leaving her to scoop babies by the armful and hide them under beds for protection.[109] By February 12, the amah in charge of sixty children left the hospital in the middle of the night screaming that she could not bear it. Some children had "screaming horrors during the shelling." It turned out that the amah was not neglecting her duty, as Williams assumed, for on February 13, she "brought all her family of thirteen people to live in a room about 10 ft. square, next door to the ward, and she gallantly remained on duty all night." The amah had "felt privileged that she had the sanctuary of the hospital." This was a privilege that many other civilians lacked, and gave Williams the power to decide who deserved protection. She admitted that "I threatened to turn out anyone of a size to work who did not do so," so she recruited the "gallant" amah's "old father and her children" to "wash the clothes, etc."[110] Labor in the service of Europeans remained a life-saving endeavor for Asian civilians.

Despite her hard work, Williams felt "a sinister augury for the future."[111] This was the result of seeing "a couple of young Australians whose consumption of beer was so prodigious, and whose protestations of the offensive spirit were so vapid" that she could not help but see defeat as inevitable. In Singapore, "[l]ooting was going on" and "the Japanese who had been interned" were now "at liberty," taking "affairs into their own hands." During the last week before surrender, Williams lamented that "everything became more and more harassing and disintegrated" as the city filled with "evacuating and deserting soldiers, most of them Australians looking utterly disorganised and defeated." Many soldiers threw off their equipment, looted shops, and pushed "women and children out of the way to get behind the bunding when bombs were falling near by [*sic*]." Some even shoved "women and children off the boats that were getting away . . . It was a terrible show."[112] Those soldiers so accustomed to being treated like kings in Singapore failed to perform paternalism and self-control in the empire's final moments.

While "literally dozens of the Europeans" sat around and "did nothing," Williams found that "the Asiatic nurses worked very hard." Still, she criticized the "Mental Hospital amahs" who "stole everything they could and did very little work."[113] Even as she celebrated the tireless and self-sacrificing labors of Asian nurses, she condemned Asian women for not working hard enough—"stealing" and doing "very little work" despite the trauma and privation caused by the British retreat. After the surrender, Williams's journey to internment was delayed by a bout of dysentery, which sent her back to the hospital.[114] Here, she once again depended on the labor of Asian women: "The Asiatic nurses were doing their best, but they were suffering severely from the scatters."[115] On her previous departure, Williams gave "most of my remaining possessions to the nurses and to Ah Yong, whom I asked them to keep on at the hospital as an amah."[116] When Williams returned to the hospital, "Ah Yong returned to me like a homing pigeon, and insisted on my taking back sheets, clothes and oddments which proved invaluable." Williams showed her gratitude by getting Ah Yong another job serving as "domestic help" for a Bishop.[117] This freed Ah Yong from the exhausting labor of being the hospital's only amah and also secured her passage back to her family in Ipoh. Dedicated and exemplary service to white people became Ah Yong's key to survive and rejoin her family—things previously granted to white Europeans by default.

In emphasizing how valuable Asian labor was for her own comfort and survival, Williams also indicated the moral ambiguity and dangers of performing medical labor during the occupation. Many of the women, including Ah Yong, who cared for her while she was sick could have faced punishment for doing so. Williams got a sense of this when, in July 1942, she got to leave Changi prison and return to the hospital for a "pleasant interlude," in her words, of having a hysterectomy.[118] She enjoyed being able "to see again many of my old friends among the nurses and doctors" who were kind and provided her with food and fruit. However, one person, Lim Po Lan, had already faced pressure from the Military Police and "never dared to come and see me." Nonetheless, Lim Po Lan sent Williams a daily present.[119] Continuing to support, feed, and care for white bodies was a personal risk for Asian personnel, but something that Williams regarded as unambiguous "friendship."

Throughout the invasion and evacuation, the lack of leadership, planning, and accountability among Europeans was ever-present. Only a few, Williams lamented, "continued to do their jobs." In the last days before the surrender, Williams, hospital staff, and patients relocated to the Outram Road Prison, where they had the protection of thick walls but a severe lack of sanitary arrangements and water. As deaths increased, bodies piled up. In the prison, Williams noted that there were "nurses, orderlies, coolies, all their relatives, and a pretty heavy sprinkling of deserting soldiers, British, Australian and Indian, all taking shelter, doing no work, grabbing the food, trampling on the helpless."[120] Williams remained steadfast and determined not only to survive but to continue her duty as a doctor—no doubt assuaging her continued anxieties about abandoning her post. Again and again, she encountered the colony's former leaders crumbling in the face of difficulty and behaving cruelly. Defeat felt earned.

SURRENDER

When Mehervan Singh heard of the British capitulation on February 15, 1942, twenty-seven years to the day after the Singapore Mutiny, he and many Indians believed that "the British had let us down."[121] Holman recalled greeting an Indian soldier, who was viscerally overwhelmed by the horror of surrender: "I could see from the agonised expression in his eyes that he was struggling to put his feelings into English words . . . he just stood there in front of me with tears pouring down his brown cheeks."[122] Eurasian teenager Sheila Allan similarly witnessed a soldier sit down and "unashamedly buried his face in his hands and wept as if his heart would break."[123] Dolores Ho recalled that her family, who migrated to Malaya from China to flee the war against Japan, felt "abandoned" by the British.[124] Jack Turner remembered the eerie sound of silence after so long under constant bombardment.[125] When Dr. Williams heard news of the armistice, her response was "'Why?' 'Who has given in?'" The reply she received was "We have."[126] The surrender shook the confidence of British colonial leaders and subjects alike. At the same time, it had immediate and traumatic consequences for populations left to fend for themselves because of the chaos of the British evacuation.

The large presence of military personnel and materials that once made F. Spencer Chapman optimistic revealed itself to be "an illusion."[127] Poor planning for war resulted in a shortage of ships, tanks, planes, anti-tank guns, and anti-plane guns. Despite Singapore's reputation as an "impregnable fortress," it floundered just one week after Japanese forces crossed onto the island. After the surrender, military officers could not help but feel, in the words of Major I. A. McDonald, that "Malaya was sacrificed—had to be sacrificed because arms, planes and our Navy were required elsewhere."[128] For Chapman, the worst blunder was that there were "not enough men."[129] For McDonald, by contrast, it was "a crime to allow all those Divisions to get caught in Singapore."[130] While the former saw insufficient men to combat the invasion, the latter felt it was an unnecessary for soldiers to be "sacrificed." Both men failed to grasp that British leaders expected civilians and military personnel to bear the burden of military failure. In fact, civil and military suffering in Singapore was inherent in Winston Churchill's plan to win the war. Rather than surrender, he encouraged military personnel to avoid any "thought of saving the troops or sparing the population" because the "battle must be fought to the bitter end at all costs."[131] Saving Britain meant sacrificing Singapore.

As traumatic as the surrender was for British leaders and soldiers, the most immediate consequences were for the civilian population. It was not, as Williams speculated, white Europeans who were most vulnerable to attack following the Japanese triumph. Rather, Chinese civilians bore the brunt of violence from Singapore and Malaya's new colonial overlords. Japanese military personnel killed at least 30,000 Chinese civilians by March 1942, assuming that they might be, or were working with, communists or other political resisters.[132] In Chinese, the period has been referred to as *Sook Ching*, which means "purge through cleansing." The Japanese called it *Dai Kensho*, or "great inspection."[133] The Japanese had waged continuous war in China since 1931, and the prevalence of guerilla warfare in the Sino-Japanese War (1937) made it difficult to tell the difference between a civilian and a combatant, increasing military violence against soldiers and civilians alike.[134] The result was mass death and trauma.

According to Japanese leaders, the *Sook Ching* was a consequence of misunderstanding rather than an intensification of racial-military praxis in development since Japan's ascent as a colonial power. General Yamashita Tomoyuki claimed after the war that he ordered his four area commanders that the "Chinese population were to be mustered in Concentration areas" where they were to be screened, and that undesirable elements including "those with anti-Jap[anese] sentiments, ex-Government employees etc; were to be taken away and killed."[135] This action was intended to be completed by February 23, 1942. Colonel Oishi Masayuki apparently gathered men of the 25th Army at Fort Canning "to carry out large scale round-ups and to collect the Chinese at certain areas." He told his men that "the Army HQ were very much in favour of killing all undesirables" so that "Japanese occupational force" would not be "endangered." The emphasis was on "purging recalcitrant elements, anti-Jap[anese] and Communist elements since they affect peace and order largely."[136] General Yamashita also ordered the Kempeitai, or military police, to maintain "order in the city" by killing "bad characters, such as robbers and those in possession of weapons." When he learned that "many hundreds, even thousands, of innocent civilians had been among those killed, and that the 'crime' of most of them was solely that they were young and Chinese," he insisted that this treatment should have been directed to "only the robbers and those with arms.'"[137] During the postwar trials, an interrogator assisted Yamashita's testimony by suggesting that the Kempeitai should be held responsible, rather than Yamashita, because the latter was "too senior an officer to be troubled with such trifling matters."[138] To both Japanese leaders and the British courts prosecuting them, the murder of thousands of Chinese people was a "trifling matter" caused by miscommunication.

Chinese civilians found the experience neither accidental nor trifling. Singapore resident Lim Chuan Kim recalled the difficulty of a brief but rigorous internment, which included seeing those "who were not released (my tortured friend was among them)" being "taken in lorries for unknown destinations and, we strongly believe, massacred" because "none of them has ever been heard of again." He learned from friends and mutual acquaintances that many Chinese people were bound together on beaches and machine-gunned. One man told Mr. Lim that he escaped by diving into the water.[139] Equally frightening, businessman Ong Foot Yeong saw seven lorries carrying "children, old and young males and females" followed by the sounds of gunshots.[140] Chinese farmer Mr. Neo Kuay Leh lived on Changi Road and also saw "seven trucks pass our house and they carried men, women and children, all Chinese."[141] He found it especially noteworthy that some of the captured women "had their hair permanent waved; and from their manner dress [*sic*] these people belonged to the better class of Chinese." This put them in the same group of people, described by Holman as "higher classes," who enjoyed Singapore's pre-invasion luxuries. Mr. Neo also saw the local schoolmaster on board the lorries but felt powerless to help him. Japanese forces buried these civilians in shallow graves that were made of former British trenches to defend the island. Mr. Neo could both see and smell the graves from his home. Local villagers petitioned Japanese leaders for permission to add another layer to the mounds themselves, burying the bodies of their former friends and neighbors.[142]

Another Chinese Singaporean civilian, Lim Bee Giok, recalled the terror of her husband being detained for three days—when thousands of Chinese civilians never returned. Her own brother-in-law was a volunteer and "called up by the [Japanese] few days after the Fall of Singapore."[143] By October 1945, she still had no news about his whereabouts. Elizabeth Choy had a similar experience and vividly remembered the pain of being separated from men for days or weeks and worrying about her younger brother, who failed to come home.[144] Due to her father's anguish, she went looking for news of her brother and soon found "wives, sisters, mothers looking for their lost ones too." She never learned what happened to her brother, though she speculated that he was among those taken in a lorry near the sea, shot, and buried. She also lost an uncle, who had been a wireless operator, to the occupation when Japanese forces killed him, and never heard about a cousin, who was taken by the Japanese.[145] Lim Chuan Kim remembered hearing that "one Japanese Officer was understood to have stated that at first they had orders to kill every Chinese man, woman and child that they should come across in Singapore." As a result, they "massacred a number of families in one of the villages."[146] He reasoned that Japanese troops in the early days of the occupation "were then in a ferocious mood and bloodthirsty" because of the difficult campaign down the peninsula.[147]

Especially troubling was that those who served the British were among the most vulnerable. Japanese forces targeted members of the Straits Settlements Volunteer Force (SSVF), which aided the British in suppressing the 1915 rebellion. In the initial days of the surrender, Japanese leaders told members of the SSVF that they would be pardoned if they came forward.[148] Wong Sin Joon had a very different experience. He recalled being "packed like Sardines" along with "quite a few thousands" of people.[149] Eventually, Japanese troops separated the men of the SSVF and sent them to Drill Hall. On arriving, they met a lorry full of Japanese soldiers who were "armed with Bren guns, and told us to stand up in two rows of 35 each, then simply tied our hands behind our backs and told us to go out to the empty truck." Initially the men assumed that they would go to Changi jail, but on approaching, "to our surprise they kept on moving, then we knew of our fate, that we are going to be shot." They arrived at their destination and men were "told to go down to the beach. (Just like a flock of sheep going to the slaughter). [*sic*] We could hardly move when we saw the firing squad. Some of us cried, some calling for their parents." The green water immediately turned red. After getting shot, almost drowning, pretending to be dead, and using the bodies of his friends for support, Wong Sin Joon eventually found two other men who survived, and they escaped together.[150]

Fearing death, many colonial subjects pointed fingers at one another. Mr. Lim complained about his neighborhood being ransacked not only by Japanese troops but "by the Malays who had a grand time of it." As a former British government employee, he blamed the Malay population, rather than British leaders or Japanese troops, for the invasion and surrender. He explained, "It is believed that it was partly through the treachery of some of the Malays, who led the Jap[ane]s[e] through the jungle behind the British lines of defence, that we were so easily conquered."[151] Chin Kee Onn came to a similar conclusion in *Malaya Upside Down*, published shortly after the war. He maintained that every single Japanese person in Malaya, from "photographer, fisherman, planter, farmer, taxidermist, trader, barber, and dentist abroad" was a likely spy for the Japanese.[152] Through their recruiting efforts, he believed that "Javanese, Sumatrans, and other Indonesians" worked to recruit "kampong-Malays and the Sakais [Indigenous Orang Asli] of the jungle" before moving on to the cities. Before long, they had "Indonesians, Malays, Indians, Formosans, Chinese, and Thais" spread throughout Malaya offering information to the Japanese.[153] He characterized the "cosmopolitanism of Malaya" as a key reason for the Japanese success, because of the absence of a "national consciousness." This made it easy for Japanese leaders to take "advantage of the outward resemblances of the Asiatic races in Malaya," which enabled Japanese soldiers to disguise themselves as "Chinese or Malay farmers or fishermen."[154] Here, Chin translated Malaya's diversity from a wonderland of inclusivity to a hotbed of diverse enemy agents. F. Spencer Chapman had a different view. He noted that early after the surrender "there was no question of the Chinese or Malays collaborating, but both were obviously frightened to death and it was clear that the Jap[ane]s[e] were completely ruthless and would have had no compunction in cutting off their heads."[155]

While Chapman recognized that fear was universal, many white soldiers blamed colonial subjects for the invasion. Writing after the war, Turner recounted a story of a dancing cabaret for the soldiers" in Malacca that was managed by "what we believed was a Chinaman." This man "was very good to the boys, filling them up with beer and whisky and then casually enquiring of their movements and doings and finding out the mens' individual units." After the capitulation, however, they found "this so-called Chinaman turned up at our POW camp in the uniform of the Japanese Army and wearing the rank of a Japanese Major." For Turner, this revealed the duplicity of the Japanese and the complicity of other Asian civilians. He insisted that "the native population of Malaya and Singapore had listened to much propaganda by the Jap[ane]s[e] and really believed they would have a wonderful time if the Jap[ane]s[e] could root the British out of these countries." In turn, he believed that many Asian subjects "gave every assis- tance to the Jap[ane]s[e] in leading them through the jungle" while "hampering the British."[156] He did not consider that the lived reality of colonial rule made Asian subjects crave an alternative. He also failed to acknowledge how white soldiers' inability to distinguish between Japanese soldiers and Asian civilians put the latter at greater risk. Governor Shenton Thomas even learned from a war correspondent that "in the nick of time he had prevented a British soldier" from "shooting a Gurkha." The war correspondent "stressed how difficult it was for our men unused to the jungle and to Asiatics, to distinguish between one Asiatic and another; and of course it was. The Japanese would disguise themselves as Malays or even as Indian soldiers."[157] In other words, the same racism and uncertainty about identities that made it difficult to distinguish mutineers from loyal sol- diers in 1915 continued in 1942, as British military personnel failed to differentiate Asian friends and foes.

Before 1942, many white soldiers believed that Asian civilians possessed un- wavering "loyalty" that made them ready and willing to provide endless labor. These same soldiers mobilized their bitterness and hostility about the British surrender to blame those they expected to serve them at all costs, while also putting them in greater danger. Yet the invasion and occupation inverted pre- occupation patterns of racialized labor. After being detained for hours in the sun with other Chinese men and boys, Lim Chuan Kim recalled a Japanese officer instructing them to clean the town and bury the dead, undermining their class position as former British employees.[158] Similarly, British imperial soldiers who became POWs tended to the massacred. Australian soldier Turner recalled that "[a] gruesome job" was to "bury hundreds of unfortunate Chinese families in the sand at Changi beach." Interned soldiers had to dig holes containing as many as one hundred people per hole. He regarded these deaths as a result of "an ingrained hatred," reiterating the belief that Asian violence was perennial and thus unpreventable.[159] Japanese leaders quickly racialized Singapore's pop- ulation, marking Chinese people as either useful laborers or dangerous dissi- dents who needed to be destroyed. Britain's former foot soldiers and ruling elite became the laborers serving another imperial power to clean up the mess of mass death.

FORGOTTEN TIES

Reflecting on life in Singapore and Malaya before the war, American missionary Preston Peach claimed that "the Christian religion" brought together "all the races."[160] However, he, like many other white civilians, employed a large fleet of Asian laborers who would suffer disproportionately during the invasion. While living at Kuala Lumpur, Penang, and Ipoh, Peach employed a Malayan ayah (nursemaid) whom his children "loved . . . very much." A Tamil employee— Mutto—worked with them for fifteen years and "became a real part of our family—cook and house boy." A "Chinese boy," Teng Boon, "remained faithful to us in our home as a house boy." Yet Peach and his family left all of these "familial" servants behind to face an invading army. Despite being "a real part of our family," Mutto stayed on a rubber estate to live with Tamil workers. "Faithful" Teng Boon remained to work as house boy for a missionary. They "never did know what happened to Teng Boon."[161] Their "most faithful servant and companion," a Eurasian woman named Rachel, stayed at their mission home. She apparently remained there when the Japanese made it a torture chamber for European prisoners. In the face of war, promises of inclusivity and familial belonging withered. Whether "faithful" servants were Eurasian, Malay, Chinese, or Indian, they all faced abandonment by white leaders and civilians. This cognitive dissonance is perhaps best explained by Singapore internee A. E. Fawcett, who felt "shame and humiliation, shame at having left ones [*sic*] staff behind" but also "[h]umiliation at having been defeated, nay routed, by the little beasts we loathed."[162] These perceptions of Asian people—as either helpless victims that needed British protection or beasts seizing power—enabled white people to justify their actions.

Over the two months of the Japanese invasion, white soldiers and civilians constantly demanded the continued labors and loyalties of Asian civilians to facilitate their own evacuations and escapes. Many refused to do so. Those who did often faced the brunt of Japanese invasion without protection or support. When Japanese forces instituted their own racialized labor regime, many of those who served the British, whether willingly, reluctantly, or by force, now had to contend with Japanese perceptions of the value of their life and labor. British leaders convinced themselves that their own presence was a detriment to Asian civilians and that the best thing they could do was evacuate quickly. However, it was Asian civilians—and the Chinese community in particular—who endured the most severe hardships from the surrender. The "high classes" of Chinese people who navigated upward mobility in a colonial space to share the privileges and luxuries of British colonizers faced even more violence during the Japanese surrender. The Asian police and military servicemen who helped interwar British leaders root out internal "enemies" became primary targets of the Japanese. The "Chinese boys" so frequently laboring in the service of British soldiers and civilians had to put the city back together after Japanese and British imperial forces destroyed it. Malay, Indian, Eurasian, and other racialized colonial subjects made quick decisions about where they belonged and how they could survive. The people who loved and labored in Singapore prior to and following its capitulation lived with the tenuous uncertainty of racial hierarchy and colonial violence across military regimes.

The trauma and dislocation of the invasion led to reversals in racialized patterns of server/served or colonizer/colonized. Japanese leaders stepped into the places formerly occupied by British ruling and military elite. Civilians looked to their neighbors and former friends—within and beyond their ethnic, religious, or linguistic communities—as fifth column or collaborators, laying the foundations for long-term hostilities. Many others could not stop worrying about the friends and family fighting on various battlefields, imprisoned, interned, or missing— and blamed who they could for their absence. The war not only fundamentally altered the laboring conditions of the colony, but also the means of securing safety, security, and comfort. In its absence, many turned on one another, without any other means of feeling whole. Some sought to redefine and recultivate intimacy to survive, rising from the ashes of an uncaring colonial-military state that left them to burn.

FOUR

Labored Intimacies

Following the British surrender in Singapore in 1942, at least 130,000 European civilians and 200,000 allied prisoners of war (POWs) faced internment by the Japanese military until 1945. In this, Japanese leaders followed British and other European military officials, who used internment and concentration camps to control supposedly criminal, diseased, or enemy populations within and beyond colonial spaces since the nineteenth century.[1] Yet the Second World War camps in Southeast Asia gained a notorious reputation. Popular portrayals emphasized inherent Japanese cruelty as the reason for widespread suffering.[2] However, as many scholars have argued, Japanese forces had followed international protocols and even gained praise for their humane treatment of POWs in previous conflicts.[3] By the Second World War, the traumas of the Sino-Japanese war, and the chaos and logistical burden of creating and maintaining massive camps, quickly forced Japanese authorities to secure food, water, and housing while carrying out military operations around the world. In response, individual Japanese leaders ignored directives and resorted to harsh treatment.[4] This worsened as resources spread thin and the tide turned in the Pacific, enabling allied forces to cut off Japanese supply lines. By 1943 and 1944, internment conditions worsened as provisions dwindled for British and Japanese personnel alike. In the midst of this widespread suffering, individual people had to make hard choices about how to survive and rebuild for a life after war.

This chapter examines internment from the perspective of those caught between British and Japanese colonial ideologies of race and gender. This includes people like seventeen-year-old Sheila Allan, who developed a fond attachment to Dr. Elinor Hopkins, the Liaison officer and Camp Commandant, while interned at the Changi women's prison in Singapore.[5] Allan admitted to her diary in May 1942 that she kept "thinking I wish she is my mother—how I'd like my mother to be—my Dream Mother."[6] Romanticizing a white British "Dream Mother" while living under Japanese occupation challenged Singapore's newest imperial occupiers. At the same time, Allan was a racialized woman with a white Australian father, an estranged Malay birth mother, and a Siamese (Thai) stepmother. She worked hard to impress Hopkins and other internees to prove that she was truly "British." Yet many white women resented the fact that Asian and Eurasian women outnumbered white women internees. As camp commandant and a leading doctor, Hopkins's willingness to become a "mother" to Allan influenced Allan's ability survive in a camp ruled by the Japanese but run by white internees. The division of camp labor reflected the wider expectation that Asian and Eurasian women perform labor for current and past colonial overlords. Many white women saw Allan's hard work as taking her rightful place as a "coolie." Working hard to earn Hopkins's esteem offered Allan a path for survival in a colonial world built on racial labor.[7]

Despite the many differences between camps, Changi gained a notorious reputation due to the number of high-ranking British and European officials held there and the torture of military POWs at Changi Barracks. Many soldiers went on to endure further trauma building the notoriously brutal Thai-Burma Railway. However, some POWs called Changi "POW Heaven" or a "Phoney Captivity" compared to the hardships they faced elsewhere.[8] Meanwhile, Asian and Eurasian civilians living outside of camps endured constant fear and uncertainty.[9] Compared to wartime alternatives, therefore, Changi Gaol was a best-case-scenario for Allan. Being an interned civilian meant a higher likelihood of survival.[10] It still exposed her to forced labor, food shortages, poor sanitation, and a lack of privacy while negotiating powerlessness and trauma. A key to survival was finding where to belong, yet acceptance was a scarce and fragile resource. Many felt they had to labor to live.

Tracking how people in Singapore and Malaya navigated labor and intimacy within and outside of internment camps shows both the fragility and perseverance of British hierarchies. Japanese rule struck down the patriarchal family units that served the raced, classed, and gendered needs of the British colonial state through gender-segregated camps, coercive labor regimes, death, and displacement. At the same time, the perseverance of British civilians' expectations and demands for Asian labor during the evacuation and invasion continued during the occupation. This chafed against Japanese colonial and military leaders' attempts to impose their own gender and ethnic hierarchies.[11] For captives, personal identity became inseparable from the traumas of racial and gender segregation, shifting and divergent British and Japanese colonial hierarchies, and the lived reality of trauma, privation, and loss. While ample scholarly and public attention has been paid to the traumatic conditions of Japanese POW and civilian internment camps across Southeast Asia, few have considered how the idea and articulation of intimacy, and its relationship with colonial labor regimes, changed under these conditions.[12]

A LIFE OF LABOR

As a young girl, Sheila Allan often wondered about her place in the world. Born in Taiping and raised in Ipoh and Penang, she had only faint memories of her estranged Malay birth mother. She spent most of her time in convents while her Australian father, John Charles Allan, worked as a dredge master in Siam (Thailand). In 1941, he hoped to send her to Australia to continue her education. However, while vacationing together in the Cameron Highlands with Allan's new Siamese (Thai) stepmother, Vichim, they received news of the Japanese invasion. Allan immediately expressed her delight: "There was a time I had envied other girls in the services and wished I was one of them." The war now gave her "my chance to do my duty. Suddenly I felt brave and excited at the prospect of having to fight."[13] All Allan knew of war was what she read behind the cloistered walls of convents that praised service ideals among women. It also fulfilled her Australian father's sense that hard work was a key to inclusion. He often told her, "Hard work never killed you but doing nothing will."[14] War, therefore, felt like an exciting adventure—an opportunity to do her bit and prove her worth through hard work. However, as she made her way to Singapore to evade Japanese troops, she realized that hard work would not always protect her.

Initially, Allan and her family benefited from her father's class position and access to whiteness. When they arrived at Allan's mine, they found it "deserted but for servants looking after bosses' house." Ah Juan, "our Chinese boy," apparently remained eager to cater to their needs, fixing them a good meal.[15] As the journey continued, though, Allan's father's struggled to retain his privileged access to Asian labor. During their journey, they encountered raiders, missed a train, and traveled via a packed "refugee train" from Penang, sleeping in a waiting room. When they arrived at Petaling, their Indian driver called out for "Tuan [Boss] Allan." Allan's father stepped forward but the driver "shook his head as if he didn't believe Dad." Allan suspected that it was because they were covered with soot and had two filthy dogs. By failing to perform the bodily cleanliness of their class position, Allan's father nearly lost the labor of Asian people to which he previously felt entitled.[16]

Throughout their journey, Allan also navigated feelings of familiarity and foreignness, particularly in her encounters with soldiers. Allan observed soldiers with "wonderment of teenage hero-worship." She was fascinated by these "men from another planet." Convent life ensured that, apart from her father, "I knew little of man and his ways so I guess I wouldn't know what to say if one of them had spoken to me."[17] Some soldiers made her feel cheerful by flashing victory signs and maintaining positive attitudes. Others made her uncomfortable. While staying at a "Chinese hotel," Allan heard marching and "[r]ushed to the window, looked out onto the narrow street. What I saw made me feel cold." What she found was not the arrival of Japanese troops, but rather "the Punjabs, [*sic*] guns and vicious looking knives, were marching four abreast." She felt that "[t]heir faces were hard and grim. The civilians scuttled indoors."[18] One civilian urged Allan and her family to leave because this "army of Punjabs" was there to fight against a likely Japanese landing. Even though Indian soldiers were in Malaya to protect and defend civilians like Allan and her family, they made her feel uneasy.

Allan's testimony suggests that, at least initially, she regarded Asian soldiers as dangerous and white soldiers as cheerful protectors. This was reinforced by a gunner in the Australian Imperial Force offering to tow them to Tampin when their car broke down. By contrast, Allan was dismayed by "an Indian" who "came towards us with a nasty gleam in his eyes which were blood-shot." The Australian gunner told him "to push off but he refused," so the Australian threatened him with his bayonet and rifle. Allan's "heart stood still and silently I prayed that there was not going to be a fight." The Indian man turned away "muttering to himself." The Australian soldier followed and fired a shot in the air, so "[t]he man took fright and ran down the street as if the very devil was after him."[19] After this experience, a police officer blamed Allan's father for not evacuating Sheila and Vichim, noting their gendered vulnerability. However, this encounter earned them additional protection. The police officer accompanied them to Singapore, where they arrived mid-January 1942. This gave them official aid not often provided to Asian women without attachments to white people. As a result, Allan continued to associate whiteness with safety. By contrast, she perceived Asian identity with unease and uncertainty.

Arriving in Singapore challenged Allan's racial assumptions. Her family stayed at the Rex Hotel under relentless bombing, including one that fell through their roof. Rather than feeling excited to serve and fight, Allan now felt "stripped of my sensitive covering—I feel naked—I have no place to hide my tearful face, my knowledge of the evil that has erupted in this world that I am born into." She saw dead bodies all over the city, including many mangled by bombing. Providing comfort, rather than fear, were Chinese men who gave her coffee and were everywhere "helping the people, dead and alive."[20] By contrast, white men proved threatening. She described one planter, Mr. M., who made her feel "uncomfortable" because of his habit of brushing up against her. She indicated, "For some reason I feel nervous with him about—It's a feeling I'm not sure I like having." His efforts became so intrusive that he tried to kiss her and grab her during a bombing, causing her to hit her head. Even gentler men had their own motives. One young man, Leslie, hastily proposed marriage to Allan, suggesting that "if I married him, the Jap[ane]s[e] wouldn't assault me." She scoffed at the thought of "[a]nother one trying to protect me!"[21] Both Leslie and Mr. M. used the fear of invasion to force Sheila's compliance. The prewar world made white men feel entitled to Asian and Eurasian women's bodies and left Allan vulnerable. This deepened the emotional trauma of the invasion by forcing her to navigate the threat of sexual violence from someone on the same "side." Several encounters with men—soldiers and civilians—heightened her sense of danger before ever seeing a Japanese soldier.

These experiences made Allan even more fearful when she first saw Japanese forces marching into the city on the day of surrender. She worried about "the women population—are we going to be safe from them?"[22] Yet it was racialization as an Asian woman that exposed her vulnerability. En route to the Central Police Station to register for internment, she witnessed Japanese soldiers "beating Chinese women and men."[23] When trying to cross a bridge to their hotel, a Japanese sentry allowed Allan's white father to pass but "roughly pushed" her back, putting a bayonet prick in her back and pushing her along. Allan recalled that "I had an Asian face" so "the Japanese thought I was Chinese."[24] It took the intervention of an Indian interpreter for her to escape—turning Indian men she once feared into allies and protectors. Meanwhile, she witnessed the bombed city, nearly depleted water supply, and absence of toilet facilities leaving many Europeans "drowning their sorrows."[25] Among them was her tormenter, Mr. M., who spent all morning crying and drinking.

Allan's experience fleeing the Japanese invasion forced her to make a hasty transition from a cloistered world of religious women into a world of martial men at their worst. She found that men—soldiers and civilians, Asian and European—expected to consume and enjoy women like her, increasing her vulnerability. She joined many other Asian and Eurasian civilians in learning how to survive a colonial world designed to use and discard her. At the same time, Allan's connection to her white father gave her initial protection and the opportunity for internment. Most Asian women had to fight to survive without such protections as soon as the invasion began.

FORGING COMFORT

Sheila Allan's quick initiation into a world of sexual danger reflected Asian women's precarious position during the Japanese occupation. Despite her difficult experiences, Allan felt "thankful for having been in Changi prison" because "I doubt whether I would have survived if I had lived out."[26] She felt safe because of the "women running the camp," which included Dr. Hopkins, who "were so protective of us." This prevented "shocking brutality and rapes" common at other camps.[27] A. E. Fawcett, interned at Changi, was relieved that "the Nip[pone]s[e] never molested our women" but acknowledged that "the Chinese an [*sic*] Eurasian women were not so lucky."[28] Sexual violence, and the coercion of forced sexual laborers euphemistically referred to as "comfort women," was a horrifically common feature of the occupation period.[29] As a result, Japanese leaders, Asian civilians, and European internees had very different ideas of what "comfort" meant. While Allan found protection in Changi, many civilians struggled to navigate traumas that would outlive the conflict.

The pervasive threat of sexual violence during the Japanese occupation stemmed from British and Japanese imperial and military cultures.[30] Takashi Fujitani has argued that Japanese military leaders promoted ethnic inclusivity among military men through a shared belief that women had to serve military needs through forced conscription as sexual laborers.[31] The commodification of sex under British rule also aided Japanese leaders' access to forced sexual encounters. Many cabarets that previously delighted British imperial servicemen were, according to Singapore resident Lim Chuan Kim, "ordered to be closed down and the proprietors were asked to open up brothels instead."[32] Others admitted that places like New World Amusement Park employed women for sex work prior to the Japanese occupation. Many Cantonese "sing-song" women also faced sex trafficking during British rule to entertain wealthy Chinese businessmen. One of these women was Ho Kwai Min, who worked in the "Blue Triangle" of Chinatown starting in 1940. During the occupation, Chinese collaborators forced her and other women to work for the Japanese.[33] Sometimes civilian women took it upon themselves to recruit former sexual laborers. Madam Seow Guat Beng recalled the frequency of rape near her home in Penang and threats of sexual violence by a Japanese officer. As a result, she went to Ayer Hitam, where many women formerly employed in sex work resided. She begged them "please come back and work and do your profession," offering them a home, protection, and food to encourage their return.[34] Even women outside of sexualized professions faced pressures to work in cafés and offices where they faced constant sexual coercion.[35] The Japanese wartime demand for sex echoed British soldiers' entitlement to prewar pleasure, intensifying the multiple threats faced by civilian women.

The reality of sexual violence often made spaces of previous safety and comfort into sites of trauma. Singapore resident Lim Chuan Kim noted, "The Jap[ane]s[e] began by entering our houses on the first day." Whenever this happened, "[o]ur womenfolk would hide under the beds" because "raping was going on everywhere, and in some districts you could hear women screaming throughout the night."[36] Facing these pressures, many Asian and Eurasian women, or families with daughters, fled to the margins of Malayan towns to hide young women in the rubber estates or fields.[37] Feng Su Qiong recalled hiding in mountain caves with her mother.[38] Guan Ying hid with communist guerillas fighting the invasion and occupation, leading many to regard communists as "heroes and protectors of the people."[39] Others took measures into their own hands. Eurasian nurse Sybil Kathigasu disguised her twenty-year-old daughter Olga with a "close crop" haircut, trousers, a torn shirt, and a smeared face. If Japanese soldiers came to their neighborhood, Olga started "sweeping out the drains." Kathigasu maintained that "he" was her younger brother who was "deaf, dumb and an idiot."[40] Wong Wai Kwan used another strategy: urging her eighteen-year-old sister-in-law to marry "a boy whom she knew very little about" in the hopes of keeping her safe.[41] For some, marriage and family offered protection. For many others, it was impossible to escape the fear and uncertainty of an invading army. They sought whatever means possible to protect themselves and those they loved.

Pre-occupation intimacies sometimes offered protection. Indian Christian Rasammah Bhupalan recalled feeling vulnerable because her family consisted of her mother, Nancy, her sister, and herself—three women alone. Because of this, they moved in with a lawyer, Mr. Chin Sween Oon, and Margaret Chin, her mother's former student. Since Mr. Chin worked for the Japanese Peace and Goodwill Committee, the entire household gained a letter protecting them from assault by military forces.[42] Despite their personal security, they could not escape the sounds of women screaming at night. They also benefited from protections from the Secretary and Interpreter for the Japanese Governor because Nancy was her son's teacher before the war and stood up for him when he faced bullying for being Japanese.[43] This helped shelter them from the everyday uncertainty of violence. Yet friendship and protection proved fragile. As Sybil Kathigasu recalled, "Under the Japanese, the informer was everywhere, and everywhere was hated and feared." Anyone from telephone operators, maids, rickshaw pullers, and waiters could be commissioned to report to the Japanese, leaving Kathigasu to remark that "one never felt safe." She lamented that friends "had betrayed friends, sons and daughters had betrayed parents." As a result, she "learnt to trust nobody."[44] Protection and betrayal defied simplistic categorizations of loyalty and disloyalty and rarely followed clear ethnic, class, or familial lines. Anyone could be a friend or an enemy.

These uncertain paths to protection complicated allegations of collaboration. Mrs. Tan Choo Quee recalled Japanese soldiers demanding food and shelter in her uncle's plantation in Paya Lebar District on February 14, 1942, the day before the surrender.[45] Mrs. Tan explained that the Japanese captain warned her uncle "to keep all his young daughters in a safe locked-up-place, as he and his soldiers were going to sleep in his hall and balcony." The young girls hid in an air-raid shelter and "only came out for baths, etc under the watchful eyes of the family men-folks when the soldiers had gone out roaming in the daytime." For his troubles, her uncle received a "Protection Letter." In turn, several neighbors asked her uncle "to safeguard their teenaged daughters in his air-raid shelter." Aiding the "enemy," therefore, became an asset for a community lacking other protections. However, it did not always work. One day, an armed soldier came "looking for young girls" and ignored the protection letter. The unmarried women in the house "quickly hid under the bed in the back ground floor room" and managed to evade being touched when he put his gun under the bed to find them.[46] In these tense moments, people made quick decisions for themselves, their families, and their communities, enduring trauma and violence no matter what path they took.

The emphasis on "protection letters" hints at how some civilians saw tenuous alliances with Japanese soldiers as the only way to escape violence. Dolores Ho's family, for instance, fled China in a small boat to escape the Japanese military. They traveled from Hong Kong to Singapore and Penang only to find that the Japanese had already invaded Malaya. After the surrender, they hid in a banana plantation to avoid anti-Chinese violence. They later found a "home" in a chicken coop. However, it was a Japanese soldier, rather than other civilians, who bicycled by and threw rice over their fence so that they would not starve.[47] Some Japanese soldiers tried to make Malaya and Singapore into a home by enmeshing themselves in existing networks. Indian Malayan nurse Sybil Kathigasu recalled that the first-line troops to arrive in and around Ipoh and Papan "all spoke Malay" and were instructed to "behave with courtesy and consideration towards the local population, with a view to winning their loyalty," though many fell short of this directive.[48] Mr. Lim described one Japanese businessman who "married one of the local Chinese girls and told us that he intended to settle down here after the war." Mr. Lim found him "very much attached to his Chinese wife."[49] In many ways, Japanese leaders followed British predecessors in tensely asserting supremacy while also trying to win over, extract privileges from, or forge intimate bonds with the civilian population.

Some white women also relied on Asian employees to protect them from sexual violence. This was the case of Nona Baker, who lived behind enemy lines with the aid of former workers at her brother Vin's mining estate. Chief among her protectors was Cheng Kam, a "trusted" estate foreman of more than thirty years.[50] Repeatedly, Cheng Kam emphasized Nona's vulnerability, suggesting that if they surrendered to the Japanese, Nona would be "debased in front of a gaping crowd." He shared rumors of "white women" being "driven naked through the streets." This reflected, in part, Cheng Kam's fears for his own wives amidst pervasive "stories about the cruelty of the Jap[ane]s[e] towards the Chinese." As a Chinese man facing very real threats of violence, Cheng Kam assumed that the Bakers were just as vulnerable. By contrast, the Bakers dismissed Cheng Kam's fears of the Japanese as perennial enmity: "the two peoples hated each other." They also lacked concern for the risk he took in sheltering them. The Bakers worried that he "might be tortured," not because he would suffer, but because he might "break down and give us away." They proved their indifference to his safety when he was wanted by the Kempeitai, the Japanese secret police. They urged him to turn himself in rather than risk giving away their position. Cheng Kam returned having experienced torture, but the Bakers were more concerned with bad news about the war. Ultimately, a plantation employee blackmailed Cheng Kam for protecting them. As a result, they left him and joined the orang bukit—a colloquial name for "hill people," often communists.[51] In their efforts to survive and avoid sexual violence, the Bakers proved indifferent to the traumas and worries of the Asian people who helped them.

Other white women volunteered Asian women for sexual labor. White Australian nurses held at camps near Palembang protested Japanese soldiers' efforts to force them to work in clubs by suggesting that there were "a number of Eurasian girls in the camp" who were "more than willing to fill the part."[52] White nurses were ready to offer up Eurasian women as sexual sacrifices, echoing a common view that Eurasians were by-products of sin and illegitimacy and therefore predisposed to sexual laxity.[53] Teenager Betty Kenneison, a Eurasian girl with a convent education, remembered the trauma of her teenaged friend reluctantly agreeing to work in the Japanese club in exchange for food and clothing. This could hardly be considered "more than willing."[54] Yet other white women, such as Changi internee Constance Sleep, understood things in these terms when she singled out "quite a number" of "Eurasian and native girl friends [*sic*] of some of the Nip[pone]s[e]."[55] White women claimed to have autonomy and rights over their bodies, while insisting that Asian or Eurasian women were outlets for men's sexual needs. They framed this as a reflection of the "degraded" or "willing" nature of Asian women to maintain the prestige of white womanhood.

Throughout the invasion and occupation, violence remained raced and gendered. Some people reached out to offer aid to those they viewed as vulnerable. Women and girls responded to the very real threat of sexual violence and depended on considerable aid from their communities to avoid it. Not all efforts were successful, and many women endured extreme traumas as a result of their experiences. Yet these stories indicate that while colonial boundaries could be transgressed, with neighbors helping neighbors and sheltering those they saw as vulnerable, other hierarchies remained firmly in place. Asian colonial subjects had a variety of reasons for aiding white Europeans. Their own access to survival, including long-term material compensation, was one of them. However, white Europeans continued to assume that their lives were a guarantee of future prosperity for anyone who aided them. This maintained the unequal hierarchies of the colonial period throughout the occupation, and emboldened white women to feel that their bodies, but not Asian women's, deserved aid and protection.

WHITE WOMEN COOLIES

White women's sense of entitlement to Asian labor influenced patterns of work within internment camps. Prior to her internment, Dr. Cicely Williams worked in Singapore hospitals where she lamented during the invasion that there was "lots of coolie work, carrying water, cooking food, cleaning latrines—with little time for anything except coolie work."[56] The absence of Asian laborers forced Williams to do the work of a "coolie," inverting the racial labor pattern of British colonialism. Williams also went on to become a commandant of the women's camp at Changi, replacing Allan's "Dream Mother," Dr. Hopkins. Her resentment at becoming a "coolie," in turn, echoed throughout the testimonies of interned white women. Many clung to the notion that white femininity represented the height of purity and prestige in colonial spaces. As Ann Laura Stoler has suggested, the class-based notion of whiteness made both women and poor whites the most

FIGURE 3.   White women bowing as they did for Japanese guards while
interned. Argus (Melbourne, Vic.) Australia. Dept. of Information.
Courtesy of State Library Victoria, www.slv.vic.gov.au

vulnerable to losing their status.[57] In turn, white internees repeatedly emphasized
the indignity of performing labor previously undertaken by Asians. Internment
therefore heightened the biases of white women, who resented their captivity
and saw Asian internees as a key to their suffering. They harshly condemned
Asian women for performing too little or too much labor for either Britons or the
Japanese. Emphasizing that white women had become "white coolies" was about
ensuring the restoration of an old racial order so that they, but not Asian women,
would be exempt from such treatment ever again.

A noteworthy feature of the civilian camps was their diversity. Roughly 2,000
men, and 300 women and children, of all ethnicities faced initial internment in
Singapore. After two years, these numbers swelled to roughly 3,000 men and 650

women and children, confined together in a prison built for 700. By the end of the war, Japanese leaders held over 4,000 men and 1,350 women and children in the camp at Sime Road.[58] Asian and Eurasian women vastly outnumbered white women, with Eurasian women and children alone outnumbering white women seven to one.[59] The inclusivity of the Singapore camps proved life-saving, as integrated camps had higher survival rates than those that were more segregated.[60] Yet many white women fixated on their suffering as "coolies." Australian nurse Veronica Clancy lamented that white women toiled like "the poorest paid coolies" and lost "their former prestige."[61] Constance Sleep complained about doing "heavy work usually done by coolies."[62] Betty Jeffrey, an Australian nurse, wrote a novel entitled *White Coolies*, foregrounding the upheaval of racialized labor as a key to women's suffering.[63] During this time, many white women saw their performance of manual labor as an outrage because "coolies," to them, meant Asian laborers. "White Coolies," therefore, were against the "natural" imperial order of British colonialism. White women's feelings of becoming "coolies" influenced how they responded to the labor expectations of camp life, and the presence of the Asian and Eurasian people living beside them.

Among white women internees, the diversity of inmates was a recurring concern. Nursing Sister Early recalled seeing the "most heterogenous collection of people" and numerous Eurasian families.[64] This added to her stress of living "in an awful state of overcrowding and semi-starvation," particularly during their initial internment in a cluster of houses at Katong prior to the march to Changi. She noted that internees consisted of all "nationalities with any connection by blood or marriage to Britishers—all colours—creeds and classes. Majority non white."[65] Dr. Williams similarly described the initial group as "a motley assembly. Some were born British, some had achieved Britishness, and some had had it thrust upon them."[66] The women's camp was "far more mixed" than the men's because it included many "[n]on-European wives, mostly with children, of men who were interned, military and civilian." These women lived alongside a large collection of predominantly white nurses, doctors, and other professional women who "had remained to look after the sick and distressed" and the wives of the civil and military men who stayed behind. Williams found it inevitable that among "so many and so varied standards, social, domestic, moral and racial, there was bound to be considerable friction." For this she blamed the internees themselves, among whom she found few "with any aptitude for community life." Even the children were "a great problem" because they "were mostly drawn from the more undisciplined strata of society."[67] The camp's ethnic and class diversity added to white women's assumptions that internees racialized as Asian, Euraisan, and Jewish were a burden and had to prove their worth.

As soon as internees arrived at Katong, Williams noted, "women had to do all the work."[68] This included the indignity of "burying the night soil in the small garden" before enduring the difficult march to Changi. Williams believed that such labors were a deliberate effort of the Japanese to "excite the derision of the local population" through the "'degradation' of the white people."[69] For Constance Sleep, the problem was that white women were completely unprepared and unsuited to perform camp labor.[70] She wrote that "we must do all the work of the camp. I have never minded work, but I never thought I should have to do such work as cleaning drains, and other heavy work usually done by coolies." She justified prewar racialized labor with familiar arguments that: "White women cannot do hard work in the tropics for long, and if they have already lived over 20 years in the tropics as so many of us had done, they are not very fit."[71] Later in her internment she complained again that white women "work hours every day just like coolies." She demonstrated some self-awareness about comparing wartime internees to prewar laborers, clarifying that "in peace time no coolie would have stood such conditions."[72] Here, Sleep walks a fine line between portraying white women as ill-prepared for the rigors of "coolie labor" but also insisting that prewar British leaders treated Asian laborers well. This emphasized the brutality, in her mind, of the Japanese, compared to the benevolent British who maintained a supposedly necessary and natural labor hierarchy.

White women's hostility about becoming "coolies" intensified when some women earned additional compensation by working for the Japanese. In Changi this included a match factory and a military clothing factory. Working in these positions usually granted workers extra food and the opportunity to buy eggs, sugar, and coffee, which they often resold to the camp "at a large profit."[73] One consequence was that women not working for the Japanese took on additional chores, without the benefit of additional pay. Dr. Williams suspected that Japanese leaders offered these "to sow dissension in both camps." She believed that many women did this work "to provide more food for their children" or because they lacked access to friends and neighbors locally and therefore "had little other opportunity of obtaining any extras." Still, Williams speculated that many women worked for the Japanese "for purely selfish reasons."[74] While Williams did not racialize women working for the Japanese, other white women saw this as a problem specific to Asian women. Constance Sleep blamed "native and Eurasian women" for working in the match factory. She claimed that "very few white women have touched either the match work or the sewing, and of those few, some of them have excused themselves on the ground that they must have food for their children, and others have been honest and said it was for their own stomachs." She claimed to speak for others in saying that "we don't think that excuses them."[75] White women might earn private scorn for such labor, but not a loss of access to Britishness or their place in the camp.

In reality, white women worked for the Japanese in numerous capacities. After the surrender, Japanese leaders demanded continuity with "essential services, such as hospitals, sanitation, fire-fighting, burial of the dead," making Dr. Williams, by default, an employee of the Japanese occupation.[76] She noted that most of the nurses were unwilling to work "under Asiatic doctors" and "preferred internment." By contrast, most of the doctors wanted to remain in their positions, though many like Williams eventually faced internment as well.[77] Still, in September 1942, Williams got to leave camp life to work for Mr. Asahi writing a report on food in Changi. For four months, she lived in a flat in Singapore, enjoying "all possible necessaries and many luxuries." She got to work in the Raffles Museums and dined with Japanese leaders.[78] These connections earned her books for the internees at Changi, helping her evade criticisms for her potentially disloyal actions.[79] This time outside camp also gained her further labor and support from the Asian population not enjoying the protection of internment. She received "many kindnesses from the population in general, ricksha [*sic*] pullers who refused to take money from us, and shopkeepers and market sellers who gave us presents." The only interruption to this idyllic period, she noted, was the proximity of the Raffles Museum to the Kempeitai headquarters at the YMCA building, where "we heard noises that left us in no doubt of the way in which the Kempei treated its victims"—a fate that would, eventually, befall Williams.[80] At a time when white women resented Asian women for taking additional work, Williams enjoyed fine dining with Japanese leaders and free rides from Asian civilians, being only occasionally reminded of the occupation with the screams of prisoners.

Once Williams returned to internment, Japanese leaders encouraged her to replace Elinor Hopkins as commandant because Hopkins's "manner annoyed them in some way."[81] Williams continued to enjoy working alongside Japanese leaders Naito and Asahi, whom she considered "by far the two best individuals we ever had to deal with." As commandant, she appreciated going toe-to-toe with Japanese military leaders. She saved her resentments for "the party squabbles and disloyalties in the camp" among internees, which "made the job unpleasant." After enjoying a comfortable life dining with and working for Japanese officials, her own loyalties were never questioned. Instead, she enjoyed a dignified and respected position, with even Sikh guards being "very kind to me and showed me nothing but sympathy, though they were very frightened."[82] As a white woman, Williams labored tirelessly in ways that benefited both Japanese and British rule without losing her status or access to Britishness. It gave her mobility and proximity to power that did not exist for most Asian civilians. Most of the Asian women who labored endlessly to protect white bodies failed to receive protection and care in return.

In contrast to Williams's treatment, many white women saw Asian women's ability to work for and gain favors from the Japanese as a sign of their inherent immorality. Nurse Early lamented feeling watched and "aggravated" with "the presence of spies (official or self appointed) and girl friends [*sic*] in our camp."[83] She attributed this dynamic to her belief that "the more well to do of all races left before capitulation," leaving them with "the dregs of humanity. Comfort girls—keeps [mistresses] etc." Consequently, in her view, "Brawls were f. frequent [*sic*] and these people did not hesitate to fraternize with Sikhs, Jap[ane]s[e], etc."[84] Despite her own friendliness with Japanese dining companions, Dr. Williams similarly resented those who "fraternised unreservedly with our captors, who acted as spies in the camp and reported other internees to them, who encouraged drunken sentries to come into the women's camp at night." This made camp discipline difficult, and led to "much disquiet and resentment."[85] Nurse Early agreed that Japanese guards "of course had girl friends [*sic*] whom they visited at night in the huts. Most unpleasant."[86] White women's perceptions that Asian women earned extra benefits for their labor, sexual or otherwise, made it impossible to hold these women to whatever standards white women demanded. Such perceptions repeatedly depended on the racialization of Asian women as sexually immoral compared to white women. Even though white women engaged in the same behavior, and Williams herself worked for the Japanese, the dominant perception of Asian women's willing intimacy heightened simmering resentments.

Due to these alliances, many white women concluded that Asian women could never be truly loyal to the British. Nurse Early noted that many Asian internees initially "did make an effort to be truly British but the effort proved too great over a long period."[87] In her mind, the Britishness of Asian and Eurasian women was a façade during British rule. Over time, these women apparently lost interest in proving their Britishness. Instead, self-interest prevailed, inspiring them selfishly to secure food at a time "when camp was starving." Rather than helping the camp, apparently, these women "bought and straight away sold [food] at Black Market prices."[88] What these women did not consider was that Asian internees' proximity to whiteness and British rule could have trained them to embrace this mercenary outlook. British economic and imperial policies of extracting resources for the highest profit and securing positions within imperial hierarchies dominated prewar life in colonial Singapore and Malaya. White women were offended to see Asian women embrace these values so readily at a time when they felt it was important to stick together. In reality, white women were unaccustomed to being the losers, rather than beneficiaries, in a contest for comfort.

Despite their resentments toward Asian women, white women often measured their own value through hard work, particularly when it served white men. Nurse Early noted that building a garden in Changi "kept me sane during the most trying year."[89] She found that in the camps, women were more fortunate than the men because they could occupy themselves with sewing, knitting, and mending socks and blankets. These were skills often taught to white and Asian women in Christian schools, further emphasizing the demand for gendered labor.[90] Nurse Early even lamented not getting to finish all of the sewing she wanted to do before the war ended. However, the men appreciated whenever women made things for them, which "kept us always busy."[91] Men also performed labor for the women, such as "making the food more palatable—mending our shoes with scraps, bits of tyre rubber, making trompahs, spectacle rims out of tooth brush handles—medicine out of herbs and so on."[92] By Early's account, white people labored as long as they felt like they were part of a mutual and reciprocal economy of care. For most Asian and Eurasian women living in proximity to white Europeans, the precarity of life under colonialism had already divested them of such illusions.

After the move to Sime Road, white women found it easier to maintain working relationships with white men. Dr. Williams noted that in October 1944, nursing sisters were able to assist in the men's hospital. While this "added greatly to their work," the women took it on "cheerfully and gladly." The men, in turn, were "exceedingly grateful" at seeing women in "carefully preserved and laundered white uniforms and caps."[93] Women performing care and comfort in the service of white men earned praise and gratitude for maintaining prewar gender norms in exceptional circumstances. To address men's needs, they also took on a few Voluntary Aid Detachments (VADs) to do much of the cleaning, Sheila Allan among them. According to Nurse Early, these women "varied in their enthusiasm" but proved necessary as their "work greatly increased." This hard work bonded some of the medical women closer together. Nurse Early recalled that at Sime Road, Miss Stewart worked tirelessly without a break, but "[i]t has been grand working for her and she has looked after us well."[94] Labor and mutual support was a pathway for securing and maintaining intimacy and belonging for white medical women.

Despite this enthusiasm for intimate labor in Sime Road, camp life remained tense because of an ever-increasing number of internees. While camp numbers increased throughout the occupation, in March 1945 there was a "large influx of new internees." This increased the number of men by roughly two hundred and nearly doubled the number of women and children, bringing the total camp numbers near five thousand. Williams noted:, "The new accessions were nearly all Jews, together with a few Eurasiansand [*sic*] Chinese."[95] Like Williams, Nurse Early claimed that the new internees in March 1945 were "Jews from Arab Street, Salegie Road, and wherever the Singapore Ghetto was," which included a "dreadful sense of sordidness in overcrowded Jewish huts." She found these women "huge masses of female bulk" who were "all completely undisciplined until they were terrot [*sic*] stricken by Nip[pone]s[e] a few times for breaking rules."[96] Although internees never knew the reason for the added numbers, Williams speculated that it was "an excuse to seize their houses and their goods, or possibly to provide more cover for the 'foxholes' and gun-encampments." The consequence was "afurther [*sic*] reduction in food" because "the produce of the gardens" had to be "divided among greater numbers." Worse still, new internees brought an "influx of Nipponese currency" that caused "a big increase in black market prices."[97] This further encouraged white internees to blame their suffering on Asian, Eurasian, and Jewish "others."

As several internees hinted, the existence of black markets exposed the intersection of financial and racial animosity. Nurse Early racialized the black market as "chiefly run by Jews and Prison Warders (European Internees)."[98] This increased existing hostility toward those who, in Williams's words, "made large fortunes out of the distress of their fellow countrymen."[99] While there was an acknowledgment of "fellow countrymen" being responsible, most emphasized Asian, Eurasian, and Jewish women as the problem. For example, Nurse Early loathed Jewish women who arrived in March 1945 for bringing "Kerosene tins of Nip[pone]s[e] money" and many possessions. This meant that they could "buy everything they wanted." As a result, "we old internees quickly dropped out of running" when haggling for goods on the black market. The men had to resort to cashing checks "chiefly with Jews" who had been "buying and selling" with the Japanese.[100] This racialization and antisemitism reflected white internees' bitterness at being on the losing side of a competitive and unequal financial system. Interned since the surrender, they felt marginalized and unable to compete with those who, apparently, continued to amass resources while living outside the camps. Once again, it was the rare experience of being the financial "losers," and no longer receiving racial privilege, that heightened white internees' resentments.

While white women were certain that Jewish, Asian, and Eurasian internees had access to superior resources, those who experienced life both within and outside camps had very different experiences. Eurasians outside of camps faced racial discrimination and violence. They struggled to secure food, jobs, and housing while being singled out with armbands that were meant as a "passport" to avoid being persecuted as European.[101] Some Eurasian women previously living outside of Changi saw internment as a safe option that might facilitate repatriation after the war.[102] Others participated in Japanese resettlement plans in Bahau, which targeted Eurasians as well as Chinese and Indian Catholics, with the promise of fresh food. However, the fatality rate among settlers was roughly 25 percent—comparable to the highest death rates in Japanese camps.[103] Mrs. Barbara Clunies-Ross, who experienced life in both Bahau and the Sime Road internment camp, described the latter as more well-organized and better supplied than the former. In Bahau, which was under the leadership of Catholic church officials, people could only eat what they could afford, whereas at Sime Road, everyone got food.[104] Mrs. Clunies-Ross's insistence that life in Changi and Sime Road was more equitable and well-provisioned further exposed the relative privilege of internment and white women's continued indifference to the suffering of others.

Despite many hardships, Nurse Early ultimately saw the internment experience as a triumph of whiteness: "We much despised Orang Putch [*sic*] maintained discipline in a camp of 5000 souls of all types some hardened criminals and ex convicts."[105] While the Japanese "boasted they'd make coolies of us," the white internees "anticipated them voluntarily." This, she believed, represented European pluck and determination: "It must have astonished them to find that the Europeans were the first to voluntarily make coolies of themselves. The work had to be done and we all did it unhesitatingly."[106] For Nurse Early, a willing performance of labor indicated pride and self-sufficiency. This gave her, and other white women, the opportunity to see their own labor as just and necessary. The hardships and frustrations of camp life faded away behind a memory of overcoming the selfishness of "criminal" Asian "companions" comparatively unwilling "to live communally." This made her certain that "[h]ad this been a purely English camp our problems would have been practically non existent [*sic*]."[107] To Nurse Early, Asian and Eurasian civilians with the most proximity to prewar British leaders were too devoted to self-interested capitalism to succeed in internment life, recalling Homi Bhabha's formulation that Indigenous elites were "almost the same, but not quite."[108] The need and desire to live "communally" became a virtue of white people who knew how to work hard and mutually support one another in wartime.

FIGURE 4. White women re-creating the labor they performed while interned. Argus (Melbourne, Vic.) Australia. Dept. of Information. Courtesy of State Library Victoria, www.slv.vic.gov.au

After the war, many films, articles, and memoirs joined white women in commemorating the plight of white internees. Photographs and newspaper articles depicted white women's experiences in prison camps to emphasize that servility— especially in the service of an Asian "enemy"—was at odds with white femininity.[109] Nurse Early participated in a series of postwar photographs taken of the women "in our work attire—Ooo what a picture that will be for you at home seeing a lot of white coolies at their chores." Meanwhile, she celebrated the end of what she found to be humiliating labor: "No longer have to clean drains, bathrooms, lavatories, splash lalang, play at nursing in a make shift hospital, queue for food, save the mark, do my personal chores, wash, mend, and cobble, and make do with rags."[110] Despite the diversity of the camps, only white women were included in these photos. By contrast, in December 1945, the *Straits Times* published images of Asian women working in fields to redeem themselves from their past as coerced sexual laborers.[111] While labor brought indignity to white women, hard work apparently redeemed the perceived immorality of Asian women. If the worst sin of the war was reducing white women to "white coolies," then many would ensure that all future laborers would remain Asian.

LABORING TO BELONG

Many white women cast their experiences of being "white coolies" as a temporary indignity, but Sheila Allan eagerly labored to earn the love of her "Dream Mother," Dr. Elinor Hopkins. Allan's early life of attending various Malayan convents shaped her expectations of a life among white women. She converted to Catholicism before the war because the French and Irish nuns were "so kind and so gentle and so serene and I thought perhaps being a Catholic might make me like that."[112] She processed this through religious rather than racial terms. However, her Muslim Malay mother, Buddhist Chinese amah, and Siamese (Thai) stepmother all failed to represent the unconditional love that she craved, unlike the white nuns and doctor. Her love and admiration for Dr. Hopkins only deepened her equation of whiteness with ideal, loving femininity at a time when Asian leadership and intimacy evoked fear, violence, and neglect.[113] After spending her early life in convents with white women, she was optimistic that hard work, faith, and community spirit, which white internees prized as "British" qualities, would grant her acceptance and inclusion. Ultimately, she struggled to retain the conditional belonging she found during internment, creating lasting traumas of laboring for love.

As soon as Allan's internment journey began, she labored for inclusion among her fellow internees. She shared their horror at their living conditions at Katong, noting: "What a life! Mosquitos terrible! Our latrines stink!"[114] However, she gave more precise details about emptying latrines three times daily because her chore was to dig holes and bury the rubbish. Once they arrived in Changi, she helped with morning teas and acted as first drain sweeper. The equation of people with labor was so important that Allan noted in her diary the names of people and their jobs to help her keep track of everyone. In turn, Allan used work to find acceptance. The first person to catch her admiration was Miss Josephine Foss, who served as representative on her floor, A3. When Miss Foss asked Allan to assist a pregnant woman, Allan agreed because for her, "I would do anything."[115] This was no small ask, since Allan witnessed a Japanese sentry murder a baby

FIGURE 5.   White women re-creating the vigorous physical labor they performed while interned. Argus (Melbourne, Vic.) Australia. Dept. of Information. Courtesy of State Library Victoria, www.slv.vic.gov.au

during the invasion and thought of this every time she heard a baby cry.[116] While she continued to regard Miss Foss as a "nice lady," she soon admitted her admiration for Dr. Hopkins. She noted that she was "attracted to Dr. Hopkins—I think she's beautiful—Gray hair, blue eyes that can look straight through you and a smile that lights up her face."[117] This attraction to, and fascination with, a camp commandant and doctor shaped the rest of her time in internment and her understanding of the need to labor for love.

At a time when white women complained about performing "coolie" labor, Allan was grateful for everyone's work. This included not only the "self-sacrifice" of teachers, nurses, and doctors, but also praiseworthy were "all the sweepers, drain workers who work tirelessly to keep the camp clean" and the kitchen squad who fed them.[118] She lamented the hostility between women, noting "some un-charitable females in here" and the inability to "escape from malicious tongues!" Such tensions made her thankful for "the friends that I have made," especially those "around my age" who made her feel that "we are in this together and we depend on each other to boost our morale and strange to say we seem to be blessed with a sense of humour!" This sense of mutual obligation earned her an invitation to join in "elevenses" by "Mrs Freddie Bloom." While Allan was acutely aware of her own suffering, feeling included in a community of care made the experience bearable.[119]

At other times, inclusion and recreation amplified Allan's difference. During one Christmas show, white women dressed in various costumes to perform as and mock Asian women. Allan observed that Mrs. Lancaster "looked really 'Indian' in her dress. Mary Winters looked cute as a 'Chinese.'" Mrs. Macindo also dressed in a costume to look like a "Javanese." Rather than expressing dis-comfort at this racial drag, Allan appreciated the collective feeling of forget-ting about their internment for the first time.[120] Meanwhile, she maintained her laboring spirit, noting that she reproduced the programs for concerts, circuses, and other camp performances. Allan even performed occasionally, often in roles that emphasized her marginalization. During one performance of the Merchant of Venice she was picked to play "Tubal, 'the Irish Jew.'"[121] These spectacles of race and gender amplified her exclusion while also offering conditional inclusivity hinging on continued performances of otherness.[122] Proving Britishness included dressing up as racialized others for amusement. Performances that enabled other internees forget the hardships of their situation forced Allan to maneuver be-tween alterity and inclusion.

Official record-keeping within camps, and white women's perceptions of Allan as "Eurasian," also added to her exclusion. Nominal rolls at Changi had over a dozen categories, including Australian, British, and Eurasian—all of which could have applied to Allan.[123] In April 1944, Allan learned that "other children" were listed "under fathers' nationality" but hers was listed as "Eurasian." She spoke with a Mrs. Brooks about it, who assured her that she could have this changed to Australian, like her father. This categorization became especially stressful, when on one occasion in 1945 there was a "special roll call" that segregated people into four groups: "Br. UK, Br. Eurasian, Br. Jews and Indetermines."[124] Also adding to her hardships, many internees clearly resented Eurasians. Constance Sleep, interned in Changi alongside Allan, felt that "I don't despise the Eurasians as such. In fact, I have known some very admirable people amongst them, but I do despise the European men who are responsible for bringing them into the world."[125] Allan may have passed Sleep's test of being a "very admirable" person individually. Yet Sleep belittled her father—her most intimate family connection and her key to white imperial privilege—for creating her. Nurse Clancy, who shared Allan's Australian identity but was held at camps near Palembang, condemned Eurasian children as "the victims of these marriages between the East and West." She maintained the common view that "Eurasions [*sic*] . . . are not wanted by either people."[126] White women often treated Eurasians as a burden and a nuisance in camps to deflect the humiliation of surrender.[127] For Allan, categorization as "Eurasian" could literally be a matter of life and death.

These tense circumstances make it unsurprising that Allan found comfort in emphasizing her "British" identity.[128] During the arduous eight-mile march to Changi, she described marching "in the true 'British spirit'—singing." This included the patriotic refrain, "There will always be an England."[129] This also made Dr. Hopkins the ideal woman. According to one observer, Hopkins was "very 'English' in voice, manner and outlook." Some internees, and Japanese leaders, found this "extremely irritating."[130] To Allan, it was a source of comfort, aspiration, and desire. Her Anglophile tendencies may have chafed against Japanese rule and their perception of her as Eurasian. Yet her devout association with Britishness helped her assimilate into camp. Assimilation was also, in her father's eyes, a key to long-term survival. During a treasured New Year's meeting in 1943, Allan's father, John, advised her to talk with Dr. Hopkins or Miss Foss to discuss medical work.[131] For John, Allan's ability to make positive connections with white colleagues gave her long-term prospects for claiming Britishness and professional opportunities after the war. Despite this advice, Allan wanted to be a writer. She kept her diary and won a tin of peaches for her submission in a camp literary competition in April 1943, which was a thinly-veiled story describing her love of Hopkins.[132] Meanwhile, she took on the responsibility of looking after many of the children, a task assigned to some of the "older girls."[133] Intimate, gendered care remained a key to her belonging, and following white women into medicine was meant to secure her future.

Despite her inroads finding community, loneliness was a recurring part of Allan's internment experience. By December 1943, she wrote a poem about her prewar life, recalling, "As companions, two dogs or more,/ A cap, perhaps, that is not a bore—They are often better than company of men and women/ Who let you down again and again."[134] The feeling of being let down by people no doubt exacerbated the loneliness and desperation of camp life. By then, Allan realized that reasons for exclusion could be petty. While some women fought over accusations of sex with guards, others got in arguments about things like snoring.

Allan wrote a poem with the lines "You might have been the best internee/ And first rate at every chore" but "the only thing that mattered/ Was, my lady, did you snore?"[135] Here, Allan emphasizes that even excellent work "at every chore" did not spare women from resentment and hostility. Camp tensions gave Allan repeated reminders of how fragile belonging could be.

The move to Sime Road in Bukit Timah in May 1944 gave Allan a new sense of purpose and more opportunities to prove her worth to the camp. Men and women were allowed to meet twice daily and circulate letters, giving Allan the important job of working as assistant to the postwoman.[136] By the end of the month, Allan asked Dr. Williams if she could train in nursing, and arranged for three other young women to do so as well, fulfilling her father's wish that she go into medicine. However, things became more stressed, as other internees noted, in March 1945 with new arrivals. Allan had observed two years earlier that the "whole place is so crowded already and tempers do fray frequently!"[137] Rather than lamenting the burden of these arrivals or racializing their behavior, like other internees, Allan helped collect everyone's names and hut numbers, facilitating their entry into camp life.[138] Allan noted that new internees added to her hospital labor, with many suffering from dysentery. They also stressed the housing situation, with thirty-two people now living in her hut. As a result, "tempers [were] not improved by this situation and personal possessions are jealously guarded—naturally accusations are flung in all directions. What a bitchy lot of females we have become!!!"[139] Despite these setbacks, Allan never blamed the new arrivals for joining the camp. She noted only that their presence caused great resentment among other internees.

Ultimately, Allan's inclusion at Sime Road was limited by fears for her father. She learned that his mental and physical health deteriorated after he stole a knife and got into a fight, which she noted made "the second time Dad has been in a sort of disgrace." During this difficult time, Dr. Hopkins continued to be a source of inspiration. She promised Allan that she would be able to visit her father, giving Allan a look that made her heart "leap." This feeling of intimacy—her beloved "Dream Mother" ensuring her access to her father—was soon undermined by the racism of other prisoners. In the same entry she noted hearing that she has been referred to as "That slit-eyed C----!'" by other internees.[140] Despite Allan's meticulous efforts to labor for respectability and be an asset to camp life, the arrival of other marginalized prisoners, her father's behavior, and the racism of other internees still set her apart.

When Allan's father passed away a few months before the end of the war, she recognized the depths of her loneliness and vulnerability. This loss temporarily bonded her with her stepmother. However, it was Dr. Hopkins who provided the most immediate support. She arranged for Allan's identity to be listed as Australian, solidifying her connection to her father. Hopkins also arranged for Allan to continue nursing after the war, fulfilling her father's wishes. While Allan was excited about the end of the war, she also felt "rather sad in midst of laughter" because she knew that she would lose Hopkins. She lamented that "very soon we will part, perhaps, never more to meet." She felt she would always be at Hopkins's side "in spirit." When her stepmother journeyed back to Ipoh alone, Allan felt even more isolated and turned to work to sate her loneliness. She hoped to secure a job as soon as possible to support herself so that she would "not be a burden to anyone longer than I can help." She felt confident in her skills but worried about "how the world is going to treat me."[141] Despite the temporary inclusion she earned as a hard worker in Changi and Sime Road, her uncertain fate as an unattached and racialized woman meant that she would continue to labor for love after the war.

Allan realized that the hard work that gave her a sense of inclusion would not guarantee her intimacy and belonging after the war ended. Still, the connections she made helped her find employment. She had difficulty gaining a nursing spot because there were far more applications than vacancies. In response, P. B. Marriott, who knew her father in the camps, arranged for her housing in convents and other expenses until she could find employment.[142] While Allan felt grateful for the aid, she could not help worrying about having her future "mapped out for me."[143] Nursing only added to her feelings of isolation. Most of her patients were soldiers who refused to talk to "outsiders" about their experiences, even as she heard "them crying with the pain of their dreadful memories."[144] Yet her experience in the camps did help her serve them. When one former Dutch POW got into trouble for hiding food, she remembered how it felt to be so hungry and helped him get extra food. After spending the war laboring for love, work seemed like the only thing she could count on.

Despite losing her father and "Dream Mother," Allan was able to find a place in the world. Her Aunt Grace arranged to bring her "home" to Australia, where she had never been before.[145] This came as a surprise, since Allan had wished to live with Aunt Grace, but Grace initially expressed hesitancy. She only agreed after learning that it was Allan's father's wish for Allan to live there.[146] In response to the news, Allan made one last, sad journey back to Sime Road. There, she realized that this was the only "'bit' of a home I had left and I knew I would be there on my own and 'lick my wounds.'"[147] While other internees saw the end of the war as an unambiguous end to suffering, and an opportunity to return home, Allan realized that the only real home she had was in the camp with the people she loved. On arrival in Australia, she found some relief in finding her aunt Grace was "not unlike Dad."[148] Yet it was difficult for her to feel "at home" because "everything's so strange." The home her father once lived in had been "mortgaged." While she enjoyed learning about her family and seeing pictures of her dad when he was young, she also experienced cruelty. For instance, while Allan was buying stamps, "the girl was very nasty." Many people "look at me in their quizzical way."[149] However, she found some comfort in the Chinese grocer who had lived in Singapore for three years. Even working as a nurse, which gave her temporary inclusion in Changi, did not make her feel welcome in Australia. Some patients told to "Go back to Japan" while she nursed them.[150]

When Allan looked back on her internment decades later, she maintained that racism did not play a large role in her treatment. The only people who were not treated well, in her view, were those "who wouldn't work or tried to get out of work."[151] As the testimonies of white women indicate, the situation was more complex. Allan sometimes took jobs that other women did not want — and clearly felt that they should have — to do. This earned her both the designation of a "hard worker" but also maintained the racial prejudices of many white women. Allan's acceptance into Britishness was conditional on her willingness to work—an expectation that did not exist for white people. However optimistic Allan was that her hard work prevented her from facing discrimination, though, many women used racial difference to explain value. Constance Sleep was certain that Eurasians were "liabilities in the Camp. They either won't or can't take their share of running of the Camp."[152] Allan was considered lazy by default and had to perform "coolie" labor to prove that she deserved access to British spaces. This earned her relative exemption from the abuse that other Eurasian women faced at the hands of white prisoners. Yet for Allan, the end of the war also meant separation from her "Dream Mother" forever. Losing Hopkins meant losing the person who made her feel hope among a not-always welcoming group of internees. Internment allowed Allan to fortify her connections to British women and survive not only her Japanese captors but also her fellow internees. It did not guarantee permanent inclusion within the British Empire.

THE MODEL WORKER

In contrast to Allan, Elizabeth Choy's hard work and suffering endeared her to the British imperial world. During the war, Choy took a leading role in supporting and sustaining interned Europeans by smuggling goods and medicine into camps. Dr. Williams recalled being "[d]eeply indebted" to "many of our Chinese and Eurasian friends" including "Elizabeth Choy and her husband, and various nurses in the hospitals." She recognized that they "took, and knew they were taking, very great risks, and many of them paid for it later with their lives, and suffered torture and imprisonment." Her efforts ensured that internees "were in relatively good condition and able to withstand the hardships."[153] Many Asian and Eurasian people, like Choy, took risks to sneak medicine, food, and other supplies into camps such as Changi and Sime Road. These dangerous labors reflected pervasive religious and educational training that encouraged self-sacrificing service. Many men and women put themselves at risk to continue serving a colonial state that had crumbled. Few earned praise for doing so. Yet as one of the few people to gain British favor, Elizabeth Choy's story is a necessary contrast to Allan's for understanding what British leaders valued in a hard-working Asian woman.

Born in North Borneo, Choy came from the elite Yong family of Khek/ Hakka[154] Chinese Christians that valued being "hardy, sturdy, and self-reliant." From a young age she learned that "all work is noble" and lived in a community where everyone "was very hardworking." She received an English education from missionaries, where the aim was "to train young girls to be good Christians, good housewives and people—hardy and so on." Daily activities included manual labor, such as "keeping the lawn trimmed, chopping wood and carrying water, and doing all the housework in the whole boarding school." She remembered being "unhappy over these chores," but in hindsight she reasoned that it was "the only way to learn to be hardy."[155] She received various levels of instruction in English and Chinese, before securing a place in the Convent of the Holy Infant Jesus, the same group that supported Sheila Allan's studies.[156] Many of the women graduates pursued nursing or teaching, and had opportunities for charitable work, giving Choy a solid foundation in ideas of Christian service. She emphasized that her own family had priests and preachers in the ranks, instilling her with the importance of helping "those in need."[157]

While Allan longed for a "Dream Mother," Choy took inspiration from her own "ideal mother, gentle, kind, soft-spoken and very loving."[158] Experiencing this love gave her a "great desire to help those without mothers," setting her on a course to help Allan and other internees. It started with her coming to the aid of "British soldiers looking so desperate" during the invasion. They were "tired and thirsty," so she boiled water and made them tea.[159] This did not grant her inclusion. During intense bombing, Choy sought refuge in Po Leong Kok on York Hill, where one missionary who worked with her previously, Miss Foss, took in girls. When Choy arrived with her parents, grandparents, and children, Foss turned them away. They watched from the hill as Singapore city went up in flames. Despite this rejection, Choy continued to demonstrate her value. She turned from teaching to nursing, as many schools became hospitals overnight.[160] She and her family managed a canteen at Woodbridge Hospital before moving to Tan Tock Seng Hospital. She soon learned that British internees "lacked medicines, food, and news of friends." As a result, she used the canteen to enable friends and family members of internees to "send them medicines, food, money, messages and so on, using an ambulance that used to run between the internment camp and the hospital." For these efforts, she and her husband were taken by the Kempeitai and "very badly tortured."[161]

Choy and her husband were implicated in the notorious Double Tenth incident of October 10 (10/10), 1943, during which Dr. Williams was also imprisoned. This event saw Japanese leaders capture and torture civilians whom they believed supplied information that contributed to a string of significant Japanese losses. Choy and her husband took it as a compliment even though they were not "connected with some kind of espionage." Rather, "all we did was help those in distress to live through their internment."[162] This put her in further touch with Europeans from the internment camp who were "interrogated and tortured very severely," some of whom died as a result. She remembered seeing Sir Robert Scott "so disfigured, so wounded, his face all puffed up and his body swollen" that they "never thought he would be able to live after that." Choy herself endured electric shock torture and being stripped. She claimed to never blame the Japanese, believing instead that "their military obligations" made them "so cruel and heartless."[163] While she was released from confinement after two hundred days, her husband remained in prison until the British return. Laboring for British internees made her more vulnerable to the Japanese and forced her to endure torture.

Ultimately, torture marked Elizabeth Choy as someone deserving praise. After liberation, Lady Mountbatten invited Choy to the surrender ceremony at City Hall. She then spent a month in Indonesia, visiting internment camps at Jakarta and visiting President Sukarno's palace. She also received an invitation to "recuperate their health" in England.[164] In 1946, she earned the Bronze Cross, the highest award in the Girl Guide movement for valor, which was bestowed by Lady Baden-Powell. She received a private audience with the Queen Mother, accompanied by Sir Shenton and Lady Thomas. She enjoyed an invitation to a party at Buckingham Palace, where she met "many old friends" including Earl and Lady Mountbatten. The latter was "very sweet and I was impressed by her warmth and friendship," which included introducing Choy to her two daughters.[165] She later received an invitation to Buckingham Palace to meet Princess (later Queen) Elizabeth, who was interested in celebrating the nurses of Singapore, for whom Choy was to serve as representative. She received an invitation to the coronation banquet, where she met "great leaders of the world." Finally, she took a course in domestic science, taught at a London Council School, and felt that she "seemed to meet the best people."[166]

Despite Choy's Christianity, war experience, and elite upbringing, she often felt out of place in Britain. She regarded herself as "almost a Wild Woman from Borneo, walking into Buckingham Palace and meeting such a great Queen!"[167] The queen apparently laughed at Choy's desire to attend the London School of Oriental Languages to learn Chinese, or to take up domestic science, because the queen believed that "all Chinese were very good in domestic work." Choy rebounded by suggesting that she wanted to learn more about "English ways of life," which the queen felt was "very good." Initially, Choy experienced homesickness and only felt better after going to Chinese restaurants and chatting with strangers. She recalled: "It was strange that talking to people of your own race in a foreign country should cheer you up, even though they were perfect strangers. It just shows how clannish we were at home."[168] While Choy stayed in England for four years, instead of her originally planned six months, the comfort she found in Chinese establishments did more than prove "clannishness" back home.[169] It showed that, despite her positive encounters and common experiences with many Britons, she still felt different and longed for those with a shared sense of home.

Being treated like a British dignitary gave Choy a renewed faith in British colonialism. She noted that prior to the Japanese arrival "we regarded the British as our rulers and benefactors, and our protectors, we went about our business in a very contented way."[170] However, after being welcomed with open arms for her suffering, she viewed British rule as egalitarian and liberatory. She was "impressed by the attitude of the English people," whom she found "friendly, warm, and ever ready to help."[171] She speculated that when "we have a common enemy, we become very friendly and anxious to help one another." If she had not visited England, "my idea of English ways would be very different."[172] Her experience was influenced by the fact that "there were many internees from Singapore now returned to Britain who asked me to visit their homes, and we would have a talk about the Occupation days."[173] Shared suffering made her feel like she belonged. Seeing "all the war damage in the city" and hearing people "talking about what they had gone through in such a cheerful way" made her realize "why the British had been great for so long—because of their sturdy power of endurance and the qualities necessary to become great people." She even saw rationing in England as a sign of greatness, because in Singapore "we had no organization," so those "who could not get food starved."[174] Strikingly, she processed this not as the difference between how British leadership treated the metropole versus a colony. Instead, she saw it as evidence of superiority. While Choy's suffering gave her a place in England, England's tales of heroic suffering made her forget the colonial power that fled.[175] After the war, she became an important international voice in advocating for the British Commonwealth's unity and need to fight communism.[176]

Unlike Choy, many women colonial subjects never got to enjoy the spoils of inclusion because they did not survive the war. Sybil Kathigasu was tortured by the Japanese for aiding communists and then died from resulting medical complications. Geoffrey Cater, former Agent for Malaya in London, still claimed that Kathigasu "was proud to be a British subject." As a devout Catholic, she believed that the Japanese worshipped "material success as incarnate evil" making it her duty as a "Christian to oppose and defy."[177] Kathigasu echoed this narrative, citing holy visions inspiring her to resist.[178] Like Choy, her willingness to provide not only medical labor to those fighting the occupation, but also to sacrifice her body for the resistance, was the necessary ticket to inclusion. Others toiled under the knowledge that no amount of loyalty or labor would gain them a place in colonial society. When Winsome Mayo returned to Malaya at the end of the war, she found many upset that Europeans received three years' worth of back pay while Eurasians and other local staff received it for just three months. She later saw this dynamic as "a great spur to the Malayan insurgency: so far as the Eurasians and Asians could see, they had been willing to lay down their lives, had seen the sacrifice of family members who had died, and then they were insulted by being valued at one-twelfth of a European."[179] While many colonial subjects showed that they were willing to labor for love and inclusion, few British leaders extended it beyond the war. It was not enough for colonial subjects to labor for the empire. They had to suffer for it.

FRACTURED MEMORIES

When British power returned to Singapore and Malaya, many reflected on the legacy of the Japanese occupation for British colonialism. Nurse Early believed that the Japanese occupation was "the best possible propaganda for the British." This was because the "Asiatic Community no matter how Anti British previously" now realized that the Japanese "treated the natives as no Britisher ever would."[180] Accusations of violence, coercion, and exploitation under British rule, for Early, meant nothing compared to Japanese brutality. Others were more ambivalent. Dr.

Williams observed that during a victory parade, "the local population showed, in no uncertain manner, that, whatever they thought of the British, they much preferred them to the Nipponese." She found it heartening to receive a warm welcome from "our Asiatic friends, whose trials and tribulations had been on the whole far worse than anything we had endured in the shelter of internment, was affectionate beyond description." She noted that this was "beyond anything we felt we could have deserved."[181] While British rule benefited from being less traumatic than the Japanese occupation, many recognized that this was not clear and uncritical praise for the British. Rasammah Bhupalan remembered her father saying that colonial "masters were never or very rarely benevolent." Rather, the British were "the best of a bad lot."[182] Many British leaders returned to power hoping that that would be good enough, and that the memories of suffering under British, rather than Japanese, rule would just fade away.

The Japanese invasion represented a reversal of the laboring conditions of the British Empire. For a time, white soldiers and civilians toiled in the service of Asian overlords. In these conditions, hard work became the primary measure of value. For whom one worked (Japanese or British) determined whether they deserved care or scorn. This made people like Sheila Allan believe that if she worked hard she would gain a permanent place of love and acceptance among the British. Some, like Elizabeth Choy, enjoyed the fanfare that came with laboring and suffering for conditional acceptance. Most did not. The Asian civilians who tirelessly served British bodies and interests during the fall of Singapore endured vulnerability during the occupation, far exceeding that of white internees. Yet the preoccupation with white women's suffering contributed to the desire to restore white womanhood to its prewar prominence. Many Asian women navigated the racialized and gendered ideas of labor and hard work to increase their chances for survival amidst heightened threats of racial and sexual violence. In many cases this amplified existing patterns of colonial violence as people competed for few opportunities to evacuate, or contended for survival with those who felt entitled to it. Evacuation at once made everyone feel vulnerable—and exposed the unequal, intersecting vulnerabilities of civilians simultaneously facing an invading army and a retreating colonial power.

For many former captives, the journey home intensified the desire to return to normal—which many cast as a return to the hierarchies that eluded them in the camps. For Australian nurse Veronica Clancy, this meant a newfound confidence in racial exclusion, such as the "White Australia" policy. She wrote: "According to Educationalists all races are equal. I do not know, but we always said that we would be prepared to do almost anything if it would help to keep Australia White.

We all endorsed the Japanese idea of Asia for the Asiatics. One girl remarked, 'Who would want to live with them, anyway.' [*sic*] So why not Australia for the Australians?"[183] The commitment to "White Australia" after the war meant that many who longed to flee Southeast Asia after the occupation were unable to do so. Eurasians who tried to evacuate were often turned away even before the occupation, and continued to face difficulties migrating after the war.[184] Eurasian veteran George Hess'e was refused entry to Australia, despite his service resisting the Japanese with undercover British and Australian officers in Force 136, because he was "dark skinned." Eurasian women such as Esme Kenneison gained entry only after invasive physical inspections and her ability to "pass" as white.[185]

Some experiences of internment crossed lines of class, race, and faith and had the potential to challenge colonial hierarchies. At times, this created new understandings about community, family, and intimacy in a context of war, occupation, forced labor, and internment. Yet for many white civilians, Japanese internment signified a temporary loss of status. It emboldened their feelings that if whiteness fell from its exalted status as a mark of rule, then the alternative of Black, Brown, Asian, or Indigenous leadership would be even more brutal and exclusionary than European colonialism. Returning to societies marked by white supremacy, they came "home" to spaces in which whiteness offered status, inclusion, and citizenship. Memories of living beside Asian and Eurasian colonial subjects in filthy, traumatic conditions conflated these two realities—making them crave pristinely clean, and exclusively white, spaces. Asian and Eurasian subjects reconciled the trauma of their experiences with memories of temporary inclusion. The enthusiasm engendered by the end of the war proved to be short-lived, as colonial subjects encountered the postwar realities of delayed repatriation, migration bars, and turbulent transitions to post-colonial nation-states. The Second World War offered a moment where prewar hierarchies met their doom. The experience of wartime internment, however, made alternatives to the prewar colonial world seem even worse. Experiencing a prolonged, traumatic war created false memories of, and nostalgia for, the prewar world. At the same time, many kept their dreams of a better tomorrow alive. They hoped and believed that peace would, and could, bring them a sense of inclusion without brutality, a place in the sun without suffering. For others, the fight continued.

FIVE

Making and Unmaking "Martial Races"

In early 1946, British Major and War Crimes Defending Counsel P. R. Mursell insisted that Indian soldiers' testimonies were unreliable evidence to condemn Japanese soldiers. He alleged that if the trials took place in British courts, rather than in Singapore, their accounts "would be rejected as not constituting evidence at all."[1] The problem, in his view, was that soldiers had returned home to India, leaving no witnesses to take the stand in Singapore. He asked the court if they were truly willing to accept the account from "an Indian whom you have never seen, in flat contradiction to all that is just and fair?" In Mursell's view, Indian soldiers' absence meant that the court "cannot accuse" Japanese soldiers "of a crime at all" because "the victim cannot confront his accuser, and give him the lie to his face." For Mursell, the person accused of the crime, rather than the person hurt by it, was the "victim." Indian soldiers who were unwilling or unable to confront their former prison guards after years of trauma, in turn, were "lying" about their experiences. This was a particularly troubling assertion in a trial concerned with a Japanese officer who allegedly beheaded an Indian soldier, Ghafoor, for stealing food. Mursell did not dispute that this occurred. Instead, he found it "the just penalty for a mean and detestable act of knavery." Beheading an Indian soldier was "just." Stealing food while starving was the "detestable act of knavery."[2] Mursell's response revealed how soldiers' experiences as prisoners of war undermined their claims to racialized codes of military masculinity that underpinned British rule in Asia.

Mursell's defense was part of the more than 2,240 trials against roughly 5,700 people prosecuted for war crimes in over fifty locations across Asia-Pacific.[3] Many scholars and participants have discussed how hastily-collected evidence, discrepancies between translated testimonies, and scholars' reliance on prosecutor testimonies shaped the outcomes and memories of the war crimes trials in Asia.[4] Yet Mursell's vivid and accusatory tone toward Indian troops, who endured suffering due to their association with the British Empire, shows that Indian men had a difficult time finding justice from British leaders after the war. By contrast, when Mursell defended another Japanese soldier from causing the deaths of seven British POWs, he criticized the method of securing the defendant's testimony and the defendant's lack of personal responsibility but not the conduct of the men killed.[5] Such discrepancies revealed how the war crimes trials reflected colonial racial hierarchies by limiting who had the ability to claim suffering in wartime. It became more than an issue of British legal practices ascribing guilt or innocence to Japanese soldiers, but a contested, multi-sited experience of guilt and trauma that spanned the colonial world. In fact, many of the people collecting evidence were members of Force 136, a diverse group of locally-recruited Indian, Chinese, and Eurasian soldiers who fought behind enemy lines and had their own postwar hopes of inclusion. Mursell's defense therefore hints at a much larger problem of the complexity of POW and wartime experience, with Asian troops struggling to gain the support or sympathy of colonial leaders. This reflected the contested nature of wartime battles for martial masculinity and racial supremacy.

During the three and a half years of Japanese occupation, many soldiers fought in vain to claim and fulfill their assigned status as "martial" communities. Indian and Australian soldiers, whose service in the First World War solidified their "martial" reputations in the British Empire, were more than half of the soldiers captured after capitulation. In addition to the humiliation of surrender, they endured repeated hardships that challenged their ability to claim military masculinity and "racial" supremacy. As captives, they journeyed across Asia-Pacific in forced labor conditions that supported Japanese war aims, joining roughly 200,000 other forced laborers.[6] While white women resented being treated like "coolies" and lashed out at Asian women, soldiers often resented the British leaders who abandoned them. For Australians, the experience underlined the frailty of British power and their own tenuous claims to whiteness. For South Asian soldiers, it was yet another betrayal of imperial promises of inclusivity. Asian civilians, meanwhile, recognized that the surrender undermined the status of "martial races." Chinese civilian Chin Kee Onn found British and Australian troops during the invasion "shaky and insipid" and lacking "camaraderie."[7] While the Australians felt they had been "let down by the British," the British regarded Australians as "shirkers." Chin felt Indian troops were completely discredited for being "contaminated by discontent and alienation by fifth columnists already active within their ranks." Compared to this sorry lot, Chin found Japanese soldiers among the "toughest and fiercest" in the world. He marveled at how they fought with "fanatical ferocity."[8] The surrender called into question the imperial military ethos of "martial races," leading colonial subjects to challenge the racial exclusion that underpinned military presence and colonial rule.

From 1941 to 1945, many martial men vied for supremacy in the shadow of failing British power. Japanese General Tomoyuki Yamashita earned the name "Tiger of Malaya" due to his prompt conquest of Malaya and Singapore. Throughout the occupation, the Imperial Japanese Army exercised its own multi-ethnic colonial military praxis, relying on colonized Korean troops and locally recruited Indian and Malay police formerly serving the British. Also beneficial to Japanese goals were members of the Indian National Army (INA), who saw the Japanese invasion as an opportunity to break free from British colonialism. Many former British Indian Army personnel joined the INA to fight with the Japanese to liberate India. Yet Japanese rule also faced many challengers. Chinese men who had long feared Japanese colonialism rushed to defend Singapore by joining Dalforce, or the Singapore Overseas Chinese Anti-Japanese Volunteer Army, in December 1941. They held the line while formally conscripted British, Australian, and Indian troops retreated. Joining Dalforce and continuing the fight after capitulation were the Malayan People's Anti-Japanese Army (MPAJA), which included many communists previously imprisoned by the British. By 1943, they had the aid of Force 136, comprised of locally-recruited Asian and Eurasian military personnel and British and Australian soldiers and officers trained in jungle warfare to fight behind enemy lines. In each military unit, men demanded to be taken seriously for their martial prowess, dismantling or reinforcing exclusionary British norms of martial masculinity.

This chapter explores how captured soldiers and colonial subjects struggled to redefine or redeem martial masculinity during the Japanese occupation of Singapore and Malaya. Using war crimes trial testimonies, memoirs, oral history interviews, and soldiers' petitions, it shows how British colonial norms and expectations about military masculinity influenced soldiers' responses to the occupation and shaped their methods of fighting for or against it. Some Indian men tried to rekindle the martial race ethos through service to the Indian National Army, which allied with the Japanese in the hopes of "liberating" India. Asian and Eurasian men in units such as Force 136 and Dalforce resisted Japanese power

FIGURE 6.   Asian troops rushing to defend Singapore during the Japanese invasion. Argus (Melbourne, Vic.) Australia. Dept. of Information. Courtesy of State Library Victoria, www.slv.vic.gov.au

and hoped for British imperial honor and inclusion. Chinese communists became unlikely martial allies to British power for their tireless efforts resisting Japanese rule. As Asian fighters strove to succeed where Britain failed, they became a source of inspiration for fighting Japanese—as well as British—imperialism.

SOLDIERS INTERNED

When British leaders surrendered to the Japanese on February 15, 1942, over 100,000 soldiers from across the British Empire immediately became prisoners of war (POWs). Ultimately more than 200,000 allied POWs faced internment in this region.[9] Wartime lines of race, rank, ethnicity, and unit shaped but did not wholly determine soldiers' treatment. Australian POW Jack Turner identified several hardships that were regular features of POW experiences, including the long march to Changi POW camp and shortages of food.[10] At Changi, soldiers erected their own barbed wire fencing. Some had to bury Chinese civilians killed by Japanese soldiers. Those who tried to escape were beaten, flogged, imprisoned, and never heard from again. Even more traumatic conditions came when soldiers were relocated away from Singapore. Frequent movement on trains and ships forced them to endure food and water shortages and poor sanitation in cramped quarters, piled alongside the bodies of their fellow men-of-arms. Ships brought the added uncertainty of submarines and torpedoes. Many POWs then worked in forced labor conditions on railways intended to connect Japan's rapidly expanding empire. There, they endured maladies such as cholera, malnutrition, beriberi, malaria, and dysentery. Beatings increased over time, as did demands to work while sick and wounded. Many soldiers contemplated escape while fearing recapture and contracting tropical diseases. Turner realized the insignificance of his survival in the eyes of his captors when Japanese soldiers loaded themselves into lifeboats without offering any aid to POWs when his ship sank.[11] Even before the surrender, soldiers fought in impossible conditions without much support from British military or civilian leadership. For their efforts, they bore the brunt of the humiliation of surrender and endured the traumas of war.

Facing British and then Japanese indifference, many soldiers depended on civilians for survival, further reducing their exalted status as men of arms. Turner and Jack Williams left internment in Burma and snuck down to villages where they made friends with two Chinese brothers, a Thai gardener, and a Burmese man who provided bananas, cigarettes, breadfruit, coffee, and pawpaws.[12] Planter R. L. Inder, who served as a Sapper in the Johore Volunteer Engineers before working on the Thai-Burma Railway, remembered Tamil, Chinese, and Malay people throwing fruit into their trucks to help keep the workers alive.[13] Rasammah Bhupalan lived near a POW camp in Ipoh and recalled that her mother, Nancy, gave Nepali POWs fruit whenever they returned from their workdays. She admired their dignity—a characteristic she found rare among other POWs.[14] Chint Singh, captured in Singapore, similarly recalled that after relocation to Yakano, New Guinea, an Indigenous couple found him dying in the jungle and provided pumpkin, fish, bananas, sac sac, and sac sac cake to save his life.[15] They provided these amenities for weeks because his unit suffered from food deprivation and supply shortages. Sometimes the dynamics were opposite—in Burma, civilians relied on Australian and American soldiers killing and selling them rats because the Japanese had taken or destroyed so much food.[16] Facing the uncertainties and indignities of war, soldiers and civilians relied on one another to survive. This gave civilians repeated exposure to soldiers' frailties, underlining the loss of British power.

Despite white soldiers' dependence on Asian civilians, racial assumptions and efforts to reclaim status remained. Turner complained frequently about living in mixed POW camps, residing in former housing of Tamil rubber plantation workers, and being unable to compete for resources with civilians.[17] He hated Korean guards because, he speculated, they had been treated badly by the Japanese and enjoyed having power. He did not make a similar assumption about Indian soldiers who became their guards. Instead, he found comfort in German officers in Singapore. One spoke fluent English and gave several men tins of bully beef and some bread and sausage sandwiches. The German also "expressed his sorrow" at how Japanese soldiers treated white men, noting that "the Germans had no time for the Japanese." This white camaraderie between ostensible wartime enemies enabled Germans to retaliate against the Japanese when British and Australian soldiers could not. When cars with Japanese officers passed a work party, an NCO failed to call men to attention to salute. As a result, the Japanese officer "smacked our POW Sergeant across the face." One German sailor saw this and landed "a beautiful punch on the chin of the Japanese officer knocking him on the ground."[18] The Japanese officer simply got in the car and left. Despite British official and civilian fears that white people would receive the worst treatment from the Japanese, and Britain's own war against Germany, whiteness still carried currency for uniting Europeans during the occupation.

Such racial solidarities contrasted the treatment of Indian soldiers. Most white soldiers recognized that Indian men had different, and often more difficult, fates after the fall of Singapore. British Captain A. Weale acknowledged that the "poor Indian boys have had a dreadful time" because "brutal torture, beatings and killings had been their every day [*sic*] lot."[19] Turner, similarly, described Indians as being placed in a separate, fenced area, starved for a week, and given the "choice" to either starve or join the Indian National Army or Imperial Japanese Army. By his account, "Many hundreds of Indians were true to the colours of the red, white and blue and refused."[20] In response, Japanese soldiers severed fingers, forced water into their stomachs, and carried out other forms of torture. Despite such hardships, Turner was glad that a "few hundred Indians who loved and were true to the British" endured such things but "did not join up with the Japanese." He was heartened when Indian transport drivers shared "cigarettes and food" with prisoners "whenever the opportunity arose." Some Indian soldiers assured him that when "the time comes for the retaking of Singapore these Indians will give the British all the aid possible."[21] Indian soldiers' perceived "loyalty," and willingness to aid the British, was a prerequisite for Holman to view their suffering as unjust.

British and Japanese racism added to Indian officers' hardships. While laboring on the Thai-Burma Railway, Turner observed that British officers did not have to do work.[22] By contrast, neither British nor Japanese forces honored distinctions between Indian officers and men. Major Naranjan Singh Gill trained at the Royal Military Academy at Sandhurst and received a rank equal to British

FIGURE 7.   A starving Indian prisoner of war. Argus (Melbourne, Vic.)
Australia. Dept. of Information. Courtesy of State Library Victoria,
www.slv.vic.gov.au

officers. However, he recalled that under the Japanese, "Indian officers and men would be separated from the British; instead of the normal rule that officers of all nationalities are put in one camp, men of all nationalities are put in other camp."[23] Gill remembered a British colonel telling him that "we are handing you to the Japanese and you must now comply with their orders." Gill had to translate the order and disseminate it to the men, who felt acutely that the "British did not care what happened to us." Instead of taking care of them, British officers said, "All right, we will give them to you, the Japanese."[24] This indifference had dire consequences. According to Chint Singh, officers only gained special notice for punishment and humiliation.[25] A Japanese nursing orderly, Pte. Maida, suffered from dysentery, and his "boots became dirty with his uncontrollable motion." In response, he ordered an Indian officer, Kitial Singh, to clean them. Singh obeyed but when a little dirt remained, Maida beat him over the head with a stick until he became unconscious. Singh remained unwell for a month before dying. Similarly, when food disappeared, Japanese guards blamed Indian officers and "beat them severely," threatening them with death. If Japanese soldiers tried to instruct Indians in drill or in the Japanese language, soldiers intentionally refused to learn. As a result, "We were severely beaten, especially the officers."²⁶ Achieving officer status was a hard-earned milestone for Indian men after the First World War. After the British surrender, however, it offered no protection and created additional hardships.

Indian officers' treatment widened the distance between British and Indian experiences of the war. Captain Nirpal Chand earned the admiration of his men for organizing food-stealing campaigns and supporting those who could not march to new locations due to fatigue and illness. Chint Singh eulogized him after his execution, stating: "His loss is irreparable to us. He has guided us through many dangers of life and used to encourage us during the time of bombing and shelling."²⁷ Captain Chand had served for fifteen years, fought in the Indian borderlands, and came from a military family, including a father who fought in France and Mesopotamia in the First World War. He embodied everything that the colonial Indian soldier had once been: a generational warrior with years of distinguished service. His suffering and sacrifice endeared him to his men—a common trait of Indian officers who tried to help their men amidst risks of torture or execution.²⁸ By contrast, British officers' absence meant that they could not and did not advocate for them. Indian soldiers' reverence for their Indian officers created unity between Indian men of arms and isolation from the British leaders who abandoned them.

Wartime hardships also meant that many Indian men oscillated between enthusiasm and ambivalence for Japanese rule. According to Major E. L. Sawyer of the 22nd Mountain Regiment, Gurbaksh Singh Dhillon of the 1/14 Punjab Regiment, M. A. K. Rana of the Kapurthala State Infantry, and Havildar Sawarn Singh of the 1/14 Punjab Regiment worked as guards in Changi and "showed very marked anti-British feelings."²⁹ Rana apparently partook in a firing squad that executed two British and two Australian POWs. Nursing Sister Early found Sikh guards "beastly" and "much more intolerant" than Japanese guards because they lived in fear of reprisals, echoing Turner's perception of Korean guards. She detested that all "were very sorry for themselves." Even when they aided internees, she still believed that "NONE were to be trusted" and "we loathed" them.³⁰ Even when Sikh guards behaved kindly toward white internees, they could not avoid being "loathed," reversing a century-old fondness for "loyal Sikh" clichés.³¹ In turn, Indian service to the Japanese was rarely an unambiguous display of loyalty or disloyalty to either imperial power. Indian soldiers lived in ever-evolving circumstances that made it difficult to survive. Some decided that fighting would bring salvation.

FORGING A "NATIONAL" ARMY

Facing the indignity of surrender and imprisonment, some South Asian soldiers fought to retain their claims to "martial race" supremacy. One method was to join the Indian National Army (INA), founded by intelligence officer Major Iwaichi Fujiwara of the Imperial Japanese Army and Sikh officer Mohan Singh of the 1/14 Punjab Regiment of the Indian Army.[32] Many scholars have discussed the INA's role in the Indian independence movement, its charismatic leader S. C. Bose, the innovative all-women "Rani of Jhansi" unit, the broken promises of Japanese leaders, and its limited successes on the battlefield.[33] However, the INA also represented a simultaneous rejection of British imperialism while embracing many of its core tenets of racial military recruitment. Its initial creation supported two battalions of one hundred men each. Ultimately, tens of thousands of Indian men and women participated in the Japanese occupation or fought in campaigns against British and British imperial troops, most famously along the Indo-Burmese border. Those serving in the INA often believed that the British let them down and that the Japanese were earnest in their support of Indian independence. Others found the Japanese their best chance of survival. Ultimately, many INA personnel saw Japanese leaders as inheritors to, rather than opponents of, Britain's racial military rule in Asia. Nonetheless, challenging British power enabled some South Asian fighters to imagine a world after empire.

After capitulation, Japanese military leaders gathered about 40,000 Indian prisoners at Farrer Park in Singapore to give them the "choice" of becoming POWs or fighting for independence.[34] Many answered the call with ambivalence. Indian officer Gill could not help but notice the "domineering and arrogant attitude" of Japanese soldiers. He joined the INA to address the housing and health of POWs, which included tens of thousands of men lying in an area of roughly two football fields with no sanitation, no latrines, and no water.[35] Similarly, Shah Nawaz Khan had a long family tradition of service in the Indian Army but joined the INA to protect POWs from execution.[36] While some men joined voluntarily, many others did so after being subjected to torture by Japanese or INA soldiers. Many POWs felt trapped in an impossible "choice" between joining the INA or remaining prisoners. When they did not comply, Japanese leaders denied them the treatment and status of other POWs.[37] The fall from desirable "martial race" to prisoner, laborer, or collaborator proved difficult and traumatic for many men. Some hoped that fighting for independence would redeem them.

One aim of the Indian National Army was to revitalize South Asian masculinity from the stain of colonial military service and surrender. In his introduction to Mohan Singh's memoir, Fujiwara called the INA "a fierce tingling of Asiatic spirit."[38] This contrasted Mohan Singh's feeling that many young men "lost their sense of adventure and initiative" under British rule.[39] He recalled that when he tried to join the army, British officers derided him for being "too young and not strong and tough enough." While he eventually proved his athleticism and gained military employment, he had to participate repeatedly in "servile ceremonies." He butted heads with British leaders who resented him for swaggering and feeling important. He found some officers "inhuman and rude." Yet it took the war to fully expose Indian soldiers' emasculation. Singh felt powerless that their "brave soldiers" had to "fight as mercenaries" under "alien rulers." He anticipated that British victory could only be achieved "through the untold sufferings of the Indian soldiers," which "further strengthened the chains of our bondage." Soldiers wrestled with "being dubbed cowards" for not fighting in the war, and so "glory or the desire to achieve higher rank" enabled their "humble submission" and "surrender of our will."[40]

Despite clear problems with their British service, not all Indian men were enthusiastic about joining the Japanese. For Mehervan Singh, most INA and Indian Independence League (IIL) personnel were not pro-Japanese at all—many had Chinese friends and opposed the Japanese due to their actions in China.[41] He compared the plight of Indian soldiers to that of the Chinese workers who supplied food to the Japanese despite Japanese military leaders' hostility toward the Chinese community. Singh remarked, "Are we to say they were pro Japanese? They had to do their jobs, maybe to save their necks."[42] Naranjan Singh Gill's impression was that only leaders like Rash Behari Bose and A. M. Nair were truly pro-Japanese.[43] In fact, sometimes Japanese critics, such as Satyanand Puri, died in mysterious ways, such as a plane crash on the way to Tokyo. Gill could not help but wonder if the Japanese had tampered with the plane. On his own visit to Japan in 1942, Gill sensed that many Indian men "were not free." In Japan they enjoyed the luxuries that British soldiers had experienced in Malaya prior to the war, with visits "to Geisha girls to entertain and gave us good eats and drinks." Still, he often felt like a subordinate because Prime Minister Tojo gave them commands, told them to forget their "British heritage," or refused to let them speak.[44] By noting their inferior treatment, Gill suggests that Japanese racism and exclusion, like that of the British, were major impediments to long-term allegiance.

Ultimately, Gill's apprehensions reflected broader tensions in the INA. He shared his hesitation with Mohan Singh in a Gurdwara in Singapore.[45] Singh promised Gill that "should it later appear that the Japanese are merely exploiting

us and we will be worse off later, then you will join me in resisting them." Singh
kept his word and stepped down from INA leadership after he suspected that
the Japanese were replacing rather than ousting the British in India. This led to
the disbandment of the INA in 1942. Gill and other skeptical Indian men were
jailed. Such experiences convinced Gill that if the British had not been so badly
defeated, the INA would not have formed at all.[46] In Gill's view, it was British
failure, more than Japanese success, that hastened the formation of the INA.
However, by 1943, Indian political leader and revolutionary S. C. Bose, along
with Lt. Col. J. K. Bhonsale, formerly of the 5 Mahrattas, revived the INA and
took over its leadership. Bose declared Singapore the "graveyard of the British
Empire" and expanded INA recruitment to the Indian civil population across
Southeast Asia, hoping to mobilize the three million people of South Asian ancestry in the region.[47] This included the formation of the all-women's Rani of
Jhansi Regiment, further blurring gendered distinctions between soldier and civilian and increasing martial enthusiasm for Indian independence.

The existence of the INA complicated Indian men's status as POWs. Those
who rushed to join the Japanese in 1942 were largely disbanded by 1943, derided as
"turncoats," and sent overseas on working parties, losing their status as soldiers.[48]
There, they faced eighteen-hour workdays, malnutrition, and beatings for their
initial enthusiasm.[49] By contrast, those who initially refused to renounce the British enjoyed better food and housing. This was largely due to the advocacy of Major
Bahadur Singh of the 4/19 Hyderabad Regiment.[50] However, Singh faced criticisms from men across political allegiances. Some Indian POWs called him too
"Nip[ponese] happy" while Sarwan Singh of the 1/14 Punjab Regiment reported
him for spreading "anti-Japanese propaganda amongst the troops." The Major
lost his ability to advocate for soldiers in October 1943 for this reason. Meanwhile,
after S. C. Bose's arrival, the INA returned to being "an endless source of worry
and anxiety to all loyal prisoners," in the words of one British officer. By the end
of 1943, conditions for Indian POWs deteriorated. Deaths of Indian POWs in
hospitals spiked in 1944, with a peak of 125 in October. Since British POW camps
had their "own troubles," they provided "no adequate assistance."[51]

Despite such shortcomings, numerous revolutionary recruits enthusiastically
joined the INA because it claimed to have egalitarian intentions to liberate India.
Mehervan Singh, a civilian who worked in revolutionary sabotage, recalled that recruitment was carried out by Mr. N. Raghovan, a Penang lawyer. He interviewed
candidates to ensure that they were not beholden to "Hindu-Sikh food fads" that
would hinder their service.[52] This was a direct wish of Mohan Singh, whose experience with segregated kitchens in the Indian Army inspired him to "introduce

common kitchens for one and all."[53] Similarly, S. C. Bose made a point of sitting on the floor and eating with INA men instead of dining at fancy tables, emphasizing his egalitarianism.[54] He refused to serve beef or pork to avoid alienating Hindus and Muslims respectively, and carefully avoided symbols, phrases, and songs that had connections to particular religious, ethnic, or political communities.[55] Yet other biases remained. Mr. Raghovan preferred a recruit who was an "intelligent young man, not labour type."[56] As a result, while men had religious plurality, with about half of the volunteers Sikh and others Christian, Hindu, and Muslim, the majority shared a background in English schools and had received their military instruction in English. As a result, men recruited for revolutionary activity in Southeast Asia mirrored the demographics of British officer recruiting in India. The growing emphasis on an English-language, interfaith force that was not "beholden" to religious or caste custom was a cornerstone of making martial men fit for British colonial service.[57] The opposition to recruiting a "labour type" also underlined sharp class and caste biases. It contrasted the composition of the women in the Rani of Jhansi Regiment—many of whom came from laboring backgrounds.[58] This amplified the gendered and classed distinctions between units, which relegated the Rani of Jhansi Regiment largely to ceremonial and supportive duties.

Despite these realities, many women of the INA's all-women Rani of Jhansi Regiment delighted in the INA's egalitarian intentions. Rasammah Bhupalan, a Ceylonese Tamil Christian teenager from Ipoh, felt that "class consciousness had been totally eliminated."[59] She remembered the "exhilarating" feeling of marching with other women and girls through the streets of Singapore in a regiment named for the Rani of Jhansi, a woman ruler who waged war against the British in 1857. While Bhupalan enjoyed a comfortable childhood in a family of teachers, she recognized that most RJR recruits previously worked as laborers. Those women "found themselves free from the drudgery and what in reality was more a life of slavery. The retreat of British management from estates at the outset of the war left them abandoned."[60] Bhupalan alleged that serving in the RJR made them "for the first time completely freed from the heavy burden of being considered an underclass of coolies. Now with heads held high, bound together with their comrades they experienced egalitarianism at its highest level. They were soldiers for India's freedom." This made them "no longer prepared to undergo the indignities of their pre-war life."[61] Ex-estate laborer Pachaimmal remembered things differently. She suggested that while life was not ideal under the British, compared to the Japanese the former "treated us fine." However, once the Japanese arrived, men "were taken to the railway and we were taken to work on dockyards to bind fences."[62] In the absence of British management, Japanese officials employed Indian estate employees as managers who often won Japanese favor by mistreating laborers.[63] Many women faced extreme sexual coercion from Japanese soldiers and newly-appointed managers. While Bhupalan's education and social position made her regard estate workers as little better than "slaves" who relished in fighting the British for liberation, estate women focused on finding a way out of their already precarious lives as conditions worsened.

As this difference of opinion suggests, not everything in the RJR was egalitarian. Bhupalan recalled being demoted by one of the RJR officers, adjutant Lt. Thaver, for being "very recalcitrant and indisciplined."[64] By contrast, S. C. Bose personally promoted her to Lieutenant, reviving her enthusiasm for the cause. Yet other inequities persisted. When the RJR arrived in Burma, Japanese soldiers mocked their insistence that they were trained soldiers, believing them instead to be "comfort women" (forced sex workers) for the INA. More frustratingly, despite their training, they were not permitted to participate in battle, even during the terrible reversals at Imphal that ultimately forced their retreat. The RJR "felt deeply that we had been denied the opportunity to prove our mettle on the front line." Adding insult to injury, two women were killed in an attack on their retreating train. This dampened their earlier enthusiasm to endure all sorts of suffering and hardships because "we were freedom fighters dedicated to the liberation of India and the ever-living memory of our Rani of Jhansi drove us on."[65] Their inability to fight, largely due to gender inequity, betrayed the promise of egalitarian liberation.

Over time it became clear that the speed and circumstances of the INA's founding hampered its success. Some worried that the immense diversity of the forces stood in the way of unity and operational effectiveness. Also concerning was that when the INA fought the British Indian Army, they could encounter units to which their men formerly belonged. Others might reunite with friends and family members. Some men only reluctantly joined the INA, so seeing familiar faces on the battlefield might awaken their desire to return. Others worried that INA men surrendered with the British and were too unmotivated, frightened, or exhausted to fight effectively.[66] While some hoped that battles for Burma—Imphal the most famous among them—would liberate India from British rule, troops faced food shortages that compelled them to eat dry rice and grass. Japanese and Indian leaders also fought constantly over chain of command, including who would get to command Indian forces. Since many recruits were civilians rather than soldiers, their limited training and unfamiliarity with harsh military punishments limited their effectiveness.[67] Things looked dire for the military prospects of the INA by July 1944 but Bose encouraged them to fight on. By 1945, facing Japanese supply shortages and lost battles, many INA units deserted to the British.

Despite the INA's ultimate failures, these were neither inevitable nor foreseen in 1942. Many South Asian soldiers willingly, reluctantly, or forcibly served Japanese aims to secure anti-colonial futures. Yet the INA's poor results forced men to endure further humiliation. Lee Kip Lim met an INA soldier named Kurana who returned to India hoping to be embraced as a liberator. Instead, he returned to Punjab, finding military men and their families who regarded INA men as traitors. At one point, Kurana was detained. Worse still, Kurana's home was in land that became Pakistan rather than India on independence in 1947, forcing him to move to Delhi. Despite his efforts to free his homeland from colonial rule, he ultimately lost his home altogether.[68] Even remaining "faithful" to the British Indian Army did not secure men a warm welcome or continued employment. Major P. S. Leathart of the 9th Gurkha Rifles recalled that "no soldier of the Indian Army who had been in Jap[anese] custody, for however short a period, was permitted to rejoin his unit or take part in any active service against the Jap[ane]s[e]."[69] Leathart reasoned that this was because of the INA, "a traitor organisation." He believed that none of his Nepali troops joined, but nonetheless, "we never again saw those men." He considered it "bad luck that no exception could be made to the rule."[70] Whether fighting for or against the British, most South Asian men lost hope for belonging or employment because of military racism.

Despite early optimism that the Indian National Army would inherit the "martial" status of the colonial forces, and create a united India free of discrimination, these hopes withered by the end of the war. Years after Indian independence, Lakshmi Saghal reflected on what had been lost with the failure of the INA: "a Free, Secular, United India." It had been a source of optimism and pride that the ranks of the INA were filled with "Christians, Hindus, Muslims and Sikhs. They hailed from Punjab, Bengal, Kerala, Tamil Nadu and Andhra."[71] For the women of the INA who, in some cases, left the "slave" conditions of plantations and mines in Malaya, the disappointment was even more acute. The "martial races" ethos was never meant to include them, and it never did. Some INA men hoped that service in an anti-colonial force would renew their "martial race" identities as a martial heritage that predated British rule. For others it was a way to rewrite who belonged as a "martial race" and who did not.

CONTESTED COLLABORATIONS

While many former Indian troops fought with the Japanese, other former colonial subjects fought against them. During the invasion, many Chinese subjects fled or faced targeted violence from the Japanese military. This left the Malayan

Communist Party (MCP) as the strongest Chinese-led political organization in Malaya during the war.[72] Its military arm, the Malayan People's Anti-Japanese Army (MPAJA), numbered roughly three to four thousand at the start of the war and nearly doubled by the end. While the MCP and MPAJA boasted Indian and Malay members, their connections with Chinese nationalism in Singapore after 1937 strengthened its Chinese composition.[73] Yet for many communists, the appeal of communism was ethical rather than nationalistic. Former guerilla Lin Guan Ying noted that "it was easy to organise the workers and farmers because they understood that they were being oppressed and exploited. There was no need for theories and persuasion."[74] Communist leader Chin Peng recalled similarly that he had a strong interest in "thinking of how to fight for justice, how to help the poor people. Sort of Robin Hood type of thing."[75] This sense of moral justice inspired a lifelong fight against both British and Japanese imperialism. For British leaders who lost their imperial vanguard, communists became their longest allies. This did not end British fears and racialization of them.

In many ways, British leaders' decision to align with communists exposed how racism undermined prewar British military preparation. In August 1941, F. Spencer Chapman, who served with the Special Training School (STS 101) in Singapore, recognized the need to train Chinese, Malay, and Indian personnel in jungle warfare to remain behind enemy lines. While his proposal received official consideration, high-ranking British leaders opposed "the employment of Asiatics" because admitting "the possibility of enemy penetration would have a disastrous psychological effect on the Oriental mind."[76] In other words, acknowledging and preparing for occupation would injure British prestige in the eyes of Asian subjects. Equally concerning, for some British officials, was that arming Chinese people would make it impossible to exclude those who "belonged to an illegal organization, the Malayan Communist Party."[77] It made no sense to British leaders, who spent interwar years combating communism, to arm them. Through concerns about the fragile "Oriental mind" and hidden communists, British racism resulted in inadequate preparation for war.

When Chapman learned of leaders' refusal to train Asian personnel in jungle warfare, he recognized it as a tactical failure. He noted that "the Chinese had already been fighting the Jap[ane]s[e] for years and had made a magnificent name for themselves in exactly the type of warfare we envisaged."[78] British leaders reassessed the project in November 1941 but reiterated that "no Asiatics in Malaya could be trained for such work." The proposal only gained approval after the invasion and bombing began on December 8. This proved reactionary to the Malayan Communist Party's own request "to form a military force to fight the Jap[ane]s[e]"

while "armed by the British." The commander-in-chief once again initially refused this proposal, given long-standing institutional resentment of communist
militarism. He eventually agreed given the dire situation of the Japanese invasion.
Soon, British leaders released communist prisoners, jailed in the interwar period,
to fight. Chapman himself went into the jungle in January 1942 on instruction
that he was would become "the liaison officer to the Chinese guerillas." However,
due to "the disorganization caused by the speed of the British retreat, nobody had
actually informed MCP headquarters of this."[79] British failures forced Chapman
to endure periods of extreme privation and loneliness living and working behind
enemy lines without a clear plan.

Chapman's early war experiences forced him to come face-to-face with British soldiers' inadequacy for jungle warfare. He stated that "the British private
soldier" was unprepared for life in the jungle and could only be expected to live
a few weeks or months in these conditions.[80] Former communist guerilla Lin
Guan Ying agreed, recalling that the British who stayed in the jungle with communists were "very pampered." Despite food shortages, they "would not eat rice
but insisted on having bread and butter. They were even too lazy to cook rice for
themselves."[81] Meanwhile, Chapman recognized that, despite his prewar life as a
rugged mountaineer and sportsman, jungle life threatened his physical strength.
He became very ill with dysentery and "fainted and rolled right down the hill to
the stream" while on the latrine. He had to be carried away by stretcher to avoid
being found by the Japanese. Ultimately, jungle life cost him his bodily strength,
reducing him from an original weight of twelve stone to "seven or eight stone"
with limbs "like chicken's legs—straight sticks with exaggerated bulges at the
joints—my ribs and shoulder bones stood out, and my face was quite unrecog-
nizable; deep hollows had appeared on my temples, and my cheek- and jawbones
protruded like a skeleton."[82] Remaining to fight cost him the physicality that
defined his masculinity.

Chapman's experience of living with guerillas also made him feel isolated
and powerless. He "suffered all the time from a sense of frustration and impotence."[83] He regularly felt like "a prisoner." He lacked "freedom of movement"
because he knew too much about the camps and so the guerillas could not risk his
capture. His poor Chinese and Malay language skills also made him feel "it was
impossible to escape." Meanwhile, his only access to news was English-language
Japanese newspapers, which exaggerated or invented information about the war.
He heard that Burma, the Dutch East Indies, the Philippines, and Australia had
all fallen to the Japanese. He read that the British fleet had been destroyed and
that the Germans and Japanese had succeeded in surrounding India. Britain had

been so badly blitzed, the news claimed, that the government fled to Canada. China allegedly had fallen. Communist news was equally exaggerated in the opposite direction. Meanwhile, the "evasion and equivocation" of communist leaders made Chapman feel incapable of knowing what was true or untrue. The result had a "depressing psychological effect" that made him wonder, "Where then could I go?"[84]

Chapman's experiences with the Menchis patrol, No. 6 Independent Anti-Japanese Regiment, beginning in July 1942 enabled him to vent his frustrations by criticizing communists. He realized that "many of the Chinese who had joined the guerillas in a fit of enthusiasm were becoming disillusioned."[85] They resented not being able to visit their homes, which had superior food compared to the camps. While many fought to keep "the Japanese out of Malaya," it appeared that the Japanese "had come to stay." As a result, many early guerillas either deserted or became Japanese informers. Chapman racialized this as a flaw of Chinese people being "single-minded in their hatred of the Japanese" but also willing to work as an "informer." He blamed "the Oriental mind" for this willingness to change sides, echoing his military commanders. Yet he was acutely aware that his own leaders had little devotion to him. For eleven months, he practically "saw no white men." This left him to feel like an ethnographic object, since many of those he encountered "had never before seen an Englishman at such close quarters, or so intimately." He had the uncanny feeling of people standing and staring at him "as if I were some new kind of animal."[86] Feeling different and vulnerable, Chapman experienced what military service felt like for colonial soldiers who fought in Singapore and Malaya. He tried to assert power by relying on racist tropes to explain the behavior of the communists who saved his life.

Working with the Menchis ultimately gave Chapman some sympathy for communist fighters that still reinforced racist assumptions. He regarded "the rank and file" as "absolutely magnificent" and admired "their courage, fortitude, and consistent cheerfulness in adversity."[87] He noted that he was "more in sympathy with the men in the camps than with their political leaders." Class played a role in Chapman's admiration. Most of the men in the Menchis were former rubber tappers, tin-mining laborers, gardeners, house servants, and other laborers. Those who supported British trade, comfort, and profitability before the war, in other words, were the communist rank and file. Among leaders, by contrast, Chapman was annoyed by men like Ah Chong, whom he felt "had been educated far beyond his intelligence," making him "a fanatic." Ah Chong's job before the war apparently was "to visit the mines and foment strikes." It did not help that Ah Chong believed that Chapman was left behind to "spy upon the activities of the M.C.P"—a reasonable concern given interwar anti-communism. Chapman also disdained group leader Low Kow as "tall and friendly, but very stupid." Low Kow had experience fighting the Japanese in Hainan but in Chapman's view he had "no military knowledge whatsoever."[88] Praising low-ranking men as brave and cheerful, while condemning educated men as "stupid" or ill-informed troublemakers, reinforced colonial tropes about Asian militarism.[89] Those who had the education, training, and power to challenge Chapman were undesirable compared to those accustomed to subservient cheerfulness. The latter were the ideal colonial subjects.

Chapman also revealed how gendered assumptions about Asian women influenced his response to camp life. He was impressed by communist women, who were "very keen to fight the Japanese" but rarely had the chance.[90] Most taught songs, filed paperwork, and nursed. Whenever they moved to a new camp, the women "carried just as heavy loads as the men and certainly showed no less fortitude." Due to their "incredible bravery," he had "the greatest admiration for these girls." He also feared them because they could be "as pitiless and cruel as the men in dealing with a captured Jap[anese soldier] or traitor." Still, he believed that "they had a certain humanizing effect on the rougher coolies who predominated in the camps." Women, it seemed, were necessary to balance the class diversity of communist recruits. At the same time, they "expected to be, and were, treated exactly like the men."[91] Communist guerilla Chen Xiu Zhu echoed this view, recalling that "in our collective way of living, there was no difference between men and women."[92] Still, Chapman was relieved that women's presence did not cause "sex complications." This did not stop him from noting that women were well-groomed and "always looked attractive" with "straight black hair . . . cut in a short bob" and "slim figures."[93] His quickness to assess women's attractiveness reiterated his tendency to claim power amidst powerlessness.

Chapman's efforts to reassert gender and racial supremacy chafed against his communist companions' awareness of British inadequacy. He felt embarrassed to "live with people who had lost every shred of faith in the British." He recognized "that they had been badly let down by us, and did not hesitate to say so. They questioned not only our military competence but our very integrity and courage." It helped that Chapman had no role in the prewar government of Malaya. Still, his comrades continually asked "why we had allowed the Japanese to develop their Malayan Fifth Column undisturbed, why the British Army in Malaya had not been equipped or trained to fight in the jungle, and above all why we had armed the Malays but had refused to train and arm the Chinese." This last point felt unjustifiable because, as Chapman had also argued, "they had been fighting the common enemy for years."[94] Chapman claimed that he remained silent and un-responsive in these conversations, unable to justify the racial exclusion that con-tributed to the defeat and surrender. Yet he clearly shared their frustrations. His memoir walked a fine line between noting that he "identified myself with them as a comrade in arms" without accepting "their party views."[95] This contrasted other British men, such as Pat Noone, who, according to Chapman, was "extremely interested in the theory of Communism" like "most intelligent people." However, Noone became "dissatisfied with the Chinese interpretation of Communism" be-cause of an "unreasonably anti-British bias."[96] Noone disappeared after challeng-ing communist teachings to the Temier (Orang Asli) people.[97] Acknowledging that "intelligent people" felt an interest in communism, but that guerilla's "anti-British bias" was an impediment to long-term enthusiasm, Chapman implied that he found some commonality with the communists who sheltered him. Yet Noone's disappearance and death reiterated that affinity was a dangerous game.

Ultimately, Chapman found purpose and community when he rejoined other white men. He had the chance to visit John Maurice Cotterill who lived in Johore with a group of "bandits" because the communists were eager to recruit them.[98] Compared to the communists, Chapman found these bandits "cheerful and like-able rogues" who "did not suffer from the political and social inhibitions which made the guerillas in some respects so infuriating to live with." Prior to the war this group distilled illegal alcohol. During the occupation they targeted "Chinese towkays who were helping the Jap[ane]s[e]." As a result, the "standard of living was much more luxurious" with the bandits. Still, Chapman noted that "discipline and organization were non-existent." He associated this with the prevalence of women, because the leader "had no control over his men" and took "the wife of a Chinese he was alleged to have shot, and she ran the camp." Roughly "half the men lived with their women in squalid shacks in the jungle edge." Unlike the egalitarian communists, Chapman found that these "likeable rogues" depended on gender vi-olence, capturing "Malay women in the jungle by firing over their heads." This ap-parently alienated some communist recruiters who visited the camp and returned with "frightful stories of the orgies and lawlessness." Despite their vices, Chapman found the bandits "first-class guerilla material, and thirsting to 'have a crack' at the Jap[anese]." Life with them was so attractive that Cotterill remained with them despite Chapman's proposal that they try to escape Malaya. Chapman reluctantly returned to the communists, believing that "my work was with Communist gueril-las and not with bandits."[99] Continuing his work rather than staying with "likeable rogues" was no doubt made more difficult by Cotterill's unwillingness to escape, reiterating that white men often failed to do their duty for the empire.

On Christmas Day, 1943, Chapman finally found white men committed to restoring British rule and fighting the Japanese occupation. John Davis and Richard Broome, along with Chapman, combined various threads of British resistance, including the 101st Special Training School, to work with Force 136, which challenged the Japanese occupation throughout Asia.[100] Force 136 was remarkable for embodying elements of Britain's colonial armies but with a greater social, ethnic, religious, and cultural diversity. Chapman noted that there was a broad range of support for such efforts, with Malay civilians seeing "the rottenness of their new over-lords" and Chinese people having high morale and supporting guerillas throughout the war.[101] This inspired British leaders to send "Europeans who knew the languages and the country" to "direct Chinese" agents to "collect information and make contact with the guerillas." A key mover in this was Lim Bo Seng, who came from a well-known Singapore family and fled to India during the war.[102] He recruited Straits-born Chinese fighters to return to Malaya by mid-1943. Force 136 also worked with Lai Teck and Chin Peng, representing the MCP and MPAJA, by January 1944.[103] Asian military allies became essential for resisting the occupation. Unlike communists, the men of Force 136 were freedom fighters who inspired civilians against the Japanese yet remained in the service of the British. This would not earn them the respect that they felt they deserved.

Unfortunately, there were signs that all was not well in Force 136. One issue was that they relied on good relations with the MPAJA. Since many men in Force 136 had been educated civilians or police before the war, they struggled to cooperate with lower-class former rubber tappers and servants bearing arms as communists.[104] Another "very big problem," according to Tan Chong Tee, was that "[e]veryone thought they were heroes."[105] He believed that many Force 136 volunteers joined to establish careers for themselves after the war. Other Force 136 members worried, much like the men of the INA did, that they had insufficient training, including ignorance about the Malay language. Like the Japanese volunteers who aided the British in 1915, Force 136 volunteers wanted assurances that they would be treated fairly and that their "pay and compensation were clarified by the British." Yet trust was a recurring issue. Tan believed that no "matter what you said, the British would always be suspicious. They would not believe you. On the surface, they displayed much goodwill. Actually, they were very scared of you." British leaders constantly feared that the men they trained were "anti-British."[106] This led some British leaders to pick favorites, including Lai Teck, a Vietnamese double agent who spied on the MPAJA for the British. Unfortunately, after his capture by the Japanese, he spied on both the MPAJA and the British.[107] A consequence was the capture and death of Lim Bo Seng, a situation that Tan regarded as "a good leader, sacrificing himself for the country."[108] Tan believed that British leaders were reluctant to investigate the death of Lim Bo Seng because of the involvement of Lai Teck, which would reveal "British responsibility."[109]

Another problem, for Tan, was that British leaders were skilled at dividing and conquering their own forces. In Tan's view, they would recruit one or two people to be close to them and "divide the organisation from within, thereby impacting the solidarity. They were scared that the Chinese would unite."[110] One of the worst culprits, he insisted, was John Davis. He found Davis to be "selfish and ambitious," which included sowing "discord among the members" and choosing "his own confidants."[111] Tan recalled: "Because Davis was biased, there was preferential treatment towards the people he favoured. Those who were not on good terms with him or were not close to him received secondary treatment."[112] He recalled that Davis tried to bribe men into compliance while also giving war spoils to his favorites. Tan insisted that Davis, not unlike the communist leaders Chapman criticized, often withheld information. By contrast, he found Broome "one of the best leaders" because he "cooperated with us" and "knew that Davis handled matters unfairly."[113] Despite finally offering diverse Asian military personnel the opportunity to defend Malaya, British distrust ensured mutual suspicion and resentment.

Tan also believed that British leaders were incapable of recognizing their debt to the Asian men of Force 136. He felt that they wanted "to recover from the disgrace of losing Singapore" by claiming that "the glory of recovering the territory belonged only to the British."[114] This stung for many colonial subjects whose anti-Japanese militarism predated the occupation. Tan had done anti-Japanese work in Singapore and China before the war—a feat which amplified his feeling that the British failed to defend the colony. During the invasion and occupation, he lost his brother and mother in the anti-Chinese violence of the *Sook Ching*. Despite having "sacrificed ourselves," Asian men felt that they "were not recognised appropriately for all our contributions and sufferings." He felt so "discontented with the British" that he refused an invitation to attend a victory parade in England. Instead, he worried that the British enabled the MPAJA to hunt down "traitors and lackeys," making postwar life "rather chaotic."[115] Administrator Wilfred Blythe agreed that the MPAJA took the opportunity to behave "in an arrogant and ruthless fashion" including "paying off old scores" and "eliminating not only so-called collaborators but all who had the temerity to oppose their demands."[116] Unlike Tan, though, he saw the negative responses to the MPAJA's task of regaining control of police and the countryside as racial antagonism. He viewed the predominantly Chinese MPAJA as "resented and feared by the

Malays" while the Chinese community always greeted them "with enthusiasm."[117] He noted that Chinese civilians equated the MPAJA with resistance to the Japanese and "symbolic of the new-found might of China herself."[118] By contrast, Tan claimed that he proposed to train and find jobs for the MPAJA so that they could reincorporate into society, but Davis apparently said they "should not think too much" about it.[119] As a result, anyone considered a "collaborator," especially Malays and women coerced into sexual labor, faced targeted violence that often verged on ethnic cleansing.[120] Men who lost family because of the British surrender and Japanese occupation, and kept fighting when British leaders fled, found themselves discarded and ignored.

Asian men's criticisms of their white officers in Force 136 did not prevent these leaders from receiving lofty praise for their efforts. Major E. H. Peacock received an award nomination that emphasized his battle with heatstroke, his "considerable exhaustion," and his rigorous efforts to save a fellow officer.[121] Lieutenant John Maurice Cotterill received a lengthy commendation for remaining behind even though he "could have got away." Instead, he led forces in the jungle, enduring an "unstable existence" from December 1941 until June 1942, when they were invited to "join a band of Chinese guerillas." He did so, the nominee insisted, only after learning that Singapore had fallen and "there was no chance of them rejoining the British Troops." Cotterill received praise for having "volunteered to remain and do a dangerous job, regardless of his own fate."[122] The nomination did not mention that he preferred living with Chinese guerillas over trying to escape with Chapman. Still, compared to the number of British leaders and officers who fled duty during the invasion, simply remaining behind became praiseworthy. Politically ambiguous actions—like abandoning his unit or joining Chinese guerillas—turned into selfless devotion. By contrast, Asian personnel in Force 136 only received award nominations when serving in active battlefields like Burma, for securing numerous fatalities, or for putting themselves in grave personal danger that exceeded living in the jungle.[123] This underlined how British leaders saw simply remaining to fight as praiseworthy for white, but not Asian, men.

As Tan suggests, the occupation years made it difficult to know who could claim the "British" victory for themselves. The first boots on the ground to recapture Malaya were often Asian, rather than British or Australian, forces. When women of the Rani of Jhansi Regiment were captured, it was Force 136 that held them.[124] Similarly, many of the men who collected testimonies from former internees and Japanese guards were also from Force 136. Indian and Nepali soldiers often liberated POW camps and disarmed guerillas, while communists took food to Changi and Sime Road prisoners in the final days of the occupation.[125] As a result, former communist guerilla Lin Guan Ying insisted that they "were the ones who defeated the Japanese; the British did not do anything. We were the ones who fought on the battlefront, not them."[126] This forced British administrator Wilfred Blythe to admit that at the surrender parade in Singapore and the official entry into Ipoh, it was not British troops but the MPAJA which received roars of acclamation from the crowds."[127] Yet communists entered a postwar world governed by a colonial state that distrusted them. Many other colonial subjects felt ambivalent about participating in or claiming victory due to their difficult memories of war and struggles for inclusion in the postwar world. This deepened the hostility, already present from the surrender, about British leaders' capacity to use, and then forget, Asian military personnel.

CONFRONTING ASIAN HEROISM

After the war, Straits Settlements Governor Shenton Thomas acknowledged British leaders' gratitude to Asian colonial subjects by reviving prewar colonial clichés. He responded to criticisms of the surrender by insisting that Malaya was a stable colony with a loyal population. He celebrated the Malay Regiment because it "fought well on Singapore island and gave little ground."[128] The broader Asian community, in his view, never complained about war taxation and gave lavishly to funds and subscriptions. He singled out Chinese people for being "intensely loyal and proud of their connection with the Throne." Many Straits-born Chinese people were "British in all but name" and "showed splendid fortitude and loyalty during the campaign and the occupation." While "they suffered terribly at the hands of the Japanese," they "started the resistance movement before Singapore fell" and became "its leaders during the following years." Because of these contributions, Shenton Thomas believed that "the success of the war effort made by Malaya was very largely due to the support given by the Asiatic population."[129] Unfortunately, this enthusiastic praise did not translate into material gratitude.

One roadblock to assigning heroic status to Asian men was prevalent rumors about fifth column activity. Many accused Malay civilians and Indian soldiers of aiding the Japanese invasion and occupation.[130] Shenton Thomas, by contrast, stated that he knew of no credible cases of fifth column activity, despite "an abundance of allegations."[131] In conversation with Shenton Thomas, Inspector General of the Straits Settlements Police Arthur Dickinson expressed that "the amount of genuine fifth-column activity in the Colony was astonishingly small. Hundreds of hysterical reports were received and investigated in the weeks preceding the capitulation." Of these reports, police and special tribunals found only a hundred worthy of investigation and only a few truly credible. Shenton Thomas regarded the numerous accusations as "war hysteria." Ultimately, he believed that military paranoia was to blame. He found that "military officers" possessed "a preconceived conviction and even fear, due to complete ignorance of the country and its peoples, that fifth column influences were everywhere at work." Racism in the military, in other words, made military personnel distrust the Asian civilian population of a country they were meant to protect. Shenton Thomas hoped that "in fairness to the great mass of the Asiatic population," military officials would stop making accusations and instead "make it clear that these activities were isolated acts which did not affect the course of the campaign."[132] Despite the governor's claims that military racism alienated civilians by exaggerating accusations, he offered no proposal to address the military's race problem. Rather, Singapore and Malaya would be governed by the British Military Administration until 1946.

In condemning military leaders, Shenton Thomas revealed his own biases. Internment left him isolated from the day-to-day realities of towns and villages under occupation. This led him to believe that disloyalty did not exist. Denying reports as "hysterical" and blaming military leaders for "pre-conceived convictions" ignored the concerns of the non-interned Asian civilians who filed them. Instead, Shenton Thomas insisted that Malaya possessed a loyal colonial population eager to serve British interests with "Malays, Chinese, and Tamils" aiding Europeans in the jungle and "rarely if ever" betraying them.[133] He found people "of all races" who helped "the resistance movements" with food, clothes, and other materials, despite fears of death. He therefore rejected the accusation that colonial subjects were "indifferent to us or that we have failed to win their confidence."[134] Kindness and mutual aid, for Shenton Thomas, were evidence of colonial subjects' unwavering support for British rule. If Asian civilians resented British authority, he reasoned, then they would have killed or abandoned British people when they had the chance. This recast civilians' life-saving instincts and gestures of humanitarian care as pro-British "loyalty." Indifference or hatred, for Shenton Thomas, meant death.

While Shenton Thomas insisted that Asian civilians were unambiguously loyal, military leaders debated whether they deserved compensation for their assistance. Lieutenant-General Arthur Ernest Percival, the General Officer Commanding the Straits Settlements, noted the importance of distinguishing between "those who had remained loyal and those who had not."[135] One point of contention was knowing if men had abandoned their posts or laid down their arms during the invasion. He believed that some of the Federated Malay States Volunteers "elected to hand in their arms and return to their homes," while certain members of the Straits Settlements Volunteer Force "deserted before capitulation." He acknowledged that some of these men received commands "to return to their homes after the capitulation" but others became POWs. This diversity of experience made it difficult to categorize men in the same unit as loyal or disloyal. However, British inaction had clear consequences. Former 1st Battalion, Federated Malay States Volunteer Force (FMSVF) Company Commander, and civil servant Mubin (M.C.ff) Sheppard observed "disappointment and a sense of neglect" among "Asiatic Volunteers."[136] The cause was a lack of equitable compensation for their service.

Unfortunately, many men received no material support after fighting for the British. Percival was left with "a most disturbing picture of what is happening" and believed that many servicemen had "a very raw deal."[137] He worried that this would "have a very serious effect on our future position in Malaya." In the absence of a clear British policy, many Asian servicemen fought to be compensated. Some approached multiple offices and got passed back and forth without concrete solutions.[138] As a result, Percival received many "indignant letters," including from Eurasians who did anti-aircraft work and Asian men in Dalforce who resented that "practically nothing has been done yet to settle their claims." Most unsettling, for Percival, was the racism of these oversights. He found it "a very disgraceful affair" that "practically all Europeans have had their accounts settled while very few Asiatics have."[139] One Downing Street official reiterated the importance for the Secretary of State to avoid "any appearance of racial discrimination."[140] Despite the fact that the Governor of the Straits Settlements claimed that victory was impossible without Asian people, they were the first to be forgotten.

Sometimes bureaucratic inefficiencies helped paper over charges of racism. Percival knew, for instance, that Dalforce "was raised as an emergency measure" so it was unlikely that the War Office knew about it. It was formed by policeman John Dalley to combat the Japanese invasion, and was known locally as the Singapore Overseas Chinese Volunteer Army.[141] While the men signed attestation forms, many intentionally destroyed these to prevent them falling into Japanese hands, leaving "no record of these men." Still, Percival noted that they were "entitled to pay the same as any other soldier" but "have so far received none."[142] Another complication was that overt or documented efforts to resist the Japanese during the occupation could have resulted in torture and death. Still, some officials demanded proof that "by virtue of having been Government employees or through pro-British activities" that a claimant was "effectively denied by the Japanese of those means of earning a livelihood which were open to the public generally."[143] In other words, Asian people had to demonstrate that they were so loyal to the British that they refused to do any work at all during the occupation, remaining unemployed and alive without arousing Japanese suspicions. Only then would they be able to prove their dedication to the British. As a result, most British leaders believed that the non-interned deserved only half of the pay of POWs, finding this "fair if not generous."[144]

In response to this discrimination, many men advocated for their fellow men of arms. Former telegraph company manager and Dalforce volunteer Mah Khong wrote to Governor Shenton Thomas about British leaders' disregard for Dalforce. He noted that during the invasion they "defended the last line in Singapore till the last minute" including fighting with and defending British, Australian, and Indian troops.[145] They were present for all of the major battles leading up to the fall of Singapore, and faced bombs, smoke, and hand-to-hand combat while poorly equipped.[146] Meanwhile, they promoted "anti-Japanese" ideas among civilians. They only left their positions "when the military authorities decided to forsake the place." The British surrender, in turn, left them extremely vulnerable. Japanese leaders recognized Dalforce as an anti-Japanese force and "made attempts to exterminate all of us." Mah Khong estimated that roughly ten thousand served but only one thousand survived the war because of "Japanese persecution." Meanwhile, words of gratitude from British leaders became evidence that their service was heroic. Mah Khong cited Brigadier McKerron for stating that Chinese volunteers "rendered the greatest contribution in the War" and "made our enemy pay a very big price in our defensive war." The Advisor of Chinese Affairs, Colonel Pagden, also felt that Dalforce men "fought and died nobly" to "destroy one of the most bestial enemies of all time." Pagden added, "Let us in Malaya never forget them in a scramble for our selfish gain."[147] Unfortunately, many in Dalforce were forgotten already.

Despite British leaders' vocal support for Dalforce, most men felt they received inadequate compensation. This disrespected their suffering, which included becoming "physically disabled" and losing families and homes while being "massacred recklessly and relentlessly by the atrocious Jap[ane]s[e]."[148] In response, Mah Kong made a full-page list of "requests." These included demobbing before Christmas, back pay for the occupation period equal to the British regular army rates, passages back to China, employment recommendations, demobilization certificates, compensation to families of the fallen, free education for children of army members, priority for allotment of agricultural land, erection of a monument, and free medical treatment.[149] He felt that the government needed to respect their demands because volunteers "represented the anti-Japanese spirit of the several million Chinese in Malaya" who "opened up the road for the armed resistance of the people against facism [*sic*]."[150] By failing to support their allies, British leaders disrespected the entire Chinese population, who remained ready to fight.

Unfortunately, British leaders did not grant these "requests." Mah Khong expressed the "unanimous dissatisfaction and seething indignation."[151] He explained that, rather than receiving three and half years of back pay, Dalforce only received offers for seven and a half months. They refused to accept these terms "with intense indignation." He reiterated Dalley's promise that they would "be treated as English Regulars." In response, they risked their lives by eliminating "traitors," spreading "anti-enemy doctrines," and participating in "guerilla skirmishes with the enemy in which many of us lost our lives." British leaders' refusal to pay them for their wartime work suggested that these men's labors and lives were "of little or no consequence." Mah Khong believed firmly that this inaction reflected racial discrimination, as such treatment would not have happened to white men who made such sacrifices. He requested "sufficient and interested consideration for those who, though not having skins as white, have certainly sacrificed blood as red and real as their compatriots who fell in Dunkirk, Italy, Arnhem and Normandy."[152]

In order to gain further support for their cause, Dalforce members distributed a circular to the wider Chinese community. They noted that Dalforce helped the British Army defend Singapore when the latter was "at the point of collapse."[153] Unlike the British, "we fought persistently to the last, after General Percival had hoisted the White Flag and surrendered with his forces." With the British interned, "our comrades had determinedly engaged in anti-Japanese underground struggles until V.J. Day." Despite these accomplishments, the men of Dalforce received no assistance with food, clothing, or living quarters, whereas British soldiers received good salaries and pay for three and a half years of service. They insisted that as far as "bravery and merits, we are not inferior to the British soldiers." Once again they noted that racism was the likely cause for this different treatment: "It is perhaps because we are of the Yellow Race that we are not treated on the same level by the British Government." This made them wonder: "The victory of the anti-Japanese war belongs to whom?" All they wanted was to be put "on an equal footing with the British P.O.Ws. who surrendered to the Japanese." In emphasizing the British surrender and their own valiant efforts to fight on, members of Dalforce claimed heroism that exceeded that of the British. Yet even their commanding officer, Colonel Dalley, "made excuses when we sent an appeal to him" and "there were armed policemen to drive us away."[154] Being rounded up by police and treated like villains, instead of heroes, underlined the futility of fighting for the British.

Eventually, Dalley took up the case of his men. In his correspondence to Shenton Thomas, he indicated that they "knew" that the men would refuse the offer of seven and a half months' pay. He recommended "immediate and generous recognition of these men's services."[155] He told the Colonial Office that the men actually deserved more than the average soldier because the men of Dalforce took up "exposed positions" with insufficient equipment and "suffered very heavy casualties. They were never disbanded."[156] Dalley also recognized the political implications of failing to compensate and celebrate them. Many were recruited "from all political parties and from all ranks of life," including college students and rickshaw pullers, from "loyal British subjects to communists." Across these differences, there was "considerable discontent" that unified them. Dalley worried that the "extremist elements, both among DALFORCE [*sic*] men and outside parties, are making considerable capital out of our lack of generosity." Demonstrations in Singapore made him fear that he would not be able to control them much longer. However, he refuted that he was being "frightened into giving them generous treatment." Rather, he believed firmly that "they earned generous treatment." He recommended that "it will pay us to treat them generously, here and now, without any further delay. There are many people in this country who have extreme political views, and these people are exploiting our apparent lack of generosity to these men."[157]

Several English and Chinese newspapers also took up the cause of Dalforce men. One Chinese language newspaper, *Chung Nan Jit Poh*, reported on the protest in front of the Chinese Secretariat.[158] It echoed that these men faced hardships that exceeded those of British regulars. While POWs and interned civilians "lost their personal freedom," the anti-Japanese forces "lost even their mental and spiritual freedom, being daily in constant fear of their lives, and having to frequently escape from detection." They found it "absurd" that an anti-Japanese army should receive no back pay despite "constant danger to their lives."[159] The press also regarded the matter as discriminatory. The *Morning Tribune* printed Mah Khong's statement about the injustice of possessing the same red blood but being denied the treatment of those with white skin. They added that such "discrimination against Asiatics" was shortsighted on the part of the War Office because it made it difficult to imagine that "the local peoples" would ever again "assist in the defence of the country."[160] They mentioned that even "a number of widows" squatted outside the Chinese Secretariat to protest their treatment, showing unified support across colonial society. They wondered on what "moral ground" this "glaring discrimination" could be "justified." They found it obvious that "those who were on active service" should be given the same treatment of those "who had the misfortune to become prisoners."[161]

After receiving information from Dalley, Percival concluded that the "whole thing certainly looks pretty dishonest."[162] Despite his earlier sympathy, he had "no recollection of them being promised pay at the British rates." This failure of memory was unsurprising given his three and half years in internment. Still, he advocated for Dalforce men to receive three and half years' salary at volunteer rates and allowances for dependents of those who died.[163] Finally, men got what they had earned after a long and hard-fought battle. Yet their case bears remarkable similarity to the aftermath of the 1915 rebellion. Yeo Bian Chuan fought for over a decade to receive the compensation that British leaders promised him. He died without receiving it, despite gaining the support of the Chinese community. Percival's reluctant decision to give Dalforce men what British leaders promised showed that Chinese activism had grown even more powerful from the war. British leaders had no choice but to hear it.

OLD BEGINNINGS

After the war, Major P. S. Leathart felt that all civilians in Singapore and Malaya, "be they Chinese, Malay or Indian," were "obviously pleased to see the British back."[164] He formed this impression during his work in Kota Bharu monitoring communists. When he relocated to Taiping, he carried out surveillance on the "predominantly Chinese" population to counter MCP activities. To Leathart, this represented "getting things back to normal after the trauma of the Japanese occupation."[165] Hunting communists and monitoring Chinese people, for Leathart, was normal. The only traumas of military occupation and imperial war, he insisted, were caused by the Japanese. Signaler Dennis Newland disagreed. He arrived in Singapore in September 1945 feeling that the local population resented British military presence because of their failure to protect Malaya when it mattered. He believed that communists had won the confidence of civilians that British leaders lost.[166] Echoing this sentiment, James Puthucheary, who had served in the Indian National Army, admired communists because they seemed "more committed" than any other party.[167] As the fight against communism resumed, military leaders like Leathart cast British military personnel as heroic defenders against Japanese, and then communist, aggression, rewriting the lived reality of war and colonialism.

As Leathart suggests, postwar efforts to return to "normal" chiefly benefited the British men who could enjoy their pleasure palaces once again. Governor Shenton Thomas's charges of military racism did not prevent white soldiers from returning to monitor the population that he defended as resolutely "loyal." This made it easy to dismiss and undermine colonial subjects who resisted a swift return to the prewar colonial world. For Leathart, any anti-British activity was a symptom of the Japanese spreading "virulent anti-European propaganda" and "arming and encouraging all the riff-raff who were inclined to accept their preaching."[168] He did not consider that many of these "riff-raff" had been armed by the British and fought as their allies. Instead, he cast the prewar government as "respected as benevolently paternalistic and incorruptible." This led to a "genuine joy at our return" and proved "that rule by other Asians was no more than a cruel tyranny."[169] For Leathart, anti-British sentiment did not exist. Asian leadership was inevitably more brutal and exclusionary than British colonialism. Communists were the evil enemies preventing peace-loving civilians from returning to normal. This chafed against the unresolved racial hierarchies and inequities of those who fought for Malaya and Singapore and had not forgotten the horror and indignity of the surrender.

Echoing these narratives, British leaders cast the war as part of a longer history of British imperial heroism and sacrifice. Field Marshall Archibald Wavell regarded Chapman's tale of living behind enemy lines as "a story of endurance and survival" possessing "daring, initiative, and ingenuity" akin to the famed First World War insurgent "of Arabia," T. E. Lawrence. He believed that both men were "worthy representatives of our national capacity for individual enterprise."[170] However, Chapman's stories of feeling physically inadequate, and unable to answer for the British surrender, showed the true limitations of being an imperial "hero." Living with communists made Chapman confront the realities of the British surrender. Not only did he see his own plans ignored by shortsighted leaders more concerned with saving face in front of Asian subjects than protecting them, he also confronted communist criticisms of British incompetence. His own body and mind suffered from remaining behind enemy lines, uncertain if he would be abandoned to the same fate of Asian colonial subjects. While he fervently criticized communist leaders and ideas, he also developed admiration for low-ranking men. Seeing their determination to fight the Japanese contrasted his inability to find Europeans willing to do the same. Encountering jungle fighters made it impossible to deny that white martial masculinity had fallen from grace. This was Chapman's true similarity with Lawrence, though Lawrence lamented his inability to protect the independence of those he fought beside.

The true legacy of romanticizing men like Lawrence and Chapman was to repeat the mistakes of the First World War by emphasizing the need for greater intelligence to make targeted brutality more impactful.[171] India-born British policeman René Henry de Solminihac Onraet espoused this belief when he suggested that the primary cause of the British surrender had been "military collapse" stemming from military officers lacking "any knowledge of the inhabitants" or geography before the war.[172] This left them like "birds of passage whose real interests were with their regiments or their ships, going to staff college, promotions and such-like. Their hearts were never in Malaya." The reason that the British lost Malaya, therefore, was that Malaya never won the hearts and minds of white soldiers and officers. To counter this, he urged, like Chapman, that British military leaders develop "a military technique so as to use the jungles and the swamps and the tricky seaboard to our advantage, and to familiarize our soldiers with the country and its diverse population by means of a long term garrison."[173] Despite Shenton Thomas's feeling that military leaders harbored racist resentments toward the colonial population, Onraet encouraged greater military interference in people's lives. This, he believed, would redeem them from the failures and humiliations of the war. Once again, this ignored colonial subjects' perspectives.

In many ways, communists, the diverse soldiers of Force 136, and others who fought behind enemy lines against the Japanese could and should have stepped into the warm glow of "martial race" enthusiasm. By evading capture, undermining Japanese efforts, and fighting in brutal conditions, these fighters became a potential antidote to the humiliation of Britain's martial vanguard and the indifference of its military elite. Instead, the Second World War showed how colonial militarism only encouraged and deepened racialization and violence. Even anti-colonial forces, and armies of liberation, descended into jealousy, discrimination, and exclusion. Indian men forced to surrender at Singapore joined the Japanese to liberate Asia from European colonialism. Women in the Rani of Jhansi Regiment hoped to leave laboring backgrounds to find dignity and honor. The reality was enduring racism, sexism, internal disputes, and countless hardships on and off the battlefield. Many colonial subjects joined military forces to forge a place for themselves in a world within or beyond empires. What they found, again and again, was that military service to either colonizers or liberators brought violence and hierarchy. Formal militaries were not vehicles for egalitarian liberation.

Despite these realities, postwar victory celebrations in Singapore and London attempted to show the inclusivity of the empire by featuring representatives of the diverse fighting forces that aided British victory. Prewar units such as the

Federated Malay States Volunteers and Straits Settlements Volunteer Force, which British leaders privately criticized for disbanding or retreating, received public praise at the heart of the empire. Dalforce, Force 136, and communist members of MPAJA also enjoyed their moment in the sun. Meanwhile, former Changi internee Sheila Allan witnessed the victory parade in Singapore and noted that the "Chinese roared their anger" when they saw defeated Japanese officers "and wanted to rush at them," but the military police restrained them.[174] The war and occupation engendered bitterness that would not disappear overnight. As C. A. Bayly and Tim Harper have observed, "peace" only meant that European, American, and Japanese nations stopped fighting. Battles raged on because none "of the fundamental causes of the Great Asian War had been eradicated. Imperialism, grinding poverty, and ideological, ethnic and religious conflict continued to stalk the land. In many ways, they had been strengthened by the destruction and butchery of combat."[175]

Within a few years, many parade participants returned to the jungle out of bitterness over the violence of the British reoccupation.[176] Among those present at the victory parades in London in 1946 was Lau Mah, whom Chapman heard criticize the British for abandoning Malaya and was possibly connected to Pat Noone's death. Despite his participation in the victory parade, British-led security forces killed Lau Mah during the Emergency a few years later.[177] British leaders' sense that it was impossible to distinguish between those "loyal" and "disloyal" to British power meant that colonial militarism still needed enemies to legitimize itself. In a short period, the heroes of the Second World War became the enemies of the anti-communist Malayan Emergency. Longtime British promises to "protect" colonies from foreign aggression were exposed as shadowy excuses for decades of military occupation. Exalting those not formally commissioned to fight left an open wound about the nature of what it meant to fight for freedom—and who the next fights would include.

SIX

Forging the Commonwealth

In the early years of a British-led campaign against communism in Malaya, one Senior Army Liaison officer described the conflict as "a statistical war going on between the Malays, whose homeland it is, and the Chinese, who are immigrants."[1] He expressed a prevalent view among British officials during the anti-communist Malayan Emergency (1948–1960) that strict ethnic demarcation between "native" civilians and "immigrant" outsiders would root out communists, most associated with Malaya's large Chinese population.[2] An educational pamphlet echoed this view, insisting that the situation is not "a national uprising against the British" because "communist bandits" were "predominantly alien Chinese."[3] Therefore Chinese people, rather than British colonizers, were the ones stealing the Malay people's homeland. One official suggested that the only way of defending the "peace-loving" people of Malaya from a Chinese takeover was "protection" through "British arms."[4] The irony was that "British" soldiers did not carry the primary responsibility for fighting in the Emergency.

Following British narratives, many scholars have characterized the Emergency as a campaign of British leaders taking on the predominantly-Chinese Malayan Communist Party (MCP) to protect loyal Malays.[5] This demarcation between "alien" and "native," enforced by British militarism, is striking due to the diversity of Malaya's population and the international soldiers fighting on behalf of British interests. Many civilians in Malaya traced their heritage across Southeast Asia, the Arabian Peninsula, India, Europe, China, and beyond. The forces fighting in the Emergency came from Britain, Australia, New Zealand,

Fiji, East Africa, and Nepal. For some, this reflected the spirit of the 1948 British Nationality Act, which described Commonwealth and British subjects interchangeably, in effect granting full citizenship rights to former colonial subjects. While immigration reforms ultimately reversed this in subsequent decades, for a brief time, many colonial and Commonwealth subjects hoped that Britain could be an inclusive post-colonial state.[6] Unfortunately, British leaders' preoccupation with demarcating the "loyal" from the "disloyal," "native" from "immigrant," and "communist" from devoted soldier exposed the limits of inclusion. Instead, the Malayan Emergency continued existing patterns of pitting colonial subjects against one another to retain imperial control.

Casting communists as Chinese aliens obscures the fact that British leaders initially promised the Chinese community greater rights on returning to power after the Second World War. From the Japanese surrender in September 1945 until April 1946, British leaders governed Malaya and Singapore under the British Military Administration (BMA). Their first attempt at returning to civilian leadership was as the Malayan Union in 1946, which combined Malayan protectorates with the Straits Settlements. Singapore remained a separate crown colony. Under the Union, locally born Chinese and Indian civilians gained Malayan Union Citizenship alongside Malays, who already had citizenship granted by Sultans.[7] To many Chinese civilians, this recognized Chinese soldiers' and civilians' vital contributions to the war. According to administrator Wilfred Blythe, the goal was "to erase, as far as possible, the dividing lines between the different racial communities" and develop "Malaya's capacity in the direction of responsible self-government."[8] For a short time, Chinese civilians were more included in the structures of power of colonial Malaya and Singapore than ever before.

Unfortunately, cultivating a sense of "Malayan" unity also meant taking an inherently anti-Chinese stance. According to Blythe, British leaders saw locally-raised organizations "of independent Malayan origin, no matter what its political colour" valuable for "promoting local loyalties." By contrast, they viewed "any organization which had its roots in and was directed from China, whether right, left, or centre" as "a menace."[9] This undermined existing Chinese political leadership. Still, Blythe maintained that the Union failed because of colonial subjects rather than British leaders. He explained that the United Malays National Organization (UMNO) opposed the new constitution because they wanted to protect the sovereignty of Malay Sultans and secure greater power for Malays in government.[10] Tensions escalated as Chinese secret societies reemerged to assist the communist-led Malayan People's Anti-Japanese Army (MPAJA) in retaliating against Japanese collaborators, causing "further embarrassment to the

Government."[11] In places like Johore, which had been major sites of anti-Japanese activities during the war, some Malays responded by attacking the MPAJA.[12] In response to this embarrassment, and perceived Malay unhappiness, British leaders quickly reversed course on Chinese subjects, creating the Federation of Malaya in February 1948. To appease Malay politicians, it included high bars on citizenship for Indian and Chinese, but not Malay, civilians. This made it so that many people born in Malaya lacked citizenship rights if their parents were not also born there, leaving them more vulnerable to deportation.[13] Such actions made John Davis of Force 136 recognize that the "Chinese have utterly lost confidence in us owing to our clownery over forms of government during the last 3 years."[14] In just a few short years, British officials abandoned their support of racial equality in the name of peace. The Emergency started the same year.

The Malayan Emergency formally lasted over a decade, from 1948 until 1960, beyond Malaysian independence in 1957. Preceding it were many years of violence and political maneuvering. After the war, members of the Malayan Communist Party (MCP) believed that they enjoyed status as a legal organization due to wartime anti-Japanese activity, postwar aid to the British Military Administration, and British promises of freedom of association.[15] This enabled the MCP to gain even more popularity among civilians. Former guerilla Lin Guan Ying recalled that her own activism intensified when the "British imperialists came back" and began "to oppress the workers" by suppressing wages, banning newspapers, and restricting union and communist activities.[16] Further, British leaders permitted the MPAJA to regain control over police stations and the countryside. Some used this sanction to retaliate against suspected Japanese collaborators. Chinese nationalist groups like the Kuomintang (KMT), in turn, covertly supported secret societies to kill five workers, including a top communist leader, in 1947. As a result, the KMT became a key target of communists. Things also intensified when double agent Lai Teck disappeared in 1947. Many communists encouraged direct action, believing that Lai Teck only advocated the slow infiltration of communism into Malaya because he was subverting the cause.[17] Politically motivated assassinations or retributions became more common. Despite the frequency of violence in the years immediately following the Second World War, British leaders let it continue without declaring an emergency.

The situation changed rapidly when communists killed three white planters. Soon after, in June 1948, High Commissioner Edward Gent declared an "Emergency" against communism.[18] By calling the conflict an "Emergency" rather than a war, British leaders avoided UN interference and circumvented the rules of the Geneva Convention.[19] This enabled them to prioritize killing communists in the jungle and forcibly resettle hundreds of thousands of Chinese civilians into internment camps. Ultimately more than a half million people, roughly 90 percent of whom were Chinese, faced resettlement into nearly five hundred villages. Many plantations and mines also resettled over 600,000 laborers, bringing the total number of people subjected to forced resettlement to over a million.[20] The most famous leader to emerge from the conflict was General Templer, whom many credit with winning a "hearts and minds" campaign after more brutal efforts failed. While recent scholarship has acknowledged that coercion, violence, and control of civilians, rather than "winning" civilian confidence, enabled the British to claim victory, few have questioned what "winning" actually meant.[21] This chapter posits that the violent militarization and racial profiling used in the Emergency should be considered anything but a success. Rather, the Emergency represented a definitive failure of colonial militarism to win civilian confidence and forge a peaceful interracial colony. Instead, it revived martial violence and colonial racism.

For British officer J. P. Cross, Britain's "hearts and minds" approach to war was about convincing "all races that it was in their interests to help the Government and not the communists."[22] Appealing to Malaya's diverse subjects, he believed, would secure victory. By contrast, Victor Purcell, who worked in Chinese affairs, criticized the British government's tendency to pit Malay and Chinese civilians against one another.[23] In turn, this chapter examines how British officials used colonial tropes about racial inclusivity in the military to rewrite the history of colonialism in the region. As Takashi Fujitani has argued, many colonial powers, including Japan and the United States, shifted their emphasis from the "vulgar racism" of violence and segregation to the "polite racism" of integration to facilitate military recruitment during the Second World War.[24] For Britain, which had long relied on multi-ethnic fighting forces, additional challenges stemmed from uncertain wartime loyalties within and beyond colonial armies in the midst of rapid decolonization.[25] Increasingly, Emergency leaders reasserted colonial control by recasting British imperial militaries as heroic saviors against villainous communists.

The Malayan Emergency enabled British leaders to carry out a targeted race war against Chinese people by revitalizing colonial "martial race" ideas discredited during the war. This revived the notion that racial inclusivity could be achieved through colonial militarism, rather than in opposition to it. This previously unexamined dynamic of the Emergency goes beyond a binary of British colonial capitalism versus Chinese communism by foregrounding the use of racialized soldiers from around the world to fight the campaign. Throughout the

Emergency, British leaders touted their diverse fighting forces as a sign of the strength and diversity of the Commonwealth, rather than a legacy of hierarchical colonialism and racist recruiting. Comparing soldiers' experiences of military service across differences of religion, rank, region, and nationality reveals the shared consequences of racist military policies for soldiers and civilians alike. The same categorization and eugenicist certainty that regarded some men as "naturally" loyal soldiers enabled the violent crackdown on racialized "others" considered suspicious and "disloyal."[26] Britain's transition from Empire to Commonwealth hinged on the unresolved racial hierarchies that determined colonial military recruitment and permissible violence.

REDEEMING WHITE MASCULINITY

For many British leaders, the Emergency was a chance for redemption. It brought them into the jungle to show their mettle against their former communist allies, including Chin Peng.[27] Against them was not only communism, but also a not-uncommon perspective, expressed by guerilla Lin Guan Ying, that during the Second World War British leaders "literally ran away. They were real cowards; they were scared of dying."[28] Madam Seow Guat Beng recalled a Second Magistrate acting like a "very big man" during the Emergency even though he "hid under his wife's bed" when the Japanese invaded.[29] For administrator Wilfred Blythe, this proved a poor contrast to communists who showed "endurance in facing the rigours of jungle life and the dangers of torture and death if captured."[30] One key of the Emergency, therefore, was rebuilding lost confidence in British leadership and white masculinity. Hoping to do so was an influx of British police and military officials from now-independent colonies and mandates such as India and Palestine. These men felt emasculated by the loss of those colonies in 1947 and 1948 and hoped to prove that they could retain control in Malaya, even though their methods chafed against the "Old Malayan" officials eager to regain power after internment.[31] For author Han Suyin, this latter group "had been 'in the bag' together" as prisoners of the Japanese and "now stuck together, and formed the higher ranks of the official hierarchy up and down Malaya."[32] Regardless of their differences, all British police and military leaders wrestled with redeeming themselves from the Second World War and decolonization by fighting in the jungle.[33]

One immediate hurdle to success in the Emergency was that its call to fight and protect the colonial planter class seemed woefully out of touch. The postwar British government was led by the socialist-leaning Labour Party, which at least nominally prioritized decolonization and the needs of the British working classes. British and European planters, who bore the brunt of initial communist attacks in Malaya, represented a seemingly bygone class of wealth and Prestige. They were dependent on the immense labor of others and were unwilling to defend themselves or their employees when it mattered. Meanwhile, many Britons serving in the Emergency were not eager volunteers or career soldiers, but conscripts serving under mandatory National Service (1949–1963). These inexperienced men participated in unpopular policies, such as arduous jungle patrols searching for communists and the mass resettlement of Malaya's large Chinese population.[34] They also had to enforce Emergency Regulations engineered by officials formerly employed in the Palestine mandate, which gave colonial authorities the power to impose curfews, arrest people and detain them without a trail, and deport anyone considered undesirable.[35] Many servicemen even admitted that torture was a frequent interrogation tool, despite its illegality under the Geneva Convention.[36] Finding a way to win civilian confidence, while using extreme violence to maintain profitable trade, proved almost impossible.

One method of cultivating sympathy for white planters was portraying them as victims who fought for redemption. *Picture Post* made this point in 1949, estimating that "at least half" of British rubber planters "were war prisoners of the Japanese." One article highlighted Mr. A. S. Taylor, manager of a rubber estate of 1,866 acres, who "was a prisoner of the Japanese for over three years. On such men Britain's influence in Malaya depends."[37] An Army educational workbook also emphasized the hardships of planter families during the Emergency, stressing that "planters and miners and their families suffered severely" in the conflict. Only "their staunchness and determination . . . saved the situation." The workbook assignment asked, "Who are the bravest group of men you met in Malaya?" The military students had to answer "Without a doubt the tin miners (or the rubber planters)" and then explain in their own words why this was the case.[38] Planters who used, and often exploited, Asian laborers prior to the war, and either fled or were interned by the Japanese, now became staunch and determined saviors of Malaya. If the surrender revealed white men's inability or unwillingness to protect colonial subjects, the Emergency allowed them to demonstrate their perseverance.

Among police, too, internment became evidence of resilience rather than weakness. Lancelot Alban Searle died when he was just thirty-nine years old in 1954 on Emergency operations. His obituary suggested that he was among the last police ordered to evacuate Hong Kong because he stayed to prevent looting. He then had "an 'unlucky war'" by spending the duration as a POW. Due to his "outstanding physical courage," they argued, "he felt this deeply." The embarrassment of internment inspired his vigorous response to the Emergency, according to M. C. A. Henniker, Commander 63 Gurkha Infantry Brigade. Henniker elaborated: "Deprived by the fortunes of war from gaining fame in battle," Searle "was always ready and eager to take part in operations against the terrorists." The Emergency gave him the opportunity to show repeatedly "the mettle of which he was made." Some men "lacked spirit . . . stayed at home, and left the action to the soldiers," but this "was not Lance Searle's way of doing things." His decision to take an active part in operations, rather than leaving the fighting to other men, led to his death. Still, for Henniker, "personal courage was at the root of the man's makeup, and staying at home was not his way."[39] While internment cast doubt on the masculinity and courage of British men, vigorous courage in the Emergency allowed them to "show their mettle" with glorified deaths. Heroic suffering created natural leaders.

Despite these efforts to restore white masculinity, many observers found that white men fell short of their exalted status. Sgt. Richard W. Valdan managed a garrison club in Malaya and felt impressed by "our crowd, I mean Aussies and Kiwis [New Zealanders], because with them one never has a real trouble." By contrast, he found that "Pommies" (Britons) were always responsible for "rumbles." He explained that British soldiers' "favourite way of dealing with anyone, is to attack in a wolf-pack fashion, using broken bottles and kicking men's 'treasure chest.'" He regarded Maori soldiers as favorable to white Britons, because even "a hulking 17 stones Maori, drunk as Wally on a payday . . . could be led to a bed, as docile as a kitten."[40] Nepali soldiers similarly observed that British men were guilty of reckless, predatory violence or neglecting their duty. When Maitraj Limbu worked on a train that was ambushed, the British soldiers escaped, leaving Nepalis behind to fight alone. He transferred to the Gurkha military police as a result, only to find that he spent much of his time breaking up "drunken fights" between British soldiers and keeping them "away from the brothels." He lamented: "I couldn't understand why they were so worthless." White African soldiers of the Rhodesian squadron were even worse. A group of Nepali men tried to break up a fight but the men "tried to attack us." A soldier "knocked one of them out by bashing a chair over his head." The Nepalis then threw a lump of concrete on the unconscious man's face, "breaking his nose and teeth. There was never any trouble for us Gurkhas after that."[41]

These tumultuous encounters reflect the fact that violence was the metric by which British leaders measured success in the Emergency. All security forces, whether British, Commonwealth, Nepali, or Police, operated with what Caroline

Elkins has called "legalized lawlessness" that enabled commanding officers to decide in the moment what level of violence was necessary to maintain British definitions of law and order.[42] This was particularly dangerous during the Emergency, when security forces counted success by the number of CTs, or "communist terrorists," killed in combat.[43] Simeon Man has suggested that Americans' similar emphasis on "the body count of confirmed Vietnamese kills" only incentivized the production of more dead Vietnamese bodies.[44] In Malaya, this led white men to marvel at their own lethality. J. M. Miller bragged that his unit killed "203 terrorists for the loss of 7 of my men."[45] Other men meticulously preserved and stored in their personal albums graphic photos of those they killed. Periodicals often reproduced such imagery. While such photos usually depicted dead communist men, one issue of the *Straits Times* published a photo of a deceased communist woman, labeling her a "handsome girl" to lament her lost beauty. The article did not include a photo of the man killed with her, but insisted that he was "a wizened little man perhaps twice her age" who was "half-starved."[46] The death of a beautiful communist woman was less tragic than her humiliation at consorting with a thin, weak old man. Such recurring imagery of dead and tortured Asian men clearly took a psychological toll. One *Straits Times* reader, Khoo Eng Teow, wrote a letter complaining about the frequency of their publishing "pictures of those horrid-looking faces of killed bandits."[47]

Despite civilian concerns, police and military periodicals treated this violent imagery as comedic. One issue of *Police* magazine included a cartoon of a woman and a child inside of a home. On the wall was either a painting or a window that showed a man outside hanging from a tree, evoking a lynching. The mother told the girl, "Darling, how often must I ask you NOT to interfere with Daddy's work?" The daughter stood grimacing, holding a rope affixed around the neck of a dead communist.[48] These published photos and cartoons ritualized the spectacle of death. Meticulously counting communist deaths enabled journalists and military personnel to dehumanize communists as "enemies" deserving their violent fate. Yet these depictions had real consequences. Guerilla Guan Shui Lian recalled her brother's death in battle at a tin mine while looking for food. It was not enough that security forces shot him. They then "stripped off his clothes and left only his underwear on. They tied his corpse to a truck and dragged him like a dead dog" back to their camp.[49] Taking to the jungle in the Second World War enabled communists to redefine and claim the exalted masculine status long bestowed by white imperial leaders to the "martial races." Now, those previously celebrated as anti-Japanese heroes resided in areas that were challenging for British

"*Darling, how often must I ask you NOT to interfere with Daddy's work?*"

FIGURE 8. Cartoon published in *Police: The Magazine of the Malayan Police Force* (June 1952). Image printed with permission from the Royal Malaysia Police and courtesy of the National Library of Australia.

and Commonwealth troops to monitor. Brutalizing them in death undermined their claims to vitality, youth, and vigor, emasculating Asian men and asserting power over their mortality.

Sometimes, cartoons that humiliated and brutalized Asian men also hinted at inadequacies in British masculinity. One cartoon by M. P. Stephens depicted a round-bodied policeman in a crisp uniform yelling at an exhausted and aggressively perspiring policeman emerging from the jungle: "Well! Why don't you salute?" In one arm, the jungle policeman holds a rifle; in the other he grasps the hair of a thin, deceased communist.[50] The bodies of the two white men hinted at wider anxieties. The rotund man reflected concerns that white men became spoiled and lazy while serving in Asia. Policeman René Henry de Solminihac Onraet resented the cliché that service in Asia made "morons or effetes of this good British middle-class stock" and rejected the notion that service "in the East" was "a softening process."[51] The cartoon's thin, sweaty policeman, meanwhile, showed that white men's bodies withered while participating in jungle patrols, echoing Chapman's earlier concerns that white men were unprepared for jungle

"Well! why don't you salute?"

FIGURE 9.   Cartoon published in *Police: The Magazine of the Malayan Police Force* (1951). Image printed with permission from the Royal Malaysia Police and courtesy of the National Library of Australia.

warfare. However, each of these anxieties paled in comparison to a brutalized communist corpse. While white men gained or lost weight, and dignity, through their service in Asia, they still boasted triumph over dead communist men. Killing and condemning communist masculinity proved easier than redeeming white manhood.

The tortured memory of the Second World War inspired an anonymous Australian veteran to pen a poem bidding farewell to war, entitled "A Toast to Malaya." He wrote: "To your palm trees that sway in the breeze,/ and the hookworms that hook in the sand,/ to your rickshaws, your dobhy's your stingahs,/ your climate, no white man can stand./ Now gladly we farewell Malaya,/ as our ship swings around by the stern,/ We are going back home to Australia,/ And by hell, we will never return."[52] Despite this soldier's confidence about leaving Malayan service firmly in the past, the Malayan Emergency compelled many white soldiers—Australians among them—to endure Malaya's "hookworms" and "climate" once again to fight communism. Yet efforts to reclaim and redeem white masculinity ultimately failed. One reason was that many men felt they were undeserving of redemption. Han Suyin's novel . . . *And the Rain My Drink*, set during the Emergency, featured a few hard-nosed racist white officials but largely depicted military personnel as tortured men. For example, one New Village commandant possessed "the frustrated kindness of a man caught and trapped in his ignorance, knowing the system inadequate, but standing his ground." This commandant believed that all people wanted was "decent treatment, a living wage. Give it to them, and there won't be any communism." However, the more he expressed this, the more other British leaders felt he was dangerously socialistic, putting him at risk of losing touch with "esprit de corps and the impassioned conformity which mitigated their loneliness."[53] Another character, Luke Davis, was racked with doubts about marrying an Asian woman, because if he did so then the "half-formulated disaffection with his world would crystalize [*sic*]; the shaky certainties would become vague, obliterated; he would never be sure that he was doing the right thing, here and now."[54] This sensitivity was no doubt related to the fact that Han Suyin married Leon Comber, who served with the Special Branch in Malaya and resigned as a result of his wife's novel. Han Suyin's intimate knowledge of British men leading the campaign enabled her to see them as powerless to change the machinery of war around them.

Another reason that white masculinity proved difficult to redeem from the indignity of war was that white men did not bear the sole, or even primary, burden of fighting in the Emergency. Having lost the Indian Army to independence in 1947, British leaders relied on support from the entire Commonwealth—including soldiers from East Africa, Fiji, Malaya, Australia, and New Zealand—throughout the long campaign against communism. They also depended on Nepali soldiers who were neither imperial subjects nor members of the British Commonwealth. Police forces, which consisted of predominantly white officers with Malay, Chinese, and Indian rank and file, increased dramatically with the creation of new units and the influx of officials from other colonies, rising from roughly 9,000 in 1948 to 250,000 in 1953.[55] This expansion proved no easy task, since many police felt "demoralized" after serving the Japanese in the war and faced persistent accusations of graft, corruption, and desertions. One official noted that by working for the Japanese, the police had enabled "the oppression and humiliation of the Chinese and had thus earned the hatred of this community."[56] Ultimately, this hatred proved beneficial, enabling police to view the Chinese community as enemies. This eliminated the need for white men to take center stage in restoring the empire. Instead, reclaiming British dignity depended on the strength of the "martial races" they employed. The future of British power abroad hinged on celebrating the heroic virtues of Black and Asian men.

THE NEPALI PARADOX

One complication of the Emergency was that some of the first soldiers to experience active service in large numbers were neither British troops nor British subjects. They were Nepali soldiers, recruited as "Gurkhas." These soldiers' long genealogy of service in British and Indian colonial forces, particularly in India since the eighteenth century, made them one of the most paradigmatic "martial races." Common British tropes romanticized them as sturdy, happy fighters always willing to follow British men into battle.[57] By contrast, communists in the jungle often feared Gurkha soldiers for being, in the eyes of author Han Suyin, just as "ferocious and noiseless as the Japanese" with an apparent affinity for appearing "suddenly with their knives" and "cutting off heads . . . sometimes hands."[58] However, Nepali service in Malaya was not an indication of their inherent brutality or "fighting spirit." Rather, it reflected the changing geopolitics of colonialism and decolonization in the British Empire. As one of the first groups of soldiers to fight in the Emergency, their experiences of being both included and "othered" during their service showed the limitations of British inclusion.

Nepali soldiers had served alongside—or more accurately, under the command of—Britons for generations. Their pattern of service in the British Indian Army started in the early nineteenth century and continued during both World Wars, and numerous colonial campaigns, under British-Indian command. When India and Pakistan became separate, independent nations in 1947, they inherited and divided the colonial Indian Army between them. The exception was Nepalis. Eight Gurkha battalions transferred from the Indian Army to the new Gurkha Contingent of the British Army. The remainder stayed in India. In 1948, Nepali men had the choice to "opt-in" for either Indian or British service, continuing Nepal's ambiguous status. Those Nepali soldiers who opted for British service went to Hong Kong or Malaya between January and April 1948. Within a few months, the latter experienced active duty in the Emergency.

During the "opt," tensions ran high as British and Indian personnel tried to win Nepali men to their side. Major P. S. Leathart of the 9th Gurkha Rifles admitted that there were opportunities for intimidation. Each Nepali man or officer had to give their choice in front of Company commanders, the commanding officer, and Indian NCOs and officers. Still, Leathart saw it as a sign of pride rather than coercion that those serving the British declared their intention "with enthusiasm." By contrast, Leathart questioned the masculinity of those who joined the Indian Army, suggesting that only those "such as clerks and lineboys" chose Indian over British service.[59] At the same time, he noted that roughly 80 percent of the men of the 2/2 Gurkhas decided to serve in the Indian Army "for reasons which no one really understood." He speculated that it must have been because most "of the men of that Bn. had been prisoners of the Jap[ane]s[e] in Malaya for whom that country had nothing but bitter memories." If not this, he felt that perhaps "the Indian National Army (INA) anti-British propaganda to which they had been subjected had had an effect upon some of them." When the 7 Gurkha Rifles also had "a very low percentage" choosing British service, Leathart speculated that this was because Indian leaders pressured Nepali men who were close to retirement and wanted to settle in India. For Leathart, Nepali men were loyal and eager to serve the British by default. If their actions contradicted this, it was because of Japanese influence, INA propaganda, or other external pressures.

In reality, the transition from Indian to British service proved difficult for many soldiers. Khayalman Rai of the 1st battalion, 7th Gurkha Rifles (1/7 GR) recalled that, just before the redivision of troops, "those who did not want to serve with the British" were influenced by anti-colonial ideas and "caused endless trouble." By contrast, soldiers who waited to be transferred to Malaya had to keep "their heads down . . . for fear of reprisals."[60] Others bucked colonial narratives about inherent Nepali "loyalty." Most of the senior and experienced Nepali soldiers opted for Indian, rather than British, service. This created an unexpected reliance on very young men. Chandrabahadur Rana, Manbahadur Gurung, and Shamsherbahadur Rai were some of the many "boy soldiers," who were just fifteen years old when they enlisted.[61] The more experienced men who joined up with the British had some shortcomings, since many had been prisoners of war during the Second World War and lacked battle experience since 1942.[62] Other battalions were drastically reduced due to the prevalence and influence of anti-colonial sentiments.

The reorganization and relocation of regiments also drew out the biases of many British officers. Major General Boucher had "an intense dislike of Gurkhas amounting almost to a mania," even though he was tasked with commanding the Brigade of Gurkhas in Malaya. Brigadier H. A. Scone became a second in command despite "open hostility" toward Nepalis. These feelings became contagious, as other officers resented being transferred from regiments bound for India, leaving them, in one officer's view, "bitter" and "indifferent to the fate of their new Regiment."[63] Making matters worse, many British officers from the colonial Indian Army knew Hindi but not Nepali, decreasing chances for mutual respect or understanding. In one battalion, the only common language between the British gunner instructors and senior Gurkha ranks was Italian due to their shared war experience.[64] Even in 1952, Major General Hedley noted that paperwork, equipment shortages, and deficiencies in education and training made it difficult to keep "units efficient and happy."[65] One method was creating new incentives for British service. By November 1948 the first Queen's Gurkha Officers received promotion as lieutenants.[66] This was an important break from the colonial period, when all officers had been either British or, in the past few decades, Indian. This opened up further opportunities for sociability across colonial racial boundaries, as Nepali officers and their families gained entry into spaces and social gatherings afforded to their rank. Sporting events, dances, and Christmas and *Dassehra* celebrations promised social mixing, including with troops from Commonwealth nations, such as Fiji.[67]

Despite some concessions and innovations, it was very difficult for soldiers to earn recognition. As discussed, British leaders measured success in the Emergency by the number of so-called "CTs"—or "communist terrorists"—killed in combat. Nepali soldiers called these men "daku"—short for *dacoit*, or bandits. Soldiers spent most of their time on long jungle patrols searching for "daku." This afforded them few opportunities to sleep, let alone find food or take off their boots in the rugged conditions. Therefore, as soldiers such as Jasbahadur Limbu, 1/10 GR, and Tulbahadur Rai, 1/7 GR, recalled, the surest way to gain British favor was to kill real or suspected communists. Whenever there were heavy kill counts, their officers celebrated with a large feast.[68] Promotions, similarly, were most likely after kills, meaning that the men who gained the most privilege from their service had to first prove their capacity for killing.

Sukdeo Pun, 1/2 GR, was sure that killing communists would get him the honorific recognition of a *bahaduri*. During one patrol, he ended up killing two men and saving the lives of many fellow soldiers. He later learned that the honors went to the oldest man in his company instead. Bhimraj Gurung of the 2/6 GR recalled a colour sergeant who was court-martialed for messing up accounts. He tried to redeem his name by securing further kills. He was so successful that his commanding officer promised him a promotion to lieutenant—before informing him that he was dismissed from the army instead. Bhimraj remembered that after one difficult patrol, and killing numerous alleged communists, a platoon sergeant and his friends received military honors instead of the man who killed the targets. The experience of being overlooked for promotion, despite conforming to military definitions of success, was fairly standard for Nepali veterans.[69] Sometimes they lamented the lack of recognition for British officers as well. Bhimraj identified Major G. H. Walsh as one of the few British officers "who had a high standard in the jungle" but never got a *bahaduri*. He confided that "I never had any faith in the British Government" after Walsh was "given nothing."[70]

Even those men who embraced British definitions of death as "success" endured repeated disappointment. Dilbahadur Thapa, 1/10 GR, was injured in the action that won him a military medal. His officer discharged him without a pension after twelve years of service. He confided to retired officer J. P. Cross that "he would much rather have no bravery award than an arm that had hurt him for the next fifty years."[71] These accounts depict two recurring features of Nepali service in the Malayan Emergency. First, the tendency to mark success through death emphasized soldiers' success securing fatalities—rarely noting how they assessed the identity of "daku," including when they were women. This contributed to racial profiling and violence against civilian communities. Second, Nepali soldiers felt that few British officers actually took the time to learn about what *they* valued, or listened to them about their frustrations. Reflecting on his own service, Sukdeo Pun thanked Cross, who was living as a military historian in Nepal, for interviewing him, noting that no "other officer has ever bothered to ask me such questions."[72]

Nepali soldiers' frustrations contrast the accounts of British officers who detailed their efforts to ensure soldiers' happiness. The colonel-in-chief asserted in 1949 that the army took "keen interest . . . in the welfare of the Gurkhas" and did their best to "provide all necessary welfare and recreational facilities for the troops under their command."[73] A British officer of the 7 GR described soldiers and families in 1952 as living in lush, hutted accommodations decorated with gardens and grass patches. In reality, accommodations were inconsistent. Thambahadur Gurung, 1/2 GR, remembered that when he enlisted for service in 1947, "We had been told we'd be in brick buildings but we were all in tents."[74] The 6 GR, similarly, had to stay in "a very dilapidated tented camp" in Kuala Lumpur from 1948 to 1949.[75] Sukdeo Pun remembered that soldiers "were kept inside a camp that had wire around it like a lot of sheep" during training. This discouraged them from seeking contact with civilians in Malaya. As Sukdeo Pun rationalized, soldiers "weren't that interested" because they "couldn't speak the language."[76]

Major Leathart dismissed soldiers' response to hardships by celebrating their cheerful spirit. He recalled that he expected to live with his men in some of the newly built barracks in Singapore. Instead, they arrived at a camp with "a scene of greater desolation I had seldom seen." It had been raining nonstop for twenty-four hours, leaving tent roofing full of holes and torn by the wind. Most of the toilets had no doors. Despite these challenges, he was surprised by "how cheerful the men remained, for not only was the work hard and tedious, but the future prospect of living in this city of sodden tents for an indefinite period could not be contemplated with much enthusiasm." However, he racialized this as a trait common among Nepali troops: "I had found during the war that Gurkha soldiers could convert part of a wilderness into an oasis of tolerable comfort when conditions made it necessary, but they could reasonably have expected something better on joining the British Army. If they did, they never said so."[77] Once again British leaders praised Nepali men for appearing compliant in difficult circumstances.

During their service, Nepali soldiers existed in an uncomfortable intermediary position. They were not members of the British Commonwealth yet bore a heavy burden to serve its interests, continuing colonial patterns. They received promotion and decorations for a willingness to kill—without, necessarily, identifying "enemies" before their deaths. Despite being exalted as a "naturally loyal" "martial race," few men with experience of British service continued after the Second World War. Many British officers, in turn, exhibited open hostility toward them despite their "cheerful" attitudes. Still, soldiers' isolation from civilians ensured that they were an insular community within Malaya. Their disillusionment with the intentions and actions of British leaders suggests that while the fantasy of loyalty and devotion to empire had faded, its violent military consequences lived on.

OTHERING ASKARI

Nepali soldiers' experiences of frustration, disappointment in white officers, and encouragement to keep their distance from civilians set the precedent for colonial and Commonwealth troops serving in the Emergency. British leaders' stated intentions of cultivating interracial harmony did not bring an end to colonial racism and violence. Rather, widespread racism against African soldiers—including the perseverance of "martial race" thinking—suggests that soldiers' hearts and minds still needed to be won. Even more than their Nepali counterparts, East African askari fought not only in brutal military campaigns, but also against the unresolved racial hierarchies underpinning Commonwealth military engagement.

As with Nepali soldiers, martial race assumptions in East Africa predated the Malayan Emergency. In nineteenth-century Nyasaland (Malawi), Punjabi Sikh soldiers helped train African recruits.[78] Colonial officers in East Africa, as in India, perpetuated the idea that the best soldiers were uneducated and from rural backgrounds.[79] The reality was far more complex. Some soldiers came from enslaved backgrounds or service in other colonies. Most recognized that military service offered them more power and influence in colonial society.[80] The King's African Rifles (KAR), formed in 1902, recruited many of its soldiers from Nyasaland (Malawi), Kenya, Uganda, and Tanganyika (Tanzania).[81] While initially recruited for internal security and the coercion of political opponents, East African askari were active in Burma and Malaya against the Japanese during the Second World War, setting a precedent for their subsequent international campaigns. British leaders assumed that a unit's experience fighting in the difficult climate and terrain of Southeast Asia would help a subsequent generation of men fight communists in the jungle patrols of the Emergency. Many British leaders rationalized this was a "natural" feature among askari. One British officer of the KAR in Burma argued that askari had a "sixth sense" in the jungle. Another suggested that they were "absolutely at Home [*sic*] in the bush or jungle." Yet by 1951 about half of the KAR were from Kenya, which had no jungles.[82] Still, a British Movietone film emphasized that askari adapted "so readily to jungle conditions that they amazed those who had lived there all their lives."[83] Portraying these men as both "natural soldiers" and inherently adaptable to difficult conditions not only deepened assumptions about their inherent differences but reduced colonial leaders' responsiveness to their needs.

Despite the perceived experience and expertise of askari, colonial politics in East Africa initially halted their inclusion.[84] British officers remembered "much headshaking" in part because many Chinese, Indian, and Malay civilians in Southeast Asia "had never seen an African" and "received them with some suspicion."[85] Japanese newspapers during the Second World War portrayed Britain's reliance on African troops as a sign of weakness and racial degeneration.[86] Still, by 1952 British leaders requested two King's African Rifles battalions. Throughout their service, African soldiers faced anti-Black racism from both white officials and Asian civilians. Despite these challenges, askari performed well, according to British measures of success. By the time the Emergency ended in 1960, troops associated with the Central African Federation—including multiple battalions of the King's African Rifles, Northern Rhodesia Regiment, and the Rhodesian African Rifles—had served in Malaya.[87] Brigadier F. H. Brooke attested that by then, all "fears have proved completely groundless and the African is extremely popular with all races here."[88]

This popularity was hard-won. Colonel H. P. Williams remembered that when African troops arrived in Bentong, they felt the negative response "very keenly." Communists had been dealt "a very hard blow" by the 7th Gurkha Rifles prior to the KAR's arrival and responded by being "as beastly as they could." This included spreading stories that "African troops were absolutely terrible," including racist arguments about their living in trees and eating children.[89] Press reports countered these narratives by highlighting when African soldiers rescued babies from the jungle.[90] However, racism also influenced military intelligence. Troops relied on good relations with and information from civilians to locate communists in the thick jungle. Civilians who readily supplied information to Nepali troops became tight-lipped around African soldiers. Apparently, the flow of information "stopped . . . because of this Communist chat."[91]

In response to communist propaganda, military officials worked with the Chinese Association to rebrand African soldiers for civilians. This group "had a big fund" that helped to organize several events encouraging support for African soldiers, including sending a corps of "drums, flutes, and bugles—round the estates and villages." These musical displays, together with distribution of medical supplies, became ways of making the military more civilian-friendly, increasing goodwill between African soldiers and Asian civilians. However, it was the creation of children's parties at every Company location that revealed the racist dynamics of this inclusion. There, soldiers were instructed "to dress up as a horse or a wild animal and offer the children a ride on their back."[92] The reasoning was "how could any Communist allege that an African would eat children if he . . . was allowed to take their children for a ride?"[93] The children, apparently, needed little convincing, and there "was fairly keen competition to ride on the back of one of the African soldiers."[94] Williams described this policy as winning "the day" because it enabled African soldiers to kill "our share of Communists" with public support.[95] In other words, this racist spectacle facilitated a deadly campaign. The inclusion of Black men in colonial Asia, some British officers reasoned, required both dehumanization and subservience.

British leaders also emphasized how religion could recast African troops in the eyes of Asian civilians. Before the First World War, British leaders preferred the recruitment of Muslim soldiers from East Africa, due to their experiences of service and connections to Arab trading routes.[96] However, during the Emergency, many British officers preferred Christian askari, fearing radicalism among some Somali Muslims.[97] Some asserted that Christian imperial militarism created interracial harmony and advertised the Christianity of African soldiers to Chinese Christians.[98] Just as importantly, according to Colonel Williams, "Local people were invited to our Church services." At one Christmas celebration, "the African choirs sang carols together with four Tamil and ten Chinese children."[99] This made the Christianity of African troops worthy of cultivation. Christian soldiers in Malaya continued to benefit from the Second World War policy of being accompanied by chaplains. They also had access to Anglican, Catholic, and

Church of Scotland services in Malaya.[100] By contrast, Muslim soldiers had to find their own opportunities for worship among Malays at local mosques. While this likely facilitated positive soldier-civilian contact, Lt. Col. Wilson dismissed soldiers' possible difficulties by suggesting that Somalis were "seldom slow to find religious objections to things they did not want to do."[101]

Like Wilson, many British officers exposed their personal biases toward certain recruits—often with contradictory results. John Arthur Williams believed that British soldiers got along best with "the more 'military' tribes," which he described as "the nomadic ones." They apparently got along less well with what he called the "educated" tribes.[102] Others saw education as helpful for maintaining discipline. Brigadier Brooke recommended Nyasaland (Malawi) men over Kenyans because the former, in his view, had superior education.[103] In fact, many African soldiers saw military service as a way to secure education.[104] Still, some officers infantilized them. Colonel Williams noted that Nyasaland men were "the happiest and jolliest to live with" and were a "rather small man, compact and mentally very alert."[105] These perceived physical and character traits echoed language used to describe Nepali Gurkha soldiers, who were also part of an imagined genealogy of "martial races."[106] Yet not all recruiting biases were so admiring. Several officers contrasted askari to "civilized" soldiers, or insisted that they were best for fighting in so-called "uncivilised country."[107] Soldiers also faced racial slurs. VC winner Lt. Col. Wilson admitted that most officers saw African solders as inferior and referred to them as "chocolates."[108]

Martial race thinking made essential tasks, like securing rations, more challenging. Veteran Matthew Kipoin was marked for so-called "Arab rations" because, in British views, Maasai ate milk and blood—even though Kipoin was most likely of Kikuyu ancestry. Similarly, most British officers assumed that East African soldiers ate ground nuts, and made these 30 percent of soldiers' caloric intake. Military officers' efforts to change soldiers' rations were rejected by London officials because, in their view, "all Africans ate ground nute [*sic*]"—or, at least, had done so during the Second World War.[109] In reality, most African soldiers traded their rations for rice. Proposals to incorporate ration rice directly was overruled by Kenyan authorities because it was not grown locally. Instead, they supplied East African canned meat mostly fed to dogs. In times of privation, it was issued to askaris, who understandably resented being fed "dog food."[110] Once again, British officers easily slipped into treating African soldiers as animals, prioritizing colonial economies over soldiers' welfare.

This treatment makes it unsurprising that soldiers frequently criticized their service. Throughout the 1950s, soldiers drafted countless letters requesting additional compensation or other accommodations. The average KAR battalion was about four times less expensive than a British one due in large part to lower wages. Eventually, KAR soldiers received bonuses in Malaya to bring their payment up to an equal standard with Nepali and Fijian troops—a fight which, in and of itself, indicates the inequitable treatment of Black soldiers compared to other troops.[111] Racism and material inequities even made some soldiers more sympathetic to the Malayan Communist Party, which they had been commissioned to fight. Kipoin read *Das Kapital* four times in Malaya, despite the ongoing fight against communism. Similarly, many NCOs who had joined the military in the Second World War had hoped to liberate Britain's subjects first from the Japanese, and then from so-called "armed bandits." However, they realized that they were agents of British recolonization instead.[112] By contrast, Malayan communists claimed to want a "peaceful, democratic and independent Malaya," similar to the stated goals of African nationalists in the 1950s.[113] One letter to the Ministry of Defence suggested that a secret organization had formed among soldiers who threatened to go on strike. Anti-colonial sentiment was especially pervasive among units that had served in Malaya. Military service even gave them strategies for helping anti-British "Mau Mau" activists evade capture—such as alerting them about ambushes or taking hands from the dead to prevent their fingerprinting.[114]

The racial hierarchies and political and religious tensions of the Malayan Emergency reveal how African soldiers embodied the limits of imperial inclusion. If useful, their beliefs were co-opted to show the triumph of interracial, imperial Christianity. More often, their bodies could be mocked or made into a spectacle to decrease Asian civilians' fears of Black men. British officers adjusted "martial race" assumptions in East Africa in small but significant ways—recruiting men who were Christian and more educated. Yet the lingering tensions of colonial military service did not disappear. Violence, racism, and unequal service conditions remained recurring features of soldiering.

ISLANDS OF INCLUSIVITY

Perhaps no forces embodied the promise—and limitations—of martial inclusivity as much as New Zealand. Newspapers often emphasized this point, proudly showing white New Zealanders working beside Malay and Sikh police.[115] New Zealand forces stood out for having racially integrated units, where white New Zealanders served side by side with Maori soldiers, who made up an estimated 30 to 40 percent of New Zealand forces.[116] Still, Maori were long regarded as one of the "martial races" of the British Empire. Their contested history of resistance and conquest in the nineteenth century left lasting legacies for access to land, jobs, and, of course, military service. Further complicating these dynamics, a 1948 defense agreement led Fijian forces to serve under New Zealand command. Fijian troops served in Malaya starting in the 1950s. These New Zealand–led forces were often touted as the embodiment of racial integration. Still, colonial legacies of "martial race" thinking continued to encourage men to give their bodies to a violent force of arms, which often made them strangers back home.

Martial race ideas were common in New Zealand to explain and justify military service, despite frequent insistence on New Zealand's relative racial integration. This narrative was especially common in *Te Ao Hou* (*The New World*), a bilingual publication issued quarterly by the Maori Affairs Department for Maori audiences.[117] One 1960s article underlined the staying power of martial race narratives, as it emphasized historic roots of Maori military service. It argued that a "young Maori of today makes as good a soldier as his ancestors ever did. He is aggressive and enterprising and generally settles well into the disciplined, ordered existence of military life."[118] Still, the article emphasized the importance of racial integration in the army by noting essentialized differences between white New Zealanders and Maori: "They say a mixed unit is better than an all-Pakeha [white] (or all-Maori) unit. The Maoris contribute dash, elan and robust good humour. The Pakeha [white] soldier is more phlegmatic and often more consistent in his approach to training. Race relations are excellent." Despite these appeals to standard martial race tropes, the article also highlighted that many men sought an army career for educational training opportunities and employment.[119] This was a recurring feature of colonial troops' desires for military employment in the twentieth century, which should have ended "martial race" clichés about their "natural" desires to fight.

Another article, written by apparent white New Zealander Alan Armstrong, justified Maori service by imitating the perspective of a Maori veteran. It started with the line "My name is Himi Meihana. In the army I call myself plain Jim Mason." The periodical did not specify if Armstrong based this account on a real person or interviewed multiple soldiers to write a composite account. Still, it is instructive for understanding representations of Maori military service targeted at Maori readers. The article cited "ancestors" from 150 years ago who searched rivers for "enemies," while now, the soldier fought in boats "propelled by the engine of the pakeha." It emphasized interracial solidarity, noting that the men in the boat were "[w]hite and brown, together as one people." They bonded, apparently, over the "sensual pleasure in this silent game of stalking," which the author

connected to "the spirit of the warrior calling back from the generations which
have gone."[120] Despite the erotic undertones, the author claimed that "the Maori
was born to hunt and fight and the blood of the warrior is in our veins. There is a
mystic but quite indefinable feeling of returning to something which is part of the
soul of our people." The article closed with an account of a jungle battle, noting:

> For months you have slogged your guts out for just this moment and when it
> finally comes, for a short space of time you are not human. Everything that
> is primitive and basic and frustrated wells to the surface to make you a killer.
> Then it is all over. The moment of blind rage and hatred passes and again we
> are just plain Jim Mason, Sonny Pehi, Pat Onslow and the rest, just ordinary
> sorts of guys again. Our moment has passed and we are mortals once more.
> But they are wrong when they say that life is as it ever was. Nothing can be
> the same again. The warriors have been blooded.[121]

The article walks a fine line between depicting Maori martial service as inherent
in its "primitive" nature, or as a shared experience with white soldiers. At the
same time, its apparent minstrelsy of Maori voice and identity underline how
common it was to expect Maori men to embrace and tout their "natural" and
inherited martial virtues.

Another *Te Ao Hou* article written by Arena Kahi provided a slightly different
account of Maori veterans. Strikingly, it emphasized the importance of race—
not only between Maori and pakeha but between Maori and Asian civilians in
Malaya. One unique feature of Maoris' Malayan service, it argued, was that in
general, "Maoris and Malays are the same colour," which meant that some could
"pass ourselves off as Malays."[122] This made the "pakeha chaps" [white men] "the
minority"—reversing the demographics of New Zealand. The author argued further that Malays and Maori had similar "virtues" and "vices," with linguistic ties
that made it easy for Maori to learn Malay during their service. In some ways,
this article replicates the colonial pattern of comparing diverse colonial populations to better define and control them. At the same time, it does so through
the lens of colonial subjects who find affinity and connections with one another
rather than being dictated or controlled by white leaders.

Arena Kahi's account differed from other *Te Ao Hou* articles by offering critiques, rather than praise, about military race relations. The article explained that
Malays were curious about "our race relations over here" because Malays were
trying to form "one Malayan race" out of Malays, Chinese, Indians, Europeans,
and Eurasians. Maoris, apparently, admitted that not everything was "ideal in
New Zealand but we are making a good try at it." Still, Malays apparently felt
surprised and excited at the "mixing of the two groups" including "on leave and

at work." They marveled at the lack of segregation and the fact that Maori officers and NCOs could command pakeha troops, which "seemed to them a practical demonstration that in New Zealand we try and practise what we preach." Though anecdotal, this article offers an interesting insight into perceptions of race in Malaya. British officials remarked repeatedly about their efforts to maintain inclusivity, but Malays, in this account, saw racial integration in the New Zealand forces as unique and almost unfathomable. The author of the article, too, noted that military culture was unique. He confessed, "Before I went into the army I do not mind admitting that I had never learned to mix with Pakeha. I thought they were different in more ways than skin colour."[123] After serving in the military, however, he had "really close Pakeha friends" who "respect us." He could not imagine anywhere else in New Zealand where you could find "a group of Maori and Pakeha in roughly equal proportions living cheek by jowl."[124] Moments of inclusion and interracial solidarity in the military were remarkable because they were so rare and fragile.[125]

Despite the promise of racial inclusivity, there was no getting around the fact that soldiers sent to Malaya were asked to leave their homes and inflict violence, leaving many men with long-standing traumas. A poem entitled "Back to Malaya" by Dinah M. Rawiri wrote of the hardships of Maori men returning to New Zealand from Malaya. It noted veterans' sense of dislocation, including having to hear relatives who cared more about sharing their own war stories than looking after the returning veteran: "Who were these strangers/ Who cared more for their own memories/ Than for he/ Who wished now, only to rest."[126] Rather than cultivating masculinity for soldiers, the returning veteran felt that masculinity had been sacrificed by seeing "too much Of the inhumanity of man/ To man." While his cousins' eyes retained "the passion of a man" his own held only "the sadness of a woman." He lamented "that war/ Can make a youth/ Into that which is less than a man."[127] Instead, he slowly recognized that "And here are your friends, cousins . . . / To welcome a stranger to their midst . . . / A stranger . . . / Who does not know yet . . . / That he is a stranger."[128] The Maori soldier's tale of brutality and becoming a stranger in his home reflected the fact that soldiers adopted new cultural and social practices and inflicted violence against other human beings. The relative racial inclusivity that some men experienced overseas did not alleviate their longer experience of isolation and depression. The prolonged nature of the Emergency, which included lengthy patrols in jungles, gave men a sense of intimacy very different from what their friends and family experienced back home. Still, the tendency to mark success through kills encouraged men to see civilians as possible enemies, and tacitly accept the everyday violence of military occupation.

The experience of Fijian troops reveals the further tensions of New Zealand forces in Malaya. Established at the outbreak of the Second World War in August 1939, the Fiji battalion served overseas in the Pacific War before getting disbanded in 1945. Their experience in the "jungle hills of the Solomons" enabled them to receive consideration for Malayan service. They were reorganized in 1948 and remobilized in October 1951, leaving for Malaya in January 1952. They achieved notoriety in Johore and Negri Sembilan.[129] However, by 1956 they claimed a particular achievement. A weekly newsletter in 1956 celebrated the Fiji Infantry Regiment for eliminating "its 200th communist terrorist."[130] This was the latest indication of the Fiji Infantry Regiment's having "the highest rate of kills since the declaration of the Malayan Emergency in 1948." While two Gurkha Battalions had already secured over two hundred kills, it was over a longer period. Their success, according to one newspaper, was a result of the high standard set by junior officers and soldiers' "natural ability in jungle-craft" as well as their "tremendous endurance."[131] Martial race assumptions, once again, explained away these men's high kill rates as an example of good leadership by white officers and soldiers' own "natural" capacities.

Like Black and Asian soldiers, Fijian troops earned praise for their physical stature as well as their ability to secure kills. Isimeli Radrodro was a star rugby player and a boxing champion, regarded by one newspaper as "champion among a race of manly men."[132] He apparently disliked the idea of returning to Fiji after his release from the army and tried to keep boxing in Singapore. The journalist noted that "Malayans and Fijians are friendly and hospitalable [*sic*] and their outlook essentially is happy," once again reiterating the feelings of commonality apparently shared among Malay, Nepali, Fijian, and Maori soldiers and civilians. These fantasies of settlement, bolstered by notions of similarity, did not make these former soldiers "alien" or "immigrants," as British officials frequently described Chinese people whose families often lived in Malaya for generations. This emphasis on Fijians' ability to get along well with civilians apparently carried over to other troops as well. When the 1 Battalion Fiji Infantry Regiment departed Malaya, they were presented with a ceremonial gift of a kukri from the 17 Gurkha Division.[133] Like Nepali soldiers, Fijian troops received the most praise not for being "cheerful" but for securing fatalities. A nomination for a mention in despatches included Sgt. Delainukunawa, whose leadership was associated with "some of the earliest kills" at Bahau. Lance Corporal Rokovutoro received a similar recommendation for being a scout who "played a large part" in "approximately sixteen kills."[134]

When reflecting on Fijian soldiers' departure from Malaya, one newspaper argued that returning soldiers would make "courageous and resourceful future leaders" in Fiji even though many felt that they had few opportunities to "exercise influence" or "express their views." The author was relieved that among these "tolerant" and "docile people," "ideas of fanatical nationalism" had not "taken root."[135] Still, Fijian service had many unintended consequences. Indigenous Fijians were less than half of the population of Fiji, owing in part to high infant mortality and recent epidemics. In 1953, their population was estimated to be just 136,000 out of a total population of 313,000. Fiji-born Indians, most of whose ancestors migrated for plantation work, outnumbered Indigenous Fijians. Because of this, there was some resistance to sending Fijians for service overseas because they "have become a minority group in their homeland."[136] Just over 1,700 soldiers served in Malaya from Fiji, and of these approximately 1,550 identified as ethnically Fijian. Military service, therefore, demanded "one in every 12 healthy young Fijians. Nothing in the least comparable was asked of the other races in Fiji."[137] This proved pivotal for the future of returning soldiers, who missed transformative postwar years of industrialization. Many believed that military service hurt rather than helped their long-term economic position.

While Fijians returned home in 1956, New Zealanders' service continued well beyond the end of the Emergency in 1960. In the words of Gordon Ell, Army Public Relations Officer, the "end of Emergency state" did not mean that the "search for communist terrorists was over."[138] New Zealanders continued to fight in Southeast Asia against communism well into the 1960s, despite Britain's own flight from "East of Suez" after the Suez Crisis of 1956 and the independence of Malaysia in 1957.[139] Yet many *Te Ao Hou* articles were not published until after the Emergency officially "ended." This signals the true long-term goal of Commonwealth inclusivity, which was about creating the next generation of "martial races" who would take up the mantle of British militarism. The Malayan Emergency became a training ground of the Commonwealth, encouraging men from across the former empire to embrace narratives of martial upward mobility and Commonwealth inclusivity. The hope was that post-colonial nations would view Britain—and its military forces—as agents of positive change in the world.

UNEQUAL WIVES

One reason that soldiers felt disconnected from societies back home was that they experienced radically different levels of familial support. Former Royal Air Force (RAF) member and army wife Irene Simkin noted that all army wives dealt with "loneliness and frustration."[140] Yet race, class, and ethnicity also shaped their experiences. For Simkin, arriving in Penang meant living temporarily in a waterfront hotel.[141] When she finally received her housing assignment, she relished in gaining the "huge" captain's quarters. They hired "two amahs, one to do the washing and help with the children, and a cook amah who also did the housework. A part-time kebun (gardener) looked after the outside areas of the house." She saw having servants as a "necessity" because the "constant heat and humidity were such that no white woman could possibly cope with everything."[142] Living in Malaya as a white officer's wife meant a large house and plentiful servants, reinforcing the entitlement to prestige and privilege temporarily lost during the war.[143] Despite these luxuries, army wives like Simkin could not escape "anagging [sic] fear for the safety of our husbands, and life in these tropic outposts is nowhere near as privileged as civilians back home imagine it to be."[144] While white women faced very real emotional hardships, they enjoyed greater material comforts than the Asian women who accompanied their husbands overseas while negotiating the same fears and uncertainties. These inequities showed the cracks in the promise of Commonwealth inclusivity and efforts to win the "hearts and minds" of those serving the cause.

While Simkin stayed in hotels and large quarters, most Nepali families were housed in tented accommodations in the sweltering Malayan climate. Some remained in tents until at least 1952.[145] Even traveling to Malaya proved arduous. Nepali women traveled by ship from India for twenty-four hours. Rather than noting the difficulty of the journey, one white Briton of the Women's Voluntary Service remarked in 1948 that Nepali babies were "grimy" after the long voyage, some with dysentery.[146] When they arrived, their living situations varied. Soldiers and their families moved into a variety of camps—some in good condition, and others left in disrepair from the Second World War.[147] Families complained frequently about the lack of suitable cooking facilities, which were shared by multiple households—a far cry from hotel accommodations and personal servants.[148] A British officer of the 7th Gurkha Rifles explained away these difficulties by suggesting: "One's immediate reaction to family quarters . . . is like ones [sic] reaction to many other things in Army life but on reflection one supposes a wife in Malaya is better than two in Nepal."[149]

While white and Nepali wives faced very different experiences of life overseas, many other Commonwealth women did not have the opportunity to accompany their husbands at all. When Maori women visited husbands or other family members on service, they received praise for doing so if they entertained the troops.[150] Fijian families did not accompany soldiers overseas, and received

FIGURE 10.   Fijian women wave goodbye to soldiers through barbed wire.
"Fiji Troops For Malaya" (1952). Still supplied by British Pathé.

little or no official assistance while their husbands, sons, and fathers were away, creating severe economic hardships.[151] Meanwhile, a British Pathé film of Fijian soldiers leaving for Malaya foregrounded the pain of family separation. As soldiers paraded and boarded their ship, crowds of women and children wept from the sidelines. The film narration explained that the soldiers were "leaving behind the wives and mothers to their grief." It spared several moments for close-ups of women wiping their tear-stained faces. Some struggled in visible agony to grasp one last hug with their beloved soldiers through barbed wire. Instead, the "chief and his wife" kissed the soldiers as they departed. The narrators interjected that there was "perhaps, some sense of intrusion in these pictures of private sorrow except that they make real to us these unknown fellow members of our Commonwealth."[152] The filmmakers exploited Fijian women's personal grief to publicly promote the familial intimacy of the Commonwealth.

Like Fijian soldiers, those from the King's African Rifles served in Malaya without family support.[153] VC winner Lt. Col. Eric Charles Tweelves Wilson

remembered that in "peace time [*sic*] all the askaris had wives."[154] Another officer suggested that "if he hadn't got a wife one wanted to know the reason why,
because they usually got into mischief without one." Despite this expectation,
"African families were sent back to villages" when soldiers left for Malaya.[155]
This exclusion caused many issues for soldiers personally and professionally. The
army often employed women as sexual laborers or "temporary wives" for soldiers,
no doubt deepening the fears and frustrations of family back home. British officials also suspected that this arrangement increased the rate of venereal disease.
In the 1 KAR, where health and discipline was good overall, "the incidence of
venereal disease was high."[156] British leaders continued a long-standing pattern
of military control that regulated disease through women rather than men. Further, soldiers' wives, still living in East Africa, did not have access to wartime
Air Mail facilities, which meant that most could not, or did not, write to soldiers
while they were away. In turn, many wives received no support from absent husbands.[157] This had a noticeable impact on enthusiasm for the campaign. When
one African unit departed for Malaya in April 1956, an African reporter noted
that few Black civilians turned out at the train station to see them off. He observed that they "left as if they were unwanted rather like outcasts without relatives and friends."[158]

    While having family nearby provided relative comfort compared to those who
were separated, it also created hardships. Nepali soldier Tulbahadur Rai, DCM,
1/7 GR, accompanied 180 families on the move from India to Malaya. When their
ship ran aground, most families "panicked" and had to be locked in their cabins
to prevent them escaping and drowning. He considered this "the hardest single
thing I had to do" during his entire service.[159] Sometimes, families caused logistical difficulties. Shamsherbahadur Rai, 1/7 GR, learned that "a hut belonging to
a Malay 500 yards from Gurkha family lines" had been visited by communists
demanding food. Because of the proximity to soldiers' families they proceeded
cautiously, waiting a month before they made contact. When they finally opened
fire, they found "a girl, hit in the thigh and covered in blood" holding on to a tree
in one hand and a pistol in the other. They eventually captured her and held her
in the British Military Hospital for a month, where she died from gangrene.[160]

    Incidents of civilian casualties reveal the gender and racial dynamics at play
in the Emergency. White women enjoyed an elevated class position and the support of Asian labor. Nepali women earned protection, if not comfort, for being
the wives of soldiers. African and Fijian women were excluded entirely from
Commonwealth visions of familial unity in Malaya. Asian women, meanwhile,
embodied the fluidity between combatants and non-combatants. Pahalman Rai,

1/10 GR, rationalized the death of a Chinese girl by suggesting that she "was taking supplies to them and one of our bullets hit her. There was no trouble about her death as she was helping the *daku* [bandits]."[161] Another Chinese girl, seventeen-year-old Ha Kit Lim, was used "as a shield against two bandits" by special constable Mohamed bin Osman, who was later charged with murder.[162] The Chinese, Indian, and Malay women caught in the cross fire of conflict rarely earned either protection or privilege.

While Black and Asian soldiers lacked family support, the press was more interested in emphasizing their lethality, particularly in acts of violence against women. Newspapers filled with accounts of Black and Asian—but not British, New Zealander, or Australian—units involved in violence against women, sidestepping British complicity. For example, Loh Sow Lan was given the chance to surrender after getting injured by the 4th Battalion Malay Regiment even after firing on them with a sten gun.[163] Ng Ah Moi surrendered after receiving "bullet wounds in her thigh and neck" from "a Gurkha patrol."[164] When a "woman terrorist was shot dead" they mentioned that this was done by the 3rd King's African Rifles.[165] The 2nd King's African Rifles were mentioned specifically when a "girl terrorist" dropped a rifle and vegetables after getting shot in the shoulder.[166] The 1st Battalion Fiji Infantry were responsible for killing a "handsome girl."[167] Mention of the 2/6 Gurkhas occurred in an article entitled "Girl Bandit Killed by Gurkhas."[168] Newspapers rarely mentioned British police and soldiers in acts of violence against women. Instead, articles usually referenced "security forces," eliminating possible scrutiny over white soldiers killing Asian women. This replicated longer patterns of using colonial troops to implement violence that British men did not want to undertake themselves, reinforcing essentialized notions about racialized men's "natural" inclinations toward violence. Their lack of family support, however, reminds us that soldiers endured radically different conditions of service, isolation from civilians, and a constant barrage of racism. Their frustrations—which might manifest as sanctioned violence—were read by British leaders as a reflection of their natural martial prowess, rather than the pent-up rage engendered by colonial rule and military violence.

DISCARDED SOLDIERS

The racial hierarchies of the Malayan Emergency reveal how colonial soldiers were—and were not—included in military efforts to win "hearts and minds" in Malaya. Most often, military leaders treated them like props to imperial efforts to win over civilians despite continued violence. Black soldiers' bodies could be mocked or made into a spectacle to decrease Asian civilians' fears. British leaders celebrated Maori, Fijian, and Nepali soldiers as "jolly" and capable of settlement and immersion—as well as agents of violence. British officers adjusted "martial race" assumptions throughout the Emergency in small but significant ways to justify the continued service of units with deep colonial histories. Yet the lingering tensions of colonial military service did not disappear. Extreme violence, racism, and unequal service conditions remained recurring features of colonial and post-colonial military institutions. As Simeon Man suggests, "racial inclusion" in the military "did not produce an orderly free world, but its opposite: more violence, more insurgencies."[169] Soldiers endured and perpetuated trauma and violence, returning home to decolonizing nations that were often radically different from when they left. Despite the confident rhetoric of winning "hearts and minds," the hearts and minds of Commonwealth soldiers were yet to be won.

Interracial militarization ultimately failed to foster a society that could forget the racism of the colonial past and present. Some hoped that police forces, rather than Commonwealth soldiers, could guide Malaya's future. For the *Malayan Police Magazine*, "cultivating the children of Malaya" would ensure long-term bonds within the Commonwealth. These children, they believed, were "the people who will govern Malaya in the future, in all probability without British assistance, and it is to be hoped that the Police will 'win over' the children as completely as they appear to have done the adults of Malaya."[170] Children of police officers soon replaced office "peons," practiced wearing uniforms, obeyed commands, and participated in drills, creating the next generation of locally-raised martial races.[171] Still, the *Malayan Police Magazine* worried that there remained a "deep-rooted fear" of policing throughout colonial society. They speculated that this was a result of "methods employed during the Japanese regime." Since police during the Emergency "had to become strict disciplinarians" to "protect the public," this "did not make for cordial relations with the masses."[172] Police even avoided wearing their uniforms off duty so that they would not scare or intimidate civilians.[173] In response, British leaders launched Operation "Service" in 1953 to emphasize broadcasts, school speaking tours, and interviews, with an aim to create a positive image of police in the minds of children. Given the lingering and ongoing traumas of war and colonialism, British leaders prioritized winning over the next generations. Winning hearts and minds, therefore, became about controlling the future—and who could live to see it.

SEVEN

Pregnant in the Jungle

In the early years of the Cold War, a Chinese-language British propaganda cartoon warned Chinese women about giving birth in the jungle. This was in the middle of the Malayan Emergency (1948–1960), a British-led campaign against communism. The cartoon depicted a pregnant Chinese woman lying on bamboo in pain, surrounded by angry-faced communist men in uniform. The men informed a British official about their position, allowing British forces to airlift the woman out by helicopter. She then enjoyed a comfortable hospital bed under the attentive care of a smiling nurse. The newspaper explained that this imagery was inspired by a real woman, Soh Pek Yoke, who had complications with her pregnancy while in a "small jungle camp." After great suffering, including the loss of her baby, two communists surrendered, enabling a "mercy helicopter" to take her to the hospital. According to the newspaper, she received "the best medical care and treatment," recovered, and "was very grateful."[1] This optimistic depiction of surrender hints at how Britain's fight against communism deepened the gendered experience of colonial rule.

The Malayan Emergency is most well-known for popularizing a famous phrase about modern warfare: winning the "hearts and minds" of civilians.[2] Director of Operations and High Commissioner of Malaya Sir Gerald Templer (1951–1954) claimed that the key to success in the campaign "lies not in pouring more troops into the jungle but in the hearts and minds of the people."[3] What this meant for "the people" was less clear. Templer's predecessor, Sir Harold Briggs, laid the foundations for combating communism in 1950 with the two-pronged

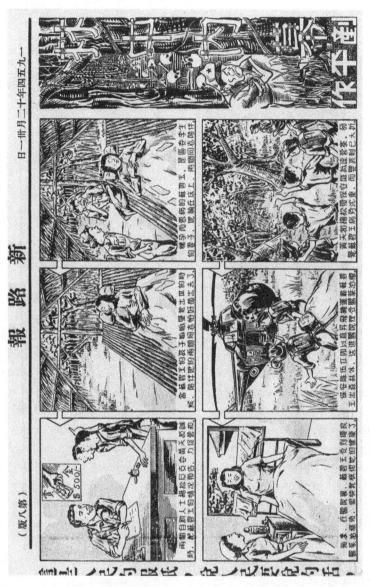

FIGURE II. Cartoon of a pregnant woman evacuated from the jungle to a British hospital. "Behind the Jungle Curtain," *Sin Lu Pau* [New Path News], No. 39 (31 December 1954). Image courtesy of the Major General Dennis Edmund Blaquière Talbot papers, Liddell Hart Centre for Military Archives.

approach of killing communists in jungles and resettling Chinese civilians.[4] Both leaders encouraged civilians to see police and military forces as agents of positive change, through upward mobility in police and military service, and the welfare offered through resettlement. The goal was to deny communists resources and recruits while creating a plan for Malaya's formal independence without communism. Yet police and military leaders often struggled with the softer side of state power. Templer rebranded many aspects of the Emergency without changing its essential components, for instance renaming "bandits" communist terrorists (CTs) and resettlement areas "New Villages." The underlying practice of extreme violence remained.[5] This chapter explores how an emphasis on civilians deepened gender and racial hierarchies by making colonial power appear less violent. In reality, the Emergency facilitated greater access to civilians, replicating longer patterns of colonial control.

This chapter will explore how a cartoon of an airlifted, happy woman smiling in a British hospital represented a recurring trope of military intervention being a source of salvation for Asian women. Using visual sources alongside military and police records, oral histories, and personal papers, this chapter reveals how the Emergency reconfigured and hardened postwar understandings of racial and gender difference. Gendered imagery depicted communist men as emaciated fanatics and communist women as irredeemable jezebels to justify violence against civilians. Yet real Asian men and women of various class, ethnic, and religious backgrounds served the British in police forces, in voluntary services, and as combatants. Reconfiguring race and gender ideals after the uncertainty and trauma of the Second World War enabled British leaders to sell the idea that colonial militarism and capitalism could be sources of stability and prosperity. Yet people's real experiences of the Emergency suggest that even the most nominally civilian-friendly military and police policies did more to perpetuate colonial violence than "win" hearts and minds.

WHITE WOMEN AND WELFARE

In many ways, white women were the preeminent symbol of imperial vulnerability.[6] This led to their ability to secure real protections, including confinement on ships in Singapore during the 1915 rebellion and their priority in evacuation during the Japanese invasion.[7] Yet many colonial subjects regarded white women in Malaya as out of touch and shameful for evacuating. Madam Seow Guat Beng emphasized this when she recalled a British woman returning to her home after the occupation, demanding to know what happened to her fine chairs and teapot.

She replied, "You dare ask me about the teapot when you all evacuated without even a word?"[8] The only people to survive with reputations relatively intact were well-respected medical women, including Elinor Hopkins and Cicely Williams, who continued to serve in internment camps. While "martial race" thinking attempted to redeem colonial masculinity, the redemption of white womanhood relied on emphasizing service-minded ideals. Advertising white women's roles as caregivers—chiefly nurses, mothers, and welfare workers—showed that they could serve the colony rather than exploit it. This contrasted the image of white women as vulnerable paragons of prestige who were incapable of doing work in a tropical climate. If white women were willing to work for the benefit of the colony, perhaps the colony could remain in British hands.

The film *Outpost in Malaya* (1952) emphasized the importance of white women for saving face after the Second World War. It became mandatory viewing for soldiers serving in the Emergency.[9] At the center of the film was a spirited fight against "bandits" by the fictional Frazer family, who were survivors of Japanese internment. While the patriarch of the family participated in an interracial fight against communists with various police and military allies, the focus was on the matriarch, Liz Frazer. She ultimately bore arms to fight communists while performing acceptable femininity. She wore white, flowing gowns and fainted when she fired weapons, collapsing into the arms of her husband. She remained a dutiful wife and mother despite her willingness to fight. The film showed that women like Liz Frazer would bare arms if they had to, but they really wanted to return to a peaceful home after years of suffering.[10] Since surrender to the Japanese made white men insecure about their inability to protect white women, the Emergency gave them—and their families—the chance to demonstrate their perseverance. Real army wife June White felt this deeply when accompanying her husband, who commanded the Third Battalion of the Royal Australian Regiment, to Malaya. They attended an ANZAC day memorial service at the military cemetery on Singapore Island "where a great number of Australian casualties from the Second World War were buried."[11] Attending such celebrations created continuity between heroic sacrifices in the Second World War and service in the Emergency. Colonial families suffered heroically for the empire and now fought to restore it.

Many real-life women in medicine and welfare similarly softened the realities of colonial militarism through compassionate care. Pamela Gouldsbury took to nursing as a pastime and wrote a detailed memoir, *Jungle Nurse*, on her efforts to provide medical assistance to Indigenous (Orang Asli) communities living in the Malayan jungles. A police officer's wife, she soon integrated herself into intelligence networks. Her efforts to "save" Orang Asli from disease and injury made her into a friendly face of British militarism, expanding the reach of the colonial state much farther than it had ventured previously.[12] As Simeon Man has suggested, this dynamic was not uncommon in Southeast Asia. Doctors and nurses in the Philippines became agents of U.S. psychological warfare by gaining the trust of community through intimate care.[13] This made it possible for many medical women to find professional opportunity in Malaya. One army educational pamphlet contended that the "Army in Malaya today is essentially a man's Army" although there were "some women and nursing claims most of them." It highlighted women's work at British Military Hospitals through organizations such as the Queen Alexandra's Royal Army Nursing Corps, the Red Cross, and St. John's Brigade.[14] The Soldiers', Sailors', and Airmen's Families Association (SSAFA) also provided assistance, with a single Sister monitoring "11 Police clinics, nine at outstations" in 1953.[15] In Malaya, welfare work recast white women as advocates and allies of Asian civilians, rather than decadent—or humiliated—beneficiaries of an empire that abandoned Malaya at the first sign of trouble. White women's efforts as nurses, welfare workers, and caregivers stressed their apparent intimacy with colonial subjects.

Periodicals were most enamored when medical women cared for soldiers' bodies. Five members of the British Women's Voluntary Service (WVS) arrived in Malaya in spring 1948.[16] An educational training pamphlet explained that women came out for eighteen-month tours and provided presents and flowers for men to send home. They also gave dance lessons and made forces' centers "as comfortable as possible with flowers, furniture, curtains etc." These women also "look after the welfare of Gurkha families."[17] Given the ubiquity of Nepali troops in the conflict, this proved to be a primary duty of WVS women. According to the Brigade of Gurkhas periodical *The Kukri*, WVS staff acted "in a welfare capacity."[18] Malaya became a regular station for Gurkha regiments after the independence and partition of India, so Nepali families were housed there in large numbers. By 1949, a single battalion of the 2 GR had ninety-five families and seventy children.[19] The WVS looked after "the health of the women and children."[20] This included issuing milk and vitamins, inspecting tents, weighing and measuring babies, and accompanying women to the clinic or hospital during pregnancy or illness. They initiated Nepali women into British customs and military life by instructing them to use sewing machines to make lighter-fabric clothing. WVS women also ran physical training courses and schools for younger children, with an emphasis on learning English.

Women's labors were critical to bringing additional welfare services to police and military personnel in Malaya. One Officer Commanding a Police Department (OCPD) recalled that welfare services in 1950 were virtually nonexistent, which contributed to low morale among Asian policemen. This worsened in 1951 when rubber prices spiked and rank-and-file Asian policemen earned less than the average rubber tapper. As a result, Asian "Police wives" had "to bargain for every article they purchased."[21] They recognized that winning over police wives maintained the productivity and happiness of policemen, despite their low salaries. Especially important were clinics for police mothers and their children, which opened in 1951 at Alor Star. It was organized and run by Che Hamzah bin Malmud, assisted by Mrs. Nevill Godwin and Mrs. Hugh Donaldson. Despite the acknowledgment of Che Hamzah bin Malmud, the article provided no further elaboration or biography. Instead, it highlighted Sister Keenan of the SSAFA, who supervised a clinic in Penang, without identifying the Asian nurse pictured with her.[22] Police erased Asian civilian women's labors to elevate and encourage further engagement from white women.

By 1951 and 1952, welfare services increased, further offsetting the financial deficiencies of police work. Canteens expanded and English classes commenced by 1952.[23] In Kedah and Perlis there were "death benefits" available for the death of a husband, wife, or child, and an additional bonus to wives whose husbands were killed in the Emergency.[24] By 1953, one anonymous contributor to the *Malayan Police Magazine*, ostensibly a police wife, claimed that "Welfare is Fun." Her article detailed women's activities, including forming clubs, organizing English lessons, volunteering to support SSAFA clinics, and offering sewing lessons. In many cases, Asian police wives served as "volunteers" to do unheralded labor—including revitalizing condemned quarters for use as a clinic in Taiping. The expectation for white women to provide uncompensated labor created a similar expectation of "volunteerism" among Asian police wives. Nonetheless, the author concluded that police wives were naturally "welfare-minded. At times we are depressed, at times we are elated, but on the whole most of us agree that WELFARE IS FUN."[25] According to these periodicals, women were instrumental in advocating for, and becoming solutions to, the morale and welfare of policemen. In turn, accolades for police wives and SSAFA women were common. A police officer cast this as a top-down model of welfare, with "the wives of our mata matas" (Asian policemen) benefiting from "the knowledge and advice of these very experienced people."[26] Some women and organizations did petition for Asian women's needs, successfully advocating for a permanent midwife and the formation of English-language courses.[27]

This emphasis on white women's roles in welfare was not always convincing for Asian women. One Malay women's organization expressed their disappointment in British wives, whom they found cold, jealous, and immature. They apparently fussed about things that Asian women did not notice, making them both bad wives and mothers.[28] British periodicals, by contrast, were reluctant to praise Asian women. One article made passing reference to the importance of local nurses and midwives, such as amahs and bidans, but emphasized that most "mothers of young families have no help in the nursery." They did acknowledge that childcare was central to overall morale: "To prevent anyone being overworked, or suffering caused among husbands and children owing to the preoccupation of the home-keeper, it is hoped to spread the burden among as many ladies as possible."[29] In other words, men who came home after long patrols to wives who were overwhelmed with housework and childcare were inefficient workers. The ultimate goal was to ensure the efficiency of police work. British leaders even explicitly connected higher morale to greater communist fatalities.[30] The acknowledgment that women were central to men's morale brought greater amenities to women. This also put a heavier burden on wives to provide uncompensated labor through social welfare to facilitate the deadliness of the campaign. Ultimately, Asian women rarely benefited from these labors. Eurasian author and doctor Han Suyin characterized hospitals for Asian women and children as sparse. She asserted that women "still don't count much in this country" because hospitals cost money and there was little to spare in the Emergency.[31] While white women received credit for the labors of Asian women, the latter received little real material support.

Some white women failed to embrace their expected roles. When June White accompanied her husband, who commanded Australian troops in Penang, she heard that "the locals would be offended, on religious grounds, by women parading around in revealing sun dresses."[32] Casting dress as a matter of offending or not offending the "religious scruples" of Asian women sidestepped the wartime concern that interned white women lost "prestige" by wearing sun tops and flimsy dresses. Meanwhile, Irene Simkin recalled that while some white women accompanying husbands coped well with living overseas, others who had just married expected "a two-year tropical honeymoon." Without men around, they "banded together to sell their favours."[33] June White similarly recalled "three of the wives were running a brothel in a married quarter." As punishment, the women "were immediately returned to Australia and the husbands given the option of accompanying them or remaining with the Battalion."[34] Simkin did not judge these women harshly, noting that "there was very little to do" apart from "seeing the occasional film, shopping and going to the swimming club." Some of the women "took courses in Indian, Chinese and Malay cooking" to pass the time, but life "could be pretty lonely and boring without the men around."[35] She saved herself from scandal by filling the time "in a welfare role" and providing assistance to "battalion wives." Other wives helped with "schools and orphanages." Ultimately, June White hoped that "never again will an Australian Government send families overseas to accompany Australian troops who will be in action. It is far too much strain to impose on all concerned."[36] Welfare work, according to these women, was a grudging alternative to boredom, worry, and prostitution.

While many white women failed to embody the military domesticity that British leaders demanded, Lady Peggy Templer became the paragon of white women's welfare work. As the wife of Field Marshal Templer, who popularized the "hearts and minds" phrase, she took seriously her role in winning over civilian confidence. This was something that even General Templer practiced. According James Neill, the General visited resettlement camps by rushing "into the labour lines" to "pick up the nearest little baby and start . . . sort of . . . chatting up mum and dad" being "very much the human contact man."[37] Meanwhile, Lady Templer acted as President of the SSAFA in Malaya, spearheading welfare initiatives during her husband's tenure as high commissioner.[38] Her service efforts were so exhaustive that police in Kuala Lumpur organized a "Lady Templer month" that focused on raising funds for her many medical initiatives through fairs, films, performances, and games.[39] In 1954, she raised over $100,000 from police families to build and support a hospital for tuberculosis. White women, therefore, were responsible for raising the funds, and constructing the infrastructure, that British leaders touted as key to their beneficence.[40] She also supported other health initiatives, such as the Welfare of the Blind Association.[41] An article in *Malayan Police Magazine* discussed one tea party in January 1954 at Kuala Lumpur that focused on the issue of police welfare, touting Lady Templer as a distinguished guest. There, she argued that women were critical to the effectiveness of police work because "hardship and trouble were often averted by women confiding their fears to the wives of officers. This confidence only came through personal contact."[42] The tacit implication was that women were crucial for monitoring the welfare and morale of police, preventing dissension and even rebellion in the ranks.

One recurring depiction of welfare work was that the Commonwealth, and its service organizations, were essentially one big family. Mr. F. K. McNamara praised the "large Police family" while advocating for police wives to help in clinics, visit families, and bring goods to police who were hospitalized.[43] Lady Templer emphasized this as a "duty," whereas McNamara suggested that "it is not asking too much" for police wives to take "an active interest in the lives and welfare of the families of the men of their husband's command."[44] Acting commissioner Nicholls also emphasized that police and their wives should "act as one large family." He suggested that women organize and participate in games and entertainment, provide comfort for sick and wounded, and take an active interest in the health and well-being of police, including attending the police clinic. Even without medical expertise, he found, police wives could weigh babies, record information, interview families, distribute comfort items, and talk to families "about their babies and children." Women who were busy in evenings could do clerical work, arrange entertainment and raise funds, or organize lectures. These efforts were essential because if "the rank-and-file feel that an interest is being taken in their personal affairs," then "their loyalty" and "the family spirit of this Service can be promoted and increased."[45] By 1952, the commissioner of police, Arthur Young, wrote to *Police* magazine "God Bless the Ladies." He also used the language of the family: "Our job in Malaya may be the most difficult in the world; we are proud that it is, but as a united and happy family what reason can we have for dismay?"[46]

By enabling British women to supervise the domestic lives of police and soldiers' wives, white women gained roles similar to missionaries, teachers, or matrons from the earlier colonial period.[47] English manners and customs were promises of civilization and uplift, regardless of training or experience. WVS women received repeated praise and mentions by name in military publications. They made only passing (and anonymous) mention of battalion "dhai amah" who served as nurses, servants, cooks, and childcare personnel. Their efforts were no doubt equally, if not more, essential for police and military families. Many photos of police clinics similarly included detailed references to the white women pictured, but rarely acknowledged or named the uniformed Asian women.[48] Welfare work encouraged interracial intimacy, and the idea of the "police" or "Commonwealth" family, while reproducing entitlement to gendered and racialized labor. Securing services for police and military families gave them the welfare and support enjoyed by comparatively few civilians, creating further distance between police/military families and other colonial subjects. At the same time, women's labors were integral to maintaining the morale of policemen and soldiers, which meant that women's work was the true backbone of retaining the "hearts and minds" that fought—and killed—for British aims.

TARGETING ASIAN WOMEN

While the film *Outpost in Malaya* emphasized the motherly heroism of white women like Liz Frazer, it also proved ambivalent toward Asian women. Scenes depicted them as either frightened but loyal servants or laborers who were preyed upon—but never joined—"bandits." One scene showed a young Tamil rubber tapper being coerced into hiding rice for "bandits," only to be discovered and roughly handled by police. Subsequent scenes never addressed her fate. In reality, many such women faced military and police violence. Real guerilla Luo Lan recalled vividly how her own aunt was a rubber tapper on their plantation when "a traitor brought many British soldiers to our place." They demanded that she "lead them to the guerillas." Her aunt knew where they were but refused to say anything, pretending that she did not know. When "the traitor" insisted that she was lying, "the British shot her on the spot." Luo Lan remembered "her corpse being carried home."[49] While white women became symbols of the beneficence of empire, many Asian women risked everything fighting against it. The consequence was violence.

Naturally, people of all genders had complex reasons for joining the communist struggle. Some joined the Malayan Communist Party (MCP) during the economic downturn of 1929 to 1933 or the Japanese occupation (1942–1945). Many early members became communists for ideological reasons, including the MCP's stated goals of improved wages and equality for women. As former guerilla Lin Guan Ying suggests, "it was easy to understand how capitalism and imperialism exploited us," but at the same time, "as women, we also wanted to join; we wanted to fight for the liberation of women."[50] Eng Ming Ching, later known as Suriani Abdullah joined the MCP in 1940, at age 16. She endured torture for anti-Japanese activities during the war and then worked as an MCP representative for the British Military Administration after 1945. With the declaration of the Emergency, however, she joined the resistance, organizing MCP unit strategy and operations.[51] Despite women's varied reasons for joining the MCP and fighting colonialism, these proved irrelevant to British officials who portrayed them as villainous communists deserving violence.

Women's experiences with communism proved just as diverse as their reasons for joining. As Mahani Musa and Agnes Khoo have shown, some women were born into communist families or in areas where communists were dominant the social, cultural, and educational forces. Lin Guan Ying recalled living in Ying Lang Lang and joining the communist party prior to the war because "the Party stood for the liberation of the poor. It stood for the poorest of the poor. We were poor and had to have many different jobs to survive." She found "no difference between exploitation and oppression by the British or the Japanese for the common people."[52] Chen Xiu Zhu similarly recalled that peasants "tended to be supportive of the revolution. Even though my family was poor, we were nevertheless willing to donate whatever money we had to the struggle." She did not formally join the guerillas until both of her parents were arrested and deported by the British. Her mother urged her to "avenge the oppressed and the exploited masses and the injustice my family had suffered."[53] Other women faced beatings and punishments from family members if they tried to join, or ran away from home to do so.[54] Some joined to follow family or friends already in the ranks or to avoid detainment after the ban on women's nationalist and labor organizations after 1948.[55] This was the case for Hajjah Haslina, also known as Siti Aishah Haji Khatib, who became a guerilla at age twenty to avoid arrest for her membership in a banned organization. She lived in the jungle for ten years. Many Malay women joined to escape poverty or took inspiration from women MCP leaders like Shamsiah Fakeh and Zainab Mahmud, whom their followers saw as carrying on the legacy of previous anti-British rebellions.[56] Malay guerilla Mak Chu even identified with her relative Datuk Bahaman, who had fought the British in Pahang in the nineteenth century. She fought because he "is my ancestor; I am his descendant. I was also fighting the British, like him, as a Communist Party member so I will not regret it if I die here."[57] The Emergency was hardly just a fight against Chinese communist men.

In many ways, women proved essential to the communist cause, serving as guerillas, trade union representatives, political party members, or in support services. Like white women, many Asian women also served in medical roles. Chen Xiu Zhu learned "how to give medical care" including "injections," "acupuncture," and helping "women comrades relieve their menstrual pains."[58] Some women faced arrests in Singapore for being teachers who spread communist messages in schools. Others aided, sheltered, and cared for MCP leaders, including Chin Peng during his move to southern Thailand in 1953. One unit on his march was comprised and led entirely by women. Other women retained his communist networks in Malaya and Singapore as the Emergency continued. Lee Meng or Lee Ten (Tian) Tai's contribution was so immense that Chin Peng singled her out as a "dedicated comrade" before the British deported her to China. Despite these contributions, many women recalled how rare it was for women to receive arms or weapons training. More often, they were passed over for men no matter their contributions.[59] Still, Chen Xiu Zhu felt "women could do everything the men did" including carrying rifles, working in factories, and going "into battle like the men."[60]

FIGURE 12.   British officials interrogate Asian women. "Malayan Women Bandits Aka Malayan Bandits Surrender" (1953). Still supplied by British Pathé.

At times, British leaders and commentators observed communist women with nervous fascination. One British Pathé newsreel depicted a group of women surrendering. It showed them marching out of the jungle and being interviewed by British leaders. The incomplete narration pondered, "Now what, I wonder, are these women thinking as they leave . . ." Rather than examining the question too deeply, the narrator suggested that they could "look forward to a new and useful life."[61] The emphasis on utility underlined that, in the minds of British leaders, the greatest contribution that Asian women could make was being useful to imperial capitalism, rather than undermining it.[62] Another film emphasized this point, depicting women workers "Feeding the Troops in Malaya." It noted the difficulty of getting soldiers access to food while they were in the jungle because they could only carry enough for two weeks. The footage came from a "factory in Kuala Lumpur" and showed the hard work of roughly eighty women who made tins and packaged food for soldiers. Jaunty music played while the exclusively female, and often very young, workers carried out their tasks diligently, declining to look at the camera. Their goal was to make tinned ration packs for Malay and Chinese security forces. Despite their hard and mechanical work in assembly lines, women retained their femininity by wearing "a fresh white apron, cap and gloves." This enabled them to work "speedily and efficiently" to produce four to five thousand tins per day. Their work ensured that unlike "terrorists, the security forces don't have to worry where their next meal is coming from." This emphasis on women's work demonstrated that British rule, and capitalism, provided women with clean, safe, and reliable working conditions. It also retained the gendered division of labor between women, associated with food preparation, and men, who served as soldiers: "By these modern methods, the soldier in the jungle can eat almost as well as he can in his own home."[63] Throughout the Emergency, British leaders tried to put Asian women in their "rightful" place of serving British militarism.

This emphasis on Asian women facilitating the meals of British-led forces obscured the fact that civilians struggled to secure food throughout the postwar and Emergency period. Civilians such as Lim Bee Giok noted the difficulty of rationing and shortages long after the war ended.[64] Meanwhile, a key tactic of the Emergency was food denial, or "starvation-restriction policy," to starve communists out of the jungle.[65] Many civilians and villagers endured frequent searches and rationing to ensure that they were not giving or selling food to communists. Luo Lan remembered riding the bus with her grandmother, who bought pork while they were out. When police entered the bus, they threw her pork out the window.[66] Similarly, Han Suyin described plantation rubber tappers as having to perform exhausting labor without nourishment because of British efforts to ensure that none of their food wound up in the jungle. This was especially difficult because depriving the jungle also meant that they had limited access to water in the hot Malayan sun.[67] Food denial also had a devastating impact on communist morale. Lo Choy, a Regional Committee member killed by security forces, reportedly wrote in his diary that he asked his leaders if "we shall starve to death," but none "of the comrades answered."[68] Chen Xiu Zhu insisted that "there were times when we did not see one grain of rice for an entire year inside the jungle."[69] As a result, communist guerillas had to grow much of their own food, which proved difficult under aerial surveillance. If they did not prepare the food properly, it could lead to mass illness in the camp, while campfires made them vulnerable to aerial surveillance.[70] This underlined women's importance, as many women ran the jungle kitchens.[71] Yet press reports only focused on their suffering. Yap Chiu Chin shared her difficulties with the *Straits Times,* insisting that "the bandits are starving."[72] Moo Yoon Kiew, interviewed on the radio, became known as the "The Starving Lady of Ipoh" after enduring two years in the jungle "on a meagre diet of tapioca, rice water and jungle seeds."[73] By emphasizing women's roles in making food, British leaders cast women's food-related suffering as an asset to the Emergency rather than a failure of colonial governance.[74]

Beyond food, women experienced multiple, intersecting dangers living in the jungle and encountering military and police forces. Feng Su Qiong, alias Xiu Ning, felt that life in the jungle was most difficult "when the enemy attacked us."[75] Aerial bombardments, for Chen Xiu Zhu, were most troubling, as "carpet-bombing went on non-stop," leaving "no respite" especially when "we were starving." Aerial surveillance also discouraged them from wearing raincoats that would make them stand out, so they got "wet when it rained and sunburnt when the sun was out."[76] In many ways, this reflected the Indian legacy of the "hearts and minds" idea, as Major General Boucher, who served in India's northwestern borderlands where the phrase was coined, readily adapted methods from India to Malaya, including aerial bombardment.[77] Yet the press rarely acknowledged the stress of living under British surveillance. When Moo Yoon Kiew was interviewed on Radio Malaya, they sexualized her being found "naked and unconscious" beside "four bandits who had starved to death."[78] She had apparently worked "as a nurse," carried messages, and collected money from villages. While she had been a strong girl when she joined, she became "a physical wreck" from her time in the jungle.[79] The Malay Regiment apparently "rescued her" and gave her a sarong and a shirt and "flew her by helicopter" to a hospital in Ipoh. As with the propaganda cartoon depicting a "rescue helicopter," Moo Yoon Kiew was photographed in the hospital, reinforcing it as a space for the redemption of Asian women. The emphasis on her physicality—a strong girl turned into a "physical wreck"—helped undermine the communist cause. Others poked fun at communist women such as S. E. P. Lijah, who, a police newsletter claimed, was "one of the big girls of her platoon" at "under 4 ft."[80] Women's stature explained why communism was destined to fail.[81]

Occasional mocking sympathy for "women bandits" contrasted the tendency of English-language newspapers to emphasize women's participation in violence if they were hurt or killed by security forces. While women sometimes led fighting units and participated in battle, as they had in the MPAJA during the war, descriptions of women's roles in combat only appeared to justify their deaths.[82] One unnamed "girl" apparently kept firing a pistol after getting hit but "would not give up" until death.[83] Another article detailed the deaths of "2 Girl Terror Chiefs," including a woman identified as "the officer-in-charge of the women's

Communist section."[84] Mak Yuen Lin was apparently a "terror boss" when security forces killed her in an ambush in 1954. Her alleged crimes included extorting money from workers and serving as a branch committee member. Killed in the same attack was Wong Yee Lan, first described a "jungle wife" of Hon Yoon. Calling her a "jungle wife" centered her sexual proximity to men rather than the fact that she was a branch committee secretary. Instead, newspapers emphasized that Wong Yee Lan's "favourite weapon" was "a hand grenade," with which she terrorized rubber tappers. Hon Yoon, of course, was never described as Wong Yee Lan's "jungle husband." He was killed in the same attack and the article mentioned his being "responsible for some of the worst incidents of the Emergency." This included "the notorious terrorist ambush" in the Bentong area in 1950, during which "Mrs. Nora Evelyn Stutchbury, wife of Mr. A. D. Stutchbury" and an unnamed "Chinese translator" were "brutally murdered." The death of Asian women became more justifiable with the context of a white woman's death.[85] Compared to the martyrdom of the "brutally murdered" Mrs. Stutchbury, newspapers described communist women as "in the bag" of kills. Emphasizing their alleged crimes avoided asking whether or not these women deserved to die.[86]

Even in cases with specious evidence or minor transgressions, Asian women faced severe consequences for associating with communists.[87] Sixteen-year-old Yap Nee Moi was sentenced to five years penal servitude for giving "supplies"—a towel and a toothbrush—to communists.[88] Four women rubber tappers were sentenced to between five and eight years in prison for failing to report a "murder gang" at Ban Seng Huat Estate, even though "the accused denied any knowledge of bandits."[89] Several women, including many teenagers, received sentences of hanging for crimes ranging from possession of a grenade, swallowing evidence, and "consorting with armed terrorists."[90] Of course, these seemingly "small" contributions may have been evidence of women's participation in Min Yuen, the People's Movement, which clandestinely provided material support for communists from within villages. At the same time, many villagers faced coercion to sustain communist jungle camps, making material support a poor sign of either complicity or innocence.

Mr. N. L. Cohen suggested why such severe punishments were meted out to so many young women. He told nineteen-year-old Chinese woman Pua Kim Eng, also known as Yit Hong, "Young persons like you must be discouraged from joining the armed opponents of the Government" when she was sentenced to three years in prison. She apparently had been "consorting with an armed bandit on Sagil estate."[91] Some Chinese civilians helped defend women against such harsh punishments. Mrs. Wee Phaik Gan, later known professionally as diplomat and lawyer P. G. Lim, was "the only Chinese woman at the English Bar." She appealed against the death penalty sentence for twenty-five-year-old "girl bandit" Lee Meng, who was instead exiled to China.[92] The Selangor Chinese Chamber of Commerce, meanwhile, petitioned to commute the death sentence given to Wong Lan, also known as Ah Har. She had been condemned as a "terrorist" in possession of a shotgun and ammunition. The petition also went to the Sultan of Selangor and Prime Minister Tunku Abdul Rahman, showing the continued importance and political sway of local leaders.[93] Some women fought hard to protect themselves. Choo Ha Yew had been "sentenced to death for offences under the Emergency Regulations." She attacked the assistant gaol matron, Mrs. D. Goetlieb, two days before her scheduled hanging. She also attempted to free herself from British "justice" through several self-inflicted injuries.[94]

Compared to such condemnation, Chinese women—and girls more specifically—received sympathy in newspapers and army pamphlets if they were killed or hurt by communists, rather than security forces.[95] A pamphlet for the Army Education Third Class Certificate emphasized the "abominable cruelty" of communists who stabbed and then beat a "Chinese girl in Perak" to death.[96] A newspaper mentioned that a "12-year-old Chinese girl" was a wounded victim of "terrorists." This followed a more detailed account of how Commonwealth aircraft targeted and killed communists with airstrikes, which included injuring a "woman bandit."[97] Newspapers leaned into the most graphic details of communist cruelty, mentioning strangulation, stabbing, and burning as communist methods of killing young Chinese girls ranging in age from six to sixteen.[98] Chinese girls only received praise if they defied communists. One "young Chinese girl" was apparently "shot dead" after resisting attempts by bandits to take her into the jungle.[99] These accounts tended to leave victims anonymous, compared to the overt sentimentality that accompanied tales of white women killed throughout the Emergency.[100] Newspapers mobilized Chinese girls' deaths to encourage Chinese civilians to see the fight against communism as an antidote to violence, rather than central to its perpetuation.

THE PIN-UP INSURGENT

One method of minimizing violence against Chinese women was by depicting communists as sexually extravagant. Military, government, and police officials were anxious about the romantic appeal and rumor of "moonlight" romances in the jungles and did what they could to portray women insurgents as immoral jezebels. This echoed a fairly common Cold War trope, as Gregory Daddis has discussed, to portray women as objects to be controlled by men for sexual gratification.[101] The irony was that many women joined the MCP because they saw it as a way to flee sexual coercion and objectification.[102] For example, Guo Ren Luan joined the MCP after hearing about the 1953 rape and murder of a girl by a man who had been addicted to pornography. This case had sparked the "anti-yellow culture" campaign which opposed the import of "immoral"—especially American—culture, which, opponents argued, led to social breakdown. This movement had an anti-colonial undercurrent as it criticized the British government for banning Asian magazines that might provide alternative—and "healthier"—depictions of gender and sexuality.[103] Leftist women's organizations such as the Singapore Women's Federation sponsored "anti-yellow culture" activities alongside campaigns for equal pay, equal employment, and the abolition of polygamy.[104] Despite communist women's fights against sexualization, the Chinese-language periodical *Sin Lu Pau* (New Path News), contended that "the jungle of South Johore" was essentially "one big brothel."[105]

Periodicals frequently sexualized "bandit" women to emphasize the redemptive masculinity of white men. As Daddis has explained, "pulp heroes" were "rewarded with beautiful, seductive women as a kind of payoff for their combat victories."[106] Similarly, one newspaper suggested that European planter H. A. Stonor captured "a pretty girl bandit" at the Ulu Remis Oil Palm estate. She had apparently handed out leaflets to workmen on nearby estates while her comrades set fire to lorries. Nonetheless, the *Straits Times* branded her a "pin-up girl."[107] The *Singapore Standard* noted that "lipstick" was found on a "pretty terrorist."[108] The *Malayan Police Magazine* published a cartoon of a beautiful Asian woman, styled as a bombshell with a low-cut communist uniform, reaching her hand out with the caption "I just thought I'd come in and surrender to you lieutenant," making light of the sexual violence that many women experienced.[109] This cavalier attitude had very real consequences. Maxwell Anthony Nolan, a New Zealander seconded to the Fiji Regiment, noted that there was an "alleged rape of Malayan women by three other soldiers." His sympathies were not with the women but with his colonel, Ron Tinker, who had to address the issue while knowing that "good relations with the public were absolutely essential to success."[110] Winning hearts and minds meant papering over the gendered violence of military and police presence. British and Commonwealth forces turned Asian women into objects of desire that needed to be "saved" from communism, with violent force if necessary.

Another *Straits Times* article, written by Bill Fish, described a deceased Chinese woman in a way that bordered on necrophilic. He explained that "even the

"I just thought I'd come in and surrender to you lieutenant."

FIGURE 13. Cartoon published in *Malayan Police Magazine*, (December 1953). Image printed with permission from the Royal Malaysia Police and courtesy of the National Library of Australia.

bullet hole in the side of her head couldn't hide the fact that she had been hand-some."[111] A "curious crowd of men, women and children" apparently came to see the "stiffening girl" who was "well-built." He noted that a "half-smile played on her foam-flecked lips" while dark "hair cascaded in a black frame round her palid [*sic*] features." By contrast, he described the man killed with her as "a wizened little man perhaps twice her age" who was "half-starved." This suggested that beautiful women who bought into the romantic allure of the jungle would be sad-dled with unattractive men. Sex with an emasculated man was a fate worse than death. Fish even romanticized the woman's death, noting that she could not "run fast enough among the rubber trees to outpace death," even as she "wrenched a hand-grenade from her waist and dropped it into the under-growth." Then she "threw a second grenade and two Fijians fell injured." However, a "Fijian machine-gun silenced the girl . . . for ever [*sic*]."[112] After specifically naming and blaming Fijian soldiers, the article closed with a close-up picture of the deceased woman, but not the man killed with her, to give readers the chance to assess the tragedy of the woman's wasted beauty.

Other journalists emphasized the danger of exploitation that communist women might face in the jungle. An article entitled "Shameful Affairs in the Jungle" detailed communists who had multiple sexual partners. B. C. M. Chee Hok Hung apparently had sex with multiple women, including Chen Tai, who was "unfortunately shot dead in the jungle." Eighteen-year-old Teoh Moi Gaik was "accused of consorting with" a "bandit" at Ji Kongsi, Sungai Bakap. When the police prepared for an ambush, she was "talking and laughing" with "the bandit."[113] Another article described a "Bandit girl" as a "poet's muse" who in-spired men to create anti-British songs and poems.[114] One cartoon depicted a woman as distracting a communist man with the promise of intimacy as secu-rity forces closed in.[115] Occasionally, articles suggested that women went into the jungle to be with other women. When Cheong Meng, also known as Ah Meng, was sentenced to ten years in prison, the *Straits Times* noted that she had been "consorting with another armed woman bandit" before getting captured in an ambush.[116] This echoed the language used in the condemnation of nineteen-year-old Soo Hoo Guat Gnoh, sentenced to four years' imprisonment for "consorting with an armed bandit."[117] Using the same language of "consorting" hinted at the possibility of intimacy between combatant women, without overtly stating that women went into the jungle to pursue these relationships. Sex as a communist woman, according to the police and military, only brought coercion, danger, hu-miliation, and death. It also evoked memories and rumors of "fraternization"

" Oh, forget party regulations, Ah Moi—this moment belongs to US."

FIGURE 14.   Cartoon published in *Malayan Police Magazine*, (September 1954). Image printed with permission from the Royal Malaysia Police and courtesy of the National Library of Australia.

during the Japanese occupation, which recycled the notion that women were pliable and corruptible outside the confines of marriage.

Sometimes, women's sexual attraction to communists became grounds for public shaming and humiliation.[118] Security forces dropped "fifty thousand leaflets" of excerpts from the love letter of a "girl" who admired Chin Lim, alias Yong Sin Poh, a political commissar of the 4th Platoon 8th Regiment. She apparently wrote that "I love you very much and will always be yours. I hope our dreams will soon come true." The leaflet then condemned Chin Lim for subjecting a girl to "masterful . . . private lessons" that led her to have "more thought for personal love than for love of the party."[119] Similarly, nineteen-year-old Wong Ong Kee's communist sympathies resulted in having her personal life splashed onto newspapers. She was sentenced to three years' imprisonment after getting arrested in 1949 for having suspicious documents in her possession and "luring men into the Communist Party."[120] Yet time in prison often amplified rather than reduced hostility to the colonial state, and after Wong Ong Kee's release she went to a girls' home where she became "an extremely evil influence."[121] As punishment, one periodical published excerpts from her confiscated diary. In it, she mentioned "the British Imperialists" using "mad round-ups and arrests, etc., to hit at us." More attention, though, focused on her love life. She admired a man she called "T" who took up a "guerilla-like life." Once he was arrested, other men pursued her, and she contemplated going into the jungle. While she vowed to only love T, she admitted to having "another lover."[122] The journalist was confused that the diary revealed her to be "intensely human" while also "imbued throughout with the barbaric inhumanity of Communist ideology." Mr. N. G. Morris, Assistant Commissioner, tried to portray her dedication to communism as irrational: "She was about 10 years old during the Japanese occupation, when the Chinese who fought in the jungle were, quite rightly, national heroes." He explained that she represented "a generation growing up which confuses the Communist bandits with those men who fought the Jap[ane]s[e]." The consequences of her teenage love and "confusion," after enduring a childhood of Japanese occupation, was being "repatriated" to Peking, even though she was born in Singapore.[123]

Newspapers that humiliated communist women for their sexuality also portrayed communists as cruel for punishing sexual relationships. Chee Hok Hung was apparently "reprimanded" for having sex with multiple women when he "already had a wife in the jungle."[124] Another article emphasized how "Bandits" kept "Lovers Apart." A man who worked with the communists left "his sweetheart in a village," but she was "dragged into his camp" and "accused" of "being a spy." They "forced" her to join them but sent her to a camp away from her lover for more than a year. The same article suggested that another man "drowned himself" because "his leader had been carrying on with his wife."[125] Communist men and women in sexual relationships apparently faced punishments—including death—for sharing blankets in the jungle, sleeping on the same bed, or continuing to meet with partners after communist leaders refused them permission to marry.[126] One man, according to *Sin Lu Pau* (New Path News), endured violence for making inquiries about his family. This was problematic, according to the press, because the "Communist Party say that family love is decadent and not to be encouraged. Love for the Party must come first."[127] Similarly, Chan Wa was apparently "shot to death" for asking "permission to go home and live with his family because he was sick of jungle life."[128] The Singapore press cast these stories as evidence of the apparently anti-family stance of communists, appealing both to British leaders and Asian civilians. Ironically, press depictions contrasted F. Spencer Chapman's wartime understanding of communists as resolutely moral and inclusive of women without "sex complications."[129] Some former communists also suggested that marriage and sex never caused issues in communist camps, while others lamented affairs by their husbands or feeling pressured to be outlets for communist leaders' lust.[130] Other women, such as Lin Guan Ying, maintained that she "did not have a wedding ceremony" only because it "was war then." Still, she insisted that they "were very serious about marriage, even though we did not have weddings."[131]

Some Asian policemen used communists' apparent sexual stringency to justify their service to the British. Police Lieutenant Wei Fei Ehr wrote an article for *Malayan Police Magazine* suggesting that communist ideas about love doomed them to failure. He evoked Plato's myths about original humans being androgynous figures, with two heads, four arms, and four legs, who got split in half, condemned to search for their "other half." He then paraphrased Confucius, who claimed that any government that ignored human nature would not last. Connecting this to communism, he gave the example of Chan Fung, an insurgent and President of the Rubber Workers' Union in Sepang Salak. In September 1948, Chan Fung met "a pretty rubber tapper about 20 years of age." Rather than running away to marry her, he kept their affair a secret. In response, communist leaders apparently "strung him up to a tree and murdered him." For the police lieutenant, "Communism gave no sympathy . . . Its whole aim is to regiment human beings to fit the Communist system, to cut human nature into a preconceived design. And that is why Communism will not survive in the world."[132] The worst sin of communism, for this police officer, was denying the apparently natural harmony of heterosexual monogamy.

Compared to these grim stories, the press suggested that happiness and love could come to former communists who surrendered. The *Singapore Standard* reported on one "ex bandit" who married "the girl of his dreams" after he surrendered.[133] A similar story described Ooi Kim Chooi, a "former comrade" of the "terrorist organization" who got to marry "the girl he loved" after surrendering.[134] Other stories detailed women who did not surrender and had to grieve the deaths of their lovers.[135] While surrender in the Second World War brought humiliation, British leaders in the Emergency suggested that surrender could fulfil sexual and romantic longings. They even encouraged communist women to pressure loved ones into surrendering. One cartoon in the *Malayan Police Magazine* lampooned an official going to the home of a Chinese couple. The cartoon woman frowned angrily as the communist man, dressed in uniform, jumped out the window to escape. The official asked the woman, "Can I interest you in a surrender policy for your husband?"[136] Another cartoon depicted two Indigenous families: one that had very few possessions and no children, and the other with a healthy child and ample possessions, including a dress, necklace, and makeup for the wife. The caption read: "Mumu dear, isn't it about time you passed on a bit of information?"[137] British leaders emphasized that surrender was salvation, and that women could gain materially and emotionally from giving up the fight.

Of course, surrender rarely brought safety. In some cases, women who surrendered received employment opportunities, particularly in domestic service for police families. This not only kept them bound to the world of policing but made them vulnerable to sexual violence and poor pay. Those who did not get such work remained in detention camps or prison. There, they were a highly visible and vulnerable minority sometimes targeted for forced sex work by police or British loyalists who, according to novelist Han Suyin, ran unchecked brothels.[138] Surrender also reanimated fears about wartime "fifth columnists," making those who surrendered or became police informants subject to retaliatory violence from those sold out or left behind.[139] Whether people feared Japanese or British persecution, betrayals felt the same. Han Suyin reflected on the pervasive anxiety caused by British leaders' reliance on informants to combat the Emergency: "For we no longer need proof, to punish; we are condemned by idle speech, by the gay words in the mouths of our friends."[140]

Despite Asian women's impossible situation, and frequent demonization as irredeemable jezebels, white women took pleasure in imitating them. Thomas Pearson wrote to his parents that he attended a fancy dress ball with his wife, Betty, and felt sad that they did not win the top prize. He reasoned that it was because they "were too realistic as bandits from Malaya: in jungle green, Betty with Chinese leaflets (properly printed & looking like Communist propaganda). She had a wooden hand grenade hanging on her belt." However, the Chief of Forestry "didn't like our costume a bit. I believe he thought our leaflets were communist."[141] By dressing as communists, the Pearsons continued a well-worn pattern of mocking Asian colonial subjects through drag, theatrical, and costume performances, as they had done during the World Wars.[142] By inviting the ire of other officials for doing so, though, the Pearsons revealed the importance of policing gender and racial boundaries during the Emergency.

Depicting communists as sexually extravagant and anti-family contrasted the idealized image of British and European planters as paragons of happy, heterosexual family units. Yet Emergency policies attacked and undermined Asian families. Malay guerilla Siti Meriyam Binti Idris, alias Atom, recalled her husband surrendering in 1959 and "leaving me behind" because he could not "stand the hardship."[143] Chen Xiu Zhu lamented her brother's arrest shortly after the birth of his son because a former comrade "pretended to be a fervent supporter of the revolution but was actually reporting to the enemy."[144] Many people struggled with resettlement plans, including a loss of ancestral lands or separation from family members.[145] Chen Xiu Zhu lost her brother, sister, father, and mother to deportation because British leaders categorized them as a "revolutionary family."[146] By contrast, white families continued to enjoy lavish estates, servants, and job opportunities that most Asian civilians lacked. Many Asian civilians turned to the jungle to protest and flee these material inequalities. However, by portraying Asian women as desirable objects pliant enough to surrender, British leaders criminalized and condemned Asian women's sexuality as a way to blame them for the violence that they experienced.

POLICE(ING) WOMEN

One way that Asian women evaded criminalization—but not sexualization—was by participating in police work. Many white women went to Malaya as police officers' wives, facilitating welfare programs. Yet an even greater number of Asian women had connections to policing. Throughout the Emergency, Asian women supported the police for several complex reasons. Some were wives of low-ranking policemen. Others worked as secretaries in the station, in intelligence, or in critical yet undervalued unofficial roles such as female searchers. Some communist women surrendered and took on police work to reduce their sentences, earn a salary, or enjoy comforts not available to them in the jungle or in their previously impoverished lives.[147] Additionally, hundreds of Asian women became police constables, bringing them further into the military culture of the Emergency. Munah bt. Husin joined the Women Special Constables to escape the threat of kidnapping in areas with intense communist activity.[148] Select women could evade violence or suspicion by embracing colonial militarism.

Women police proved essential during the Emergency because Emergency Regulations required women suspects to be searched by other women.[149] This did not prevent police from joking about sexual violence. One police magazine cartoon depicted a tall and beautiful Asian woman, completely stripped nude, standing at profile. She told the policeman, "I know it's the woman searchers' day off, Lieutenant, but there was no need to be so thorough."[150] A letter to the satirical advice column "Aunt Fanny's Advice Bureau" from "Police Lieutenant Mouthwater" asked if he could "offer my services as a Female Searcher?" Another from "P.C. Kaseh bin Sayang" asked how to convince his OCPD to let him visit his beloved Fatimah. The advice was to show the OCPD his girlfriend so that

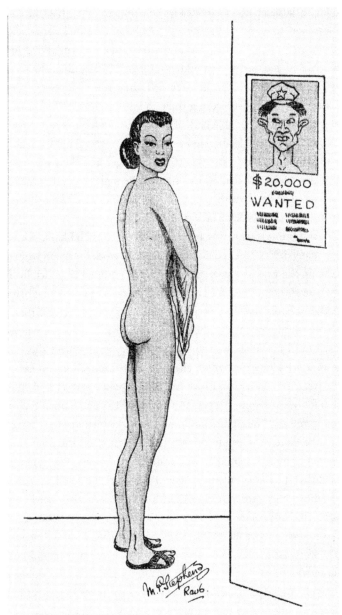

"I know it's the woman searchers' day off, Lieutenant, but there was no need to be so thorough."

FIGURE 15. Cartoon published in *Malayan Police Magazine*, (September 1953). Image printed with permission from the Royal Malaysia Police and courtesy of the National Library of Australia.

he could appreciate her beauty. Instead, the commanding officer hired her as "a Female Searcher" to work "in his office."[151] Another cartoon lampooned an over-eager policeman for lying on top of a car to flirt with a woman, asking her: "Good afternoon, Ma'm, your name and address, please!"[152] The ubiquitous imagery of police officers stopping women in streets, finding their addresses, hiring them for their attractiveness, or subjecting them to invasive searches was cast as both a humorous fantasy and a possible perk of policing. Han Suyin's 1956 novel, . . . *And the Rain My Drink*, even dramatized this with character Ah Mei, who was captured from the jungle while she was still a teenager and then worked as an informant. Her perceived sexual availability led the male Chinese informant, Lam Teck, to insist that the British police officer "should have taken liberties" with her. If he did not, then "what a slow-witted fool he is."[153]

For Mary Quintal, who was born in Borneo to a Hakka-speaking family, there were many difficulties associated with police work for Asian women. Quintal was among the first group of ten women who trained as police in Singapore in 1948, where she remained for twenty-five years. She noted that after attending Christian schools and developing a passion for sports, Peter Gross, a British police officer who knew her brother, encouraged her to join the women's force. She refused until Gross showed up at the grocery store where she worked and took her on a drive in a car, which she enjoyed because riding in cars was considered "a treat." However, he drove her to the police station and filled out an application for her, insisting: "If you don't sign you can't go home." She was "naïve and so innocent" and "wanted to go home," so she signed and "got myself shanghaied into the force."[154] Despite this deceitful beginning, she grew to enjoy the job compared to more sedentary work available to women, like typing. She also appreciated that it was the only unit of civil service that offered women equal pay as men, thanks to forward-thinking British Police Commissioner Foulger. Still, she recognized that people "were very sceptical [*sic*] about us being a success and didn't know how to take us, being women."[155] During a gambling raid, one of the men "was so astounded to be arrested by a woman" that he did not struggle when she tackled him.[156] However, she recalled little difficulty doing her work because people understood that women police were there to protect or advocate for women and children, so they rarely interfered with them.

There were, of course, some hardships being an Asian woman police officer in a male-dominated colonial institution. Quintal recalled that women's uniforms were designed by British officers' wives, so initially they consisted of unattractive skirts and very hot flannel tops with short sleeves. These proved dangerous in riots and exposed her to scratches on her arms and rioters lifting up her skirt.[157] As a result, she advocated for women to get riot gear and redesigned their uniforms to be more practical. Yet the competitive atmosphere also hurt Quintal's initial enthusiasm. Unlike male police, who were often uneducated, all women police came from educated backgrounds. She recalled one woman who was jealous of Quintal's level of education and feared that this would lead to Quintal's promotion. As a result, the woman spread rumors and isolated her from the other women, which caused Quintal to consider leaving the force. However, this other woman "got mixed up with a senior officer" so she "had to leave." While this enabled Quintal to win the day, it also hinted at women's vulnerability. Getting "mixed up" sexually with an officer, or landing on the wrong side of the wrong person, could cost them their jobs. Quintal recalled numerous women complaining about a particular British commanding officer who arrived from South Africa. Few were willing to risk the backlash of writing a formal complaint. When Quintal had to work with him, he was dismissive and complained about her lack of deference, even though Quintal had the same rank as him. While Quintal ultimately regained the upper hand by formally complaining about his behavior, she observed that he "treated the girls worse" because they were only "Woman Constable and rank and file."[158] The protection and respect she received as a high-ranking officer did not extend to most of the women in police work.

Asian women's growing incorporation into policing complicated their exposure to institutions dominated by men. By 1957, the year of Malaya's official independence from Britain, the first "batch" of fifty-four Women Police Constables took up their positions in Malaya. *Malayan Police Magazine* emphasized that these women represented "the three major races." In reality, forty-six were Malay, seven were Chinese, and only one was Indian. Their training was segregated by both gender and ethnicity.[159] Women's uniforms, with long, full skirts, also emphasized their femininity and set them apart from men.[160] Initial depictions of women police varied. For example, the 1957 Christmas issue of *Malayan Police Magazine* included an illustration of various types of police officers, with women police officers situated prominently among the group.[161] Others expressed surprise at the women's competence, noting, for example, public admiration during a parade for the women's "bearing during the long period whilst the medals were being presented."[162] Sporting events engendered both genuine praise and condescension.[163] One police ladies' cricket team handily defeated the police men's team during a "novelty game."[164] Yet their athletic prowess was less appreciated than their physical attractiveness. One spectator, Roger Brooks, left a women's sporting match but returned because the "girls are much prettier here than at the Beauty Contest."[165] Despite these dismissive attitudes, women police became popular attractions at parades and celebrations.[166]

Of course, women often struggled in their new positions. Miss Hor Pew Toh, a Woman Probationary Inspector, wrote an article for the *Malayan Police Magazine* detailing her experiences. Given the forum, it is unsurprising that her tone was overwhelmingly positive. At the same time, she hinted at the struggles that women police faced. When she first arrived at the Federal Police Depot, little had been arranged, so they spent most of the day cleaning their own barracks and classrooms.[167] Initially she felt self-conscious about her lack of training and assumed that they were "a funny sight" with their marching "out of step and our hands swinging low." Thereafter, they settled into a routine of training, drill, and physical activities in the morning, followed by classes from 9 a.m. to 1 p.m., drill in afternoons, and games in the evenings. Still, she struggled to adjust to the physical demands of training and was soon "running short of cash." She found that discipline in the Depot was "really strict" but life overall was "very interesting and full of activities." She found it "rather a tough life for a girl. With all the rules and regulations, it is so different from the life I used to lead as a teacher."[168]

Policewomen also had separate duties. Hor Pew Toh explained that their lessons focused on laws that concerned "women and girls, children and young persons" because they were expected to specialize in these areas. She rationalized: "That is why we have to undergo seven months' training instead of six."[169] Training included visits to welfare organizations such as the Blind School, homes for youthful offenders, VD clinics, and juvenile courts, which meant that Asian policewomen filled the type of welfare roles previously expected of white women. However, an unintentional indication of police women's treatment came with her article's publication. Despite giving Hor Pew Toh the space to reflect on her experience, the magazine published her article with an image of the wrong woman, replacing her with a woman who was younger and thinner.[170] By the end of the year, police periodicals also made light of women's policing due to their roles monitoring children. One *Malayan Police Magazine* cartoon showed a woman police officer bringing in a small boy who stole a chicken, riffing on a popular saying among scouts about the need to steal chickens for sustenance.[171] Policewomen's assigned duties—focusing on women, children, and welfare—made them the butt of the joke.

Sometimes policemen admitted and made light of the fact that they treated women unfairly. One *Police* magazine correspondent described his encounters with a young woman, Molly Tan.[172] He lamented that the two female searchers assigned to his headquarters were "depressing old widows." As a result, when

FIGURE 16. Cartoon published in *Malayan Police Magazine*, (June 1957). Image printed with permission from the Royal Malaysia Police and courtesy of the National Library of Australia.

Molly came in search of work, the author quickly found a position for her. His descriptions alternated between sexual desire, sympathy, annoyance, and amusement. He explained that it "would be hard to say whether Molly Tan was beautiful or pretty. Perhaps she was both." She was a young woman of twenty-four, "slim, tall for a Chinese, with a soft clear skin and bright eyes." Seeing her "in a flowered satin Chinese costume" with "a most radiant smile" allowed him to forget "the cares of the office momentarily." She explained that she needed work because her brother, who had worked in police intelligence, was killed by communists. Her

The Writer.

FIGURE 17. Incorrect photograph included with the article. *Malayan Police Magazine* (September 1957). Image printed with permission from the Royal Malaysia Police and courtesy of the National Library of Australia.

only remaining family member was her impoverished and widowed mother. She assured the policeman that she wanted to help kill those who killed her brother. He admitted that "I created a rather doubtful vacancy for Molly to fill, partly because I believed her story and sympathised, partly, I suppose, because I am as susceptible as the next man." Molly's appointment led to both amusement and gossip. Despite her "grim" desire to kill communists, he found her "a happy and friendly creature. She was neither a prude nor a wanton. She treated all men and all women alike."[173] Attractiveness, and the ability to walk the fine line between "prude" and "wanton," helped Molly navigate the financial and employment insecurity engendered by her brother's service.

Despite the OCPD's willingness to "help," he continually undermined Molly's thoughts and desires. Practically speaking, she proved her value by keeping in touch with some of her brother's contacts, providing the police with relevant intelligence. However, she repeatedly requested a pistol so that she could take an active role in the fight. He felt that she was "being silly, and I told her so."

We apologise to W.I.P. Miss Hor Pew Toh, the writer of " My First Month in the Depot " which appeared in the last issue. The photograph which appeared with that article was not that of the writer. (Anyone's ears burning in the Depot ?).

W.P.I. Miss HOR PEW TOH

FIGURE 18. The correct photograph, included in a subsequent issue. *Malayan Police Magazine* (December 1957). Image printed with permission from the Royal Malaysia Police and courtesy of the National Library of Australia.

One day, she and the other "female searchers" accompanied a Jungle Squad on a screening operation "to deal with the women." Insurgents attacked their truck, killing the driver and leaving many men injured. Molly single-handedly saved a man and watched as a wounded communist ran away. When she gave her report, she reiterated that if "I had had a pistol I could have killed him." The OCPD asked if she felt that saving the man with her was better than killing the bandit, and she replied that if she had been armed, she could have done both. Eventually, the OCPD decided that Molly deserved accolades—including a gift of a pistol. He found one from the unclaimed property and presented it to her at a parade. He noted that the pistol "was one of those vicious little small-calibre automatics, popularly carried by a beautiful spy in the top of a nylon stocking," reiterating that arming Molly only added to her sexual desirability. However, her attractiveness turned back into foolishness, as they took her to the pistol range: "As I expected, she was a rotten shot."[174]

By depicting Molly Tan as a Chinese victim of terrorism, an impoverished woman in need of rescue, a beautiful object of desire, and a foolishly headstrong woman, the article reinforced multiple tropes about Asian women in the Malayan Emergency. Undoubtedly, many men and women became *communists*—rather than police—to seek revenge or to find alternatives after the loss of livelihoods and family members. Han Suyin's . . . *And the Rain My Drink* depicted one man captured as a "terrorist" who went into the jungle because his parents were killed by the Japanese and he was too old for school.[175] Few civilians had moved past British abandonment and the suffering of the Second World War before the Emergency started. However, these motives were never articulated in police or press documents. Instead, they emphasized communist women's foolishness and lost sexual potential. They did not mourn women who had lost their family members in the war and embraced communism for survival. Whether women fought or supported communists, they faced condescension and sexualization.

EXTERMINATING COMMUNISTS

Many women could not volunteer as police or flee into the jungles because they were forcibly resettled into so-called "New Villages." Resettlement plans focused on the roughly 400,000 Chinese "squatters" who lived along the fringes of the jungle. At least 150,000 "squatters" became homeless during the economic downturn of the 1930s as laborers lost jobs from rubber estates and tin mines with no alternative for employment.[176] Their numbers increased with the Japanese occupation, as tens of thousands escaped urban centers, economic collapse, and the Japanese army's targeting of Chinese civilians. Many took up cash-crop farming during the occupation and continued to earn a living this way unchecked during the British Military Administration, which required additional supplies to curb food shortages.[177] However, with the outbreak of the Emergency, the government relocated this population so that they would not become communist recruits. Two decades of imperial capitalism and war caused the mass relocation of hundreds of thousands of Chinese civilians. While resettlement established new norms of family and community, it also revealed the true implications of the "hearts and minds" idea of war—which hinged on extermination. Focusing on New Villages shows that, despite promises for care and welfare, the Emergency exposed many women to harassment, coercion, and death.

Resettlement villages followed longer patterns of internment, concentration, and other camps in British imperial history.[178] They also showed continuity with the Japanese occupation, which also relied on the mass internment of civilians.

However, British leaders resettled more people in Malaya during the Emergency than the Japanese interned across Southeast Asia during the Second World War. By 1952, 470,509 people, 85 percent of whom were Chinese, had been resettled in 440 New Villages.[179] Ultimately another hundred thousand people would join New Villages; 1.2 million total people faced resettlement or relocation of some kind.[180] One Army educational pamphlet depicted this as a utopian model of welfare for Chinese settlers. It emphasized "building wooden houses for each family; erecting schools and clinics, putting up administrative technical and police buildings." This, apparently, enabled resettled civilians to receive "education and social services and be made to feel that they are truly part of the community."[181] One cartoon depicted the building of these communities as an easy choice: on one side a communist threatened a civilian in their home, and on the other was a peaceful hut. The label asked the reader: "This or This?"[182]

Unfortunately, many civilians remembered "villages" as little better than concentration camps. They had curfews, barbed wire, security towers, and other restrictions.[183] The infrastructure of roads and drains were often hastily built and inadequate for settler demands, creating health issues. Many struggled to maintain livelihoods in agriculture or mining given the curfews and other restrictions of village life. Conditions only improved with a rubber boom facilitated by the Korean War.[184] Yet violence remained a recurring feature of camp life. Police lived and worked within villages to monitor the population. If British officials were killed, villagers could be confined to their villages for days.[185] This made it easy for rumors and hearsay to catch the imagination of those living outside. James Desmond Howard Neill, who worked in resettlement, recalled that barbed wire urged communists to claim that the "wire fencing all around the resettlement areas was radio-active" and anyone who went near would be electrocuted.[186] Chen Xiu Zhu was certain that some of their fences "had electric currents."[187] Such methods were believable because security forces burned houses, detained squatters, or evicted people who refused resettlement. Lin Guan Ying recalled British forces rounding up villagers where her mother and child lived before they "burn[ed] down the whole village."[188] Luo Lan recalled similarly their "house was destroyed and members of my family were killed" for their activism.[189] New Villages were about control more than care.

Some British leaders admitted that New Villages were largely bait for communists rather than avenues for extending genuine welfare to civilians. One army pamphlet explained that if "the bandits want to tap these new settlements, they have to come within reach of forces ready and looking for them."[190] Settlers also were guarded by a locally-raised "Home Guard" that was separate from police and military and attempted to cultivate a civic and community spirit among villag-ers.[191] Chen Xiu Zhu remembered that both Chinese and Malay people worked in policing but the Chinese were recruited from villages and were "often the worst" because they worked for the British undercover "as plainclothes police."[192] Yet even those who worked as informants might find themselves arrested because of miscommunication. As a result, many felt that British leaders established trust by who treated them with the most deference. Doctor and novelist Han Suyin, who was married to Special Branch police officer Leon Comber, portrayed one New Village commandant as determining the treatment of prisoners not on their past actions but on "if they salute and smile, and call me Tuan, call me Sir." If they were "surly and bad-tempered, and won't answer my questions, and won't laugh," then the commandant categorized them as the worst communists.[193]

The expectation to live cheerfully chafed against daily camp life, which con-sisted of raids, searches, detentions, interrogations, and deportations without much hope for escape or redemption.[194] In fact, living in New Villages often rad-icalized people. For Han Suyin, residents became more sympathetic to commu-nists and resentful of the British because of the "muddles of ignorance, the sus-picions based on race, the heavy hand of Emergency Regulations, condemning without trial, needing not evidence but plausible suspicion."[195] This was true for Guan Shui Lian, who lived in a New Village when her mother was arrested, leav-ing them "penniless." This did not force her enthusiasm or "loyalty." Rather, she and most other villagers were "relatives or friends of the guerillas," so it became "quite logical that most of us became sympathisers and supporters of the rev-olution." Her own village was "very 'red.'"[196] Violence, therefore, was inherent in resettlement. British leaders expected settlers to become active and cheerful participants in militarization or face military reprisals.

Food denial policies also added to the violence of New Villages.[197] Emergency Regulations stated that any "Police Officer or member of H. M. Forces or of a Local Force may stop and search any vehicle, vessel or individual in any place if he suspects that food is being carried which is intended for, or may become available to CT."[198] As a result, women experienced assaults and harassment from guards who demanded strip searches under the auspices of looking for food, echoing the "jokes" found in many police magazines.[199] Han Suyin noted that many of the hastily-recruited Malay plantation police sometimes did not bother to search men but would search women "for their pleasure."[200] Guan Shui Lian recalled that "they used to harass us," making life in New Villages "a frighten-ing time for us."[201] Yet even women searchers caused problems. Chen Xiu Zhu remembered that the policewoman in her village was "very mean" and forced women to strip anytime she "suspected something." Then, she would "throw our clothes outside and the old women would have to go out naked to fetch their clothes." In response, her brother, who combated the Japanese occupation, passed food to communists through the barbed wire of New Villages. They feared for his life because if "anyone was caught assisting the Communists, they were beheaded immediately." Still, they took "crates and crates of food" including rice from New Villages to communists in the mountains, largely by soaking barrels full of food in cow urine and excrement so that guards would not want to inspect them. When that failed, they bribed the guards. In response, British leaders added "more layers of barbed wire around our village" and placed extra sentries on duty.[202] The emphasis on resettlement hid the violence of military and police action, especially toward women.

The violence of New Village life reflected the fact that some British officials viewed Chinese civilians as pests that needed to be exterminated. Sir Harold Briggs, whose "Briggs Plan" set the course for resettlement, described the relationship between squatters and communists like so: "You can kill mosquitoes in your house with a spray gun, but they'll soon be replaced by reinforcements if you don't sterilize the stagnant water pools where they breed."[203] Casting Chinese squatters as pests, and villages as breeding grounds, dehumanized Chinese civilians as a problem that could only be solved with extermination. The language of "extermination," and the need to thwart "breeding" suggests that the pregnant communist was, perhaps, the embodiment of British anxiety during the Emergency. Some officials blamed Chinese women for being too fertile, creating the "problem" of both squatters and communists. A lecture by a Senior Army Liaison officer described the total population of Malaya as 2.5 million Malays, 2 million Chinese, half a million Indians, and about 30,000 Europeans. The most prominent feature of the Chinese community, in his view, was the "rapidity with which they are reproducing their species." He described Malays as being the rightful inhabitants of their Malayan "homeland" while the Chinese were "immigrants." He then quoted a *Times* article, which apparently claimed that every "third person in Singapore today is a Chinese woman with all the prolific potentialities of her race." Malaya, in his mind, was "the first Commonwealth country in which the cold war has got hot," so it was important for "the Bandits to be exterminated as rapidly as possible."[204] Given that military units measured their successes by the number of "CTs," or communist terrorists, killed in combat, this exterminationist outlook had very real consequences for anyone who might be perceived as one.

This language of extermination, while noting the reproductive capabilities of Chinese women, paints a dire picture of British tactics for combating the

Emergency. In fact, this represented a reversal from previous British leaders' perspective on Chinese fertility. Wilfred Blythe noted that before the Second World War, "there were sufficient Chinese children being born in Malaya to satisfy all future labour needs without recourse to immigration from China. The Chinese were increasingly becoming a settled community in their Malayan habitat."[205] For Blythe, the growth and settlement of the Chinese community in "their Malayan habitat" was a positive boon for trade and could reduce the perceived problems caused by immigration. However, this did little to stop those who saw Chinese births as an uncontrolled population of pests. Educational resources for soldiers during the Emergency were even more explicit, stating that "Exterminating Communist bandits" is what "British Forces are doing in Malaya."[206] Malay-language leaflets dropped over communist camps, purportedly written by surrendered communists, made the same point. One surrendered man, Rayuan, stressed that the "Security Forces are organised to exterminate you" and gave his comrades options for surrendering.[207] Racial hierarchy and exterminationist policies betrayed the promise of Commonwealth familial unity. Chinese women, with their "prolific potentialities" exposed the genocidal logics underpinning state violence.

Despite this chilling depiction of extermination, press and propaganda emphasized communist views of pregnancy and childbirth in contradictory ways. While non-communist Chinese periodicals stressed the hardships of being a pregnant communist, one English-language newspaper stated that communists had extensive medical provisions. After the death of a Japanese communist doctor, Ah Kong Pak, at the hands of the 2/7 Gurkhas, a newspaper reported that he helped a Chinese doctor set up two hospitals, including "a maternity centre for women bandits." "Both hospitals," apparently, were "well-equipped with drugs including penicillin and morphia."[208] Given the difficulties of jungle life, communists did discourage having children. Chen Xiu Zhu recalled that at Command Headquarters "we were not allowed to have babies" so contraception was widely available.[209] If contraception failed, women were not punished but did have to endure "a difficult delivery." Luckily, in her camp, they had a doctor from China serving with them who facilitated one delivery via caesarean. The situation grew more challenging because the "enemy was closing in on us at that time." Rather than abandoning the woman and the baby, their unit took painstaking efforts to "carry her into the underground shelter on two planks of wood and continue the operation from there. It was excruciatingly painful for her and really hard for us." As opposing troops drew near, their party had to evacuate "and the baby had to be carried out of the jungle too" despite the looming fear of battle. The woman who recently gave birth via caesarean "had to run with us, over water and swamp. The others had to carry her most of the way, over the mountains and across the rivers."[210]

Chen Xiu Zhu's account suggests that communists discouraged and avoided having children because of the logistical difficulty of living in the jungle and the fear of encountering enemy troops. When it did happen, though, camps extended compassionate care and rigorous labor to send babies away for safety. Huang Xue Ying worked as a midwife and delivered over twenty babies during her time as a guerilla.[211] The most common outcome was to send children to live with grandparents, as happened to Lin Dong, Luo Lan, and Lin Guan Ying.[212] For Siti Meriyam Binti Idris, alias Atom, her husband surrendered in 1959 and then took over the care of their children himself.[213] Many women with husbands or lovers in the jungle lied about who the fathers of their children were to avoid coercion that would force them to surrender.[214] Yet the *Malayan Police Magazine* portrayed communists as disdainful toward childbirth. One cartoon depicted four racist caricatures of communist women sitting on the floor around a baby, with two communist men standing over them asking: "And whose little bit of petty bourgeois deviation is this?"[215]

Despite guerillas' efforts to care for children, many journalists suggested that British leadership could save and redeem communist babies. The *Straits Times* included information about an Indigenous woman, Cherook, who surrendered with a fifteen-day-old baby along with the baby's "terrorist father," Chong Mau Yoon.[216] Most women were not so lucky. *Sin Lu Pau* reported on Looi Lee Chai, who was "pregnant in June 1954" but was missing and presumed dead.[217] On another occasion, security forces found an "abandoned six-months-old Chinese girl" near Bentong area of Pahang near where "a Chinese woman bandit was killed."[218] The author's use of passive voice refused to name the specific branch of security forces involved in the murder of a woman with a newborn child. Another article noted that "babies abandoned by their parents have, from time to time, been found by Security Forces." Most were then "handed over to the State Welfare Home, Johore Bahru, for care." The first child was brought in November 1948 and was a "bonny child" adopted by a Chinese couple. Women who died as a result of encounters with security forces or illnesses also had their children taken by the State Welfare Home.[219] One boy called Jimmy apparently was "abandoned as a baby by terrorists" but went to London with foster parents. The adoptive parents, Mr. and Mrs. Edward Barr of Bristol, were an Admiralty official from Singapore and a former nurse, respectively, who had already adopted two other children from Malaya.[220]

" And whose little bit of petty bourgeois deviation
is this ? "

FIGURE 19.   Cartoon published in *Malayan Police Magazine,* (March 1954).
Image printed with permission from the Royal Malaysia Police and courtesy
of the National Library of Australia.

Adoption of "abandoned" communist babies embodied the true nature of
the Commonwealth "family." Giving colonial subjects' children to white parents reflected a process of "unchilding" that hinged on the death or erasure of
inconvenient parents.[221] It also proved a telling parallel to the case of Maria Hertogh, a young Dutch-Eurasian woman who had been given to Che Aminah binte
Mohamed as a child in 1943 by her birth mother after her father's internment.[222]
However, after the war, her birth parents reunited and protested that this was not
an adoption. The decision to return Maria to her European parents resulted in
massive riots and eighteen deaths in 1950. According to a Mrs. Mohamed Siraj,
it became a cause celebre among Malay Muslims, as Che Aminah was regarded

as a "very soft, very loving woman." As a result, people became "very angry with the whites, with the Englishmen or anybody who is white—European."[223] The fact that this happened during the Emergency only amplified the fact that adoption remained expensive and legally complex for Asian civilians, whereas British leaders readily rehomed Asian children to white parents. Emphasizing "abandonment," rather than death, underlined the apparently anti-family cruelty of communists. British welfare services, in this view, saved the children, erasing the violence perpetuated by security forces against their parents.

Military leaders and press described communists as irredeemable and in need of "extermination," which enabled them to justify the use of force by both police and military units, including against women. The emphasis on welfare services and resettlement "villages," by contrast, allowed British leaders to emphasize the beneficence of their rule compared to communism, particularly for improving the lives of women and children. Ironically, this meant extending many of the things that civilians had demanded for decades and which communists promised—land, jobs, resources, education, and political representation. The use of police and military power to spread these welfare services through resettlement invariably replicated the gender and racial violence of colonial rule. Perhaps for this reason, Han Suyin ended her novel . . . *And the Rain My Drink* with the primary police informant, a surrendered woman named Ah Mei, pregnant and getting married. Despite facing accusations of being a die-hard communist wielding a grenade, she got to drive into the sunset in cars that British leaders gave her to sell out her comrades. Marriage, birth, and material comfort, to British officials, became proof of her redemption, despite the narrator's knowledge of Ah Mei's continued communist loyalties.[224]

EMPIRE'S MOTHER

In 1947, the year of Indian independence and the year before the Malayan Emergency, the future Queen Elizabeth II celebrated her twenty-first birthday by insisting: "I declare before you all that my whole life, whether it be long or short, shall be devoted to your service and the service of our great imperial family to which we all belong."[225] During her coronation in 1953, the *Malayan Police Magazine* included a photo of two Malay policemen standing at attention bearing arms, carefully guarding a giant painting of Queen Elizabeth, the ultimate symbol of British rule and white womanhood.[226] In England, a British newspaper celebrated the unity of the empire with imagery of two Nepali soldiers, visiting for the coronation, walking arm-in-arm with "pretty 16-year-old Sylvia

Terry," whose father was a civil engineer in Malaya, flouting postwar anxieties about interracial relationships.[227] During her seventy-year reign, Queen Elizabeth was the ultimate paragon of motherly devotion to the empire. As decolonization accelerated in the 1950s and 1960s with Britain's retreat "East of Suez," the Queen remained the gendered embodiment of what the British nation and Commonwealth represented—what it fought for. She was the symbol meant to unify the hearts and minds of the Commonwealth long after formal decolonization. In reality, the Crown facilitated continued colonial brutality around the world. Motherly white womanhood failed to protect colonial subjects from violence. The Queen needed to be protected *from* the imperial, or Commonwealth, "family."

Despite the public outcry over the indignity that white women endured during the Second World War, including torture, forced labor, and privation, there was no comparable official outrage over Asian women's suffering during the Emergency. Worse still, there were no "homes" for Asian women to look forward to in "peace," as many faced police and military intervention in their homes. Banishment orders, resettlement, and imprisonment displaced them whether they were born in Singapore, Malaya, China, or elsewhere. The intersection of gender and racial violence proved central to the Malayan Emergency, setting the tone for global understandings of postwar militaries in the age of decolonization and the Cold War. Women's activism in the Emergency—including their willingness to resist colonial rule and support communists—forced colonial leaders to attempt to prioritize their needs. In turn, some Asian women gained greater access to food, jobs, medical care, and resources, which had not been possible in the previous decades of Japanese and British rule. British leaders stressed their inclusion, including equal pay, in previously gender-exclusionary institutions such as the police, due to the number of communist women evading detection. White women became models of care and welfare, rewriting themselves as saviors and bringers of peace. This created a feminine ideal of "military domesticity" that relied on women embracing militaries as civilizing forces against the difficult climates, terrains, and political uncertainties of overseas service. This removed the language of colonialism without losing its essential components.

Ultimately, the "hearts and minds" approach to war gave civilians the illusion of a choice: give their consent to military intervention or face the consequences of refusing. This deepened rather than alleviated the everyday traumas of colonial violence. Denying people employment, food, resources, and access to safety was intended to demoralize, just as distance from home, with plentiful amenities, enabled colonial soldiers and officials to create "homes" in colonial spaces. Deprivation was a central arm of British colonialism. Recurring periods of war and privation, however, also emboldened people to fight on. Creating unprecedented welfare and support for colonial subjects in the context of conflict did not stop violence. Entrenched racism ensured that many leaders saw Chinese civilians generally, and women especially, as a pestilence. Britain's perceived "success" in the Malayan Emergency relied not only on military strategy, but also on widening the influence of the military and militaristic institutions with violent force. British administrator Wilfred Blythe even admitted that the armed communist revolt was a boon rather than a burden to British interests. If communists had not resorted to military force, he believed, they would have infiltrated Malaya peacefully.[228] Military violence and racial exclusion from politics, therefore, ensured a non-communist political future for Singapore and Malaya. It did not secure peace and stability. As one of the earliest entwined struggles of decolonization and the Cold War, this conflict set the tone for many misguided understandings of warfare and military power in the twentieth and twenty-first centuries.

Conclusion

When F. Spencer Chapman wrote about his experiences fighting the Japanese occupation alongside communist guerillas, his memoir boldly proclaimed that the "jungle is neutral." He explained further that the jungle "provides any amount of fresh water, and unlimited cover for friend as well as foe—an armed neutrality, if you like, but neutrality nevertheless. It is the attitude of mind that determines whether you go under or survive."[1] To Chapman, the jungle's neutrality ensured that whoever harnessed the willpower of mind over matter would claim victory in Malaya. Yet his memoir also argued the opposite. He explained that "life is very precarious and unhealthy in such places even for a native, much more so for a white man."[2] The jungle, it seemed, was not neutral, and white men were particularly vulnerable. This preoccupation with white vulnerability against frightening colonial landscapes was a recurring colonial trope, made famous by fictional works such as Joseph Conrad's *Heart of Darkness* (1899).[3] However, it had particular resonance in the dense jungles of Singapore and Malaya. By the time of the Malayan Emergency, General Templer appeared on the cover of *Time* magazine with the reassuring declaration that the "jungle has been neutralized."[4] For American readers hoping to emulate British practices of jungle warfare, the neutralization of the natural, colonial world brought comfort. For colonial subjects, the jungle still offered alternatives.

British fears of "the jungle" reflected an awareness of the limitations of British rule.[5] Walter de Burley Wood noted in his 1918 history of the King's Shropshire Light Infantry that in Singapore, the "country was extremely difficult, consisting of rubber and pineapple plantations, mangrove swamps, virgin jungle." However, the "worst of all" was "ground that had been cleared during the rubber boom but allowed to lapse, and which was covered by dense growth to a height of eight feet."[6] A promise of civilization through cultivation produced land that was nearly impossible for troops to manage. In 1915, this hindered British leaders who pursued Indian soldiers into the jungles. It also hurt colonial troops protecting the island in 1941 and 1942, hastening the British surrender. Until 1945 it sheltered Chinese and Eurasian loyalists, communists, and adventure-seeking British and Australian servicepeople, including Chapman, resisting Japanese rule. When British leaders regained control over Singapore and Malaya, communists poured into the jungle once again to escape colonial violence. As a result, J. M. Miller, who journeyed to Malaya after working in the Special Operations Executive (SOE) during the Second World War, found the jungle more frightening than anything he had experienced previously. He preferred knowing "who your enemy was." By contrast, in Malaya, "your enemy could have been one of your own servants and your objectives were hidden in the dense jungle. One didn't only fight human beings, one had also to fight nature."[7] British leaders' fears and anxieties about the uncontrollable landscape of the jungle mirrored their inability to comprehend the diverse needs of their colonial subjects, whom they believed could become enemies at any time. "The jungle" embodied the insecurities of colonial militarism.

For those fighting against colonialism, the jungle offered opportunity. The title of Han Suyin's novel on the Malayan Emergency, . . . *And the Rain My Drink*, came from a Chinese ballad exclaiming the need "to go to the forest for justice." One character, a Chinese businessman and informant, even wondered "what is there for a young Chinese in Malaya but the jungle, the hellish green mouth of the jungle?"[8] For real guerillas, such as Chen Xiu Zhu, the jungle offered "revenge . . . to crush British Imperialism." Yet her frustrations were not limited to British rule. She noted that without "rifles and cannons, the enemy would never have given us independence" in 1957. Because of this, she resented Malaysia's first prime minister, Tunku Abdul Rahman, for calling "himself the Father of Independence. Shame on him!" Instead, she insisted that "independence was fought for by the CPM [Communist Party of Malaya]. Due credit should be given to the CPM yet we were treated like criminals . . . Had we not sacrificed so many of our comrades, would Malaya have ever become what it is today?"[9] For Chen, the betrayal of the post-colonial nation-state was just as, if not more, difficult than persecution under British colonialism. Zhu Ning noted similarly that she often faced questions from Singaporeans and Malaysians about

why she joined communist guerillas. She retorted that she did so after "my husband was killed by your government." If she had not joined, her "children would
have had nothing to eat."[10] To those who toiled in the jungle, post-colonial states
betrayed the promise of independence by continuing to fight communists rather
than acknowledge their role in securing national liberation. In so doing, they
followed the British Empire's model of abandoning those who fought for it.

This feeling of betrayal reflected the fact that both Malaysia and Singapore
forged national histories steeped in memories of war. As Chen Xiu Zhu suggested, Malaysian national memory tends to blame the Emergency on Chinese
communist outsiders, replicating British narratives of the conflict. While the
founders of Malaysia emphasized the need for interethnic unity, this understanding of the Emergency still enabled ethnic nationalism that excludes many
non-Malays.[11] By contrast, Singapore's national memory hinges on the idea of a
small nation-state rising from the ashes of the Japanese occupation to emerge as
a peaceful, multi-racial society.[12] Yet being a global port city with a reputation as
a pleasure palace also meant that this peaceful prosperity came in part by catering
to troops on leave from the region's many conflicts. Even places that carried significance for anti-colonial resistance became sites of post-colonial oppression. St.
John's Island, which held Indian prisoners in 1915 and Japanese internees in 1941,
became a prison for communists and other political dissenters from Singapore
after independence. Emphasizing Singapore's war-torn history, and the need to
defend their small nation from internal and external threats, enabled Singapore
to require mandatory military service, regardless of gender.[13] Both Malaysia and
Singapore, therefore, sustain nationalist histories steeped in the unresolved legacies of war and colonialism. If British leaders can be credited with "winning"
hearts and minds, it is only because postwar nationalist narratives obscured the
experiences of those who survived—or failed to survive—these conflicts. Granting independence (1957) before the formal end of the Emergency (1960) ensured
such continuity. Britain's victory in Malaya and Singapore was encouraging independent nations to preserve imperial fictions.

In truth, the history of colonial warfare in Southeast Asia was often a story
of betrayal. Sacrifices in war constantly resulted in being forgotten in peacetime
or abandoned at the next sign of trouble. Those who supported British power
were often the first to be targeted. This was true for both the Indian soldiers who
served in the First World War and the Chinese and Japanese civil and military
personnel who aided the British in the 1915 rebellion. British leaders relied on
Chinese militarism against Indian troops in 1915, left them unprotected in 1942,
and then turned them into targets of the Emergency. The problem with allying

with a military state is the inherent proximity to real and potential violence. For allies there is never enough loyalty—only future sedition. The first hearts and minds that colonial states usually lose are those of their own soldiers and allies. For Hannah Arendt, "the danger of the practice of violence, even if it moves consciously within a non-extremist framework of short-term goals, will always be that the means overwhelm the end." The reason is that if "goals are not achieved rapidly, the result will not merely be defeat but the introduction of the practice of violence into the whole body politic."[14] As a survivor of Nazi persecution, Arendt experienced firsthand how plans for swift victory enabled pervasive and targeted everyday violence. Yet she wrote her "Reflections on Violence" during the Cold War. Certainly no one could claim that the twelve-year Malayan Emergency swiftly achieved clear goals. Even though British leaders declared success in Malaya in 1960, the *Konfrontasi* (1963–1966) showed the unfinished business of decolonization and nation-state formation. Much of Southeast Asia continued to experience traumatic warfare that made it more difficult for civilians to recover from violence. In Malaysia it would take until the Peace Agreement of Hat Yai in 1989 to formally end conflict between the Malayan Communist Party and the Malaysian and Thai governments. There was no healing from war that seemed unending.

An emphasis on winning "hearts and minds" privileges the nations, empires, and militaries who state, repeatedly, their intention to wage a different kind of war. These have a farther reach on wider public consciousness than the experiences of those whose "hearts and minds," they believed, were up for grabs. Yet by declaring their intention and ability to win "hearts and minds" in war, British military and political leaders inadvertently admitted that these were lost already. Racism, militarism, and violence were the realities of colonial conflict in times of both war and "peace." "Winning hearts and minds" promised to win back the world's confidence that British military action could and would lead the world into an inclusive utopia. In reality, it further blurred distinctions between combatant and non-combatant, soldier and civilian, homefront and battlefield, which were already complex in colonial spaces.[15] As a result, the "hearts and minds" concept simply distilled existing colonial policies.

Winning the "minds" of colonial subjects was a long-standing aim of colonial rule. Schools, missions, and legal codes monitored and influenced how and what colonial subjects thought. Colonial leaders rewarded those whose thoughts and actions benefited the empire with employment and upward mobility—an exchange of compliance for material comfort. As novelist Han Suyin contended, many police believed that "any Asian who doesn't grovel and whine and thank

his stars he's got such good masters as we are is a Red." This produced "an in-
duced hypnosis of inferiority, destroying confidence and initiative, prolonging
the period of tutelage which we would like to go on for ever [sic]."[16] Race, therefore, was often the cornerstone of colonial thought as it categorized lived experiences to create safety, security, and opportunity for some, and violence and
exclusion for others. Militaries, prisons, and internment camps monitored those
who rejected colonial logics. Winning "hearts," however, was about translating
the emotional experience of colonialism from one of pain, suffering, and fear into
love and mutual care. War exploited both impulses. Emotional pride in nation,
empire, or "justice" often compelled people to fight just as much as the logical,
material benefit of doing so.

Despite its colonial origins, the "hearts and minds" phrase cast a large shadow.
During a 1965 dinner party speech in Texas, U.S. president Lyndon Johnson declared that in Vietnam, "the ultimate victory will depend upon the hearts and the
minds of the people who actually live out there."[17] This echoed British military
leaders' belief that, by preventing communists from taking over the government
of independent Singapore and Malaysia, they had achieved success in the Malayan Emergency five years prior. In the next two years, Sir Robert Thompson
(1966) and Richard Clutterbuck (1967) produced works arguing that Briggs developed, and Templer perfected, a counterinsurgency campaign more successful
at fighting communism than the coercive methods of previous leaders.[18] Such
interpretations became widespread and inspired European and American leaders
to have faith that military action could turn the tide of communist expansion.[19]
American military leaders like Edward Lansdale continued to popularize the
phrase through experiences in the Philippines and Vietnam. In so doing, they
carried on a military tradition of British colonialism that dated back to the nineteenth century. After the Cold War, American military leaders reproduced and
recycled ambiguous overtures to winning over civilian favor to justify the "War
on Terror." Still, many have questioned the realities of winning the "hearts and
minds" of those "who actually live out there." Johnson's speech featured prominently in the 1974 anti-war film *Hearts and Minds*, which went on to win the
Academy Award for best documentary. Its stark portrayal of American military
men as, at best, reluctant adventure-seekers who loved explosions or, at worst,
eager communist-killers, contrasted the quieter scenes of tearful Vietnamese civilians whose homes were destroyed by bombs. The film showed that the only
"hearts and minds" the war had won were those of Americans who eagerly signed
up to fight or took pride in the illusion of military heroism.

The traumas of war and everyday colonial violence often engendered a form of self-preservation that legitimized narrow or exclusionary concepts of identity. For this reason, war tended to harden not only colonial boundaries but also anti-colonial and nationalist visions. Prior connections and collaborations fragmented and splintered against the exigency of global tumult. Both war and colonialism encouraged isolationist thinking necessary for survival. In some cases, racial hierarchy and exclusion was a response to the uncomfortable fact of the dependence of white bodies on Black and Brown people and a refusal to build a world that acknowledged interdependence. In this way, the endemic racialization of military conflict contributed to further hierarchy and violence. The promises of British colonialism could never be won—because in times of war and peace, leaders used and then abandoned racial integration to facilitate violence.

Twentieth century anti-colonial activists—soldiers and civilians alike—protested military occupation, extractive and coercive colonial policies, and endless war. Colonial and military leaders responded by exporting their methods of combating dissent and resistance around the globe—not only to Malay, Chinese, and Indian soldiers and civilians in Southeast Asia, but also to Australians, New Zealanders, East Africans, Nepalis, and Fijians who participated in these campaigns. Americans who learned the wrong lessons adapted the "hearts and minds" approach to war, solidifying the Malayan Emergency as a "test case" for counterinsurgency among military and policy "experts."[20] However, endemic military violence continues around the world, despite repeated military and government efforts to "win" hearts and minds. Military conflicts tend to make more problems than they solve. Yet paying the nation in blood through military service remains a ticket to citizenship and upward mobility in many countries. Institutions founded under colonial and military power continue to replicate colonial patterns of violence. When states commit to "winning" at all costs, the world is lost.

NOTES

Introduction

1. Dolores Ho, interview by Kate Imy, July 2019, National Army Museum, Waiouru, New Zealand.

2. Sarah Sewall (Introduction), John A. Nagl (Foreword), David H. Petraeus (Foreword), and James F. Amos (Foreword), *The U.S. Army/Marine Corps Counterinsurgency Field Manual,* 2nd ed. (Chicago: University of Chicago Press, 2007). For a United States–focused examination of the phrase, see Elizabeth Dickinson, "A Bright Shining Slogan: How 'Hearts and Minds' Came to Be," *Foreign Policy,* August 22, 2009, https://foreignpolicy.com/2009/08/22/a-bright-shining-slogan/.

3. Quoted in Richard Clutterbuck, *The Long Long War: The Emergency in Malaya, 1948–1960* (London: Cassell, 1967), 3. For more on Templer, see Leon Comber, *Templer and the Road to Malayan Independence: The Man and His Time* (Singapore: Institute of Southeast Asian Studies, 2015).

4. Key works discussing the event include Sho Kuwajima, *First World War and Asia: Indian Mutiny in Singapore (1915)* (Osaka: Sho Kuwajima, 1988); Heather Streets-Salter, *World War One in Southeast Asia: Colonialism and Anticolonialism in an Era of Global Conflict* (Cambridge, UK: Cambridge University Press, 2017); Umej Bhatia, *Our Name Is Mutiny: The Global Revolt against the Raj and the Hidden History of the Singapore Mutiny 1907–1915* (Singapore: Landmark Books, 2020); Tim Harper, "Singapore, 1915, and the Birth of the Asian Underground," *Modern Asian Studies* 47, no. 6 (November 2013): 1782–811.

5. Key works include C. A. Bayly and Tim Harper, *Forgotten Armies: Britain's Asian Empire and the War with Japan* (London: Penguin, 2005); Brian P. Farrell, *The Defence and Fall of Singapore, 1940–1942* (Gloucestershire: Tempus Publishing Group, 2005); Patricia Pui Huen Lim and Diana Wong, *War and Memory in Malaysia and Singapore* (Singapore: Institute of Southeast Asian Studies, 2000); Lachlan Grant, *Australian Soldiers in Asia-Pacific in World War II* (Sydney: NewSouth, 2014); Ban Kah Choon and Yap Hong Kuan, *Rehearsal for War: The Underground War Against the Japanese* (Singapore: Horizon

Books, 2002); Cheah Boon Kheng, *Red Star over Malaya: Resistance and Social Conflict during and after the Japanese Occupation of Malaya, 1941–46* (Singapore: National University of Singapore Press, 2003); Karl Hack, *Defence and Decolonisation in Southeast Asia: Britain, Malaya and Singapore, 1941–1968* (Richmond, UK: Routledge Curzon, 2001).

6. Karl Hack, *The Malayan Emergency: Revolution and Counterinsurgency at the End of Empire* (Cambridge, UK: Cambridge University Press, 2021); Karl Hack, "The Malayan Emergency as Counter-Insurgency Paradigm," *Journal of Strategic Studies* 32, no. 3 (2009); C. A. Bayly and Tim Harper, *Forgotten Wars: Freedom and Revolution in Southeast Asia* (Cambridge, MA: Harvard University Press, 2010); Teng Phee Tan, *Behind Barbed Wire: Chinese New Villages during the Malayan Emergency, 1948–1960* (Petaling Jaya: Strategic Information and Research Development Centre, 2020); Syed Muhd Khairudin Aljunied, *Radicals: Resistance and Protest in Colonial Malaya* (Delkab: Northern Illinois University Press, 2015); Benjamin Grob-Fitzgibbon, *Imperial Endgame: Britain's Dirty Wars and the End of Empire* (New York: Palgrave Macmillan, 2011); Peter Dennis and Jeffrey Grey, *Emergency and Confrontation: Australian Military Operations in Malaya and Borneo 1950–1966* (Sydney: Allen and Unwin and the Australian War Memorial, 1996); Raffi Gregorian, *The British Army, the Gurkhas, and Cold War Strategy in the Far East, 1947–1954* (New York: Palgrave, 2002); T. N. Harper, *The End of Empire and the Making of Malaya* (Cambridge, UK: Cambridge University Press, 1999); Christopher Pugsley, *From Emergency to Confrontation: The New Zealand Armed Forces in Malaya and Borneo 1949–1966* (South Melbourne, Victoria: Oxford University Press, 2003); Kumar Ramakrishna, *Emergency Propaganda: The Winning of Malayan Hearts and Minds, 1948–1958* (Richmond, UK: Routledge Curzon, 2002); Anthony Short, *The Communist Insurrection in Malaya, 1948–1960* (London: Muller, 1975); Richard Stubbs, *Hearts and Minds in Guerilla Warfare—the Malayan Emergency, 1948–1960* (Oxford: Oxford University Press, 1989); Leon Comber, *Malaya's Secret Police, 1945–60: The Role of the Special Branch in the Malayan Emergency* (Singapore: Institute of Southeast Asian Studies, and Australia: Monash Asia Institute, 2008); Rory Cormac, *Confronting the Colonies: British Intelligence and Counterinsurgency* (Oxford: Oxford University Press, 2014); David French, *The British Way in Counter-Insurgency, 1945–1967* (Oxford: Oxford University Press, 2012); Christopher E. Goscha and Christian F. Ostermann, *Connecting Histories: Decolonization and the Cold War in Southeast Asia, 1945–1962* (Stanford: Stanford University Press, 2009).

7. Farish A. Noor and Peter Carey, eds., *Racial Difference and the Colonial Wars of 19th Century Southeast Asia* (Amsterdam: Amsterdam University Press, 2021), 9, 15.

8. Evelyn Brooks Higginbotham, "African-American Women's History and the Metalanguage of Race," *Signs* 17, no. 2 (Winter 1992): 251–74; Ann Laura Stoler, "Sexual Affronts and Racial Frontiers: European Identities and the Cultural Politics of Exclusion in Colonial Southeast Asia," *Comparative Studies in Society and History* 34, no. 3 (July 1992): 514–51.

9. Kristy Walker, "Intimate Interactions: Eurasian Family Histories in Colonial Penang," *Modern Asian Studies* 26, no. 2 (2012): 324.

10. Higginbotham, "African-American Women's History and the Metalanguage of Race."

11. Ann Laura Stoler, "Rethinking Colonial Categories: European Communities and the Boundaries of Rule," *Comparative Studies in Society and History* 31, no. 1 (January 1989): 134–61, at 136–7.

12. Anne Spry Rush, *Bonds of Empire: West Indians and Britishness from Victoria to Decolonization* (Oxford: Oxford University Press, 2011).

13. Kate Imy, *Faithful Fighters: Identity and Power in the British Indian Army* (Stanford: Stanford University Press, 2019).

14. John Mitcham, *Race and Imperial Defence in the British World, 1870–1914* (Cambridge, UK: Cambridge University Press, 2016), 2.

15. Olivette Otele, *African Europeans: An Untold Story* (New York: Basic Books, 2021); Tiffany Florvil, *Mobilizing Black Germany: Afro-German Women and the Making of a Transnational Movement* (Champaign: University of Illinois Press, 2020).

16. Anne Anlin Cheng, *Ornamentalism* (Oxford: Oxford University Press, 2019).

17. David Atkinson, *The Burden of White Supremacy: Containing Asian Migration in the British Empire and the United States* (Chapel Hill: University of North Carolina Press, 2017); Madeline Y. Hsu, *The Good Immigrants: How the Yellow Peril Became the Model Minority* (Princeton: Princeton University Press, 2015).

18. For more on Eurasian identities, see Stoler, "Rethinking Colonial Categories"; Liesbeth Rosen Jacobson, "The Eurasian Question: The Colonial Position and Postcolonial Options of Colonial Mixed Ancestry Groups from British India, Dutch East Indies and French Indochina Compared," *Historische Migratiestudies* 6 (PhD diss., University of Leiden, 2018), 14, https://openaccess.leidenuniv.nl/handle/1887/62456.

19. Han Suyin, *. . . And the Rain My Drink* (London: Jonathan Cape, 1956), 252.

20. "Plan of the Town of Singapore by Lieut Jackson," Survey Department, Singapore (1828), National Archives of Singapore, accessed July 2, 2023, https://www.nas.gov.sg/archivesonline/maps_building_plans/record-details/f9926418-115c-11e3-83d5-0050568939ad; Bonny Tan, "Raffles Town Plan (Jackson Plan)," National Library Board, last modified 2016, https://eresources.nlb.gov.sg/infopedia/articles/SIP_658_2005-01-07.html.

21. Lynn Hollen Lees, *Planting Empire, Cultivating Subjects: British Malaya, 1786–1941* (Cambridge, UK: Cambridge University Press, 2017), 182; Lim Teck Ghee, "British Colonial Administration and the 'Ethnic Division of Labour' in Malaya," *Kajian Malaysia* 2, no. 2 (1984): 28–66; Colin E. R. Abraham, "Racial and Ethnic Manipulation in Colonial Malaya," *Ethnic and Racial Studies* 6, no. 1 (1983): 18–32; Sandra Khor Manickam, "Race and the Colonial Universe in British Malaya," *Journal of Southeast Asian Studies* 40, no. 3 (October 2009): 593–612.

22. Lees, *Planting Empire, Cultivating Subjects*, 217.

23. For more on 1857, see Vera Nünning, "'Daß Jeder Seine Pflicht Thue.' Die Bedeutung der Indian Mutiny für das Nationale Britische Selbstverständnis," *Archiv für Kulturgeschichte* 78 (1996), 373; Marina Carter and Crispin Bates, *Mutiny at the Margins: New Perspectives on the Indian Uprising of 1857* (New Delhi: Sage Publications, 2013); Heather Streets, *Martial Races: The Military, Race, and Masculinity in British Imperial Culture 1857–1914* (Manchester: Manchester University Press, 2004), 28–9; Kim A. Wagner, *The Great Fear of 1857: Rumours, Conspiracies and the Making of the Indian*

Uprising (Oxford: Peter Lang, 2010), 27–8; Avril Powell, *Muslims and Missionaries in Pre-Mutiny India* (New York and London: Routledge, 1995).

24. Malcolm H. Murfett et al., *Between Two Oceans: A Military History of Singapore from 1275 to 1971* (Singapore: Marshall Cavendish Editions, 2011).

25. Netusha Naidu, "'Sly Civility' and the Myth of the 'Lazy Malay': The Discursive Economy of British Colonial Power during the Pahang Civil War, 1891–1895," in *Racial Difference and the Colonial Wars of 19th Century Southeast Asia*, ed. Noor and Carey, 193.

26. Lees, *Planting Empire, Cultivating Subjects*, 168–9.

27. Nadzan Haron, "Colonial Defence and British Approach to the Problems in Malaya," *Modern Asian Studies* 24, no. 2 (1990): 275–95.

28. There is a rich and robust scholarly dialogue about the "Martial Races." See for example, Streets, *Martial Races;* Kaushik Roy, *Brown Warriors of the Raj: Recruitment & the Mechanics of Command in the Sepoy Army, 1859–1913* (New Delhi: Manohar, 2008); Gavin Rand and Kim Wagner, "Recruiting the 'Martial Races': Identities and Military Service in Colonial India," *Patterns of Prejudice* 46, nos. 3–4, (2012); Gajendra Singh, *The Testimonies of Indian Soldiers and the Two World Wars: Between Self and Sepoy* (London: Bloomsbury, 2014); David Omissi, *The Sepoy and the Raj: The Indian Army, 1860–1940* (London: Macmillan, 1994).

29. Singh, *The Testimonies of Indian Soldiers*, 12–13.

30. Mrinalini Sinha, *Colonial Masculinity: The "Manly Englishman" and the "Effeminate Bengali" in the Late Nineteenth Century* (Manchester: Manchester University Press, 1995); Streets, *Martial Races.*

31. Michelle Moyd, *Violent Intermediaries: African Soldiers, Conquest, and Everyday Colonialism in German East Africa* (Athens, OH: Ohio University Press, 2014), 210, 10–11.

32. Timothy Parsons, *The African Rank-and-File: Social Implications of Colonial Military Service in the King's African Rifles, 1902–1964* (Portsmouth, NH: Heinemann, 1999), 5–6, 55.

33. Simeon Man, *Soldiering through Empire: Race and the Decolonizing Pacific* (Berkeley, University of California Press, 2018), 12.

34. Quoted in B. D. Hopkins, "The Problem with 'Hearts and Minds' in Afghanistan," *Middle East Report* 255 (Summer 2010), https://merip.org/2010/05/the-problem -with-hearts-and-minds-in-afghanistan/. See also T. H. Thornton, *Colonel Sir Robert Sandeman: His Life and Work on Our Indian Frontier* (London: John Murray, 1895), letter dated April 19, 1891, title page.

35. Nivi Manchanda, *Imagining Afghanistan: The History and Politics of Imperial Knowledge* (Cambridge, UK: Cambridge University Press, 2020), 8.

36. Stubbs, *Hearts and Minds in Guerilla Warfare*, 1.

37. Simon Smith, "General Templer and Counter-Insurgency in Malaya: Hearts and Minds, Intelligence, and Propaganda," *Intelligence and National Security* 16, no. 3 (2001): 60–78. Thompson and Clutterbuck focus on the impact the Emergency had on American militarism in Southeast Asia: Robert Thompson, *Defeating Communist Insurgency: Experiences from Malaya and Vietnam* (London: Chatto & Windus, 1966); Clutterbuck, *The Long Long War.*

38. Florvil, *Mobilizing Black Germany*, chap. 1, Kindle.

39. Gauri Viswanathan, *Masks of Conquest: Literary Study and British Rule in India* (New York: Columbia University Press, 2014).

40. Ashis Nandy, *The Intimate Enemy: Loss and Recovery of Self Under Colonialism* (Delhi: Oxford University Press, 1983); Homi Bhabha, *Location of Culture* (London: Routledge, 1995), 65; Gayatri Chakravorty Spivak, "Can the Subaltern Speak?" in *Colonial Discourse and Post-Colonial Theory: A Reader*, ed. Patrick Williams and Laura Chrisman (New York: Columbia Univesity Press, 1994), 66–111.

41. Singh, *The Testimonies of Indian Soldiers*, 19.

42. Singh, *The Testimonies of Indian Soldiers*, 82; James C. Scott, *Weapons of the Weak: Everyday Forms of Peasant Resistance* (New Haven and London: Yale University Press, 1985).

43. Francis Loh Kok Wah, *Beyond the Tin Mines: Coolies, Squatters and New Villagers in the Kinta Valley, Malaysia, c. 1880–1980* (Singapore: Oxford University Press, 1988); Agnes Khoo, *Life as the River Flows: Women in the Malayan Anti-Colonial Struggle* (Monmouth, Wales: Merlin Press, 2004); Tan, *Behind Barbed Wire*; Mahani Musa, "Women in the Malayan Communist Party, 1942–89," *Journal of Southeast Asian Studies* 44, no. 2 (June 2013): 226–49.

44. Sandra C. Taylor, *Vietnamese Women at War: Fighting for Ho Chi Minh and the Revolution* (Lawrence: University Press of Kansas, 1999), 7, 17, 18.

45. Joan Scott, "The Evidence of Experience," *Critical Inquiry* 17, no. 4 (Summer, 1991): 773–97, at 777. See also Keat Gin Ooi, "The 'Slapping Monster' and Other Stories: Recollections of the Japanese Occupation (1941–1945) of Borneo through Autobiographies, Biographies, Memoirs, and Other Ego-Documents," *Journal of Colonialism and Colonial History* 7, no. 3 (Winter 2006).

46. Teng Phee Tan, "Oral History and People's Memory of the Malayan Emergency (1948–60): The Case of Pulai," *Sojourn: Journal of Social Issues in Southeast Asia* 27, no. 1 (2012): 84–119, at 86. See also Kah Sengh Loh, Ernest Koh, and Stephen Dobbs, *Oral History in Southeast Asia: Memories and Fragments* (New York: Palgrave Macmillan, 2013).

47. Yasmin Khan, *India at War: The Subcontinent and the Second World War* (Oxford: Oxford University Press, 2015); Singh, *The Testimonies of Indian Soldiers*; Tarak Barkawi characterizes Indian soldiers as cosmopolitan in *Soldiers of Empire: Indian and British Armies in World War II* (Cambridge, UK: Cambridge University Press, 2017).

48. Lees, *Planting Empire, Cultivating Subjects*; Rachel Leow, *Taming Babel: Language in the Making of Malaysia* (Cambridge, UK: Cambridge University Press, 2016); Loh Kok Wah, *Beyond the Tin Mines*; Timothy P. Barnard, *Contesting Malayness: Malay Identity across Boundaries* (Singapore: NUS Press, 2018); Anthony Milner, *The Invention of Politics in Colonial Malaya: Contesting Nationalism and the Expansion of the Public Sphere* (Cambridge, UK: Cambridge University Press, 1995).

49. Tim Harper, *Underground Asia: Global Revolutionaries and the Assault on Empire* (Cambridge, MA: Harvard University Press, 2021); Streets-Salter, *World War One in Southeast Asia*; Maia Ramnath, *Haj to Utopia: How the Ghadar Movement Charted Global Radicalism and Attempted to Overthrow the British Empire* (Berkeley and Los Angeles:

University of California Press, 2011); Moon-Ho Jung, *The Rising Tide of Color: Race, State, Violence, and Radical Movements Across the Pacific* (Seattle: University of Washington Press, 2014).

50. Ranajit Guha, *Elementary Aspects of Peasant Insurgency in Colonial India* (Durham: Duke University Press, 1999); Ranajit Guha, *Dominance without Hegemony: History and Power in Colonial India* (Cambridge, MA: Harvard University Press, 1998); Ranajit Guha, "The Prose of Counter-Insurgency," in *Selected Subaltern Studies,* ed. Ranajit Guha and Gayatri Chakravorty Spivak (Oxford: Oxford University Press, 1988), 45–86; Samuel Moyn, *Humane: How the United States Abandoned Peace and Reinvented War* (New York: Farrar, Straus and Giroux, 2021); Taylor Sherman, *State Violence and Punishment in India* (New York: Routledge, 2010); Elizabeth Kolsky, *Colonial Justice in British India: White Violence and the Rule of Law* (Cambridge, UK: Cambridge University Press, 2011); Caroline Elkins, *Legacy of Violence: A History of the British Empire* (New York: Penguin, 2022).

51. Elkins, *Legacy of Violence,* 13.

52. Bayly and Harper cite the larger number, though 30,000 is the more common reference. Bayly and Harper, *Forgotten Wars,* 25.

53. Elkins, *Legacy of Violence,* 14.

Chapter One

1. Frank Kershaw Wilson to family, February 20, 1915, MSS. Ind. Ocn. S. 162, Bodleian Library, Oxford.

2. For more on British fears of Indian Muslim soldiers more broadly, see Kate Imy, "Kidnapping and a 'Confirmed Sodomite': An Intimate Enemy on the Northwest Frontier of India, 1915–1925," *Twentieth Century British History* 28, no. 1 (November 2016): 29–56.

3. Surprisingly little scholarly attention has been paid to the role of colonial racism and soldier-civilian relations in 1915 Singapore. Many excellent works analyze the event's place in the First World War, Indian Army culture, Indian nationalism, and anti-colonial networks across Asia-Pacific. Kuwajima, *First World War and Asia;* Singh, *The Testimonies of Indian Soldiers;* Streets-Salter, *World War One in Southeast Asia;* Bhatia, *Our Name Is Mutiny;* Mary Brown and Edwin A. Brown, *Singapore Mutiny: A Colonial Couple's Stirring Account of Combat and Survival in the 1915 Singapore Mutiny* (Singapore: Monsoon Books, 2015); Murfett et al., *Between Two Oceans.*

4. Bonny Tan, "Convict Labour in Colonial Singapore," National Library Singapore, accessed November 26, 2021, https://biblioasia.nlb.gov.sg/vol-11/issue-3/oct-dec-2015/convict; Vernon Cornelius-Takahama, "Indian Convicts' Contributions to early Singapore (1825–1873)," National Library of Singapore, November 26, 2021, https://eresources.nlb.gov.sg/infopedia/articles/SIP_39_2005-02-02.html.

5. Lees, *Planting Empire, Cultivating Subjects,* 173–4, 179, 189, 209.

6. Lees, *Planting Empire, Cultivating Subjects,* 203.

7. Leow, *Taming Babel.*

8. This created a notorious demographic imbalance in the army, with Punjabi Sikhs, less than 1 percent of India's population, comprising 20 percent of the army. David

Omissi, *Indian Voices of the Great War: Soldiers' Letters, 1914–18* (New York: Palgrave Macmillan, 1999); Daniel Marston, *The Indian Army at the End of the Raj* (Cambridge, UK: Cambridge University Press, 2014); Streets, *Martial Races;* Santanu Das, *India, Empire, and First World War Culture: Writings, Images, Songs* (Cambridge, UK: Cambridge University Press, 2018). For additional excellent studies on non-Indian colonial soldiers, see also Moyd, *Violent Intermediaries;* Richard Fogarty, *Race and War in France: Colonial Subjects in the French Army, 1914–1918* (Baltimore: The Johns Hopkins University Press, 2008).

9. Harper, *Underground Asia*; Ramnath, *Haj to Utopia*; Streets-Salter, *World War One in Southeast Asia.* Umej Bhatia and Farish Noor have examined the racism against Indian men and Muslims: Bhatia, *Our Name Is Mutiny*; Farish Noor, "'Racial Profiling' Revisited: The 1915 Indian Sepoy Mutiny in Singapore and the Impact of Profiling on Religious and Ethnic Minorities," *Politics, Religion & Ideology* 12, no. 1 (2011): 89–100.

10. Gajendra Singh's work is especially useful for understanding the utility of these sources. Singh, *The Testimonies of Indian Soldiers.*

11. Marisa Fuentes, *Dispossessed Lives: Enslaved Women, Violence, and the Archive* (Philadelphia: University of Pennsylvania Press, 2016).

12. Paraphrase of cypher cable from Governor Young to Secretary of State, December 6, 1914, FCO 141/16205, National Archives of Singapore (henceforth NAS).

13. Report, in Connection with "Mutiny of 5th Light Infantry at Singapore 1915," Part I—"Proceedings of Court of Enquiry"; Part II—"Report by His Excellency the Governor of the Straits Settlements and the General Officer Commanding at Singapore" (Simla: Government Central Branch Press, 1915), 143, IOR/L/MIL/7/7191: 1915–37 (henceforth Mutiny Report), 29–30.

14. Streets-Salter, *World War One in Southeast Asia*, 64, 98; Karen A. Snow, "Russia and the 1915 Indian Mutiny in Singapore," *South East Asia Research* 5, no. 3 (1997): 295–315.

15. Mutiny Report, 31, 76

16. Mutiny Report, 433.

17. Streets-Salter, *World War One in Southeast Asia*, 28; Kuwajima, *First World War and Asia*; Darshan S. Tatla, "Incorporating Regional Events into the Nationalist Narrative: The Life of Gurdit Singh and the Komagata Maru Episode in Postcolonial India," *South Asian Diaspora* 8, no. 2 (2016): 125–46; Rita Kaur Dhamoon et al., eds., *Unmooring the Komagata Maru: Charting Colonial Trajectories* (Vancouver: UBC Press, 2019).

18. Mutiny Report, 284.

19. Mutiny Report, 285, 293–4.

20. Mutiny Report, 307.

21. MSG demographics in December 1914 were: 550 Sikhs, 90 Punjabi Muslims, 210 Pathans, 3 Hindus, 1 Malay. C. H. B. Lees, "Report of the Malay States Guides for the Year 1914" (March 3, 1915), 1–2, 7, NAB1960_0278_0361_0084, CAB 11/64, received at NAS.

22. "Malay States Guides" (January 16, 1915), CO 273/435, NAS.

23. "Notice," CO 273/435, NAS. See also Sana Aiyar, *Indians in Kenya: The Politics of Diaspora* (Cambridge, MA: Harvard University Press, 2015); Antoinette Burton, *Africa in the Indian Imagination: Race and the Politics of Postcolonial Citation* (Durham: Duke

University Press, 2016). Rishma Johal and Heena Mistry also have researched aspirational Indian settlement in Africa during and after the First World War.

24. R. Reade, The General Officer Commanding the Troops, Straits Settlements, to The Secretary, War Office, London, December 9, 1914, CO 273/435, NAS.

25. Anonymous address from "Men of the Guides" to The General Officer Commanding, Singapore, Straits Settlements, December 1914, CO 273/435, NAS.

26. G. Badham Thornhill, Captain, SO, CF, to Commandant, Malay States Guides, CO 273/435, NAS.

27. C. H. B. Lees, Comdg. Malay States Guides to the Staff Officer to Local Forces, Straits Settlements, Singapore, December 6, 1914, CO 273/435, NAS.

28. Zaman commanded the battery for several months and visited India for additional training, which earned him praise from his officers. F. E. Spencer, Capt, R. A., Commanding Mountain Battery, MSG, "Annual Report, 1913," NAB1960_0278_0361_0084, CAB 11/64; "Report of the Malay States Guides for the Year 1914;" Zaman also shows up on Mutiny Report, 325.

29. "Report of the Malay States Guides for the Year 1914," 4.

30. Lees to Staff Officer to Local Forces, December 6, 1914.

31. Tim Harper discusses how police reports often circulated agreed-upon stories and thus reflected what people believed at the time, rather than what was real. Harper, *Underground Asia*, xxix.

32. Lees to Staff Officer to Local Forces.

33. Lees to Staff Officer to Local Forces.

34. Mutiny Report, 433.

35. Mutiny Report, 203.

36. "Local Northern Indians. Meeting of a Committee held at Kuala Lumpur on the 14th January 1915," FCO 141/16054, NAS.

37. "Local Northern Indians," 2–3.

38. B. B. Cubitt to the Under Secretary of State for the Colonies, January 7, 1915, CO 273/435, NAS.

39. War Office, "Garrison of the Straits Settlements, Secret 4564," January 1915, CO 273/435, NAS.

40. Major General Reade to His Excellency The Governor, Straits Settlements, January 15, 1915, FCO 141/16054, NAS.

41. Paraphrase of cypher cable sent to Secretary of State, January 1915, FCO 141/16054, NAS.

42. "Local Northern Indians," 3.

43. Reade to Governor, January 15, 1915; Brown and Brown, *Singapore Mutiny*, 17.

44. Unsigned note to Y. E. [Your Excellency], January 16, 1916, FCO 141/16054, NAS.

45. "Local Northern Indians."

46. Heather Streets-Salter has provided an excellent reconstruction of these events: Streets-Salter, *World War One in Southeast Asia*. Strength of the regiment reported in Paraphrase of cypher to Viceroy, February 22, 1915, FCO141/16539, NAS. The fifth light infantry departed Nowgong for Singapore in March 1914, arriving in April of that year. Mutiny Report, 284.

47. Mutiny Report, 3–4, 18–19, 77–8; Streets-Salter, *World War One in Southeast Asia*, 19–20, 22, 33.

48. Copy of Regimental Order No 100 (February 15, 1915), WO32 9560, The National Archives (UK) (henceforth TNA).

49. Sepoy Kandha of E Company also heard "everybody saying the regiment was going to Europe," Mutiny Report, 53; see also Mutiny Report, 49, 46. For discussion of the belief that Egypt was the destination. See Paraphrase of cypher from Governor Arthur Young to Viceroy of India, February 28, 1915, FCO141/16539, NAS, and Mutiny Report, 208.

50. Mutiny Report, 20, 145.

51. Mutiny Report, 144; Paraphrase of cypher from Governor Arthur Young to Viceroy of India, FCO141/16539, NAS.

52. Brown and Brown, *Singapore Mutiny*, 17.

53. L. A. Thomas, "Mutiny of the 5th Light Infantry, (Indian). Singapore, 1915" (undated), MSS. Ind. Ocn. S. 106, Bodleian Library.

54. Mutiny Report, 41–2, 77, 146–7, 185.

55. Mutiny Report, 38–9.

56. Mutiny Report, 55; see also Mutiny Report, 39.

57. Mutiny Report, 57, 74.

58. Brown and Brown, *Singapore Mutiny*, 18.

59. Mutiny Report, 51.

60. Mutiny Report, 27, 40.

61. Mutiny Report, 47.

62. For more on laborers in the Indian Army, see Radhika Singha, *The Coolie's Great War: Indian Labour in a Global Conflict, 1914–1921* (London: Hurst, 2020).

63. Mutiny Report, 90.

64. Mutiny Report, 74.

65. Mutiny Report, 87, 89.

66. Mutiny Report, 346.

67. Mutiny Report, 174.

68. Mutiny Report, 34.

69. Mutiny Report, 15–16.

70. Mutiny Report, 346, 32–3, 54.

71. Brown and Brown, *Singapore Mutiny*, 122.

72. Mutiny Report, 22.

73. Mutiny Report, 50.

74. Mutiny Report, 42, 85.

75. Cable from Young to the Viceroy, February 18, 1915, FCO141/16539, NAS.

76. Mutiny Report, 31, 41, 59. See also "The Mutiny Trials," *The Singapore Free Press and Mercantile Advertiser*, April 10, 1915, 5.

77. Mutiny Report, 60.

78. "The Mutineers," *Straits Times*, March 1, 1915, 6.

79. Mutiny Report, 82.

80. Brown and Brown, *Singapore Mutiny*, 37, 41, 101–2, 109.

81. Sng Choon Yee, interview by Lim How Seng, March 26, 1981, Accession Number 000064 Oral History Centre, National Archives of Singapore (henceforth NAS), Reel 11, 26:30, and Reel 12, 82 and 85, https://www.nas.gov.sg/archivesonline/oral_history_interviews/record-details/df70f1cc-115d-11e3-83d5-0050568939ad?keywords=Sng%20Choon%20Yee&keywords-type=all.

82. "The Alarmists," *The Singapore Free Press and Mercantile Advertiser,* May 18, 1915, 10.

83. "Houseboys and the Mutiny," *Straits Times,* May 17, 1915, 8; Press Extracts regarding Mutiny, *Singapore Free Press,* February 17 to March 3, 22–2-15, TNA WO32 9560, received from National University of Singapore.

84. "The Alarmists," 10.

85. Mutiny Report, 25, 46–7.

86. Mutiny Report, 25.

87. Sng Choon Yee, interview by Lim How Seng.

88. Mutiny Report, 273.

89. For Ball, Mutiny Report, 26–7; Tilak Raj Sareen, *Secret Documents on Singapore Mutiny, 1915* (New Delhi: Mounto Publishing House, 1995), 271.

90. Mutiny Report, 112.

91. Herbert Smith, "An Account of What I Saw and Did, Mutiny Day 15th February 1915," in Sareen, *Secret Documents,* 280.

92. Mutiny Report, 118, 74, 112.

93. "The Mutineers," 6; "The Mutiny," *Straits Times,* March 6, 1915, 7.

94. Sareen, *Secret Documents,* 273.

95. Kuwajima, *First World War and Asia,* 4.

96. "Dear Sir Arthur," dated April 22, 1915, from Dudley Ridout.

97. Kate Imy, "Queering the Martial Races: Masculinity, Sex and Circumcision in the Twentieth Century British Indian Army," *Gender & History* 27, no. 2 (August 2015): 374–96.

98. Tim Harper, "Singapore, 1915, and the Birth of the Asian Underground," *Modern Asian Studies* 47, no. 6 (November 2013): 1782–811, at 1806.

99. Walter de Burley Wood, *The History of the King's Shropshire Light Infantry in the Great War, 1914–1918* (London: Medici Society, 1925), 100.

100. Mutiny Report, 172–3.

101. Mutiny Report, 22.

102. Brown and Brown, *Singapore Mutiny,* 69.

103. de Burley Wood, *The History of the King's Shropshire Light Infantry,* 100.

104. Smith, "An Account of What I Saw and Did, Mutiny Day 15th February 1915," 279.

105. Sareen, *Secret Documents,* 280, 267, 270, 275.

106. Mutiny Report, 100 (slur removed by author).

107. B. A. M. papers, University Library Cambridge, NAB0473_0006_012_0007.

108. Preston L. Peach, "Recollections Based on Actual Experiences during the Singapore Mutiny of 5th Light Infantry," NAB0466_0721_0747_0027.pdf, 3, 16, NAS.

109. Press Extracts regarding Mutiny, *Singapore Free Press,* February 17 to March 3, 18–2-15, WO32 9560, TNA.

110. Mutiny Report, 95.

111. Mutiny Report, 101.

112. Harper, *Underground Asia*, 242–3.

113. Mutiny Report, 115.

114. Thomas, "Mutiny of the 5th Light Infantry," 1–2.

115. Brown and Brown, *Singapore Mutiny*, 24.

116. Singh, *The Testimonies of Indian Soldiers*, 155.

117. Mutiny Report, 117.

118. Mutiny Report, 22.

119. Mutiny Report, 4.

120. Mutiny Report, 5–6.

121. Sareen, *Secret Documents*, 271.

122. Mutiny Report, 39.

123. Sareen, *Secret Documents*, 271, 281.

124. Sareen, *Secret Documents*, 279.

125. Sareen, *Secret Documents*, 280.

126. Christine Doran, "Gender Matters in the Singapore Mutiny," *Sojourn* 17, no. 1 (2002): 76–93.

127. Mrs. Marjorie Binnie, "Account of the Mutiny by the 5th Light Infantry in Singapore," B. A. M. papers, University Library Cambridge, NAB0473_0006_012_0007.

128. Sareen, *Secret Documents*, 271–2.

129. Sareen, *Secret Documents*, 280.

130. Sareen, *Secret Documents*, 284.

131. Secret Documents, Mrs. Robinson, wife of Captain T. Robinson, 276–7.

132. Secret Documents, Mrs. Robinson, wife of Captain T. Robinson, 276–7.

133. Peach, "Recollections Based on Actual Experiences during the Singapore Mutiny," 3.

134. Thomas, "Mutiny of the 5th Light Infantry," 1.

135. Extract from *Times of Malaya,* January 24, 1928, FCO 141/16015, NAS.

136. Author photo from National Museum of Singapore (May 2021).

137. Author photo from National Gallery of Singapore (June 2021).

138. Noor, "'Racial Profiling' Revisited."

139. "A Proclamation under Martial Law" (February 20, 1915), WO32 9560, TNA.

140. Singh, *The Testimonies of Indian Soldiers*, 154.

141. Cable secret to Viceroy from Young, February 18, 1915, FCO141/16539, NAS.

142. Singh, *The Testimonies of Indian Soldiers*, 153, 262n1.

143. Cypher to Governor of Hong Kong, February 15, 1915, FCO 141/16536, NAS.

144. Cypher to Governor of Hong Kong, February 15, 1915.

145. General Officer Commanding the Troops, Straits Settlements, to the Secretary, War Office, HQ Singapore, March 3, 1915, WO32 9560, TNA.

146. Mutiny Report, 109.

147. For more on speculation about Sikhs, see Mutiny Report, 110, 108, 120.

148. Mutiny Report, 113.

149. Enclosure No. 2. Reference to Report signed by General Hoghton, May 11, 1915, and General Officer Commanding the Troops, Straits Settlements to the Secretary, War Office, Whitehall London, August 26, 1915, CO 273/435, NAS.

150. Sng Choon Yee, interview by Lim How Seng, Reel 11, 26:30. See also Imy, *Faithful Fighters*, for more on Indo-Afghan anti-colonial revolution.

151. Sareen, *Secret Documents*, 280; Mutiny Report, 74, 331, 112.

152. Mutiny Report, 99.

153. Mutiny Report, 5.

154. Mutiny Report, 136; Sareen, *Secret Documents*, 276.

155. Sareen, *Secret Documents*, 276.

156. "The Mutiny," *Straits Times*, 7.

157. Mutiny Report, 140–1; Sareen, *Secret Documents*, 284.

158. Mutiny Report, 5.

159. Mutiny Report, 5.

160. Sareen, *Secret Documents*, 275.

161. Mutiny Report, 49–50.

162. Mutiny Report, 20–1.

163. "The Mutiny," *Straits Times*, 7. See also "The Mutiny Trials," *The Singapore Free Press and Mercantile Advertiser*, April 7, 1915, 10.

164. Ramnath, *Haj to Utopia*.

165. Sng Choon Yee, Reel 11, 26:30.

166. Press Extracts regarding Mutiny, *Singapore Free Press*, February 17 to March 3.

167. Press Extracts regarding Mutiny, *Singapore Free Press*, February 17 to March 3.

168. Arthur Young to Lewis Harcourt, Colonial Office, March 11, 1915, TNA WO32 9560.

169. Scholars often agree with this conclusion. Murfett et al., *Between Two Oceans*.

170. Young to Harcourt, March 11, 1915.

171. Peach, "Recollections Based on Actual Experiences," 3.

172. Brown and Brown, *Singapore Mutiny*, 46.

173. Mutiny Report, 35.

174. Brown and Brown, *Singapore Mutiny*, 67.

175. Singh, *The Testimonies of Indian Soldiers*, 150; Streets-Salter, *World War One in Southeast Asia*, 22–3.

176. Mutiny Report, 5.

177. Binnie, "Account of the Mutiny by the 5th Light Infantry in Singapore," 5.

178. Binnie, "Account of the Mutiny by the 5th Light Infantry in Singapore," 5.

179. Enclosure by Hoghton (May 11, 1915).

180. Binnie, "Account of the Mutiny by the 5th Light Infantry in Singapore," 5.

181. Streets-Salter, *World War One in Southeast Asia*, 23.

182. Emphasis in original.

183. "The Mutiny," *Malaya Tribune*, March 23, 1915, 8, Newspaper SG, National Library of Singapore.

184. Thomas, "Mutiny of the 5th Light Infantry," 2.

185. Malcolm Bond Shelley, "Brief Account of the Happenings in Singapore" (1927), cited in Singh, *The Testimonies of Indian Soldiers*, 154.

186. A. M. Thompson, "Record of Promulgation and execution of sentences on 45 mutineers of the 5th Light Infantry, carried out at the Criminal Prison, Singapore on 25/3/1915" (March 26, 1915), FCO141/16530, NAS.

187. Mutiny Report, 331–2, 36.

188. General Officer Commanding, Straits Settlements, to War Office, February 22, 1915, CO 273/435, NAS.

189. Press Extracts regarding Mutiny, *Singapore Free Press*, February 17 to March 3.

190. Mutiny Report, 165–7, 162.

191. Mutiny Report, 85.

192. Syed Muhd Khairudin Aljunied, "The Prison and the Anti-Colonialist in British Malaya," *Journal of Historical Sociology* 25, no. 3 (September 2012): 386–412.

193. R. C. D. Bradley, "An Eye-Witness Account of the Mutiny Compiled by British Advisor Johore State in 1933" (September 28, 1933), in Sareen, *Secret Documents*, 782–3.

194. Singh, *The Testimonies of Indian Soldiers*, 151.

195. *The Singapore Free Press and Mercantile Advertiser*, June 23, 1915, 4.

196. Paraphrase of a Cypher telegram sent to the Secretary of State for the Colonies from Young, August 9, 1916, FCO 141/16116, NAS.

197. Dudley Ridout, Memorandum submitted to H. E. the Governor, August 8, 1916, FCO 141/16116, NAS.

Chapter Two

1. Spelling appears as both Tsukada and Tsukuda in various sources. Quoted in Murfett et al., *Between Two Oceans*, 140. See also Sareen, *Secret Documents*, 776, and Extract from the book by Koji Tsukuda, "Nanyo Yori" as translated by the Foreign Office, Foreign Department, Ext. B. See B. Confidential B. of 1918, Nos. 41–60, National Archives of India (henceforth NAI), Annexure I.

2. Sareen, *Secret Documents*, 776, 781.

3. L. A. Thomas, "Mutiny of the 5th Light Infantry, (Indian). Singapore, 1915" (undated), MSS. Ind. Ocn. S. 106, Bodleian Library.

4. General Staff assessment of the Japanese role in the suppression of the Mutiny (September 23, 1917), in Sareen, *Secret Documents*, 781.

5. Sareen, *Secret Documents*, 776, 780.

6. Xu Guoqi, *Asia in the Great War* (Oxford: Oxford University Press, 2017), 185.

7. Sareen, *Secret Documents*, 776–7, 780–81.

8. Tarak Barkawi, *Soldiers of Empire: Indian and British Armies in World War II* (Cambridge, UK: Cambridge University Press, 2017); Chandar Sundaram, "Grudging Concessions: The Officer Corps and Its Indianization, 1817–1940," in *A Military History of India and South Asia*, ed. Daniel P. Marston and Chandar S. Sundaram (Westport, CT, and London: Praeger Security International, 2007), 88–100; Marston, *The Indian Army and the End of the Raj*.

9. Leow, *Taming Babel*.

10. "To Towkay Yeo Bian Chuan," from Mr. H. Knott, Mr. R. W. Reeder, Mr. J. Dessett, Mr. W. E. Gibson, Mrs. W. J. Trowell, Mrs. H. Knott, Mrs. R. W. Reeder, Mrs. W. E. Gibson, Miss Kate Trowell, Miss D. Trowell, Mr. A. Trowell, Mr. F. Keller, Mr. D. D. Mackie Jr., Mr. A. Callwood, Mr. J. Downes, Mr. A. W. Hoy, FCO 141/16015, received at NAS.

11. Ann Laura Stoler, "'In Cold Blood': Hierarchies of Credibility and the Politics of Colonial Narratives," *Representations* 37 (1992): 151–89.

12. "Towkay Yeo Bian Chuan's Account of What Took Place at His Bungalow on the Night of February 15th, 1915," FCO 141/16015, NAS. This document is typed and is most likely a copy. It is unclear if it was altered or translated.

13. W. Geoge Maxwell to Mr. Collins, November 22, 1920, FCO 141/16015, NAS.

14. Maxwell to Collins, November 22, 1920; A. C. C. Parkinson to Sir Laurence Guillemard, November 24, 1920, FCO 141/16015, NAS.

15. "Papers in Reference to Grant of Naturalization to Mr Yeo Bian Chuan" (February 1921), FCO 141/16015, NAS.

16. Dudley Ridout, January 22, 1921, FCO 141/16015, NAS.

17. "Notes of an Interview with Mr. D. D. Mackie Sr.," FCO 141/16015, NAS.

18. D. D. Mackie to David Beatty, January 27, 1921, FCO 141/16015, NAS.

19. H. F. Knott to D. Beatty, January 27, 1921, FCO 141/16015, NAS.

20. F. Keller to D. Beatty, January 28, 1921, FCO 141/16015, NAS.

21. Keller to Beatty, January 28, 1921.

22. Mr. Herbert Smith, "An Account of What I Saw and Did, Mutiny Day 15th February 1915," in Sareen, *Secret Documents*, 278.

23. Keller to Beatty, January 28, 1921.

24. Keller to Beatty, January 28, 1921.

25. A. Callwood to the Acting Colonial Secretary, January 29, 1921, FCO 141/16015, NAS. The 1915 testimony of Mrs. G. J. Marshall stated that she "[s]pent the night in Chinese house" with "twenty Europeans." Sareen, *Secret Documents*, 285.

26. Callwood to the Acting Colonial Secretary, January 29, 1921.

27. Callwood to the Acting Colonial Secretary, January 29, 1921.

28. "Towkay Yeo Bian Chuan's Account."

29. Unsigned note, February 2, 1921, FCO 141/16015.

30. L. N. Guillemard to A. C. C. Parkinson, February 5, 1921, FCO 141/16015.

31. F. S. James to Mr. Yeo Bian Chuan, November 14, 1921, FCO 141/16015.

32. A. W. Still to Mr. Marriott, March 3, 1925, FCO 141/16015.

33. A. W. Still to Mr. Marriott, February 20, 1925, FCO 141/16015.

34. Private letter to Mr. Still, February 27, 1925, FCO 141/16015.

35. Still to Marriott, March 3, 1925.

36. E. L. Talma to Mr. Marriott, May 14, 1926, FCO 141/16015.

37. Mr. Marriott to E. L. Talma, May 19, 1926, FCO 141/16015.

38. "A Mutiny Night: A Chinese New Year Echo," *Straits Times*, January 19, 1928, FCO 141/16015.

39. "A Mutiny Night: A Chinese New Year Echo."

40. "Good Work Unappreciated," extract from *Times of Malaya*, January 24, 1928.

41. "Good Work Unappreciated."

42. Wilfred Blythe, *The Impact of Chinese Secret Societies in Malaya: A Historical Study* (London: Oxford University Press, 1969), 1–2.

43. Blythe, *The Impact of Chinese Secret Societies in Malaya*, 5, 280.

44. Blythe, *The Impact of Chinese Secret Societies in Malaya*, 281.

45. Secret. Issue No. 65 Copy No. 43, "The Malayan Bulletin of Political Intelligence" (October 1928), IOR/L/PJ/12/108, File 6320/22, NAS.

46. Leonard David Gammans, "Rotary in Malaya," MSS. Ind. Ocn. S. 178 (henceforth Gammans papers), Bodleian archives, 9.

47. Suyin, . . . *And the Rain My Drink*, 255.

48. Blythe, *The Impact of Chinese Secret Societies in Malaya*, 284.

49. D. Beatty, "Annual Report of the Protector of Chinese. S. S. 1919," PPMS 31/FILE 4, NAS.

50. Priya Satia, *Spies in Arabia: The Great War and the Cultural Foundations of Britain's Covert Empire in the Middle East* (Oxford: Oxford University Press, 2008), 201.

51. Beatty, "Annual Report of the Protector of Chinese. S. S. 1919."

52. H. W. Firmstone, "Administration Report. Penang. 1919," PPMS 31/FILE 4, 1900–1937, NAS.

53. "FMS. Annual Reports. 1921," PPMS 31/File 5, NAS.

54. S. S. Annual Reports, 1921. Report of the Secretary for Chinese Affairs. Immigration. Chinese Protectorate, 1921, PPMS 31/FILE 4, NAS.

55. D. Beatty, "Annual Report of the Secretary for Chinese Affairs, S.SS 1922," February 15, 1923, PPMS 31/FILE 4, NAS.

56. P. T. Allen, "Annual Report: Protector of Chinese. 1920," PPMS 31/FILE 4, NAS.

57. SCA/SS Annual Report, 1922, PPMS 31/FILE 4, NAS (capitalization in original).

58. W. George Maxwell, "Chief Secretary's Report. 1923," May 26, 1924, PPMS 31/File 5, NAS; "Annual Report on the Police Force and the State of Crime. 1924. SSs.," by G. C. Denham, CIE, CBE, IGP/SSs.

59. G. C. Denham, "Annual Report on the Police Force and the State of Crime. 1924. SSs.," PPMS 31/FILE 4, NAS.

60. Blythe, *The Impact of Chinese Secret Societies in Malaya*, 2.

61. H. Fairburn, "State of Crime and the Straits Settlements Police" (1927), PPMS 31/FILE 4, NAS.

62. Other articles refer to her as Wong Sung, Wung Sung, or Wong Sang. See for example: "The Bomb Outrage," *The Singapore Free Press and Mercantile Advertiser*, February 4, 1925, 78; "The Bomb Outrage," *The Singapore Free Press and Mercantile Advertiser*, March 25, 1925, 179; "The Bomb Outrage," *Straits Times*, March 23, 1925, 9. Tim Harper uses "Wong Sang" when discussing this case. Harper, *Underground Asia*, 512.

63. "Woman Confesses," *The Singapore Free Press and Mercantile Advertiser*, January 28, 1925, 52.

64. "The K. L. Bomb Affair," *The Singapore Free Press and Mercantile Advertiser*, January 28, 1925, 16; "Bomb Outrage. Protector of Chinese Seriously Injured," *Straits Budget*, January 30, 1925, 7.

65. Su Lin Lewis, "Cosmopolitanism and the Modern Girl: A Cross-Cultural Discourse in 1930s Penang," *Modern Asian Studies* 43, no. 6 (November 2009): 1385–419; Harper, *Underground Asia*, 510; Rachel Leow, "Age as a Category of Gender Analysis: Servant Girls, Modern Girls, and Gender in Southeast Asia," *The Journal of Asian Studies* 71, no. 4 (November 2012): 975–90.

66. Harper, *Underground Asia*, 512–13. See also J. L. H. Davis to his mother and father, August 7, 1931, Private Papers of Colonel J. L. H Davis (henceforth Davis papers), Documents.16593, Imperial War Museum (henceforth IWM). These discuss many Chinese men's fears that being sent home would lead to their deaths.

67. "Bomb Outraged. Bobbed Haired Woman Charged With Attempted Murder," *Straits Budget*, February 6, 1925, 16; "The Bomb Outrage," *The Singapore Free Press and Mercantile Advertiser*, February 4, 1925, 67.

68. "Bomb Outrage. Protector of Chinese Seriously Injured," *Straits Budget*, January 30, 1925, 7.

69. Blythe, *The Impact of Chinese Secret Societies in Malaya*, 5, 8.

70. W. T. Chapman, "FMS. Annual Reports. 1925. Report of the SCA for 1926" (March 1926), PPMS 31/File 5, NAS.

71. Harper, *Underground Asia*, 513.

72. Some articles say five years. "The Bomb Outrage," *Straits Times*, March 23, 1925, 9; "Echo of K. L. Bomb Outrage," *Malaya Tribune*, March 24, 1925, 6.

73. Chapman, "FMS. Annual Reports. 1925."

74. Harper, *Underground Asia*, 519.

75. H. Marriott, "Straits Settlements. 1925. Annual Report," PPMS 31/FILE 4, NAS.

76. A. M. Goodman, "Annual Report of the Secretary for Chinese Affairs, 1926. S.Ss.," PPMS 31/FILE 4, NAS, 348.

77. C. W. H. Cochrane, "Perak Administrative Report. 1927," PPMS 31/File 5, NAS.

78. Blythe, *The Impact of Chinese Secret Societies in Malaya*, 282.

79. Cochrane, "Perak Administrative Report. 1927"; J. W. Simmons, "Negri Sembilan Administration Report. 1928," PPMS 31/File 5, NAS.

80. Blythe, *The Impact of Chinese Secret Societies in Malaya*, 282–3.

81. John Scott, "Straits Settlements Administration Report. 1928," PPMS 31/FILE 4, NAS.

82. Andrew Caldecott, "Negri Sembilan Administration Report. 1929," PPMS 31/File 5, NAS.

83. H. Fairburn, "Annual Report of the State of Crime and the Straits Settlements Police. 1929," PPMS 31/FILE 4, NAS. Capitalization per original.

84. Harper, *Underground Asia*, 617–18.

85. Lees, *Planting Empire, Cultivating Subjects*, 171, 174. For more on rubber, see John H. Drabble, *Malayan Rubber: The Interwar Years* (London: Macmillan, 1991).

86. A. M. Goodman, "Annual Report of the Secretary for Chinese Affairs, Straits Settlements. 1930," PPMS 31/FILE 4, NAS.

87. A. M. Goodman, "Annual Report of the SCA/Straits Settlements, 1932," PPMS 31/FILE 4, NAS.

88. Lees, *Planting Empire, Cultivating Subjects*, 214.

89. C. W. H. Cochrane, "FMS Annual Reports. 1930," PPMS 31/File 5, NAS.

90. C. H. Sansom, "FMS Report on the State of Crime and the Administration of the Police Force for the Year 1931," PPMS 31/File 5, NAS.

91. Cochrane, "FMS Annual Reports. 1930."

92. A. Caldecott, "Selangor Administration Report, 1930," PPMS 31/File 5, NAS.

93. P. T. Alen, "Report of the SCA/FMS for 1930," PPMS 31/File 5, NAS.

94. Blythe, *The Impact of Chinese Secret Societies in Malaya*, 282–4.

95. Sansom, "Annual Report of the Police. 1934."

96. Khoo, *Life as the River Flows*, 203.

97. William Arthur Campion Haines (henceforth Haines papers), Kings College Liddell Hart Centre for Military Archives (henceforth LHCMA), 73–4.

98. See for example the police "types" included in T. Q. Gafikin papers, Box 6, MSS. Ind. Ocn. 97, Bodleian Library.

99. Leela Gandhi, *Affective Communities: Anticolonial Thought, Fin-de-Siècle Radicalism, and the Politics of Friendship* (Durham: Duke University Press, 2006).

100. Imy, "Queering the Martial Races."

101. Haines papers, 3, 12, 18, 24–25, 52.

102. J. L. H. Davis to his mother and father, March 1, 1931, Davis papers; J. L. H. Davis to his mother and father, October 16, 1931, Davis papers.

103. J. L. H. Davis to his mother and father, September 18, 1932, Davis papers.

104. J. L. H. Davis to his mother and father, August 7, 1931, Davis papers.

105. J. L. H. Davis to Geof, February 20, 1931, Davis papers.

106. Haines papers, 3, 12, 18, 24–5, 52.

107. Blythe, *The Impact of Chinese Secret Societies in Malaya*, 283; Heather Streets-Salter, "The Noulens Affair in East and Southeast Asia International Communism in the Interwar Period," *Journal of American-East Asian Relations* (November 26, 2014): 394–414; Harper, *Underground Asia*, 625.

108. Haines papers, 121.

109. Haines papers, 147–8.

110. Haines papers, 169.

111. C. H. Sansom, "Annual Police Report. 1935," PPMS 31/File 5, NAS.

112. A. B. Jordan, "Annual Report of the Secretary for Chinese Affairs. Malaya. 1936," PPMS 31/File 5, NAS.

113. Alen, "Report of the SCA/FMS for 1930."

114. C. H. Sansom, "Annual Police Report. FMS. 1936," PPMS 31/File 5, NAS.

115. R. H. de S. Onraet, "Annual Report on the Straits Settlements Police and the State of Crime, 1936," PPMS 31/FILE 4, NAS.

116. Sansom, "Report on the State of Crime and Administration of Police. 1937," 2.

117. R. H. de S. Onraet, "Annual Report of the Straits Settlements Police and the State of Crime. 1937," (June 30, 1938), PPMS 31/FILE 4, NAS; Jordan, "Annual Report of SCA/Malaya for the year 1937."

118. Ernest Koh, "Remembrance, Nation, and the Second World War in Singapore: The Chinese Diaspora and their Wars," in *Oral History in Southeast Asia: Memories and*

Fragments, ed. Kah Seng Loh, Ernest Koh, and Stephen Dobbs (New York: Palgrave, 2013), 61; Lucian Pye, *Guerilla Communism in Malaya: Its Social and Political Meaning* (Princeton: Princeton University Press, 1956), 47.

119. "Federated Malay States, Police Report, 1939," PPMS 31/File 5.

120. "Federated Malay States, Police Report, 1939," PPMS 31/File 5.

121. "Annual Report of the Secretary for Chinese Affairs Malaya for the Year 1937," PPMS 31/FILE 4, NAS.

122. de S. Onraet, "Annual Report of the Straits Settlements Police and the State of Crime. 1937."

123. "Annual Report of the Secretary for Chinese Affairs Malaya for the Year 1937."

124. A. B. Jordan, "Annual Report of SCA/Malaya for the year 1937," PPMS 31/File 5, NAS.

125. C. H. Sansom, "Report on the State of Crime and Administration of Police. 1937"; J. V. Cowgill, "Negri Sembilan Administrative Report. 1937"; and C. D. Ahearne, "Report of the Federal Secretary to Government. 1937," all in PPMS 31/File 5, NAS.

126. "Police Reports. 1937," PPMS 31/File 5, NAS.

127. "Annual Report of the Secretary for Chinese Affairs Malaya for the Year 1937."

128. Sansom, "Report on the State of Crime and Administration of Police. 1937," 2.

129. Sansom, "Report on the State of Crime and Administration of Police. 1937," 2.

130. Tan Chong Tee, interview by Lye Soo Choon, June 7, 2005, Accession Number 002944, NAS, Reel 1.

131. Tan, interview by Lye, Reel 2.

132. Lees, *Planting Empire, Cultivating Subjects,* 194–5.

133. Preston L. Peach, "Recollections of 35 Years as a Missionary Teacher in Malaya," BAM IV/26, NAS, 11–12.

134. Peach, "Recollections of 35 Years," 14–15.

135. Peach, "Recollections of 35 Years," 13.

136. Hayden Bellenoit, "Missionary Education, Religion and Knowledge in India, c.1880–1915," *Modern Asian Studies* 41, no. 2 (2007): 369–94.

137. Lees, *Planting Empire, Cultivating Subjects,* 228.

138. Peach, "Recollections of 35 Years," 13.

139. Lees, *Planting Empire, Cultivating Subjects,* 230–1; Viswanathan, *Masks of Conquest.*

140. Blythe, *The Impact of Chinese Secret Societies in Malaya,* 12.

141. Leonard David Gammans, "Rotary in Malay," Gammans papers, 14–16.

142. Leonard David Gammans, "Confidential. Economic Development" (undated, c. 1930–34), Gammans papers.

143. Gammans, "Rotary in Malay," 11–12.

144. See for example David Arnold, "Touching the Body: Perspectives on the Indian Plague, 1896–1900," *Selected Subaltern Studies* (1988): 391–426.

145. Lees, *Planting Empire, Cultivating Subjects,* 196.

146. C. Elaine Field, "The Development of Paediatrics in Singapore" (undated), Williams papers.

147. Lenore Manderson, "Colonial Desires: Sexuality, Race, and Gender in British Malaya," *Journal of the History of Sexuality* 7, no. 3 (January 1997), 372–88, at 385–6.

148. Lees, *Planting Empire, Cultivating Subjects*, 196.

149. Ida M. M. Simmons, "Pioneer Maternity and Child Welfare Work in Rural Singapore from 1927 to 1938," Williams papers.

150. An army educational training pamphlet said that "squatters" came from the "world slump in the early thirties when immigrant Chinese labour on the rubber estates and in the tin mines turned to the land for livelihood." "Army Education Third Class Certificate: General Studies Assignments Part I, Emergency in Malaya," 3/12 to 3/19 Box 5 of 7, Talbot papers, KCL LHMA, 5; Teng Phee Tan, "'Like a Concentration Camp, Iah': Chinese Grassroots Experience of the Emergency and New Villages in British Malaya," *Chinese Southern Diaspora Studies* 3 (2009): 216–28, at 216.

151. Simmons, "Pioneer Maternity and Child Welfare Work."

152. Simmons, "Pioneer Maternity and Child Welfare Work."

153. Cicely D. Williams, "Conditions in Trengganu," Williams papers, 6.

154. Unsigned letter to the Chief Medical Officer, Singapore, January 3, 1938, Williams papers.

155. Cicely D. Williams, "Milk and Murder," lecture given to Rotary Club, Singapore, 1939, Williams papers.

156. Williams, "Milk and Murder," 2.

157. Williams, "Milk and Murder," 2.

158. Williams, "Milk and Murder," 3–4.

159. Newspaper excerpt: "Woman talks to Rotary: Care of Children Essential," *Morning Tribune* (July 15, 1937).

160. Cicely D. Williams, "Conditions in Trengganu," Williams papers.

161. Williams, "Conditions in Trengganu."

162. Private Papers of Veronica Ann Turner (nee Clancy), Australian War Memorial, MSS1086 (1940–45), 26, henceforth Clancy Papers. For the full lyrics to the "Glorious Malaya" song, see Papers of Sergeant S. L. Gilmore, 2/20 Bn, AIF. PR89/051, AWM.

163. Clancy papers, 29.

164. Clancy papers, 33–34.

165. "My Autobiography by Elizabeth Choy Su-Mei as told to Shirle Gordon," *Intisari: The Research Journal of Wider Malaysia* 4, no. 1 (1973): 15–65, held at NUS library, 17–18.

166. Cicely D. Williams, "Scheme for Health Work (Part II)," Williams papers, 20.

167. Williams, "Scheme for Health Work," 21.

168. Khoo, *Life as the River Flows*, 83.

169. Arunima Datta, *Fleeting Agencies: A Social History of Indian Coolie Women in British Malaya* (Cambridge, UK: Cambridge University Press, 2021).

170. S. E. Nicoll-Jones, "Report on the Problem of Prostitution in Singapore," MSS. Ind. Ocn. S. 27, Bodleian Library, 43.

171. Nicoll-Jones, "Report on the Problem of Prostitution in Singapore," 1, 3–4, 33, 39–40.

172. Tan Beng Hui, "'Protecting' Women: Legislation and Regulation of Women's Sexuality in Colonial Malaya," *Gender, Technology and Development* 7, no. 1 (2003): 1–30.

173. Nicoll-Jones, "Report on the problem of prostitution in Singapore," 1, 3–4, 33, 39–40.

174. de S. Onraet, "Annual Report on the Straits Settlements Police and the State of Crime, 1936."

175. Lenore Manderson, "Colonial Desires," 375.

176. R. H. de S. Onraet, "Annual Report of the Straits Settlements Police and the State of Crime for 1935."

177. C. H. Sansom, "The FMS, Report on the State of Crime and the Police Force. 1933," PPMS 31/File 5, NAS.

178. Arthur John Moore Bennett, "Leaves from a Life," papers of Arthur John Moore Bennett (henceforth Moore Bennett papers), Mss Eur F594/10/12, 155. Capitalization per original.

179. Moore Bennett papers, 246.

180. Moore Bennett papers, 162.

181. Moore Bennett papers, 190.

182. "Secret. Issue No. 54 Copy No. 43. The Malayan Bulletin of Political Intelligence," (October/November 1927), IOR/L/PJ/12/108 File 6320/22, NAS, 3.

183. Moore Bennett papers, 156.

184. Moore Bennett papers, 168, 170 (slur removed by author).

185. Moore Bennett papers, 182.

186. Moore Bennett papers, 182, 227, 247, 248.

187. Moore Bennett papers, 227.

188. Moore Bennett papers, 184.

189. Moore Bennett papers, 168, 184, 209, 231, 244, 249.

190. Moore Bennett papers, 168, 231, 249.

191. Moore Bennett papers, 194.

192. Moore Bennett papers, 200.

193. Imy, "Queering the Martial Races"; Liam J. Liburd, "Beyond the Pale: Whiteness, Masculinity and Empire in the British Union of Fascists, 1932–1940," *Fascism: Journal of Comparative Fascist Studies* 7, no. 2 (October 2018), https://brill.com/view/journals/fasc/7/2/article-p275_275.xml#d1611169e415.

194. Moore Bennett papers, 183.

195. Moore Bennett papers, 204, 218.

196. Moore Bennett papers, 294.

197. Moore Bennett papers, 209, 230, 231, 264.

198. "Extracts from Despatch on Far East by Air Chief Marshal Sir Robert Brooke-Popham" (undated, 1941), Box 2 File 4, Papers of Sir Thomas S. W. Thomas, GB 0162 MSS.Ind.Ocn.s.341, Bodleian Library.

Chapter Three

1. See chapter 2.

2. William Arthur Campion Haines (henceforth Haines papers), Kings College Liddell Hart Centre for Military Archives (henceforth LHCMA), 174, 181. Haines

evacuated his wife on a ship bound for Australia. Unfortunately, it was "bombed, machine-gunned and sunk by aircraft." In his words, she "did not survive this totally unnecessary and murderous attack by the Japanese aircraft."

3. Haines papers, LHCMA, 169.

4. Excerpt from A. H. Dickinson, "Obituary," *The Shield*, included in S. E. Nicoll-Jones papers, MSS. Ind. Ocn. S. 27, Bodleian Library.

5. Joseph Kennedy, *When Singapore Fell: Evacuations and Escapes, 1941–42* (New York: St. Martin's Press, 1989); Paul Kratoska, *The Japanese Occupation of Malaya, 1941–1945* (Honolulu: University of Hawaii Press, 1997).

6. Bayly and Harper, *Forgotten Wars,* 10.

7. F. Spencer Chapman, *The Jungle Is Neutral* (New York: W. W. Norton & Company, 1949), 13.

8. Chapman, *The Jungle Is Neutral*, 13.

9. Susanne Hoeber Rudolph, Lloyd L. Rudolph, and Mohan Singh Kanota, eds., *Reversing the Gaze: Amar Singh's Diary, A Colonial Subject's Narrative of Imperial India* (Boulder, CO: Westview Press, 2002).

10. Sir Shenton Thomas, "Comments on Sir R. Brooke-Popham's Report" (undated, c. 1946), Box 2 File 4, Papers of Sir Thomas S. W. Thomas (henceforth Shenton Thomas papers), GB 0162 MSS.Ind.Ocn.s.341, Bodleian Library.

11. Thomas, "Comments on Sir R. Brooke-Popham's Report."

12. Jack Wilfred Turner, "A True Autobiography of My Life as a Prisoner of War from 15 February 1942 till 12 September 1944. Also of My Experiences from 12 September 1944 till arrival in Australia" (henceforth Turner papers), PR00651, Australian War Memorial (henceforth AWM), preface.

13. Jack Wilfred Turner, Diary, March 14, 1941, Turner papers, AWM. For the sexual implications of such encounters and gift-giving, see Imy, "Queering the Martial Races."

14. Turner, Diary, September 3, 1941.

15. Turner, Diary, February 19, 1941.

16. Private Papers of A. J. S. Holman (henceforth Holman papers), Docs7877, Box No: 98/19/1, Imperial War Museum (henceforth IWM), 68–9, 71.

17. His emphasis. Holman papers, 31, 72.

18. Holman papers, 31.

19. Holman papers, 55, 32.

20. Holman papers, 65.

21. Holman papers, 65–6, 34, 51.

22. R. H. de S. Onraet, "Extracts from Onraet's Police background," Box 2, File 4, Shenton Thomas papers.

23. Holman papers, 65–6.

24. Allison Abra, *Dancing in the English Style: Consumption, Americanisation and National Identity in Britain, 1918–50* (Manchester: Manchester University Press, 2017); Wendy Webster, *Mixing It: Diversity in World War Two Britain* (Oxford: Oxford University Press, 2018), 213; Sonya Rose, *Which People's War? National Identity and Citizenship in Wartime Britain 1939–1945* (Oxford: Oxford University Press, 2003).

25. Holman papers, 67, 68.

26. Lyal Lever to his mother (undated), Private Papers of Private Lindsay William (Bill) Lever and Private Alfred Lyal (Lyal) Lever (henceforth Lever papers), PR01514, AWM.

27. Lyal Lever to his father, August 5, 1941, Lever papers (slur removed by author).

28. A. L. Lever to his mother, April 4, 1941, Lever papers (slur removed by author).

29. Lever to his father, August 5, 1941.

30. Lyal Lever to his mother, January 3, 1942, Lever papers.

31. Holman papers, 56, 87.

32. Holman papers, 77–8.

33. Holman papers, 42, 43, 45.

34. Imy, *Faithful Fighters.*

35. Holman papers, 47, 53, 79, 80.

36. Holman papers, 76, 79.

37. Turner, Diary, May 31, 1941.

38. Jonathan Saha, "Whiteness, Masculinity and the Ambivalent Embodiment of 'British Justice' in Colonial Burma," *Cultural and Social History* 14, no. 4 (2017): 527–42.

39. Turner, Diary, July 9, 1941.

40. Holman racialized such violence, such as when a fight broke out before him at the seafront Straits Cabaret, he described "An enormous buck negro" who used his "huge black paws" against another. Holman papers, 66.

41. Lever to his mother, April 4, 1941 (slur removed by author).

42. A. L. Lever to his father, September 15, 1941.

43. Turner, autobiography, preface.

44. A. L. Lever to his father, December 14, 1941.

45. Mehervan Singh, interview by Pitt Kuan Wah, Accession Number 000553, NAS, Reel 17, transcript pg 2.

46. Transcript of an oral history interview with Shri Naranjan Singh Gill, interview by Shri S. L. Manchanda for The Nehru Memorial Museum and Library, April 11, 1972, Mss Eur F729/7/1, British Library, 16–17.

47. General Mohan Singh, *Soldiers' Contributions to Indian Independence: The Epic of the Indian National Army* (New Delhi: S. Attar Singh, Army Educational Stores, 1974), 49.

48. Gill, interview by Pitt, 16.

49. Gill, interview by Pitt, 16–17.

50. Lt-Gen. (Retd.) S. P. P. Thorat, *From Reveille to Retreat* (New Delhi: Allied Publishers Private Limited, 1985 (1988 edition)), 39.

51. Gill, interview by Pitt, 16–17.

52. Singh, *Soldiers' Contributions to Indian Independence,* 48.

53. Singh, *Soldiers' Contributions to Indian Independence,* 49–50.

54. Singh, *Soldiers' Contributions to Indian Independence,* 49–50.

55. K. A. K. Menon, *From the Diary of a Freedom Fighter* (Madras: Kavungal Anat, 1989), 17.

56. Menon, *From the Diary of a Freedom Fighter,* 18.

57. Quoted in Elkins, *Legacy of Violence,* 244.

58. Menon, *From the Diary of a Freedom Fighter,* 20.

59. Menon, *From the Diary of a Freedom Fighter,* 20–1.

60. Menon, *From the Diary of a Freedom Fighter,* 19.

61. Menon, *From the Diary of a Freedom Fighter,* 19.

62. Holman papers, 93.

63. Holman papers, 96.

64. Holman papers, 98.

65. Holman papers, 98, 100, 101, 102.

66. Holman papers, 104.

67. Imy, *Faithful Fighters,* chap. 3; Mary Katherine Des Chene, "Relics of Empire: A Cultural History of the Gurkhas, 1815–1987" (PhD diss., Stanford University, 1991).

68. Holman papers, 104.

69. Holman papers, 104.

70. Holman papers, 106–7.

71. Holman papers, 111.

72. Cicely Williams, "Retreat from Trengganu" (undated), PP/CDW/B2, Papers of Doctor Cicely Williams (henceforth Williams papers), Wellcome Library collection, held at NAS, 1.

73. Williams, "Retreat from Trengganu," 1–2.

74. Williams, "Retreat from Trengganu," 1–2.

75. Williams, "Retreat from Trengganu," 2–3.

76. Williams, "Retreat from Trengganu," 3.

77. Sheila Allan, "Journey to Changi and Down Under . . . Diary of Events between 8th December, 1941 to 24th. November, 1945, Written by a Seventeen Year Old Girl," unpublished manuscript, Private Papers, Australian War Memorial, PR00666 (1942–1992) (henceforth Allan papers), 3.

78. Chapman, *The Jungle Is Neutral,* 218.

79. Williams, "Retreat from Trengganu," 3.

80. See for example Indian military men who adopted disguises and had limited success: Khan Bahadur Risaldar Shahzad Mir Khan, O. B. I., 11th K. E. O. Lancers (Probyns Horse), *A Right Royal World Tour,* tr. Lt. Col. C. A. Boyle, D. S. O., Probyns Horse (Simla: The Army Press, 1934), British Library, Urdu 14110.cc23., 48–50; Imy, "Queering the Martial Races," 383.

81. Williams, "Retreat from Trengganu," 2, 3.

82. Private Papers of Major I. A. McDonald, 10035, IWM, 7–8.

83. A. E. Percival to Sir Shenton Thomas, April 22, 1947, Shenton Thomas papers, 1.

84. Williams, "Retreat from Trengganu," 3.

85. Dorothy Thatcher and Robert Cross, *Pai Naa: The Story of Nona Baker* (Constable: London, 1959), 25.

86. Haines papers, 172

87. McDonald papers, 3.

88. Sybil Kathigasu, *No Dram of Mercy* (London: Wyman & Sons Ltd., 1959), 24.

89. Williams, "Retreat from Trengganu," 2.

90. Williams, "Retreat from Trengganu," 3.

91. Williams, "Retreat from Trengganu," 11.

92. Williams, "Retreat from Trengganu," 3.

93. Williams, "Retreat from Trengganu," 4, 5, 8.

94. Williams, "Retreat from Trengganu," 5.

95. Williams, "Retreat from Trengganu," 8, 11.

96. Williams, "Retreat from Trengganu," 14.

97. Williams, "Retreat from Trengganu," 14.

98. Mrs. Pereira was "Ceylonese." Williams, "Retreat from Trengganu," 17.

99. Williams, "Retreat from Trengganu," 19.

100. Williams, "Retreat from Trengganu," 6.

101. Williams, "Retreat from Trengganu," 6.

102. Williams, "Retreat from Trengganu," 7.

103. Williams, "Retreat from Trengganu," 3.

104. Williams, "Retreat from Trengganu," 11.

105. Williams, "Retreat from Trengganu," 3.

106. Williams, "Retreat from Trengganu," 4, 10, 14.

107. Williams, "Retreat from Trengganu," 15–16.

108. Williams, "Retreat from Trengganu," 16, 18.

109. Williams, "Retreat from Trengganu," 19.

110. Williams, "Retreat from Trengganu," 18–19.

111. Williams, "Retreat from Trengganu," 15.

112. Williams, "Retreat from Trengganu," 18.

113. Williams, "Retreat from Trengganu," 23–4.

114. Cicely Williams, "Personal Notes" (February 23, 1942), Williams papers, 39.

115. Williams, "Personal Notes," 39.

116. Williams, "Retreat from Trengganu," 24.

117. Williams, "Personal Notes," 39.

118. Williams, "Personal Notes," 39.

119. Williams, "Personal Notes," 39.

120. Williams, "Retreat from Trengganu," 21.

121. Singh, interview by Pitt, transcript 9.

122. Holman papers, 113.

123. Allan papers, 15.

124. Dolores Ho, interview by Kate Imy, July 2019, National Army Museum, Waiouru, New Zealand.

125. Turner, autobiography, 1.

126. Williams, "Retreat from Trengganu," 21.

127. Chapman, *The Jungle Is Neutral*, 13.

128. McDonald papers, 7.

129. Chapman, *The Jungle Is Neutral*, 13.

130. McDonald papers, 7.

131. Quoted in Elkins, *Legacy of Violence*, 246.

132. Karl Hack and Kevin Blackburn, "Japanese-Occupied Asia from 1941 to 1945: One Occupier, Many Captivities and Memories," in *Forgotten Captives in Japanese-Occupied Asia*, ed. Karl Hack and Kevin Blackburn (New York: Routledge, 2008), 10.

133. Tan Tik Loong Stanley and Tay Huiwen Michelle, *Syonan Years, 1942–1945: Living Beneath the Rising Sun* (Singapore: National Archives of Singapore, 2009), 15. See also Stephanie Ho, "Operation Sook Ching," National Library Board, June 17, 2013, https://eresources.nlb.gov.sg/infopedia/articles/SIP_40_2005-01-24.html.

134. Hack and Blackburn, "Japanese-Occupied Asia," 13–14.

135. "Abstract of Evidence," in "Various Documents Relating to Chinese Massacre Trial—Charge Sheet of Maj Mizuno Keiji," WO235/1004, Received from Ward, Ian,1/1993, NAS.

136. Major Onishi Satarou, "Conditions of Every Military Policeman," in "Various Documents Relating to Chinese Massacre Trial—Charge Sheet of Maj Mizuno Keiji," WO235/1004, Received from Ward, Ian,1/1993, NAS.

137. Major C. H. D. Wild, "Report on Interrogation of General Tomoyuki Yamashita," E Group, SEAC, at Manila, (October 28, 1945), WO 325/30: "Killing of Chinese of Straits Settlements Volunteer Force in Singapore," received at NAS, 2–3.

138. Wild, "Report on Interrogation of General Tomoyuki Yamashita," 3.

139. Letter to Bell from Lim Chuan Kim, (January 8, 1946), Private papers of Lim Bee Giok (henceforth Lim Bee Giok papers), 3DRL/74157, AWM.

140. Summary of Examination of Ong Foot Yeong, WO 325/30, received at NAS.

141. Summary of Examination of Mr. Neo Kuay Leh, (January 7, 1946), WO 325/30, received at NAS.

142. Summary of Examination of Mr. Neo Kuay Leh.

143. Giok to Bell, October 12, 1945, Lim Bee Giok papers.

144. "My Autobiography by Elizabeth Choy Su-Mei as Told to Shirle Gordon," *Intisari: The Research Journal of Wider Malaysia* 4, no. 1 (1973): 15–65, held at NUS library, 33.

145. "My Autobiography," 33, 34, 27–8.

146. Lim Chuan Kim to Bell, January 8, 1946, Lim Bee Giok papers.

147. Lim to Bell, January 8, 1946, 13.

148. Main HQ, "E" Group via "E" Group SAGSEA, September 11, 1945, WO 325/30, received at NAS.

149. Wong Sin Joon, Statement made to Major W. Totman (February 23, 1946), WO 325/30, received at NAS.

150. This episode only reinforced the racialization to come, as he noted that they tried but failed to gain assistance from "well dressed [sic] Malays" who refused to help them. Wong, Statement to Totman, 2, 4.

151. Lim to Bell (January 8, 1946), 8.

152. Kee Onn Chin, *Malaya Upside Down* (Singapore: Jitts & Co., 1946), 4.

153. Chin, *Malaya Upside Down*, 5.

154. Chin, *Malaya Upside Down*, 6.

155. Chapman, *The Jungle Is Neutral*, 32.

156. Turner, autobiography, preface.

157. Sir Shenton Thomas, "Comments on Sir R. Brooke-Popham's Report."

158. Lim to Bell, January 8, 1946.

159. Turner, autobiography, 4.

160. Preston L. Peach, "Recollections of 35 Years as a Missionary Teacher in Malaya," BAM IV/26, NAB0466_0721_0747_0027, NAS, 15.

161. Peach, "Recollections of 35 Years," 8, 19–20.

162. A. E. Fawcett, "Personal memories of Malaya and internment in Singapore, 2 vols," Mss. Ind. Ocn. r. 1, 2, Bodleian Library, received at NAB0735-0005-0063-0059, NAS.

Chapter Four

1. Aidan Forth, *Barbed-Wire Imperialism: Britain's Empire of Camps, 1876–1903* (Berkeley: University of California Press, 2017).

2. See for example films such as Bruce Beresford, *Paradise Road* (Twentieth Century Fox, 1997); Jonathan Teplitzky, *The Railway Man* (Lionsgate, 2013); Angelina Jolie, *Unbroken* (Universal Pictures, 2014).

3. Felicia Yap, "Prisoners of War and Civilian Internees of the Japanese in British Asia: The Similarities and Contrasts of Experience," *Journal of Contemporary History* 47, no. 2 (2012): 322; Sarah Kovner, *Prisoners of the Empire: Inside Japanese POW Camps* (Cambridge, MA: Harvard University Press, 2020); Kaori Maekawa, "The Heiho during the Japanese Occupation of Indonesia," in *Asian Labor in the Wartime Japanese Empire: Unknown Histories*, ed. Paul H. Kratoska (New York: Routledge, 2005).

4. Hack and Blackburn, "Japanese-Occupied Asia," 13–14; Paul H. Kratoska, *Food Supplies and the Japanese Occupation in South-East Asia* (New York: St. Martin's Press, 1998).

5. Discussions of Allan combine interviews and Sheila Allan's published and unpublished materials. Allan, "Journey to Changi and Down Under"; Sheila Allan, *Diary of a Girl in Changi* (Pymble, NSW: Kangaroo, 2004). According to the nominal rolls, Dr. Hopkins is forty-two-year-old Dr. M. E. Hopkins from the United Kingdom. "Changi and Sime Road Civilian Internment Camps: Nominal Rolls of Internees," Cambridge University Archives, RCMS 103/12/22 (1942–1967), https://cudl.lib.cam.ac.uk/view/MS-RCMS-00103-00012-00022/183, 183.

6. Allan papers, 21.

7. Sections of this chapter have been published in Kate Imy, "Dream Mother: Race, Gender, and Intimacy in Japanese-Occupied Singapore," *Journal of Southeast Asian Studies* 52, no. 3 (2021): 464–91.

8. The number 130,000 was for "western" POWs—which roughly translates to white POWs. This number was assembled by the Tokyo War Crimes Trials. Hack and Blackburn, "Japanese-Occupied Asia," 4, 8, 11, 17.

9. Yap, "Prisoners of War and Civilian Internees," 320; Felicia Yap, "Eurasians in British Asia during the Second World War," *Journal of the Royal Asiatic Society* S3, 21, no. 4 (2011): 495.

10. Civilian death rates averaged around 5 percent across all camps. POW deaths ranged from 16 to 36 percent. Hack and Blackburn, "Japanese-Occupied Asia," 15.

11. Women and men in Changi were separated by a courtyard, with the exception of occasional mixing for labor and cooking. Allan papers, 19.

12. See for example Bayly and Harper, *Forgotten Armies;* Catherine Kenny, *Captives: Australian Army Nurses in Japanese Prison Camps* (St. Lucia: University of Queensland Press, 1986); Christina Twomey, *Australia's Forgotten Prisoners: Civilians Interned by the*

Japanese in World War Two (Cambridge, UK: Cambridge University Press, 2007); Yuki Tanka, *Hidden Horrors: Japanese War Crimes in WWII* (Boulder, CO: Westview, 1996); Bob Moore and Barbara Hately-Broad, eds., *Prisoners of War, Prisoners of Peace: Captivity, Homecoming and Memory in World War II* (Oxford: Berg, 2005); Gavan Daws, *Prisoners of the Japanese* (New York: William Morrow & Co., 1994); Kovner, *Prisoners of the Empire*.

13. Allan papers, 2.

14. Interview with Sheila Bruhn, Australians at War Film Archive number 1998, University of New South Wales (2004), part 3, 0:30 (henceforth UNSW interview), part 1, 12:00.

15. Allan papers, 2.

16. Allan papers, 5–6.

17. Allan papers, 3.

18. Allan papers, 7–8.

19. Allan papers, 7–8.

20. Allan papers, 11–12.

21. Allan papers, 14–16.

22. Allan papers, 15.

23. Allan papers, 16–17.

24. UNSW interview, part 2, 30:00.

25. Allan papers, 15.

26. UNSW interview, part 6, 11:30.

27. UNSW interview, part 3, 14:30.

28. A. E. Fawcett, "Personal Memories of Malaya and Internment in Singapore, 2 vols," Mss. Ind. Ocn. r. 1, 2, Bodleian Library, received at NAB0735-0005-0063-0059, NAS, 30.

29. Most scholars and activists use the Japanese term *jugun ianfu* (military comfort woman) or *ianfu* (comfort woman). Women who endured the experience described it as sexual enslavement or repeated rape. Katharine McGregor, "Emotions and Activism for Former So-called 'Comfort Women'" of the Japanese Occupation of the Netherlands East Indies," *Women's Studies International Forum* 54 (2016): 67–78; Yoshiaki Yoshimi, *Comfort Women: Sexual Slavery in the Japanese Military during World War II* (Cambridge, UK: Cambridge University Press, 2002); Pui Huen Lim and Wong, *War and Memory in Malaysia and Singapore*; Choon and Kuan, *Rehearsal for War*; Muta Kazue, "The 'Comfort Women' Issue and the Embedded Culture of Sexual Violence in Contemporary Japan," *Current Sociology Monograph* 64, no. 4 (2016): 620–36.

30. Manderson, "Colonial Desires," 373.

31. Takashi Fujitani, *Race for Empire: Koreans as Japanese and Japanese as Americans during World War II* (Berkeley: University of California Press, 2011), 371.

32. Lim Chuan Kim to Bell, January 8, 1946, Private papers of Lim Bee Giok (henceforth Lim Bee Giok papers), 3DRL/74157, AWM, 27.

33. [Anonymized for WHR peer review], "The 'Comfort Women' of Malaysia and Singapore as Transnational History and Memory," *Women's History Review* (forthcoming): 7, 9–10.

34. Madam Seow Guat Beng, interview by Miss Ooi Yu Lin, July 8, 1989, transcript transcribed by Roger Khong, 1992, Accession number 001048, NAS, Reel 15, 224, 226; Reel 17, 253.

35. Lim to Bell, January 8, 1946, 27.

36. Lim to Bell, January 8, 1946, 1–2.

37. Kenneison, *Playing for Malaya*, 146–7, 151.

38. Khoo, *Life as the River Flows*, 230.

39. Khoo, *Life as the River Flows*, 12, 54.

40. Sybil Kathigasu, *No Dram of Mercy* (London: Wyman & Sons Ltd., 1959), 26–7.

41. Wong Wai Kwan, interview by Soo Aili Jasmine, October 2004 (Oral History Collection, National Institute of Education, Nanyang Technological University), quoted in [Anonymized], "The 'Comfort Women' of Malaysia and Singapore," 17.

42. Aruna Gopinath, *Footprints on the Sands of Time: Rasammah Bhupalan: A Life of Purpose* (Kuala Lumpur: Arkib Negara Malaysia, 2007), 36.

43. Gopinath, *Footprints on the Sands of Time*, 36, 38–9.

44. Kathigasu, *No Dram of Mercy*, 37–8.

45. "An Account by Mrs Tan Choo Quee," Private papers of Mrs. Tan Choo Quee, PR83/235, file 419/52/19, AWM.

46. "An Account by Mrs Tan Choo Quee," 2.

47. Dolores Ho, interview by Kate Imy, July 2019, National Army Museum, Waiouru, New Zealand.

48. Kathigasu, *No Dram of Mercy*, 25–6.

49. Lim to Bell, January 8, 1946, 11.

50. Dorothy Thatcher and Robert Cross, *Pai Naa: The Story of Nona Baker* (Constable: London, 1959), 24.

51. Thatcher and Cross, *Pai Naa*, 51, 30, 35, 37, 40, 69.

52. Private Papers of Veronica Ann Turner (nee Clancy), Australian War Memorial, MSS1086 (1940–45) (henceforth Clancy papers), 115.

53. Yap, "Eurasians in British Asia," 489.

54. Rebecca Kenneison, *Playing for Malaya: A Eurasian Family in the Pacific War* (Singapore: NUS Press, 2012), 102–4.

55. Private Papers of Constance Sleep and Arthur Sleep, MSS. Ind. Ocn. S. 127–33, ff. 29–39, Bodleian Library, Oxford University Archives (henceforth Sleep papers), 13, 17.

56. Williams, "Retreat from Trengganu," 21–2.

57. See for example Jane Haggis, "Gendering Colonialism or Colonising Gender? Recent Women's Studies Approaches to White Women and the History of British Colonialism," *Women's Studies International Forum* 13, nos. 1–2 (1990): 105–15; Raka Shome, "'Global Motherhood': The Transnational Intimacies of White Femininity," *Critical Studies in Media Communication* 28, no. 5 (2011): 388–406; Anne McClintock, *Imperial Leather: Race, Gender, and Sexuality in the Colonial Contest* (New York: Routledge, 1995); Stoler, "Rethinking Colonial Categories," 139.

58. Williams, "Synopsis," 26, 27.

59. Yap, "Eurasians in British Asia during the Second World War," 486; Yap, "Sex and Stereotypes," 86.

60. Bernice Archer, "The Internment of Western Civilians under the Japanese 1941–1945," in *Forgotten Captives in Japanese-Occupied Asia,* ed. Karl Hack and Kevin Blackburn (New York: Routledge, 2008).

61. Clancy papers, wallet 2 of 3, 360.

62. Sleep papers, 3, 16.

63. Betty Jeffrey, *White Coolies* (Sydney: Angus & Robertson, 1954).

64. Miss S. Early to Miss P. Early, August 22, 1945, WO 203/2374, received at NAS, 2.

65. S. Early to P. Early, August 22, 1945, 2, 4.

66. C. D. Williams, "Synopsis" (September 29, 1945), Williams papers, NAS, 26.

67. Williams, "Synopsis," 27–8.

68. Williams, "Synopsis," 26.

69. Williams, "Synopsis," 26.

70. Sleep papers (March 21, 1945), 19.

71. Constance Sleep to Hugh, May 25, 1942, Sleep papers, 3.

72. Sleep papers (July 10, 1944), 16.

73. Williams, "Synopsis," 33.

74. Williams, "Synopsis," 33.

75. Sleep papers (March 21, 1945), 19.

76. Williams, "Synopsis," 26.

77. Williams, "Retreat from Trengganu," 24.

78. Williams, "Personal Notes," 40.

79. Williams, "Personal Notes," 40–1.

80. Williams, "Personal Notes," 42.

81. Williams, "Personal Notes," 42.

82. Williams, "Personal Notes," 43.

83. S. Early to P. Early, August 22, 1945, 4.

84. S. Early to P. Early, August 22, 1945, 4.

85. Williams, "Synopsis," 33.

86. S. Early to P. Early, August 22, 1945, 7.

87. S. Early to P. Early, August 22, 1945, 4.

88. S. Early to P. Early, August 22, 1945, 4.

89. S. Early to P. Early, August 22, 1945, 7.

90. Mary Tshu En nee Quintal, interview by Jason Lim, November 6, 1999, transcript edited by Ms Chew Hui Min, transcribed 2006, Accession Number 002219, NAS, Reel 1, pg. 5.

91. S. Early to P. Early, August 22, 1945, 5.

92. S. Early to P. Early, August 22, 1945, 7.

93. Williams, "Synopsis," 32.

94. S. Early to P. Early, August 22, 1945, 5.

95. Williams, "Synopsis," 32.

96. S. Early to P. Early, August 22, 1945, 6.

97. Williams, "Synopsis," 32.

98. S. Early to P. Early, August 22, 1945, 5.

99. Williams, "Synopsis," 30.

100. S. Early to P. Early, August 22, 1945, 6.

101. Kathigasu, *No Dram of Mercy*, 45.

102. Yap, "Sex and Stereotypes," 82–3.

103. This relates specifically to resettlement plans in Bahau organised by Mamoru Shinozaki. Despite plans and expectations for better food and living conditions, approximately a quarter of the Bahau settlers died. See for example Kenneison, *Playing for Malaya*, 156–7. See also Hack and Blackburn, "Japanese-Occupied Asia," 2; Yap, "Sex and Stereotypes," 82.

104. Barbara Clunies-Ross, interview by Zarina bte Yusof, Accession Number 002742, Oral History, NAS, transcript, 31.

105. S. Early to P. Early, August 22, 1945, 7.

106. S. Early to P. Early, August 22, 1945, 3.

107. S. Early to P. Early, August 22, 1945, 7.

108. Homi K, Bhabha, *The Location of Culture* (London: Routledge, 1994), 86.

109. See for example the numerous press cuttings in the private papers of C. A. Harness, MSS. Ind. Ocn. S. 25, Bodleian Library.

110. S. Early to P. Early, August 22, 1945, 8.

111. "New Job for Comfort Girls," *Straits Times*, December 10, 1945, cited in "The 'Comfort Women' of Malaysia and Singapore."

112. UNSW interview, 34:00.

113. Laura Doan, *Disturbing Practices: History, Sexuality, and Women's Experience of Modern War* (Chicago: University of Chicago Press, 2013).

114. Allan papers, 17.

115. Allan papers, 21, 19.

116. She alludes to this in Allan papers, 100, and recounts the story also in her NAS Archive interview: Sheila Bruhn-Allan, interview by Zarina bte Yusof, Oral History, Accession no. 002740, NAS, transcript, 12–13.

117. Allan papers, 21.

118. Allan papers, 56.

119. Allan papers, 56, 68, 79, 86, 83.

120. Allan papers, 33.

121. Allan papers, 28, 91.

122. Jialin Christina Wu, "'A Life of Make-Believe': Being Boy Scouts and 'Playing Indian' in British Malaya (1910–42)," *Gender & History* 26, no. 3 (November 2014): 589–619.

123. "Changi and Sime Road Nominal Rolls," 11.

124. Allan papers, 105, 120.

125. Sleep papers, 4.

126. Clancy papers, 103. Allan discussed this view in UNSW interview, part 4, 18:00.

127. Yap, "Eurasians in British Asia," 501.

128. She also identified with Australia, choosing, for example, to embroider a map of Australia with a kangaroo on a quilt that the women in Changi made during internment. UNSW interview, part 5, 39:30.

129. Allan papers, 15–18; UNSW interview, part 2, 5:30 and 33:00.

130. Archer, "The Internment of Western Civilians under the Japanese," 143.

131. Allan papers, 33.

132. Allan papers, 71–3. See Imy, "Dream Mother," for a fuller description of the gender and sexual dynamics at play.

133. Allan papers, 56.

134. Allan papers, 95–6.

135. Allan papers, 83, 86.

136. Allan papers, 107.

137. Allan papers, 108, 95.

138. Like others, Allan noted that they were "Jews & Jewess mostly" but also "Indians, Malays, Chinese & few foreigners." Allan papers, 122.

139. Allan papers, 123.

140. Allan papers, 124–5 (slur removed by author).

141. Allan papers, 133, 141.

142. Allan papers, 138.

143. Nursing provided some protection. One Eurasian family gained additional support for entry to Australia after the Second World War, due to the women of the family having served as nurses. F. G. Galleghan, to the Director, Canberra A. C. T., "Eurasian Family in Malaya Re Admission to Australia" (August 29, 1946), A373, 11763, National Archives of Australia.

144. Allan papers, 145–6.

145. Allan papers, 150.

146. Loose leaf diary, August 28, 1945, Allan papers.

147. Allan papers, 150.

148. Allan papers, 154.

149. Allan papers, 154.

150. UNSW interview, part 4, 19:00.

151. UNSW interview, part 3, 32:00, and part 4, 19:45.

152. Sleep papers, 4.

153. Williams, "Synopsis," 29.

154. Choy uses the term Khek but others describe her as Hakka, which she considered interchangeable. "My Autobiography by Elizabeth Choy Su-Mei as told to Shirle Gordon," *Intisari: The Research Journal of Wider Malaysia* 4, no. 1 (1973): 15–65, held at National University of Singapore library, 13, 22.

155. "My Autobiography," 19, 21, 22, 24, 27.

156. Mrs Elizabeth Choy, interview by Miss Tan Beng Luan, August 23, 1985, transcribed by Mrs. Wong-Yong Lee Yoong, November 7, 1985, NUS Library, DSS599.51. Cho.O 1985.

157. Choy, interview by Tan, transcript, 2.

158. "My Autobiography," 26.

159. "My Autobiography," 26, 33.

160. Choy, interview by Tan, transcript, 6, 3.

161. "My Autobiography," 34.

162. "My Autobiography," 35.

163. "My Autobiography," 36, 37, 38.

164. "My Autobiography," 40.

165. "My Autobiography," 42.

166. "My Autobiography," 39, 42, 38, 44.

167. "My Autobiography," 42.

168. "My Autobiography," 42.

169. "My Autobiography," 38.

170. "My Autobiography," 38.

171. "My Autobiography," 40.

172. "My Autobiography," 38.

173. "My Autobiography," 42.

174. "My Autobiography," 39.

175. See also Stephanie Barczewski, *Heroic Failure and the British* (New Haven: Yale University Press, 2016).

176. E. Choy, "Notes on Singapore for U.S.-Canada Lecture Tour Jan 1954–Apr 1954" and "Notes—for Lecture Tour of U.S.A. & Canada—on Behalf of the Foreign Office—London. Jan–Apr. 1954," NUS Library.

177. Geoffrey Cater, "Preface," in Kathigasu, *No Dram of Mercy*, 5.

178. Kathigasu, *No Dram of Mercy*, 28.

179. Kenneison, *Playing for Malaya*, 215–16.

180. S. Early to P. Early, August 22, 1945, 8.

181. Williams, "Synopsis," 33–4.

182. Gopinath, *Footprints on the Sands of Time*, 33.

183. Clancy papers, 6.

184. Yap, "Sex and Stereotypes," 78.

185. Kenneison, *Playing for Malaya*, 216, 218.

Chapter Five

1. Major P. R. Mursell, "Defence Counsel's Address," War Crimes Case Files, Defendant: Okamura Hideo, (c. February 8, 1946), WO 235/820, National Archives of Singapore (henceforth NAS).

2. Mursell, "Defence Counsel's Address."

3. Yuma Totani, *Justice in Asia and the Pacific Region, 1945–1952: Allied War Crimes Prosecutions* (Cambridge, UK: Cambridge University Press, 2015).

4. Barak Kushner, *Men to Devils, Devils to Men: Japanese War Crimes and Chinese Justice* (Cambridge, MA: Harvard University Press, 2015); Totani, *Justice in Asia and the Pacific Region;* Colin Sleeman, *Trial of Gozawa Sadaichi and Nine Others* (London: William Hodge & Co, 1948); Philip R. Piccigallo, *The Japanese On Trial: Allied War Crimes Operations in the East, 1945–1951* (Austin: University of Texas Press, 1979).

5. Kazunori Hashimoto, "Constructing the Burma-Thailand Railway: The War Crimes Trials and the Shaping of an Episode of WWII" (PhD thesis, SOAS University of London, 2022), 266–71; "Aoki Toshio," Singapore War Crimes Trials, accessed July 4, 2023, https://www.singaporewarcrimestrials.com/case-summaries/detail/011.

6. Hack and Blackburn, "Japanese-Occupied Asia," 17. For more on Japanese labor regimes during the war, see Paul H. Kratoska, *Asian Labor in the Wartime Japanese Empire: Unknown Histories* (New York: Routledge, 2005).

7. Chin, *Malaya Upside Down*, 9.

8. Chin, *Malaya Upside Down*, 9.

9. POW numbers often excluded 60,000 Indian soldiers and 45,000 Filipinos. Hack and Blackburn, "Japanese-Occupied Asia," 4, 8, 11.

10. Jack Wilfred Turner, "A True Autobiography of My Life as a Prisoner of War from 15 February 1942 till 12 September 1944. Also of My Experiences from 12 September 1944 till arrival in Australia," (henceforth Turner papers) PR00651, Australian War Memorial (henceforth AWM), 1–3.

11. Turner, "Autobiography," 6–7, 10, 20, 25, 31, 87, 88.

12. Turner, "Autobiography," 13.

13. R. L. Inder, diary, Private Papers, Documents 16730, Box 09/17/1 (June 26, 1942), Imperial War Museum (henceforth IWM).

14. Aruna Gopinath, *Footprints on the Sands of Time: Rasammah Bhupalan: A Life of Purpose* (Kuala Lumpur: Arkib Negara Malaysia, 2007), 44.

15. Chint Singh, "A Certified Copy of Story by Chint Singh: A Brief Sketch of the Fate of 3000 Indian P.O.W. in New Guinea," Wewack, New Guinea (November 4, 1945), Micro-MS-Coll-08-1249, National Library of New Zealand, 17.

16. Turner, "Autobiography," 51–2.

17. Turner, "Autobiography," 24, 83.

18. Turner, "Autobiography," 35, 78–80, 83.

19. Private Papers of Captain A. Weale, Docs 11279, IWM.

20. Turner, "Autobiography," 8.

21. Turner, "Autobiography," 8.

22. Turner, "Autobiography," 27.

23. Transcript of an oral history interview with Shri Naranjan Singh Gill, interview by Shri S. L. Manchanda for The Nehru Memorial Museum and Library, April 11, 1972, Mss Eur F729/7/1, British Library, 29.

24. Gill, interview by Manchanda, 29–30.

25. Singh, "A Brief Sketch of the Fate of 3000 Indian P.O.W. in New Guinea," 3.

26. Singh, "A Brief Sketch of the Fate of 3000 Indian P.O.W. in New Guinea," 4, 7, 24–25.

27. Singh, "A Brief Sketch of the Fate of 3000 Indian P.O.W. in New Guinea," 9.

28. Singh, "A Brief Sketch of the Fate of 3000 Indian P.O.W. in New Guinea," 16.

29. E. L. Sawyer, "The Growth of the Indian National Arm and the General Conditions of Indian Prisoners of War in Singapore From 1942 to 1945," Private Papers of Lt. Colonel E. L. Sawyer 88/33/1 (henceforth Sawyer papers), IWM, 2.

30. S. Early to P. Early, August 22, 1945.

31. Imy, *Faithful Fighters*.

32. Singh, *Soldiers' Contributions to Indian Independence*, 34.

33. Chandar S. Sundaram, "Seditious Letters and Steel Helmets: Disaffection among Indian Troops in Singapore and Hong Kong, 1940–1, and the Formation of

the Indian National Army," in *War and Society in Colonial India*, ed. Kaushik Roy (Oxford: Oxford University Press, 2006), 126–60; Sugata Bose, *His Majesty's Opponent: Subhas Chandra Bose and India's Struggle against Empire* (Cambridge, MA: Harvard University Press, 2012); Joyce Chapman Lebra, *Women against the Raj: The Rani of Jhansi Regiment* (Singapore: Institute of Southeast Asian Studies, 2008); Lt. General Fujiwara Iwaichi, *F Kikan: Japanese Army Intelligence Operations in Southeast Asia during World War II*, trans. Akashi Yoji (Hong Kong: Heinemann Asia, 1983); Kalyan Ghosh, *The Indian National Army* (Meerut: Meenakshi Prakashan, 1969); Leonard Gordon, *Brothers against the Raj* (New York: Columbia University Press, 1990); T. R. Sareen, *Japan and the Indian National Army* (Delhi: Agam Prakashan, 1986); Daniel P. Marston and Chandar S. Sundaram, *A Military History of India and South Asia* (Westport, CT, and London: Praeger Security International, 2007); Marston, *The Indian Army and the End of the Raj*; Mohammad Zaman Kiani, *India's Freedom Struggle and the Great INA* (Delhi: Reliance, 1994); Hugh Toye, *The Springing Tiger* (Oxford: Oxford University Press, 1959).

34. One British leader described this as their being "immediately subjected to Indian Independence propaganda." Sawyer, "The Growth of the Indian National Arm and the General Conditions of Indian Prisoners of War in Singapore From 1942 to 1945," Sawyer papers, IWM.

35. Gill, interview by Manchanda, 32.

36. Lebra, *Women against the Raj*, 45–6.

37. Sawyer, "The Growth of the Indian National Army and the General Conditions of Indian Prisoners of War in Singapore from 1942 to 1945," 1–2.

38. Iwaichi Fujiwara, introduction to *Soldiers' Contributions to Indian Independence*, by Mohan Singh.

39. Singh, *Soldiers' Contributions to Indian Independence*, 11.

40. Singh, *Soldiers' Contributions to Indian Independence*, 15, 17, 22, 27–8, 42.

41. Mehervan Singh, interview by Pitt Kuan Wah, Accession Number 000553, NAS, Reel 18, pg 2 and Reel 17, pg 4.

42. Singh, interview by Pitt, Reel 18, pg 3.

43. Gill, interview by Manchanda, 38.

44. Gill, interview by Manchanda, 34–5.

45. Gill, interview by Manchanda, 33.

46. Gill, interview by Manchanda, 3, 19, 33, 42.

47. Sawyer, "The Growth of the Indian National Arm and the General Conditions of Indian Prisoners of War in Singapore From 1942 to 1945," 3; Lebra, *Women against the Raj*, 48. For more on S. C. Bose, see Bose, *His Majesty's Opponent*; Nilanjana Sengupta, *A Gentleman's Word: The Legacy of Subhash Chandra Bose in Southeast Asia* (Singapore: Institute of Southeast Asian Studies, 2012).

48. Sawyer, "The Growth of the Indian National Arm and the General Conditions of Indian Prisoners of War in Singapore From 1942 to 1945," 3.

49. Singh, "A Brief Sketch of the Fate of 3000 Indian P.O.W. in New Guinea," 25–6.

50. Sawyer, "The Growth of the Indian National Arm and the General Conditions of Indian Prisoners of War in Singapore From 1942 to 1945," 3.

51. Sawyer, "The Growth of the Indian National Arm and the General Conditions of Indian Prisoners of War in Singapore From 1942 to 1945," Annexure K, 3.

52. Singh, interview by Pitt, Reel 18, pg 4.

53. Singh, *Soldiers' Contributions to Indian Independence*, 33, 100.

54. Gopinath, *Footprints on the Sands of Time*, 75.

55. Lebra, *Women against the Raj*, 56–7.

56. Singh, interview by Pitt, Reel 18, 4–5.

57. Imy, *Faithful Fighters*.

58. Lebra, *Women against the Raj*, 60–2; Datta, *Fleeting Agencies*, 125.

59. Gopinath, *Footprints on the Sands of Time*, 95.

60. Gopinath, *Footprints on the Sands of Time*, 68, 74–5, 95.

61. Gopinath, *Footprints on the Sands of Time*, 68, 74–5, 95.

62. Quoted in Arunima Datta, "Social Memory and Indian Women from Malaya and Singapore in the Rani of Jhansi Regiment," *Journal of the Malaysian Branch of the Royal Asiatic Society* 88, no. 2 (December 2015): 77–103, at 85; Ravindra K. Jain, *South Indians on the Plantation Frontier in Malaya* (New Haven: Yale University Press, 1970). See also Datta, *Fleeting Agencies*.

63. Datta, "Social Memory and Indian Women from Malaya and Singapore in the Rani of Jhansi Regiment," 83.

64. Gopinath, *Footprints on the Sands of Time*, 69.

65. Gopinath, *Footprints on the Sands of Time*, 69, 75, 82, 84.

66. Annexure 2 to "S" section CSDIC (I) (June 1, 1942), Digitized Document, PP_0000000111165, File No. 75/INA National Archives of India.

67. Lebra, *Women against the Raj*, 52–4.

68. Lee Kip Lin, interview by Low Lay Leng, May 29, 1984, Accession Number 000016, Reel 15, NAS, transcript page 168.

69. Private Papers of Major P. S. Leathart, PP/MCR/311, Reel 1, Documents.7896 (henceforth Leathart papers), IWM, 54.

70. Leathart papers, 54.

71. Lakshmi Sahgal, foreword (April 13, 1988) to *From the Diary of a Freedom Fighter*, by K. A. K. Menon, (Madras: Kavungal Anat, 1989).

72. Cheah Boon, *Red Star over Malaya*, 56–7.

73. Cheah Boon, *Red Star over Malaya*, 62, 68–70; Malay members include the mother of Siti Meriyam Binti Idris, alias Atom, who served in the MPAJA during the Japanese occupation. Khoo, *Life as the River Flows*, 207.

74. Khoo, *Life as the River Flows*, 55.

75. C. C. Chin and Karl Hack, eds., *Dialogues with Chin Peng: New Light on the Malayan Communist Party* (Singapore: Singapore University Press, 2005), 71.

76. Chapman, *The Jungle Is Neutral*, 15.

77. Chapman, *The Jungle Is Neutral*, 15.

78. Chapman, *The Jungle Is Neutral*, 15–16.

79. Chapman, *The Jungle Is Neutral*, 157.

80. Chapman, *The Jungle Is Neutral*, 125.

81. Khoo, *Life as the River Flows*, 61.

82. Chapman, *The Jungle Is Neutral*, 139, 141, 142.

83. Chapman, *The Jungle Is Neutral*, 177.

84. Chapman, *The Jungle Is Neutral*, 178–6, 196.

85. Chapman, *The Jungle Is Neutral*, 152, 155.

86. Chapman, *The Jungle Is Neutral*, 152, 155–6, 180.

87. Chapman, *The Jungle Is Neutral*, 161.

88. Chapman, *The Jungle Is Neutral*, 159–61.

89. Ironically, this gave Chapman commonality with the Japanese. According to MPAJA leader Chin Peng, Japanese leaders checked the hands of Chinese people to see if they were intellectuals or laborers. If they were intellectuals, they were often questioned and tortured. Having dirty hands on one occasion freed him from Japanese scrutiny. Chin and Hack, *Dialogues with Chin Peng*, 89.

90. Chapman, *The Jungle Is Neutral*, 161.

91. Chapman, *The Jungle Is Neutral*, 161–2, 165.

92. Khoo, *Life as the River Flows*, 81.

93. Chapman, *The Jungle Is Neutral*, 161–2, 165.

94. Chapman, *The Jungle Is Neutral*, 177.

95. Chapman, *The Jungle Is Neutral*, 180–1.

96. Chapman, *The Jungle Is Neutral*, 263.

97. Bernard Randolph Morrison, "Biography: Frank T Quayle MBE," Published in New Zealand, 2000, Accession No 2003.379, National Army Museum of New Zealand, 23. Miller claimed to have learned the truth about Noone's passing and recounted a story of Noone getting killed by a poison dart and beheaded because of a love triangle. Private Papers of J. M. Miller, Documents.20349, Box 12/47/1, IWM, 7–8.

98. Chapman, *The Jungle Is Neutral*, 201–2.

99. Chapman, *The Jungle Is Neutral*, 206, 208, 209, 210.

100. Chapman, *The Jungle Is Neutral*, 231. See also Rebecca Kenneison, *The Special Operations Executive in Malaya: World War II and the Path to Independence* (London: Bloomsbury Academic, 2019).

101. Chapman, *The Jungle Is Neutral*, 234.

102. Chapman, *The Jungle Is Neutral*, 234.

103. Cheah Boon, *Red Star over Malaya*, 73, 84.

104. Bayly and Harper, *Forgotten Wars*, 37.

105. Tan Chong Tee, interview by Lye Soo Choon, Accession Number 002944, Reel 7, NAS.

106. Tan, interview by Lye, Reel 11.

107. Cheah Boon, *Red Star over Malaya*, 59–62; Tan, interview by Lye, Reel 4; Bayly and Harper, *Forgotten Wars*, 32.

108. Tan, interview by Lye, Reel 5.

109. Tan, interview by Lye, Reel 4.

110. Tan, interview by Lye, Reel 11.

111. Tan, interview by Lye, Reel 5.

112. Tan, interview by Lye, Reel 11.

113. Tan, interview by Lye, Reel 5.

114. Tan, interview by Lye, Reel 5.

115. Tan, interview by Lye, Reels 4 and 5.

116. Blythe, *The Impact of Chinese Secret Societies in Malaya*, 331.

117. Blythe, *The Impact of Chinese Secret Societies in Malaya*, 330–1.

118. Blythe, *The Impact of Chinese Secret Societies in Malaya*, 331.

119. Tan, interview by Lye, Reels 4 and 5.

120. Bayly and Harper, *Forgotten Wars*, 42.

121. Recommendation for Award for E. H. Peacock, Regiment: Force 136, WO 373/34/230, The National Archives (UK) (henceforth TNA).

122. Recommendation for Award for John Maurice Cotterill, WO 373/102/664, TNA.

123. See for example Recommendation for Award for Saw Kyaw Yin Rank: Levy Naik Regiment, WO 373/101/196; Recommendation for Award for Tin Win Rank: Subadar Regiment: Force 136, WO 373/101/189; Recommendation for Award for Saw Shwe Paw Rank: Levy Regiment: Force 136, WO 373/101/200; Recommendation for Award for Saw Shwe Byu Rank: Levy Regiment: Force 136, WO 373/101/192; Recommendation for Award for Po Kya Aye, Saw Rank: Levy Jemadar Regiment, WO 373/146/325, TNA.

124. Lebra, *Women against the Raj*, 96–7.

125. William Arthur, "The Padang, the Sahib and the Sepoy—The Role of the Indian Army in Malaya, 1945 to 1946" (PhD diss., Oxford University, 2013), 126–7, 142; Allan, "Journey to Changi and Down Under," 133.

126. Luo Lan similarly recalled, "Both my parents were involved in the anti-Japanese army. They won the war." Khoo, *Life as the River Flows*, 59, 121.

127. Blythe, *The Impact of Chinese Secret Societies in Malaya*, 330–1.

128. Sir Shenton Thomas, "Comments on Sir R. Brooke-Popham's Report" (undated, c. 1946), Box 2, File 4, Papers of Sir Thomas S. W. Thomas (henceforth Shenton Thomas papers), GB 0162 MSS.Ind.Ocn.s.341, Bodleian Library.

129. Shenton Thomas, "Comments on Sir R. Brooke-Popham's Report."

130. See for example: Chapman, *The Jungle Is Neutral*, 125, 143, 217; Tan, interview by Lye, Reel 14.

131. Shenton Thomas, "Comments on Sir R. Brooke-Popham's Report."

132. Shenton Thomas, "Comments on Sir R. Brooke-Popham's Report."

133. Shenton Thomas, "Comments on Sir R. Brooke-Popham's Report."

134. Shenton Thomas, "Comments on Sir R. Brooke-Popham's Report."

135. A. E. Percival to Sir Shenton Thomas, June 4, 1946, Shenton Thomas papers.

136. Percival to Shenton Thomas, June 4, 1946.

137. Percival to Shenton Thomas, June 4, 1946.

138. Arthur Percival to Shenton Thomas, July 5, 1946, Shenton Thomas papers, 1.

139. Percival to Shenton Thomas, July 5, 1946, 1.

140. Downing Street to Shenton Thomas, July 23, 1946, Shenton Thomas papers, 2.

141. Bayly and Harper, *Forgotten Wars*, 30.

142. Percival to Shenton Thomas, July 5, 1946, 2.

143. Downing Street to Shenton Thomas, July 23, 1946, 2.

144. Newspaper clipping, "Back Pay for Volunteers," February 20, 1947, newspaper title not included, Box 2, File 3, Shenton Thomas papers.

145. Mah Khong, Chairman of Dalforce, to Sir Shenton Thomas, December 20, 1946, Box 2, File 3, Shenton Thomas papers, 4, 7.

146. Mah Khong to Sir Shenton Thomas, December 20, 1946, 6.

147. Mah Khong to Sir Shenton Thomas, December 20, 1946, 2, 3, 7–10.

148. Mah Khong to Sir Shenton Thomas, December 20, 1946, 2.

149. Mah Khong to Sir Shenton Thomas, December 20, 1946, unnumbered page titled "Requests."

150. Mah Khong to Sir Shenton Thomas, December 20, 1946, 3.

151. Mah Khong on behalf of the Singapore Overseas Chinese to the Officer-in-Charge, War Department, March 10, 1947, Box 2, File 3, Shenton Thomas papers, 1.

152. Mah Khong to the Officer-in-Charge, War Department, March 10, 1947, 2.

153. Translation of a Circular issued by the Singapore Overseas Chinese Anti-Japanese Volunteer Corps (DALFORCE), the Defenders of Singapore of 1942, March 28, 1947, Box 2, File 3, Shenton Thomas papers, 1.

154. Translation of a Circular by the Singapore Overseas Chinese Anti-Japanese Volunteer Corps, March 28, 1947, 1–2.

155. John Dalley to Shenton Thomas, April 8, 1947, Box 2, File 3, Shenton Thomas papers, 1.

156. John Dalley to Major J. L. Yeatman, April 8, 1947, Box 2, File 3, Shenton Thomas papers, 1.

157. Dalley to Yeatman, April 8, 1947, 1.

158. Translation of an Editorial entitled: "A Second Appeal on Behalf of Dalforce," from *Chung Nan Jit Poh*, March 28, 1947, Box 2, File 3, Shenton Thomas papers, 1.

159. "A Second Appeal on Behalf of Dalforce," March 28, 1947, 1–2.

160. Extract from "Morning Tribune," March 28, 1947, Box 2, File 3, Shenton Thomas papers, 1.

161. Extract from "Morning Tribune," March 28, 1947, 1.

162. A. E. Percival to Sir Shenton Thomas, April 17, 1947, Box 2, File 3, Shenton Thomas papers.

163. Percival to Shenton Thomas, April 17, 1947.

164. Leathart papers, 108–9.

165. Leathart papers, 113, 121.

166. Dennis Newland, "What Did You Do in the War, Dad? Military Service in the 1939/1945 War by Dennis Newland," Private Papers of D. Newland, Box Number 03/22/1, Documents. 12197, IWM.

167. James Joseph Puthucheary, interview by Lim How Seng, June 15, 1985, Accession Number 000570, Reel 1, NAS, 5–6. See also https://eresources.nlb.gov.sg/infopedia/articles/SIP_1471_2009-02-24.html; https://www.jamesputhucheary.org/quek-peng-cheng/.

168. Leathart papers, 98.

169. Leathart papers, 98.

170. Field Marshall Archibald Wavell, preface to *The Jungle Is Neutral*, by Chapman, v–vii.

171. Satia, *Spies in Arabia.*

172. R. H. de S. Onraet, "Extracts from Onraet's Police Background," Box 2, File 4, Shenton Thomas papers.

173. Onraet, "Extracts from Onract's Police Background."

174. Allan papers, 139.

175. Bayly and Harper, *Forgotten Wars*, 7–8.

176. Suyin, . . . *And the Rain My Drink*, 58.

177. Morrison, "Biography: Frank T Quayle MBE," 3.

Chapter Six

1. "Lecture by Senior Army Liaison Officer," Private papers of Dennis Talbot (henceforth Talbot papers), 3/11 Box 5 of 7, Kings College Liddell Hart Centre for Military Archives (henceforth LHCMA), 2.

2. For further reading on the Emergency, see the introduction. Hack, "The Malayan Emergency as Counter-Insurgency Paradigm"; Jeremy Taylor, "'Not a Particularly Happy Expression': 'Malayanization' and the China Threat in Britain's Late-Colonial Southeast Asian Territories," *Journal of Asian Studies* 78, no. 4 (November 2019): 789–808; Jeremy E. Taylor and Lanjun Xu, eds., *Chineseness and the Cold War: Contested Cultures and Diaspora in Southeast Asia and Hong Kong* (London: Routledge, 2021); Florence Mok, "Disseminating and Containing Communist Propaganda to Overseas Chinese in Southeast Asia through Hong Kong, the Cold War Pivot, 1949–1960," *The Historical Journal* (2021), 1–21; Donald M. Nonini, "'At That Time We Were Intimidated on All Sides': Residues of the Malayan Emergency as a Conjunctural Episode of Dispossession," *Critical Asian Studies* 47, no. 3 (2015): 337–58.

3. "Army Education Third Class Certificate: General Studies Assignments Part I, Emergency in Malaya," Prepared by the R. A. E. C. Malaya. 1, 3/12 to 3/19 Box 5 of 7, Talbot papers, LHCMA, 4.

4. William Donald Horne, "Note" (1951), MSS. Ind. Ocn. S. 128, Bodleian Library.

5. For a recent example, see Elkins, *Legacy of Violence*, 460–1. See also Short, *The Communist Insurrection in Malaya*; Blythe, *The Impact of Chinese Secret Societies in Malaya*, 419, 437.

6. Ian Sanjay Patel, *We're Here Because You Were There: Immigration and the End of Empire* (London and New York: Verso Books, 2021).

7. Elkins, *Legacy of Violence*, 466.

8. Blythe, *The Impact of Chinese Secret Societies in Malaya*, 334.

9. Blythe, *The Impact of Chinese Secret Societies in Malaya*, 336–7.

10. Blythe, *The Impact of Chinese Secret Societies in Malaya*, 335.

11. Blythe, *The Impact of Chinese Secret Societies in Malaya*, 338.

12. Blythe, *The Impact of Chinese Secret Societies in Malaya*, 403.

13. Elkins, *Legacy of Violence*, 468, 493.

14. J. L. H. Davis to his mother and father, December 17, 1948, Private Papers of Colonel J. L. H Davis (henceforth Davis papers), Documents.16593, IWM.

15. Musa, "Women in the Malayan Communist Party," 236–7; Bayly and Harper, *Forgotten Wars*, 32; Blythe, *The Impact of Chinese Secret Societies in Malaya*, 354.

16. Khoo, *Life as the River Flows*, 60.

17. Blythe, *The Impact of Chinese Secret Societies in Malaya*, 383, 391, 419.

18. See also Roger C. Arditti, *Counterinsurgency Intelligence and the Emergency in Malaya* (New York: Palgrave Macmillan, 2019); John Newsinger, *British Counterinsurgency* (New York: Palgrave Macmillan, 2015); Grob-Fitzgibbon, *Imperial Endgame*; Souchou Yao, *The Malayan Emergency: Essays on a Small, Distant War* (York, PA: Maple Press, 2016); Hack, *Defence and Decolonisation*.

19. Elkins, *Legacy of Violence*, 21.

20. Elkins, *Legacy of Violence*, 505.

21. French, *The British Way in Counter-Insurgency*; Low Choo Chin, "The Repatriation of the Chinese as a Counterinsurgency Policy during the Malayan Emergency," *Journal of Southeast Asian Studies* 45, no. 3 (October 2014): 363–92; Low Choo Chin, "Immigration Control During the Malayan Emergency: Borders, Belonging and Citizenship, 1948–1960," *Journal of the Malaysian Branch of the Royal Asiatic Society* 89, no. 1 (2016): 35–60.

22. J. P. Cross, "The Role of the Brigade of Gurkhas in the British Army: Operational, Administrative and Personnel Aspects Relating to the British Army and Nepal: From 1948 to 1982," B-37, The Gurkha Museum.

23. V. W. W. S. Purcell, *Malaya, Communist or Free?* (Stanford: Stanford University Press, 1954); Bayly and Harper, *Forgotten Wars*, 524.

24. Fujitani, *Race for Empire*.

25. Imy, *Faithful Fighters*.

26. Christi Siver, "Enemies or Friendlies? British Military Behavior Toward Civilians During the Malayan Emergency," in *Military Interventions, War Crimes, and Protecting Civilians* (New York: Palgrave, 2018), 2–8.

27. Chin and Hack, *Dialogues with Chin Peng*; Aloysius Chin, *The Communist Party of Malaya: The Inside Story* (Kuala Lumpur: Vinpress, 1994); Chieh Sze Jason Ng, "Nostalgia and Memory: Remembering the Malayan Communist Revolution in the Online Age," in *The Asia-Pacific in the Age of Transnational Mobility: The Search for Community and Identity on and through Social Media*, ed. Catherine Gomes (Cambridge, UK: Cambridge University Press, 2017); J. A. Stockwell, "Chin Peng and the Struggle for Malaya," *Journal of the Royal Asiatic Society* 16, no. 3 (November 2006): 279–97.

28. Khoo, *Life as the River Flows*, 59.

29. Madam Seow Guat Beng, interview by Miss Ooi Yu Lin, July 8, 1989, transcribed by Roger Khong (1992), Accession number 001048, NAS, Reel 15, 232.

30. Blythe, *The Impact of Chinese Secret Societies in Malaya*, 331.

31. Elkins, *Legacy of Violence*, 470.

32. Suyin, *. . . And the Rain My Drink*, 79.

33. For discussions of military and colonial masculinities, see Gregory Daddis, *Pulp Vietnam: War and Gender in Cold War Men's Adventure Magazines* (Cambridge, UK: Cambridge University Press, 2020), 1; Barczewski, *Heroic Failure*.

34. For more on resettlement, see Karl Hack, "Detention, Deportation and Resettlement: British Counterinsurgency and Malaya's Rural Chinese, 1948–60," *The Journal of Imperial and Commonwealth History* 43, no. 4 (2015): 611–40; David Baillargeon, "Spaces

of Occupation: Colonial Enclosure and Confinement in British Malaya," *Journal of Historical Geography* 73 (2021): 24–35; Tan, *Behind Barbed Wire;* Elkins, *Legacy of Violence*, 21.

35. Loh Kok Wah, *Beyond the Tin Mines*, 106; Elkins, *Legacy of Violence*, 472.

36. Elkins, *Legacy of Violence*, 511–13.

37. "A Planter in Malaya's Terror," *Picture Post* 43, no. 4 (April 23, 1949), 7–3-21, Talbot papers.

38. "Army Education Third Class Certificate."

39. *Malayan Police Magazine* 22, no. 2 (June 1954): 73.

40. Richard Valdan to Frank Lawrence, October 28, 1958, Papers of Francis Lawrence, PR91/115, AWM.

41. J. P. Cross and Buddhiman Gurung, eds., *Gurkhas at War: Eyewitness Accounts From World War II to Iraq* (London: Greenhill Books, 2007), 222.

42. Elkins, *Legacy of Violence*, 14–15.

43. These were not uncommon dynamics of the era. See Man, *Soldiering through Empire*, 88; Brian Drohan, *Brutality in an Age of Human Rights: Activism and Counterinsurgency at the End of the British Empire* (Ithaca and London: Cornell University Press, 2017); Gert Oostindie, Ben Schoenmaker, and Frank Van Vree, *Beyond the Pale: Dutch Extreme Violence in the Indonesian War of Independence, 1945–1949* (Amsterdam: University of Amsterdam Press, 2022).

44. Man, *Soldiering through Empire*, 88.

45. Private Papers of J. M. Miller, Documents.20349, Box 12/47/1, IWM, 7.

46. Bill Fish, "A Handsome Girl Meets Her Doom," *Straits Times*, November 16, 1952, 6.

47. "A Layman to a Minister," *Straits Times*, June 10, 1950, 9.

48. Untitled Cartoon, above "Gun-Shot Wounds" article, *Police: The Magazine of the Malayan Police Force* (June 1952), 46, Box 9, Harrison papers, NLA.

49. Khoo, *Life as the River Flows*, 284.

50. M. P. Stephens, untitled cartoon, *Police: The Magazine of the Malayan Police Force* (1951), Box 9, Harrison papers, unnumbered page (last page in the issue).

51. R. H. de S. Onraet, "Extracts from Onraet's Police background," Box 2, File 4, Shenton Thomas papers, GB 0162 MSS.Ind.Ocn.s.341, Bodleian library.

52. Papers of Sergeant S. L. Gilmore, 2/20 Bn, AIF. PR89/051, AWM.

53. Suyin, . . . *And the Rain My Drink*, 93, 163.

54. Suyin, . . . *And the Rain My Drink*, 84.

55. Tan, "Like a Concentration Camp, Iah," 218; Comber, *Malaya's Secret Police.*

56. Blythe, *The Impact of Chinese Secret Societies in Malaya*, 331.

57. Imy, *Faithful Fighters;* Des Chene, "Relics of Empire"; Gregorian, *The British Army, the Gurkhas and the Cold War Strategy in the Far East.*

58. Suyin, . . . *And the Rain My Drink*, 56.

59. Private Papers of Major P. S. Leathart, PP/MCR/311, Reel 1, Documents.7896 (henceforth Leathart papers), IWM, 130.

60. Cross and Gurung, *Gurkhas at War*, 196.

61. Cross and Gurung, *Gurkhas at War*, 199–201.

62. Cross and Gurung, *Gurkhas at War*, 178–9.

63. Typed copy of Lt. Colonel R. M. J. N. Ryan's notes for the Digest of Services, 2nd Battalion 2nd King Edward VII's Own Goorkhas, 1948–49, *2nd King Edward VII's Own Goorkhas, 2nd Bn Malaya & Singapore, Vol. 1 1950–57*, The Gurkha Museum.

64. Cross and Gurung, *Gurkhas at War*, 178–9, 183.

65. Major General R. C. O. Hedley, "Special Order of the Day" (undated), in *The Kukri: The Journal of the Brigade of Gurkhas* 4 (August 1952): front matter, The Gurkha Museum.

66. "7th Gurkha Rifles," *The Kukri* 1 (May 1949): 61–2.

67. See for example *The Kukri* 5 (September 1953): 41.

68. Cross and Gurung, *Gurkhas at War*, 187, 195.

69. Cross and Gurung, *Gurkhas at War*, 183, 184, 201. Maitaraj Limbu, 2/10 GR, similarly "lost heart" when "[s]ome who had joined the army after me were promoted," so he transferred to the Gurkha Military police.

70. Cross and Gurung, *Gurkhas at War*, 184.

71. Cross and Gurung, *Gurkhas at War*, 211.

72. Cross and Gurung, *Gurkhas at War*, 182.

73. "A Message from the Colonel-in-Chief," *The Kukri* 1 (May 1949): 1–2.

74. Cross and Gurung, *Gurkhas at War*, 203.

75. Update on the 6 Gurkha Rifles, *The Kukri* 1 (May 1949): 42.

76. Cross and Gurung, *Gurkhas at War*, 180.

77. Leathart papers, 132.

78. Colonel Humphrey Williams, Unpublished manuscript (henceforth Humphrey Williams papers), MSS. Afr. S. 1715. Box 19 (300), Bodleian Library.

79. Timothy Parsons, "Dangerous Education? The Army as School in Colonial East Africa," *The Journal of Imperial and Commonwealth History* 28, no. 1 (January 2000), 112–34, at 113.

80. Moyd, *Violent Intermediaries*, 67; Parsons, *The African Rank-and-File*, 91.

81. Parsons, "Dangerous Education?," 112.

82. Parsons, *The African Rank-and-File*, 7, 54, 55.

83. "King's African Rifles Return From Malaya," British Movietone (March 3, 1955), http://www.aparchive.com/metadata/youtube/323d27f9f3ee4837b7e2b0af76163de1.

84. Colonel H. P. Williams, interview by Dr. William Beaver, October 15, 1979, MSS. Afr. S. 1715. Box 19 (300), transcript, Humphrey Williams papers, 18–19.

85. Brigadier F. H. Brooke to Brigadier Ap [*sic*] Rhys Pryce, February 1953, MSS. Afr. S. 1715. Box 19 (300), Humphrey Williams papers; Speech by H. P. W. on Radio, BBC edition, (1953), Humphrey Williams papers.

86. Excerpt from a Japanese newspaper, 2nd King Edward VII's Own Goorkhas, 2nd Battalion Records 1919–45, Gurkha Museum.

87. Timothy John Lovering, "Authority and Identity: Malawian Soldiers in Britain's Colonial Army, 1861–1964" (PhD diss., University of Stirling, September 2002), 39.

88. Brooke to Pryce, February 1953.

89. Humphrey Williams, interview by Beaver, 18–19.

90. "Jungle Troops Rescue Abandoned Baby," *Indian Daily Mail*, September 26, 1952, Microfilm Reel NL7321, 1.

91. Humprey Williams, interview by Beaver, 20.

92. Speech by H. P. W. on Radio (1953).

93. Humprey Williams, interview by Beaver, 18–19.

94. Speech by H. P. W. on Radio (1953).

95. Humprey Williams, interview by Beaver, 18–19.

96. Parsons, *The African Rank-and-File*, 61.

97. Speech by H. P. W. on Radio (1953).

98. Lovering, "Authority and Identity," 220.

99. Speech by H. P. W. on Radio (1953).

100. Lovering, "Authority and Identity," 221.

101. Survey of VC winner Lt. Col. Eric Charles Tweelves Wilson, Humphrey Williams papers.

102. Survey completed by John Arthur Williams, Humphrey Williams papers.

103. Brooke to Pryce, February 1953.

104. Parsons, "Dangerous Education?," 113.

105. Speech by H. P. W. on Radio (1953).

106. Humprey Williams, interview by Beaver.

107. The Training of the Askari, Ref. Query by the C. I. G. S. (April 1953), Humphrey Williams papers.

108. Survey of Wilson.

109. "Oxford Development Records Project. The Role of British Forces in East Africa. Serving Officer: Colonel Williams, RAMC," Humphrey Williams papers.

110. "Oxford Development Records Project."

111. Parsons, *The African Rank-and-File*, 1, 93.

112. Tim Stapleton, "'Bad Boys': Infiltration and Sedition in the African Military Units of the Central African Federation (Malawi, Zambia and Zimbabwe) 1953–63," *The Journal of Military History* 73, no. 4 (October 2009): 1167–93, 1192.

113. Stapleton, "Bad Boys," 1175, 1178.

114. Matthew Mataiyan Kipoin, interview by Timothy Parsons. Notes from interview provided by Parsons to author.

115. Papers of Gordon Ell, 2016–262–1, National Army Museum of New Zealand.

116. Hoia, "Maoris in Uniform," *Te Ao Hou* 46 (March 1964): 41, National Library of New Zealand (henceforth NLNZ). This estimates that the number was 30 to 40 percent Maori but notes that no official count has been taken. Many Maori and white New Zealanders even served as part of the Fiji battalion in Malaya; for example, George Nepia, son of a Maori footballer, died on service while serving with the Fiji battalion, *Te Ao Hou* 10 (1955): 2.

117. Extract from Roger Robinson and Nelson Wattie, eds., *The Oxford Companion to New Zealand Literature* (Auckland, NZ: Oxford University Press, 1998), http://teaohou .natlib.govt.nz/journals/teaohou/about.html.

118. Hoia, "Maoris in Uniform," 41.

119. Hoia, "Maoris in Uniform," 41–2.

120. Alan Armstrong, "The Blooding of the Warriors," *Te Ao Hou*, 42 (March 1963): 8.

121. Armstrong, "The Blooding of the Warriors," 11, 13.

122. Arena Kahi, "Maori Soldiers in Malaya," *Te Ao Hou* 40 (September 1962): 21.

123. Kahi, "Maori Soldiers in Malaya," 21, 22.

124. The intention of the article may have been to criticize growing calls for all-Maori units because it would end the racial harmony that he believed existed in the army. Kahi, "Maori Soldiers in Malaya," 22.

125. Man, *Soldiering through Empire*, 12.

126. Rawiri, "Back from Malaya," *Te Ao Hou* 66 (March 1969): 20.

127. Rawiri, "Back from Malaya," 21.

128. Rawiri, "Back from Malaya," 21 (ellipses included in original).

129. The 1st battalion served for seventeen months in the Second World War before being hit hard by illness, when it was withdrawn from active service in 1944. In Malaya, they specifically served in Bahau, Batu Pahat, and Yong Peng. Pamphlet entitled "Presentation of Colours to the First Battalion Fiji Infantry Regiment" (June 25, 1956), includes a "Brief History of the Battalion" section, pages unnumbered, Petersen papers, 89-074-02 B, NLNZ.

130. "First Battalion Weekly Newsletter NO I5 Batu Penat Wednesday, 25 January 1956," Petersen papers, NLNZ.

131. J. K. Stone, "'Now What?' For Fijian Heroes," n.d. and publication info not included, article excerpt, Petersen papers, NLNZ.

132. Isa Lei, "'We Want to be Back' is Fijian Chorus as they Sadly Leave," *Straits Times*, June 1, 1956, Petersen papers, NLNZ.

133. "Farewell Gift for the Fijians" (May 23, 1956) and "Gurkhas to Fijians—A Kukri" (May 25, 1956), article excerpts from Petersen papers, NLNZ.

134. HQ, 1 FIR, "Mentions in Despatches—Nominations" (April 15, 1954), Petersen papers, NLNZ.

135. Stone, "'Now What?' For Fijian Heroes."

136. Stone, "'Now What?' For Fijian Heroes."

137. Stone, "'Now What?' For Fijian Heroes."

138. Papers of Gordon Ell (pages unnumbered).

139. Dennis and Grey, *Emergency and Confrontation*.

140. Private papers of Irene Simkin (henceforth Simkin papers), PR90/056, Australian War Memorial (AWM), 1.

141. Simkin papers, 3.

142. Simkin papers, 4.

143. See chapter 4.

144. Simkin papers, 6, 8.

145. *The Kukri* 4 (August 1952): 22.

146. "Gurkha Family Welfare," *The WVS Bulletin* 103 (July 1948): 4, WVS Archive.

147. Cross and Gurung, *Gurkhas at War*, 203; Update on the 6 Gurkha Rifles, *The Kukri* 1 (May 1949): 42.

148. Update on 2 Gurkha Rifles, *The Kukri*, 17.

149. Update on 1st Battalion, 7 GR, *The Kukri* 4 (August 1952): 32.

150. Ell papers, newspaper clipping of Maori wives, papers unnumbered.

151. Rates of pay for Fijian soldiers was 3s, 9d per day and allowance for wives was 2s od. Brij V. Lal, *Broken Waves: A History of the Fiji Islands in the Twentieth Century* (Honolulu: University of Hawaii Press, 1992), 151; "'Now What?' For Fijian Heroes," newspaper clipping, Petersen papers, National Library New Zealand.

152. "Fiji Troops For Malaya," British Pathé (1952), https://www.youtube.com/watch?v=L-opOa8H1IE.

153. Lovering, "Authority and Identity," 39; Humphrey Williams, interview by Beaver, 18–19; Brooke to Pryce, February 1953.

154. Survey of Wilson, 9–11.

155. Humphrey Williams, interview by Beaver, 7.

156. Chief of Staff, General HQ, Far East Land Forces, to General Officer Commanding East Africa Command Nairobi, Kenya, April 24, 1953, Humphrey Williams papers.

157. Lovering, "Authority and Identity," 225.

158. Stapleton, "Bad Boys," 1175.

159. Cross and Gurung, *Gurkhas at War*, 191, 195.

160. Cross and Gurung, *Gurkhas at War*, 217; "Adjutant's Quarterly News Letter" for November 1956–March 1957 (April 12, 1957), *1/7 Gurkha Rifles Newsletter 1954–70*, The Gurkha Museum.

161. Cross and Gurung, *Gurkhas at War*, 219.

162. "I Used Girl As Bandit Shield," *Straits Times*, November 30, 1949, 8.

163. "Call to Bandit Girl," *Straits Times*, April 28, 1957, 17.

164. "Girl Red Gives Up: She's No. 4 in Johore," *Straits Times*, October 24, 1955, 1.

165. The connection to communism was unclear, apart from the mention that "[e]ight terrorists fled after exchanging a few shots with two Area Security Units" and that they had recovered a Japanese rifle. "Bandit girl Shot in Jungle," *Straits Times*, May 25, 1953, 5.

166. "Girl Bandit Hit—But She Escapes," *Straits Times*, August 28, 1954, 4.

167. "A Handsome Girl Meets Her Doom," *Straits Times*, November 16, 1952, 6.

168. "Girl Bandit Killed by Gurkhas," *Straits Times*, December 17, 1955, 1.

169. Man, *Soldiering through Empire*, 13.

170. Urquhart, "Operation 'Service' and the Children," 74.

171. "Police of the Future," *Malayan Police Magazine*, Coronation Issue, June 1953, 93, Box 10, Harrison papers, NLA.

172. Denise Urquhart, "Operation 'Service' and the Children," *Malayan Police Magazine*, Coronation Issue, June 1953, 74, Box 10, Harrison papers, NLA.

173. Mary Tshu En nee Quintal, interview by Jason Lim, November 6, 1999, transcript edited by Ms Chew Hui Min, transcribed 2006, Accession Number 002219, NAS, Reel 2, 26.

Chapter Seven

1. She was married to D. C. M. Lee Sang. "Behind the Jungle Curtain," *Sin Lu Pau* [New Path News], translation of Issue No. 39 (December 31, 1954), 15 (page 8 in Chinese original), Maj. Gen. Dennis Edmund Blaquière Talbot papers, GB0099 KCLMA

Talbot, Box 7, file 3/21 (henceforth Talbot papers), Liddell Hart Military Archives (henceforth LHCMA).

2. For recent historiographical discussion on the Malayan Emergency, see chapter 6 and Bernard Z. Keo, "A Small, Distant War? Historiographical Reflections on the Malayan Emergency," *History Compass* 17, no. 3 (February 2019). The only works to discuss women and gender at length are Khoo, *Life as the River Flows,* and Musa, "Women in the Malayan Communist Party."

3. Quoted in Clutterbuck, *The Long Long War,* 3.

4. Two works that portray the success of this approach are Thompson, *Defeating Communist Insurgency,* and Clutterbuck, *The Long Long War.*

5. Elkins, *Legacy of Violence,* 524, 526.

6. Arunima Datta, "Negotiating Gendered Spaces in Colonial Press: Wives of European Planters in British Malaya," *Journal of Colonialism and Colonial History* 18, no. 3 (Winter 2017); Ann Laura Stoler, "Making Empire Respectable: The Politics of Race and Sexual Morality in 20th Century Colonial Cultures," *American Ethnologist* 16, no. 4 (1989): 634–60; Nupur Chaudhuri, "Memsahibs and Their Servants in Nineteenth-Century India," *Women's History Review* 3, no. 4 (1994): 549–62; Margaret Strobel, *European Women and the Second British Empire* (Bloomington: Indiana University Press, 1991).

7. See chapters 1 and 4.

8. Madam Seow Guat Beng, interview by Miss Ooi Yu Lin, July 8, 1989, transcribed by Roger Khong (1992), Accession number 001048, NAS, Reel 17, 256.

9. Brigadier George Lyon Mansford AM (Rtd) (2 RAR), interview by Colonel David Chinn MBE (Rtd), March 26, 2003, S02869, AWM.

10. *Outpost in Malaya* [The Planter's Wife], directed by Ken Annakin (Pinnacle Productions, 1952).

11. June White, "Some Memories of a Wife Overseas with an Infantry Battalion in Action 1957–1959," Private Record of June White (henceforth June White papers), PR90/056, AWM, 2.

12. Pamela Gouldsbury, *Jungle Nurse* (Norwich: Jarrolds, 1960).

13. Man, *Soldiering through Empire,* 51.

14. Army Education Third Class Certificate: General Studies Assignments Part 2, Malayan Background, Prepared by the R. A. E. C. Malaya, Box 5 of 7, Files 3/12 to 3/19, Talbot papers.

15. "Welfare is Fun—the Story of Perak," *Malayan Police Magazine* (December 1953), 190, Box 10, Harrison papers, National Library of Australia (henceforth NLA).

16. *The Kukri* 1 (May 1949), 46, The Gurkha Museum (henceforth TGM); "W. V. S. Help For Gurkha Families," *Straits Times,* March 17, 1948, 3, National Library Singapore (henceforth NLS).

17. "Army Education Third Class Certificate," Part II.

18. "The WVS with the Brigade of Gurkhas," *The Kukri* 1 (May 1949), 46, 47.

19. Update on the 2 Gurkha Rifles, *The Kukri* 1, (May 1949), 13.

20. "The WVS with the Brigade of Gurkhas," 47.

21. Anonymous OCPD "Police Welfare at District Level," *Malayan Police Magazine* (1952), 142, Box 9, Harrison papers, NLA.

22. "Fun and Welfare—Where it Began," *Malayan Police Magazine* 20, no. 2 (June 1954), 82.

23. Anonymous OCPD, "Police Welfare at District Level," *Malayan Police Magazine* (December 1952), 144, Box 9, Harrison papers, NLA.

24. In 1953 alone, $9,000 had been paid through this scheme. Di-Keliling Liku, "Whiteness and Welfare," *Malayan Police Magazine* 20, no. 2 (June 1954), 102. In this context, "Whiteness" actually refers to "White" areas, meaning areas free of communist activity.

25. "Welfare is Fun—the Story of Perak," *Malayan Police Magazine* (December 1953), 190–2, Box 10, Harrison papers, NLA.

26. "Johore Letter," *Malayan Police Magazine* 20, 2 (June 1954), 98–99.

27. Kathleen Stockdale, "Police Depot Wives' Club" *Malayan Police Magazine* (December 1952), 140, Box 9, Harrison papers, NLA.

28. "SSAFA IN MALAYA, 1952–62," excerpts from Magazine (January 1961), 15–16, notes provided by volunteer archivist, Juliet Chaplin, accessed June 2020, with the help of Selina Cuff, SSAFA, the Armed Forces charity.

29. *Malayan Police Magazine* 20, no. 1 (March 1954), 13.

30. "Police Welfare at District Level," 142.

31. Suyin, . . . *And the Rain My Drink*, 23.

32. White, "Some Memories of a Wife Overseas," 1.

33. Private papers of Irene Simkin (henceforth Simkin papers), PR90/056, AWM, 6.

34. White, "Some Memories of a Wife Overseas," 3.

35. Simkin papers, 6.

36. Simkin papers, 3.

37. James Desmond Howard Neill, interview by Liana Tan, December 2, 1981, Accession Number 000114, NAS, Reel 4, 36.

38. "Welfare in K. L.—A New Era Begins," *Malayan Police Magazine* 20, no. 1 (March 1954), 11, Box 10, Harrison papers, NLA.

39. *Malayan Police Magazine* 20, no. 2 (June 1954), 88–9.

40. I am grateful to Melissa Shaw for her analysis of women's material contributions to activism. Melissa N. Shaw, "'Women Who Used to Run the UNIA Hall': Black Canadian Women's Garveyite Leadership in Toronto's UNIA Division #21, 1919–1939," forthcoming.

41. Trengganu letter: "Fewer and Smaller Terrorists," *Malayan Police Magazine* 20, no. 2 (June 1954), 100.

42. "Welfare in K. L.—A New Era Begins," 11.

43. For expansion numbers, see for example "Federation of Malaya Police Its Functions and Difficulties" (undated), Box 8, Harrison papers, NLA.

44. "Welfare in K.L.—A New Era Begins," 11.

45. "Welfare in K.L.—A New Era Begins," 12.

46. Arthur Young, "A Message from the Commissioner," *Police: The Magazine of the Malayan Police Force* (June 1952), 40, Box 9, Harrison papers, NLA.

47. Lee Kam Hing, "A Neglected Story: Christian Missionaries, Chinese New Villagers, and Communists in the Battle for The 'Hearts and Minds' in Malaya, 1948–1960," *Modern Asian Studies* 47, no. 6 (2013): 1977–2006.

48. See for example "Fun and Welfare—Where It Began," 82. The image caption is "Sister Keenan and her young patients." See also Trengganu letter: "Fewer and Smaller Terrorists," 100.

49. Khoo, *Life as the River Flows*, 122.

50. Khoo, *Life as the River Flows*, 56.

51. Musa, "Women in the Malayan Communist Party," 229.

52. Khoo, *Life as the River Flows*, 51.

53. Khoo, *Life as the River Flows*, 68, 71, 73.

54. This was the case for Huang Xue Ying; Khoo, *Life as the River Flows*, 57, 187–8.

55. Syed Muhd Khairudin Aljunied, "Against Multiple Hegemonies: Radical Malay Women in Colonial Malaya," *Journal of Social History* 47, no. 1 (Fall 2013): 153–75, at 169.

56. Myths, legends, and memories of the 1890s Pahang Rebellion were especially important. Musa, "Women in the Malayan Communist Party," 240, 232, 248, 233, 235.

57. Khoo, *Life as the River Flows*, 204.

58. Khoo, *Life as the River Flows*, 9, 77.

59. Musa, "Women in the Malayan Communist Party," 238–9, 244.

60. Khoo, *Life as the River Flows*, 81.

61. "Malayan Women Bandits (AKA Malayan Bandits Surrender)" (Selangor, Malaysia: British Pathé, 1953), film ID:2010.13, Media Urn: 62350, https://www.britishpathe.com/video/malayan-women-bandits-aka-malayan-bandits-surrende/query/bandits+women.

62. Man, *Soldiering through Empire*, 3.

63. "Feeding the Troops in Malaya" (British Pathé, 1950–1959), film ID 2646.10, Media Urn: 78760, https://www.britishpathe.com/video/feeding-the-troops-in-malaya/query/malaya+food.

64. Lim Bee Giok to Bell, January 9, 1946, Lim Bee Giok papers, 3DRL/7415, AWM.

65. One article discusses food denial related to "Operation Hawk" in 1955 and bragged that "Bandits had Rubber Seeds for Dinner." "Raub Terror Gangs Broken Up," *Straits Times*, January 3, 1955, 4. Luo Lan uses "starvation restriction policy" in Khoo, *Life as the River Flows*, 123.

66. Khoo, *Life as the River Flows*, 125.

67. Suyin, . . . *And the Rain My Drink*, 47, 97.

68. They know this because KAR killed him and took his diary from his corpse. "Radio Spotlight and Pahang Government Press Release" (c. 1954), Talbot papers, Box 5 3/9, LHCMA.

69. Khoo, *Life as the River Flows*, 74.

70. Khoo, *Life as the River Flows*, 75.

71. Khoo, *Life as the River Flows*, 77.

72. "Girl Bandit Tells of Jungle Life," *Straits Times*, March 8, 1953, 3.

73. "'Starving Lady' Tells her Tale," *Straits Times*, January 28, 1951, 1.

74. "Feeding the Troops in Malaya."

75. Khoo, *Life as the River Flows*, 239.

76. Khoo, *Life as the River Flows*, 76, 79.

77. Elkins, *Legacy of Violence*, 477.

78. She was apparently interviewed over the Blue Network of Radio Malaya on January 27, 1951. "Interview with Girl Bandit," *Straits Times*, January 27, 1951, 7.

79. "'Starving Lady' Tells her Tale," 1.

80. Excerpt from Trengganu Newsletter, *Malayan Police Magazine* 13, no. 1 (March 1957), 56, Box 10, Harrison papers, NLA.

81. Another cover of *Police* similarly mocked a report that stated "Small Deserted Bandit Found" by depicting a communist as a small child crying, towered over by two concerned policemen. *Police: The Magazine of the Malayan Police Force* 3, no. 4 Christmas Number (1951), Box 9, Harrison papers, NLA, cover image.

82. Musa, "Women in the Malayan Communist Party," 242.

83. "Bandit Girl in Desperate Last Stand," *Straits Times*, January 16, 1949, 1.

84. "2 Girl Terror Chiefs Killed," *Malaya Tribune*, March 11, 1949, 3.

85. Newspaper Excerpt "Entire Bandit Out in Ambush: Woman Terror Boss Dies in Bag of 5," *Straits Times*, March 30, 1954, 5; the article "Mrs. Stutchbury's Remains Cremated," *Singapore Standard*, August 24, 1950, 1, notes that she was Mrs. Norah Stutchbury, a "British woman" originally from Hong Kong. See also "Missing Woman Named," *Singapore Free Press*, August 16, 1950, 1.

86. "Entire Bandit Out in Ambush," 5. A very similar account is provided in "Entire Bandit Branch Wiped Out in Ambush," *Straits Times*, March 30, 1954, 5.

87. "And Bandit Girl Gets Five Years," *Straits Times*, May 7, 1952, 8; "Girl Has To Serve 7 Yrs.," *Straits Times*, November 11, 1949, 8; "Seven Years for Girls," *Singapore Free Press*, November 11, 1949, 5; "Girl Bandit Captured," *Singapore Free Press*, November 29, 1948, 5.

88. "Girl, 16, Gaoled for 5 years," *Straits Times*, February 6, 1952, 7.

89. "Didn't Report Bandit Gang," *Singapore Free Press*, November 30, 1950, 5; the other women were Tai Lean Iai, The Kar Choon, and Wong Siew Yeng, who were sentenced to five years each. "Didn't Report Bandit Gang," 5. For similar stories, see "Thoroughly Bad Girl Sentenced," *Singapore Standard*, February 6, 1952, 4.

90. "Girl Bandit to Hang," *Singapore Standard*, December 10, 1953, 2; "Girl Bandit Won't Hang," *Straits Times*, April 6, 1954, 7; "Girl Bandit, 18, Won't Hang," *Straits Times*, June 6, 1951, 1.

91. "3 years for Girl Red," *Straits Times*, January 3, 1957, 7.

92. "Lee Meng Counsel," *Straits Times*, February 23, 1953, 1. The lawyer, P. G. Lim, would also defend many in the *Konfrontasi*. See also Musa, "Women in the Communist Party," 236.

93. "Save Girl Bandit Plea to King," *Straits Times*, January 15, 1958, 7.

94. "Doomed Girl Red Attacks Matron," *Straits Times*, September 8, 1951, 1.

95. "Bandits Kill Girl," *Malaya Tribune*, February 19, 1949, 5.

96. "Army Education Third Class Certificate," Part I, 4.

97. "Planes Hit Bandits in Six States," *Straits Times*, July 17, 1951, 7. For more on colonial airstrikes, see Priya Satia, "The Defense of Inhumanity: Air Control and the British Idea of Arabia," *American Historical Review* (February 2006): 16–51; David E. Omissi, *Air Power and Colonial Control: The Royal Air Force, 1919–1939* (Manchester: Manchester University Press, 1990).

98. "6 Bandits Abduct, Strangle Girl, 16," *Straits Times*, September 19, 1951, 1; "Bandits Kill Girl of Eight," *The Singapore Free Press*, October 19, 1951, 1; "Girl of 8 Hurled to Blazing Death," *Straits Times*, September 23, 1949, 1.

99. "Girl Died Defying Terrorists," *Straits Times*, February 24, 1949, 7.

100. "Wanted Man Shot Dead," *Straits Times*, February 19, 1949, 7; "Radio Spotlight and Pahang Government Press Release" (c. 1954), Talbot papers, Box 5, file 3/9; "Reds Slay Girl of 11," *Straits Times*, September 11, 1951, 1.

101. Daddis, *Pulp Vietnam.*

102. Khoo, *Life as the River Flows*, 12.

103. Harper, *The End of Empire*, 294–9; Musa, "Women in the Malayan Communist Party," 231; Khoo, *Life as the River Flows*, 254.

104. Musa, "Women in the Malayan Communist Party," 232.

105. *Sin Lu Pau* [New Path News], Translation of Issue No. 39 (December 31, 1954), Box 7, File 3/21, Talbot papers.

106. Daddis, *Pulp Vietnam*, 4.

107. "Bandit Pin-up Girl Is Caught by planter," *Straits Times*, October 13, 1955, 1. The *Malayan Police Magazine* lampooned a sitrep (situation report) that stated that "a pot of face cream was found in one of the huts" with a cartoon of a frustrated communist man looking at a dainty communist woman painting her face. Untitled cartoon, *Malayan Police Magazine* (December 1953), 219, Box 10, Harrison papers, NLA.

108. "Lipstick Found on Pretty Terrorist," *Singapore Standard*, August 21, 1954, 1.

109. M. P. Stephens, Raub, untitled cartoon, *Malayan Police Magazine* (December 1953), Box 10, Harrison papers, NLA.

110. Maxwell Anthony Nolan, "The Sands of Time," MS-Papers-4834, National Library of New Zealand, 141.

111. Bill Fish, "A Handsome Girl Meets Her Doom," *Straits Times*, November 16, 1952, 6.

112. Fish, "A Handsome Girl Meets Her Doom," 6.

113. "Girl Aided Bandit, Court Told," *Straits Times*, November 7, 1956, 4.

114. "Bandit Girl Was This Poet's Muse," *Straits Times*, January 20, 1955) 5.

115. Cartoon by G. D. Hodgson, *Malayan Police Magazine* 20, no. 3 (September 1954), 129.

116. "Girl Red Gaoled," *Straits Times*, January 22, 1954, 7. For other accounts of women surrendering together, see also "Appeal Brings Her Out," *Straits Times*, January 28, 1953, 1, and "Girl Red Gives Up: She's No. 4 in Johore," *Straits Times*, October 24, 1955, 1.

117. "Four Years for Girl. 19," *Straits Times*, December 20, 1952, 7.

118. Newspapers often reported on the hard work that families took to persuade "girl bandits" to leave the jungle, including brothers reading appeals to their sisters. "Appeal Brings Her Out," 1; Sin Ying's family apparently "disowned" her for joining communists but visited her in the hospital after she was wounded "by bullets from a Gurkha patrol." However, the mother left her daughter behind after identifying her. "Mother Sees Wounded Bandit Girl," *Straits Times*, March 30, 1955, 4.

119. "Now They All Know She's in Love with Comrade Chin," *Straits Times* March 28, 1953, 4.

120. "Diary of Spore's Red Miss," *Straits Times*, May 21, 1950, 9.

121. "Girl Sent Back to Peking," *Straits Times*, June 1950, 7. For the impact of prison, see Aljunied, "The Prison and the Anti-Colonialist in British Malaya."

122. "Diary of Spore's Red Miss," 9.

123. For more on repatriation, see Chin, "The Repatriation of the Chinese as a Counterinsurgency Policy during the Malayan Emergency"; Chin, "Immigration Control During the Malayan Emergency: Borders, Belonging and Citizenship." See also Suyin, . . . *And the Rain My Drink*, 76.

124. An S. C. M., Ah Yip, apparently selected two women for sex, one of whom was "only 14 years old." Men such as S. C. M. Lee Kai Fatt allegedly selected a girl who "had already been secretly chosen by his own boss." "Shameful Affairs in the Jungle," *Sin Lu Pau* [New Path News], translation of Issue No. 39, December 31, 1954, 7 (page 3 in Chinese original), Box 7, File 3/21, Talbot papers.

125. "Bandits Keep Lovers Apart," *Straits Times*, July 13, 1950, 10.

126. "Red Lovers Get a Warning," *Straits Times*, November 21, 1950, 7; "Red Wanted to Wed, Was Shot Instead," *Straits Times*, September 2, 1951, 9; "Bandit Love Triangle Has Unhappy Ending," *Singapore Standard*, September 24, 1951, 3; "Bandits Hang Comrade Who Fell in Love," *Sunday Standard*, February 11, 1951, 5.

127. "The Price of Foolishness," *Sin Lu Pau* [New Path News], translation of Issue No. 39 (December 31, 1954), 7, Box 7, File 3/21, Talbot papers.

128. Their source was "captured bandit documents." "Red Wanted to Wed, Was Shot Instead," *Straits Times*, September 2, 1951, 9. See also "Bandit Love Triangle Has Unhappy Ending," *Singapore Standard*, September 24, 1951, 3.

129. For a similar dynamic among communist women, see Taylor, *Vietnamese Women at War*.

130. Musa, "Women in the Malayan Communist Party," 246–7; Khoo, *Life as the River Flows*, 200.

131. Khoo, *Life as the River Flows*, 60, 62.

132. Police Lieutenant Wei Fei Ehr, "Love in the Jungle," *Malayan Police Magazine* 3, no. 2 (1951), 33–4.

133. "Ex Bandit Weds His Dream Girl," *Singapore Standard*, January 4, 1952, 5.

134. "Love Comes to Ooi the Ex-Red," *Straits Times*, August 30, 1954, 7.

135. "Ex-Bandit's Girl Had 'Hundreds of Worries,'" *Straits Times*, July 16, 1952, 4.

136. *Police: The Magazine of the Malayan Police Force* 3, no. 2 (1951), 35, Box 9, Harrison papers.

137. *Malayan Police Magazine* 20, no. 1 (March 1954), 8, Box 10, Harrison papers.

138. Suyin, . . . *And the Rain My Drink*, 107–8, 238–9.

139. Suyin, . . . *And the Rain My Drink*, 205.

140. Suyin, . . . *And the Rain My Drink*, 223.

141. Tom and Betty to Mother and Dad, January 9, 1952, PPMS 33/FILE 30–1 1952–1953, NAB 1531_0566_0748_0094, NAS. Emphasis in original.

142. See chapter 4.

143. Khoo, *Life as the River Flows*, 209.

144. Khoo, *Life as the River Flows*, 67.

145. Tan, "Oral History and People's Memory of the Malayan Emergency," 101; Tan, "Like a Concentration Camp, Iah," 220–1.

146. Luo Lan lost her mother to deportation. Khoo, *Life as the River Flows*, 67, 74, 121.

147. See for example the character Ah Mei in Suyin, . . . *And the Rain My Drink*, 20.

148. Musa, "Women in the Malayan Communist Party," 236.

149. Malaya Command Kuala Lumpur, "The Conduct of Anti-Terrorist Operations in Malaya," 2nd ed., Part IV: Emergency Regulations (1954), 11.

150. A wanted poster of a buck-toothed, emaciated communist man hovered over the scene. Untitled cartoon by M. P. Stephens Raub, *Malayan Police Magazine* (September 1953), 19, 3, 141.

151. "Aunt Fanny's Advice Bureau," *Police: The Magazine of the Malayan Police Force* 3, no. 4 (1951), 113, Box 9, Harrison papers.

152. *Malayan Police Magazine* 20, no. 1 (March 1954), 46, Box 10, Harrison papers.

153. Suyin, . . . *And the Rain My Drink*, 20–1.

154. Mary Tshu En nee Quintal, interview by Jason Lim, November 6, 1999, transcript edited by Ms Chew Hui Min, transcribed 2006, Accession Number 002219, NAS, Reel 2, 21.

155. Quintal, interview by Lim, Reel 4, 44.

156. Quintal, interview by Lim, Reel 2, 22; Reel 4, 43 and 45.

157. Quintal, interview by Lim, Reel 3.

158. Quintal, interview by Lim, Reel 3, 31–2, 38, and 40; Reel 2, 27; Reel 4, 55 and 56–7; Reel 5, 58.

159. *Malayan Police Magazine* 23, no. 1 (March 1957), 1, Box 10, Harrison papers.

160. See for example the images included in "Women Police Constables Passing-Out Parade," *Malayan Police Magazine* 23, no. 1 (March 1957), 6, Box 10, Harrison papers, NLA.

161. *Malayan Police Magazine* (December 1957), front matter, Box 10, Harrison papers.

162. "Many Varied Activities" and "Women Police Constables Passing-Out Parade," *Malayan Police Magazine* 23, no. 1 (March 1957), 34, Box 10, Harrison papers.

163. The Federal Police Depot Women Police Recruits Hockey Team proved successful, winning most of their matches. *Malayan Police Magazine* 23, no. 1 (March 1957), 35, Box 10, Harrison papers.

164. *Malayan Police Magazine* 23, no. 2 (June 1957), 121.

165. "Women Excel at Cricket," upper-right heading of "Negri Letter," *Malayan Police Magazine* 23, no. 3 (September 1957), 226–7.

166. *Malayan Police Magazine* 23, no. 3 (September 1957).

167. Miss Hor Pew Toh, "My First Month in the Depot," *Malayan Police Magazine* 23, no. 3 (September 1957), 191–2, Box 10, Harrison papers.

168. Hor Pew Toh, "My First Month in the Depot," 191–2.

169. Hor Pew Toh, "My First Month in the Depot," 191–2.

170. "We apologise to W. I. P. Miss Hor Pew Toh, the writer of 'My First Month in the Depot' which appeared in the last issue. The photograph which appeared with that article was not that of the writer," *Malayan Police Magazine* (December 1957), 276, Box 10, Harrison papers.

171. "Churi Ayam Is No Easy Job," *Malayan Police Magazine* 23, no. 2 (June 1957), 106, Box 10, Harrison papers. Churi Ayam means "steal a chicken," which has colloquial meaning in scouts relating to the idea of stealing a chicken from a local kampong and eating it for dinner. Sylvia Toh Paik Choo, *The Complete Eh, Goondu!* (Singapore: Marshall Cavendish International Asia Pte Ltd, 2010 [1982]).

172. M. J. M. [Possibly M. J. Manning, Police Magazine correspondent for Malacca], "The Hard Streak," *Malayan Police Magazine* (December 1952), 148, Box 9, Harrison papers.

173. M. J. M., "The Hard Streak," 148.

174. M. J. M., "The Hard Streak," 148–9.

175. Suyin, . . . *And the Rain My Drink*, 37–8, 57.

176. Tan, "Like a Concentration Camp, Iah," 216.

177. Tan, *Behind Barbed Wire;* "Army Education Third Class Certificate," Part I, 4–5; Bayly and Harper, *Forgotten Armies*, 31; Loh Kok Wah, *Beyond the Tin Mines*, 102.

178. Aidan Forth, *Barbed-Wire Imperialism: Britain's Empire of Camps, 1876–1903* (Berkeley: University of California Press, 2017); "Army Education Third Class Certificate," Part I, 9.

179. "The Fight against Communist Terrorism in Malaya," issued by Reference Division, Central Office of Information, London (May 1953), 20, Box 8, Harrison papers.

180. Tan, "Oral History and People's Memory of the Malayan Emergency," 85.

181. "Army Education Third Class Certificate," Part I, 9.

182. "Army Education Third Class Certificate," Part I, 11.

183. Tan, *Behind Barbed Wire*.

184. Bayly and Harper, *Forgotten Wars*, 527.

185. Loh Kok Wah, *Beyond the Tin Mines*, 135, 137, 151.

186. James Desmond Howard Neill, interview by Liana Tan, December 2, 1981, Accession Number 000114, NAS, Reel 4, 33.

187. Guan Shui Lian had a similar story about electric currents. Khoo, *Life as the River Flows*, 68, 283.

188. Khoo, *Life as the River Flows*, 53.

189. Khoo, *Life as the River Flows*, 122.

190. "Army Education Third Class Certificate," Part I, 9.

191. Loh Kok Wah, *Beyond the Tin Mines*, 140.

192. Khoo, *Life as the River Flows*, 69.

193. See for example Suyin, . . . *And the Rain My Drink*, 51, 93.

194. Luo Lan lived near a New Village in Negri Sembilan and recalled regular raids on their home. Khoo, *Life as the River Flows*, 68, 123; Tan, "Like a Concentration Camp, Iah," 219.

195. Suyin, . . . *And the Rain My Drink*, 112.

196. Khoo, *Life as the River Flows*, 283, 285.

197. Loh Kok Wah, *Beyond the Tin Mines*, 108–9, 152.

198. "The Conduct of Anti-Terrorist Operations in Malaya," 2nd ed., Prepared under the direction of H. Q. Malaya Command Kuala Lumpur 1954, Part IV, 4–5.

199. Loh Kok Wah, *Beyond the Tin Mines*, 153.

200. Suyin, . . . *And the Rain My Drink*, 44.

201. Khoo, *Life as the River Flows*, 284.

202. Khoo, *Life as the River Flows*, 67, 69–70.

203. "Army Education Third Class Certificate," Part I, 9.

204. "Malaya: Lecture by Senior Army Liaison Officer, U. K. S. L. S.," prepared in September, 1948, brought up to date February, 1950, and again September, 1950, 2, Box 5, File 3/11, Talbot papers.

205. Blythe, *The Impact of Chinese Secret Societies in Malaya*, 322.

206. "Army Education Third Class Certificate," Part I.

207. Malay Leaflet translation: Leaflet 3486/PHG/70 Order 32/55, 36/55, Requested by SIO Pahang (January 22, 1955), Box 5, File 3/12 to 3/19.

208. "Gurkhas Bag Seven in Swoop on Bandit Camp," *Straits Times*, July 31, 1954, 1.

209. Khoo, *Life as the River Flows*, 81.

210. Khoo, *Life as the River Flows*, 81–2.

211. Khoo, *Life as the River Flows*, 183.

212. Guo Ren Luan sent her child to China at age five so she could continue her work. Huang Xue Ying put her daughter up for adoption with a Thai family and later reunited. Khoo, *Life as the River Flows*, 121, 130, 200, 202, 268.

213. Khoo, *Life as the River Flows*, 209 .

214. Suyin, . . . *And the Rain My Drink*, 32.

215. *Malayan Police Magazine* 20, no. 1 (March 1954), 44, Box 10, Harrison papers.

216. "Couple Give Up with 15-Day Baby," *Straits Times*, April 26, 1958, 1.

217. "Shameful Affairs in the Jungle," 7, 1.

218. "3 Killed, 2 Wounded in S'gor Ambush," *Straits Times*, December 6, 1950, 9. See also "Forces Save Bandit Baby," *Singapore Standard*, December 6, 1950, 3.

219. "Bandits Threw Baby Away," *Straits Times*, July 22, 1951, 11.

220. "Bandit Boy Arrives Home in Britain," *Straits Times*, November 26, 1958, 4.

221. Nadera Shalhoub-Kevorkian, *Incarcerated Childhood and the Politics of Unchilding* (Cambridge, UK: Cambridge University Press, 2019).

222. Syed Muhd Khairudin Aljunied, *Colonialism, Violence and Muslims in Southeast Asia: The Maria Hertogh Controversy and Its Aftermath* (New York: Routledge, 2009); Tom Eames Hughes, *Tangled Worlds: The Story of Maria Hertogh* (Singapore: Institute of Southeast Asian Studies, 1980).

223. Mrs. Mohamed Siraj, interview by Miss Ruzita Zaki, August 4, 1995, transcribed by Ms. Chung Lai Beng, Reel 33, 496, 498.

224. Suyin, . . . *And the Rain My Drink*, 318–19.

225. "A Speech by the Queen on Her 21st Birthday, 1947," April 21, 1947, royal.uk.

226. *Malayan Police Magazine*, Coronation Issue, June 1953, Box 10, Harrison papers. For a similar display with Welsh troops, see also 2nd Bn The Royal Welch Fusiliers Scrap Book, Wrexham archives.

227. Unlabeled newspaper clippings, c. 1953, 7 GR/10 Photo Album 3, TGM. For an analysis of interracial relationships, see Chris Waters, "'Dark Strangers' in Our Midst: Discourses of Race and Nation in Britain, 1947–1963," *Journal of British Studies* 36, no. 2 (1997): 207–38; Webster, *Mixing It: Diversity in World War Two Britain.*

228. Blythe, *The Impact of Chinese Secret Societies in Malaya*, 437.

Conclusion

1. Chapman, *The Jungle Is Neutral*, 125.

2. Chapman, *The Jungle Is Neutral*, 24.

3. Joseph Conrad, *Heart of Darkness* (Blackwood's Edinburgh Magazine, 1899).

4. *Time*, cover, December 15, 1952.

5. T. N. Harper, "The Politics of the Forest in Colonial Malaya," *Modern Asian Studies* 31, no. 1 (February 1997): 1–29.

6. de Burley Wood, *The History of the King's Shropshire Light Infantry*, 100.

7. "Letter to Colin and Alison," Private Papers of J. M. Miller, Documents.20349, Box 12/47/1, IWM, 8.

8. Suyin, . . . *And the Rain My Drink*, 3, 15.

9. Khoo, *Life as the River Flows*, 85.

10. Khoo, *Life as the River Flows*, 86.

11. Keo, "A Small, Distant War?"; Ahmad Fauzi Abdul Hamid, "Malay Anti-Colonialism in British Malaya: A Re-Appraisal of Independence Fighters of Peninsular Malaysia," *Journal of Asian and African Studies* 42, no. 5 (2007): 371–98; Sze Chieh Ng, "Nostalgia and Memory: Remembering the Malayan Communist Revolution in the Online Age," 179.

12. This narrative is on full display through placards and displays in front of the Old Hill Street Police Station, the National Museum of Singapore, and the National Gallery of Singapore (visited by author in 2021). See also Kevin Blackburn and Karl Hack, *War Memory and the Making of Modern Malaysia and Singapore* (Singapore: NUS Press, 2012); Pui Huen Lim and Wong, *War and Memory in Malaysia and Singapore*, 7; Geraldine Heng and Janadas Devan, "State Fatherhood: The Politics of Nationalism, Sexuality and Race in Singapore," in *Nationalisms and Sexualities*, ed. Parker A. M. Russo, D. Summer, and P. Yaeges (New York, London: Routledge, 1992).

13. "National Service Obligation," Ministry of Foreign Affairs, Singapore, accessed July 5, 2023, https://www.mfa.gov.sg/Overseas-Mission/Chennai/Consular-Services/National-Service-Obligation.

14. Hannah Arendt, "Reflections on Violence," *New York Review*, February 27, 1969.

15. I am indebted to many rich and rewarding conversations with Melissa Shaw, Michelle Moyd, Sue Grayzel, and Tammy Proctor, for their invaluable contributions to these discussions. See for example Michelle Moyd, "African Military Historiography," *War & Society* (advance access December 2022); Michelle Moyd, "Genocide and War," in *Genocide: Key Themes*, ed. A. Dirk Moses and Donald Bloxham (Oxford: Oxford University Press, 2022); Susan Grayzel, "Men and Women at Home," in *The First World War, Vol. III: Civil Society*, ed. Peter Winter (Cambridge, UK: Cambridge University Press, 2013).

16. Suyin, . . . *And the Rain My Drink*, 268–9, 271.

17. "Hearts and Minds," directed by Peter Davis (Burbank, CA: Warner Bros. Pictures, 1974); Hannah Gurman, "Vietnam—Uprooting the Revolution: Counterinsurgency in Vietnam," in *Hearts and Minds: A People's History of Counterinsurgency*, ed. Hannah Gurman (New York and London: The New Press, 2013), 89.

18. Thompson, *Defeating Communist Insurgency*; Clutterbuck, *The Long Long War*.

19. Wen-Qing Ngoei, *Arc of Containment: Britain, the United States, and Anticommunism in Southeast Asia* (Ithaca and London: Cornell University Press, 2019).

20. John A. Nagl, *Learning to Eat Soup with a Knife: Counterinsurgency Lessons from Malaya and Vietnam* (Chicago: University of Chicago Press, 2005); Clutterbuck, *The Long Long War*; Thompson, *Defeating Communist Insurgency*; Hack, "The Malayan Emergency as Counter-Insurgency Paradigm."

SELECT BIBLIOGRAPHY

Archives
Australians at War Film Archive, University of New South Wales (Canberra, Australia)
Australian War Memorial (Canberra, Australia)
Bodleian Library, Oxford University
British Library
British Pathé
Cambridge University Library
Gurkha Museum (Winchester, UK)
Hoover Institution, Stanford University (Stanford, California)
Imperial War Museum (London, UK)
Liddell Hart Centre for Military Archives, Kings College London (London, UK)
National Archives (Kew, UK)
National Archives of Australia
National Archives of Singapore
National Army Museum (Chelsea, UK)
National Army Museum of New Zealand
National Library of Australia
National Library of New Zealand
National Library Board, NewspaperSG (Singapore)
National University of Singapore Library
Women's Voluntary Service Archive
Wrexham Archives (Wales, UK)

Printed Primary Sources and Memoirs

Allan, Sheila. *Diary of a Girl in Changi*. Pymble, NSW: Kangaroo, 2004.

Arendt, Hannah. "Reflections on Violence." *The New York Review*, February 27, 1969.

Blythe, Wilfred. *The Impact of Chinese Secret Societies in Malaya: A Historical Study*. London: Oxford University Press, 1969.

Brown, Mary, and Edwin A. Brown. *Singapore Mutiny: A Colonial Couple's Stirring Account of Combat and Survival in the 1915 Singapore Mutiny*. Singapore: Monsoon Books, 2015.

Chapman, F. Spencer. *The Jungle Is Neutral*. New York: W. W. Norton & Company, 1949.

Chin, Kee Onn. *Malaya Upside Down*. Singapore: Jitts & Co., 1946.

Choy, Elizabeth, and Shirle Gordon. "My Autobiography by Elizabeth Choy Su-Mei as Told to Shirle Gordon." *Intisari: The Research Journal of Wider Malaysia* 4, no. 1 (1973): 15–65.

de Burley Wood, Walter. *The History of the King's Shropshire Light Infantry in the Great War, 1914–1918*. London: Medici Society, 1925.

Gouldsbury, Pamela. *Jungle Nurse*. Norwich: Jarrolds, 1960.

Iwaichi, Lt. General Fujiwara. *F Kikan: Japanese Army Intelligence Operations in Southeast Asia during World War II*. Translated by Akashi Yoji. Hong Kong: Heinemann Asia, 1983.

Jeffrey, Betty. *White Coolies*. Sydney: Angus & Robertson, 1954.

The Kukri: The Journal of the Brigade of Gurkhas.

Malayan Police Magazine.

Purcell, V. W. W. S. *Malaya, Communist or Free?* Stanford: Stanford University Press, 1954.

Singh, Mohan. *Soldiers' Contributions to Indian Independence: The Epic of the Indian National Army*. New Delhi: S. Attar Singh, Army Educational Stores, 1974.

Suyin, Han. . . . *And the Rain My Drink*. London: Jonathan Cape, 1956.

Te Ao Hou (The New World).

Thatcher, Dorothy, and Robert Cross. *Pai Naa: The Story of Nona Baker*. London: Constable, 1959.

Thorat, S. P. P. *From Reveille to Retreat*. New Delhi: Allied Publishers Private Limited, 1985.

Sareen, Tilak Raj. *Secret Documents on Singapore Mutiny, 1915*. New Delhi: Mounto Publishing House, 1995.

Secondary Sources

Abraham, Colin E. R. "Racial and Ethnic Manipulation in Colonial Malaya." *Ethnic and Racial Studies* 6, no. 1 (1983): 18–32.

Aiyar, Sana. *Indians in Kenya: The Politics of Diaspora*. Cambridge, MA: Harvard University Press, 2015.

Aljunied, Syed Muhd Khairudin. "Against Multiple Hegemonies: Radical Malay Women in Colonial Malaya." *Journal of Social History* 47, no. 1 (Fall 2013): 153–75.

Aljunied, Syed Muhd Khairudin. *Colonialism, Violence and Muslims in Southeast Asia: The Maria Hertogh Controversy and Its Aftermath*. New York: Routledge, 2009.

Aljunied, Syed Muhd Khairudin. "The Prison and the Anti-Colonialist in British Malaya." *Journal of Historical Sociology* 25, no. 3 (September 2012): 386–412.

Aljunied, Syed Muhd Khairudin. *Radicals: Resistance and Protest in Colonial Malaya*. Delkab: Northern Illinois University Press, 2015.

Arditti, Roger C. *Counterinsurgency Intelligence and the Emergency in Malaya*. New York: Palgrave Macmillan, 2019.

Arnold, David. "Touching the Body: Perspectives on the Indian Plague, 1896–1900." *Selected Subaltern Studies* (1988): 391–426.

Arthur, William. "The Padang, the Sahib and the Sepoy—The Role of the Indian Army in Malaya, 1945 to 1946." PhD diss., Oxford University, 2013.

Atkinson, David. *The Burden of White Supremacy: Containing Asian Migration in the British Empire and the United States*. Chapel Hill: University of North Carolina Press, 2017.

Baillargeon, David. "Spaces of Occupation: Colonial Enclosure and Confinement in British Malaya." *Journal of Historical Geography* 73 (2021): 24–35.

Barczewski, Stephanie. *Heroic Failure and the British*. New Haven: Yale University Press, 2016.

Barkawi, Tarak. *Soldiers of Empire: Indian and British Armies in World War II*. Cambridge, UK: Cambridge University Press, 2017.

Barnard, Timothy P. *Contesting Malayness: Malay Identity across Boundaries*. Singapore: NUS Press, 2018.

Bayly, C. A., and Tim Harper. *Forgotten Armies: Britain's Asian Empire and the War with Japan*. London: Penguin, 2005.

Bayly, C. A., and Tim Harper. *Forgotten Wars: Freedom and Revolution in Southeast Asia*. Cambridge, MA: Harvard University Press, 2010.

Bellenoit, Hayden. "Missionary Education, Religion and Knowledge in India, c. 1880 1915." *Modern Asian Studies* 41, no. 2 (2007): 369–94.

Bhabha, Homi K. *The Location of Culture*. London: Routledge, 1994.

Bhatia, Umej. *Our Name Is Mutiny: The Global Revolt against the Raj and the Hidden History of the Singapore Mutiny 1907–1915.* Singapore: Landmark Books, 2020.

Blackburn, Kevin, and Karl Hack. *War Memory and the Making of Modern Malaysia and Singapore*. Singapore: NUS Press, 2012.

Bose, Sugata. *His Majesty's Opponent: Subhas Chandra Bose and India's Struggle against Empire*. Cambridge, MA: Harvard University Press, 2012.

Burton, Antoinette. *Africa in the Indian Imagination: Race and the Politics of Postcolonial Citation*. Durham: Duke University Press, 2016.

Carter, Marina, and Crispin Bates. *Mutiny at the Margins: New Perspectives on the Indian Uprising of 1857*. New Delhi: Sage Publications, 2013.

Chaudhuri, Nupur. "Memsahibs and Their Servants in Nineteenth-Century India." *Women's History Review* 3, no. 4 (1994): 549–62.

Cheah Boon, Kheng. *Red Star over Malaya: Resistance and Social Conflict during and after the Japanese Occupation of Malaya, 1941–46*. Singapore: National University of Singapore Press, 2003.

Cheng, Anne Anlin. *Ornamentalism*. Oxford: Oxford University Press, 2019.

Chieh Sze, Jason Ng. "Nostalgia and Memory: Remembering the Malayan Communist Revolution in the Online Age." In *The Asia-Pacific in the Age of Transnational Mobility: The Search for Community and Identity on and through Social Media*, edited by Catherine Gomes, 169–96. Cambridge, UK: Cambridge University Press, 2017.

Chin, Aloysius. *The Communist Party of Malaya: The Inside Story*. Kuala Lumpur: Vinpress, 1994.

Chin, C. C., and Karl Hack, eds. *Dialogues with Chin Peng: New Light on the Malayan Communist Party*. Singapore: Singapore University Press, 2005.

Choon, Ban Kah, and Yap Hong Kuan. *Rehearsal for War: The Underground War against the Japanese*. Singapore: Horizon Books, 2002.

Clutterbuck, Richard. *The Long Long War: The Emergency in Malaya, 1948–1960*. London: Cassell, 1967.

Comber, Leon. *Malaya's Secret Police, 1945–60: The Role of the Special Branch in the Malayan Emergency*. Singapore: Institute of Southeast Asian Studies, and Australia: Monash Asia Institute, 2008.

Comber, Leon. *Templer and the Road to Malayan Independence: The Man and His Time*. Singapore: Institute of Southeast Asian Studies, 2015.

Cormac, Rory. *Confronting the Colonies: British Intelligence and Counterinsurgency.* Oxford: Oxford University Press, 2014.

Cornelius-Takahama, Vernon. "Indian Convicts' Contributions to Early Singapore (1825–1873)." National Library of Singapore. Accessed November 26, 2021. https://eresources.nlb.gov.sg/infopedia/articles/SIP_39_2005-02-02 .html.

Cross, J. P., and Buddhiman Gurung, eds. *Gurkhas at War: Eyewitness Accounts From World War II to Iraq.* London: Greenhill Books, 2007.

Daddis, Gregory. *Pulp Vietnam: War and Gender in Cold War Men's Adventure Magazines.* Cambridge, UK: Cambridge University Press, 2020.

Das, Santanu. *India, Empire, and First World War Culture: Writings, Images, Songs.* Cambridge, UK: Cambridge University Press, 2018.

Datta, Arunima. *Fleeting Agencies: A Social History of Indian Coolie Women in British Malaya.* Cambridge, UK: Cambridge University Press, 2021.

Datta, Arunima. "Negotiating Gendered Spaces in Colonial Press: Wives of European planters in British Malaya." *Journal of Colonialism and Colonial History* 18, no. 3 (Winter 2017).

Datta, Arunima. "Social Memory and Indian Women from Malaya and Singapore in the Rani of Jhansi Regiment." *Journal of the Malaysian Branch of the Royal Asiatic Society* 88, 2, no. 309 (December 2015): 77–103.

Daws, Gavan. *Prisoners of the Japanese.* New York: William Morrow & Co., 1994.

Dennis, P., and J. Grey. *Emergency and Confrontation: Australian Military Operations in Malaya and Borneo 1950–1966.* Sydney: Allen and Unwin and the Australian War Memorial, 1996.

Des Chene, Mary Katherine. "Relics of Empire: A Cultural History of the Gurkhas, 1815–1987." PhD diss., Stanford University, 1991.

Dhamoon, Rita Kaur, Davina Bhandar, Renisa Mawani, and Satwinder Kaur Bains, eds. *Unmooring the Komagata Maru: Charting Colonial Trajectories.* Vancouver: UBS Press, 2019.

Doan, Laura. *Disturbing Practices: History, Sexuality, and Women's Experience of Modern War.* Chicago: University of Chicago Press, 2013.

Drohan, Brian. *Brutality in an Age of Human Rights: Activism and Counterinsurgency at the End of the British Empire.* Ithaca and London: Cornell University Press, 2017.

Elkins, Caroline. *Legacy of Violence: A History of the British Empire.* New York: Penguin, 2022.

Farrell, Brian P. *The Defence and Fall of Singapore, 1940–1942.* Gloucestershire: Tempus Publishing Group, 2005.

Florvil, Tiffany. *Mobilizing Black Germany: Afro-German Women and the Making of a Transnational Movement.* Champaign: University of Illinois Press, 2020.

Fogarty, Richard. *Race and War in France: Colonial Subjects in the French Army, 1914–1918.* Baltimore: The Johns Hopkins University Press, 2008.

Forth, Aidan. *Barbed-Wire Imperialism: Britain's Empire of Camps, 1876–1903.* Berkeley: University of California Press, 2017.

French, David. *The British Way in Counter-Insurgency, 1945–1967.* Oxford: Oxford University Press, 2012.

Fuentes, Marisa. *Dispossessed Lives: Enslaved Women, Violence, and the Archive.* Philadelphia: University of Pennsylvania Press, 2016.

Fujitani, Takashi. *Race for Empire: Koreans as Japanese and Japanese as Americans during World War II.* Berkeley: University of California Press, 2011.

Gopinath, Aruna. *Footprints on the Sands of Time: Rasammah Bhupalan: A Life of Purpose.* Kuala Lumpur: Arkib Negara Malaysia, 2007.

Goscha, Christopher E., and Christian F. Ostermann. *Connecting Histories: Decolonization and the Cold War in Southeast Asia, 1945–1962.* Stanford: Stanford University Press, 2009.

Grant, Lachlan. *Australian Soldiers in Asia-Pacific in World War II.* Sydney: NewSouth, 2014.

Grayzel, Susan. "Men and Women at Home." In *The First World War, Vol. III: Civil Society,* edited by Peter Winter. Cambridge, UK: Cambridge University Press, 2013.

Gregorian, Raffi. *The British Army, the Gurkhas, and Cold War Strategy in the Far East, 1947–1954.* New York: Palgrave, 2002.

Grob-Fitzgibbon, Benjamin. *Imperial Endgame: Britain's Dirty Wars and the End of Empire.* New York: Palgrave Macmillan, 2011.

Guha, Ranajit. *Dominance without Hegemony: History and Power in Colonial India.* Cambridge, MA: Harvard University Press, 1998.

Guha, Ranajit. *Elementary Aspects of Peasant Insurgency in Colonial India.* Durham: Duke University Press, 1999.

Guha, Ranajit. "The Prose of Counter-Insurgency." In *Selected Subaltern Studies,* edited by Ranajit Guha and Gayatri Chakravorty Spivak, 45–86. Oxford: Oxford University Press, 1988.

Gurman, Hannah, ed. *Hearts and Minds: A People's History of Counterinsurgency.* New York and London: The New Press, 2013.

Hack, Karl. *Defence and Decolonisation in Southeast Asia: Britain, Malaya and Singapore, 1941–1968.* Richmond, UK: Routledge Curzon, 2001.

Hack, Karl. "Detention, Deportation and Resettlement: British Counterinsurgency and Malaya's Rural Chinese, 1948–60." *The Journal of Imperial and Commonwealth History* 43, no. 4 (2015): 611–40.

Hack, Karl. "The Malayan Emergency as Counter-Insurgency Paradigm." *Journal of Strategic Studies* 32, no. 3 (2009).

Hack, Karl. *The Malayan Emergency: Revolution and Counterinsurgency at the End of Empire*. Cambridge, UK: Cambridge University Press, 2021.

Hack, Karl, and Kevin Blackburn, eds. *Forgotten Captives in Japanese-Occupied Asia*. New York: Routledge, 2008.

Haggis, Jane. "Gendering Colonialism or Colonising Gender? Recent Women's Studies Approaches to White Women and the History of British Colonialism." *Women's Studies International Forum* 13, nos. 1–2 (1990): 105–15.

Hamid, Ahmad Fauzi Abdul. "Malay Anti-Colonialism in British Malaya A Re-Appraisal of Independence Fighters of Peninsular Malaysia." *Journal of Asian and African Studies* 42, no. 5 (2007): 371–98.

Haron, Nadzan. "Colonial Defence and British Approach to the Problems in Malaya." *Modern Asian Studies* 24, no. 2 (1990): 275–95.

Harper, T. N. *The End of Empire and the Making of Malaya*. Cambridge, UK: Cambridge University Press, 1999.

Harper, T. N. "The Politics of the Forest in Colonial Malaya." *Modern Asian Studies* 31, no. 1 (February 1997): 1–29.

Harper, Tim. "Singapore, 1915, and the Birth of the Asian Underground." *Modern Asian Studies* 47, no. 6 (November 2013): 1782–811.

Harper, Tim. *Underground Asia: Global Revolutionaries and the Assault on Empire*. Cambridge, MA: Harvard University Press, 2021.

Higginbotham, Evelyn Brooks. "African-American Women's History and the Metalanguage of Race." *Signs* 17, no. 2 (Winter, 1992): 251–74.

Hopkins, B. D. "The Problem with 'Hearts and Minds' in Afghanistan." *Middle East Report* 255 (Summer 2010). https://merip.org/2010/05/the-problem-with-hearts-and-minds-in-afghanistan/.

Hsu, Madeline Y. *The Good Immigrants: How the Yellow Peril Became the Model Minority*. Princeton: Princeton University Press, 2015.

Hughes, Tom Eames. *Tangled Worlds: The Story of Maria Hertogh*. Singapore: Institute of Southeast Asian Studies, 1980.

Hui, Tan Beng. "'Protecting' Women: Legislation and Regulation of Women's Sexuality in Colonial Malaya." *Gender, Technology and Development* 7, no. 1 (2003): 1–30.

Imy, Kate. "Dream Mother: Race, Gender, and Intimacy in Japanese-Occupied Singapore." *Journal of Southeast Asian Studies* 52, no. 3 (September 2021): 464–91.

Imy, Kate. *Faithful Fighters: Identity and Power in the British Indian Army.* Stanford: Stanford University Press, 2019.

Imy, Kate. "Fascist Yogis: Martial Bodies and Imperial Impotence." *Journal of British Studies* 55, no. 2 (April 2016): 320–43.

Imy, Kate. "Queering the Martial Races: Masculinity, Sex and Circumcision in the Twentieth Century British Indian Army." *Gender & History* 27, no. 2 (August 2015): 374–96.

Jacobson, Liesbeth Rosen. "The Eurasian Question: The Colonial Position and Postcolonial Options of Colonial Mixed Ancestry Groups from British India, Dutch East Indies and French Indochina Compared." PhD diss., University of Leiden, 2018. https://openaccess.leidenuniv.nl/handle/1887/62456.

Jain, Ravindra K. *South Indians on the Plantation Frontier in Malaya.* New Haven: Yale University Press, 1970.

Jung, Moon-Ho. *The Rising Tide of Color: Race, State, Violence, and Radical Movements Across the Pacific.* Seattle: University of Washington Press, 2014.

Kah Sengh, Loh, Ernest Koh, and Stephen Dobbs. *Oral History in Southeast Asia: Memories and Fragments.* New York: Palgrave Macmillan, 2013.

Kathigasu, Sybil. *No Dram of Mercy.* London: Wyman & Sons Ltd., 1959.

Kazue, Muta. "The 'Comfort Women' Issue and the Embedded Culture of Sexual Violence in Contemporary Japan." *Current Sociology Monograph* 64, no. 4 (2016): 620–36.

Kennedy, Joseph. *When Singapore Fell: Evacuations and Escapes, 1941–42.* New York: St. Martin's Press, 1989.

Kenneison, Rebecca. *Playing for Malaya: A Eurasian Family in the Pacific War.* Singapore: NUS Press, 2012.

Kenneison, Rebecca. *The Special Operations Executive in Malaya: World War II and the Path to Independence.* London: Bloomsbury Academic, 2019.

Kenny, Catherine. *Captives: Australian Army Nurses in Japanese Prison Camps.* St. Lucia: University of Queensland Press, 1986.

Khan, Yasmin. *India at War: The Subcontinent and the Second World War.* Oxford: Oxford University Press, 2015.

Khoo, Agnes. *Life as the River Flows: Women in the Malayan Anti-Colonial Struggle.* Monmouth, Wales: Merlin Press, 2004.

Kolsky, Elizabeth. *Colonial Justice in British India: White Violence and the Rule of Law.* Cambridge, UK: Cambridge University Press, 2011.

Kovner, Sarah. *Prisoners of the Empire: POWs and Their Captors in the Pacific.* Cambridge, MA: Harvard University Press, 2020.

Kratoska, Paul H. *Asian Labor in the Wartime Japanese Empire: Unknown Histories.* New York: Routledge, 2005.

Kratoska, Paul. *The Japanese Occupation of Malaya, 1941–1945.* Honolulu: University of Hawaii Press, 1997.

Kuwajima, Sho. *First World War and Asia: Indian Mutiny in Singapore (1915).* Osaka: Sho Kuwajima, 1988.

Lal, Brij V. *Broken Waves: A History of the Fiji Islands in the Twentieth Century.* Honolulu: University of Hawaii Press, 1992.

Lebra, Joyce Chapman. *Women against the Raj: The Rani of Jhansi Regiment.* Singapore: Institute of Southeast Asian Studies, 2008.

Lee, Kam Hing. "A Neglected Story: Christian Missionaries, Chinese New Villagers, and Communists in the Battle for The 'Hearts and Minds' in Malaya, 1948–1960." *Modern Asian Studies* 47, no. 6 (2013): 1977–2006.

Lees, Lynn Hollen. *Planting Empire, Cultivating Subjects: British Malaya, 1786–1941.* Cambridge, UK: Cambridge University Press, 2017.

Leow, Rachel. "Age as a Category of Gender Analysis: Servant Girls, Modern Girls, and Gender in Southeast Asia." *The Journal of Asian Studies* 71, no. 4 (November 2012): 975–90.

Leow, Rachel. *Taming Babel: Language in the Making of Malaysia.* Cambridge, UK: Cambridge University Press, 2016.

Lewis, Su Lin. "Cosmopolitanism and the Modern Girl: A Cross-Cultural Discourse in 1930s Penang." *Modern Asian Studies* 43, no. 6 (November 2009): 1385–419.

Liburd, Liam J. "Beyond the Pale: Whiteness, Masculinity and Empire in the British Union of Fascists, 1932–1940." *Fascism: Journal of Comparative Fascist Studies* 7, no. 2 (October 2018). https://brill.com/view/journals/fasc/7/2/article-p275_275.xml#d16111169e415.

Lim, Teck Ghee. "British Colonial Administration and the 'Ethnic Division of Labour' in Malaya." *Kajian Malaysia* 2, no. 2 (1984): 28–66.

Loh Kok Wah, Francis. *Beyond the Tin Mines: Coolies, Squatters and New Villagers in the Kinta Valley, Malaysia, c. 1880–1980.* Singapore: Oxford University Press, 1988.

Lovering, Timothy John. "Authority and Identity: Malawian Soldiers in Britain's Colonial Army, 1861–1964." PhD diss., University of Stirling, September 2002.

Low, Choo Chin. "Immigration Control During the Malayan Emergency: Borders, Belonging and Citizenship, 1948–1960." *Journal of the Malaysian Branch of the Royal Asiatic Society* 89, no. 1 (2016): 35–60.

Low, Choo Chin. "The Repatriation of the Chinese as a Counterinsurgency Policy during the Malayan Emergency." *Journal of Southeast Asian Studies* 45, no. 3 (October 2014): 363–92.

Man, Simeon. *Soldiering through Empire: Race and the Decolonizing Pacific.* Berkeley: University of California Press, 2018.

Manchanda, Nivi. *Imagining Afghanistan: The History and Politics of Imperial Knowledge.* Cambridge, UK: Cambridge University Press, 2020.

Manderson, Lenore. "Colonial Desires: Sexuality, Race, and Gender in British Malaya." *Journal of the History of Sexuality* 7, no. 3 (January 1997): 372–88.

Manickam, Sandra Khor. "Race and the Colonial Universe in British Malaya." *Journal of Southeast Asian Studies* 40, no. 3 (October 2009): 593–612.

Marston, Daniel. *The Indian Army at the End of the Raj.* Cambridge, UK: Cambridge University Press, 2014.

Marston, Daniel P., and Chandar S. Sundaram. *A Military History of India and South Asia.* Westport, CT, and London: Praeger Security International, 2007.

McClintock, Anne. *Imperial Leather: Race, Gender, and Sexuality in the Colonial Contest.* New York: Routledge, 1995.

McGregor, Katharine. "Emotions and Activism for Former So-Called 'Comfort Women' of the Japanese Occupation of the Netherlands East Indies." *Women's Studies International Forum* 54 (2016): 67–78.

Menon, K. A. K. *From the Diary of a Freedom Fighter.* Madras: Kavungal Anat, 1989.

Milner, Anthony. *The Invention of Politics in Colonial Malaya: Contesting Nationalism and the Expansion of the Public Sphere.* Cambridge, UK: Cambridge University Press, 1995.

Mitcham, John. *Race and Imperial Defence in the British World, 1870–1914.* Cambridge, UK: Cambridge University Press, 2016.

Mok, Florence. "Disseminating and Containing Communist Propaganda to Overseas Chinese in Southeast Asia through Hong Kong, the Cold War Pivot, 1949–1960." *The Historical Journal* (2021): 1–21.

Moore, Bob, and Barbara Hately-Broad, eds. *Prisoners of War, Prisoners of Peace: Captivity, Homecoming and Memory in World War II.* Oxford: Berg, 2005.

Moyd, Michelle. "African Military Historiography." *War & Society* (advance access December 2022).

Moyd, Michelle. "Genocide and War." In *Genocide: Key Themes,* edited by A. Dirk Moses and Donald Bloxham. Oxford: Oxford University Press, 2022.

Moyd, Michelle. *Violent Intermediaries: African Soldiers, Conquest, and Everyday Colonialism in German East Africa.* Athens, OH: Ohio University Press, 2014.

Moyn, Samuel. *Humane: How the United States Abandoned Peace and Reinvented War.* New York: Farrar, Straus and Giroux, 2021.

Murfett, Malcolm H., John N. Miksic, Brian P. Farrell, and Chiang Ming Shun. *Between Two Oceans: A Military History of Singapore from 1275 to 1971.* Singapore: Marshall Cavendish Editions, 2011.

Musa, Mahani. "Women in the Malayan Communist Party, 1942–89." *Journal of Southeast Asian Studies* 44, no. 2 (June 2013): 226–49.

Nagl, John A. *Learning to Eat Soup with a Knife: Counterinsurgency Lessons from Malaya and Vietnam.* Chicago: University of Chicago Press, 2005.

Newsinger, John. *British Counterinsurgency.* New York: Palgrave Macmillan, 2015.

Nonini, Donald M. "At That Time We Were Intimidated on All Sides": Residues of the Malayan Emergency as a Conjunctural Episode of Dispossession." *Critical Asian Studies* 47, no. 3 (2015): 337–58.

Noor, Farish. "'Racial Profiling' Revisited: The 1915 Indian Sepoy Mutiny in Singapore and the Impact of Profiling on Religious and Ethnic Minorities." *Politics, Religion & Ideology* 12, no. 1 (2011): 89–100.

Noor, Farish A., and Peter Carey, eds. *Racial Difference and the Colonial Wars of 19th Century Southeast Asia.* Amsterdam: Amsterdam University Press, 2021.

Nünning, Vera. "'Daß Jeder Seine Pflicht thue.' Die Bedeutung der Indian Mutiny für das Nationale Britische Selbstverständnis." *Archiv für Kulturgeschichte* 78 (1996).

Omissi, David. *Air Power and Colonial Control: The Royal Air Force, 1919–1939.* Manchester: Manchester University Press, 1990.

Omissi, David. *Indian Voices of the Great War: Soldiers' Letters, 1914–18.* New York: Palgrave Macmillan, 1999.

Omissi, David. *The Sepoy and the Raj: The Indian Army, 1860–1940.* London: Macmillan, 1994.

Ooi, Keat Gin. "The 'Slapping Monster' and Other Stories: Recollections of the Japanese Occupation (1941–1945) of Borneo through Autobiographies, Biographies, Memoirs, and Other Ego-Documents." *Journal of Colonialism and Colonial History* 7, no. 3 (Winter 2006).

Oostindie, Gert, Ben Schoenmaker, and Frank Van Vree. *Beyond the Pale: Dutch Extreme Violence in the Indonesian War of Independence, 1945–1949*. Amsterdam: University of Amsterdam Press, 2022.

Otele, Olivette. *African Europeans: An Untold Story*. New York: Basic Books, 2021.

Parsons, Timothy. *The African Rank-and-File: Social Implications of Colonial Military Service in the King's African Rifles, 1902–1964*. Portsmouth, NH: Heinemann, 1999.

Parsons, Timothy. "Dangerous Education? The Army as School in Colonial East Africa." *The Journal of Imperial and Commonwealth History* 28, no. 1 (January 2000).

Powell, Avril. *Muslims and Missionaries in Pre-Mutiny India*. New York and London: Routledge, 1995.

Pugsley, Christopher. *From Emergency to Confrontation: The New Zealand Armed Forces in Malaya and Borneo 1949–1966*. South Melbourne, Victoria: Oxford University Press, 2003.

Pui Huen Lim, Patricia, and Diana Wong. *War and Memory in Malaysia and Singapore*. Singapore: Institute of Southeast Asian Studies, 2000.

Ramakrishna, Kumar. *Emergency Propaganda: The Winning of Malayan Hearts and Minds, 1948–1958*. Richmond, UK: Routledge Curzon, 2002.

Ramnath, Maia. *Haj to Utopia: How the Ghadar Movement Charted Global Radicalism and Attempted to Overthrow the British Empire*. Berkeley and Los Angeles: University of California Press, 2011.

Rand, Gavin, and Kim Wagner. "Recruiting the 'Martial Races': Identities and Military Service in Colonial India." *Patterns of Prejudice* 46, nos. 3–4 (2012).

Roy, Kaushik. *Brown Warriors of the Raj: Recruitment & the Mechanics of Command in the Sepoy Army, 1859–1913*. New Delhi: Manohar, 2008.

Rudolph, Susanne Hoeber, Lloyd L. Rudolph, and Mohan Singh Kanota, eds. *Reversing the Gaze: Amar Singh's Diary, a Colonial Subject's Narrative of Imperial India*. Boulder, CO: Westview Press, 2002.

Rush, Anne Spry. *Bonds of Empire: West Indians and Britishness from Victoria to Decolonization*. Oxford: Oxford University Press, 2011.

Saha, Jonathan. "Whiteness, Masculinity and the Ambivalent Embodiment of 'British Justice' in Colonial Burma." *Cultural and Social History* 14, no. 4 (2017): 527–42.

Sareen, T. R. *Japan and the Indian National Army*. Delhi: Agam Prakashan, 1986.

Satia, Priya. "The Defense of Inhumanity: Air Control and the British Idea of Arabia." *American Historical Review* (February 2006): 16–51.

Scheer, Monique. "Are Emotions a Kind of Practice (And Is That What Makes Them Have a History)? A Bourdieuian Approach to Understanding Emotion." *History and Theory* 51, no. 2 (May 2012): 193–220.

Scott, Joan. "The Evidence of Experience." *Critical Inquiry* 17, no. 4 (Summer 1991): 773–97.

Sengupta, Nilanjana. *A Gentleman's Word: The Legacy of Subhash Chandra Bose in Southeast Asia.* Singapore: Institute of Southeast Asian Studies, 2012.

Shalhoub-Kevorkian, Nadera. *Incarcerated Childhood and the Politics of Unchilding.* Cambridge: Cambridge University Press, 2019.

Shaw, Melissa N. "'Women Who Used to Run the UNIA Hall': Black Canadian Women's Garveyite Leadership in Toronto's UNIA Division #21, 1919–1939" (forthcoming).

Sherman, Taylor. *State Violence and Punishment in India.* New York: Routledge, 2010.

Shome, Raka. "'Global Motherhood': The Transnational Intimacies of White Femininity." *Critical Studies in Media Communication* 28, no. 5 (2011): 388–406.

Short, Anthony. *The Communist Insurrection in Malaya, 1948–1960.* London: Muller, 1975.

Singh, Gajendra. *The Testimonies of Indian Soldiers and the Two World Wars: Between Self and Sepoy.* London: Bloomsbury, 2014.

Singha, Radhika. *The Coolie's Great War: Indian Labour in a Global Conflict, 1914–1921.* London: Hurst, 2020.

Sinha, Mrinalini. *Colonial Masculinity: The "Manly Englishman" and the "Effeminate Bengali" in the Late Nineteenth Century.* Manchester: Manchester University Press, 1995.

Siver, Christi. "Enemies or Friendlies? British Military Behavior toward Civilians during the Malayan Emergency." In *Military Interventions, War Crimes, and Protecting Civilians,* 57–89. New York: Palgrave, 2018.

Smith, Simon. "General Templer and Counter-Insurgency in Malaya: Hearts and Minds, Intelligence, and Propaganda." *Intelligence and National Security* 16, no. 3 (2001): 60–78.

Snow, Karen A. "Russia and the 1915 Indian Mutiny in Singapore." *South East Asia Research* 5, no. 3 (1997): 295–315.

Stapleton, Tim. "'Bad Boys': Infiltration and Sedition in the African Military Units of the Central African Federation (Malawi, Zambia and Zimbabwe) 1953–63." *The Journal of Military History* 73, no. 4 (October 2009): 1167–93.

Stockwell, J. A. "Chin Peng and the Struggle for Malaya." *Journal of the Royal Asiatic Society* 16, no. 3 (November 2006): 279–97.

Stoler, Ann Laura. "'In Cold Blood': Hierarchies of Credibility and the Politics of Colonial Narratives." *Representations* 37 (1992): 151–89.

Stoler, Ann Laura. "Making Empire Respectable: The Politics of Race and Sexual Morality in 20th Century Colonial Cultures." *American Ethnologist* 16, no. 4 (1989): 634–60.

Stoler, Ann Laura. "Rethinking Colonial Categories: European Communities and the Boundaries of Rule." *Comparative Studies in Society and History* 31, no. 1 (January 1989): 134–61.

Stoler, Ann Laura. "Sexual Affronts and Racial Frontiers: European Identities and the Cultural Politics of Exclusion in Colonial Southeast Asia." *Comparative Studies in Society and History* 34, no. 3 (July 1992): 514–51.

Streets, Heather. *Martial Races: The Military, Race, and Masculinity in British Imperial Culture 1857–1914*. Manchester: Manchester University Press, 2004.

Streets-Salter, Heather. "The Noulens Affair in East and Southeast Asia International Communism in the Interwar Period." *Journal of American-East Asian Relations* (November 26, 2014): 394–414.

Streets-Salter, Heather. *World War One in Southeast Asia: Colonialism and Anticolonialism in an Era of Global Conflict*. Cambridge, UK: Cambridge University Press, 2017.

Strobel, Margaret. *European Women and the Second British Empire*. Bloomington: Indiana University Press 1991.

Stubbs, Richard. *Hearts and Minds in Guerilla Warfare—the Malayan Emergency, 1948–1960*. Oxford: Oxford University Press, 1989.

Tan, Bonny. "Convict Labour in Colonial Singapore." National Library Singapore. October 1, 2015. https://biblioasia.nlb.gov.sg/vol-11/issue-3/oct-dec-2015/convict.

Tan, Teng Phee. *Behind Barbed Wire: Chinese New Villages during the Malayan Emergency, 1948–1960*. Petaling Jaya: Strategic Information and Research Development Centre, 2020.

Tan, Teng Phee. "'Like a Concentration Camp, Iah': Chinese Grassroots Experience of the Emergency and New Villages in British Malaya." *Chinese Southern Diaspora Studies* 3 (2009): 216–28.

Tan, Teng Phee. "Oral History and People's Memory of the Malayan Emergency (1948–60): The Case of Pulai." *SOJOURN: Journal of Social Issues in Southeast Asia* 27, no. 1 (2012): 84–119.

Tan, Tik Loong Stanley, and Tay Huiwen Michelle. *Syonan Years, 1942–1945: Living Beneath the Rising Sun.* Singapore: National Archives of Singapore, 2009.

Tanka, Yuki. *Hidden Horrors: Japanese War Crimes in WWII.* Boulder, CO: Westview, 1996.

Tatla, Darshan S. "Incorporating Regional Events into the Nationalist Narrative: The Life of Gurdit Singh and the Komagata Maru Episode in Postcolonial India." *South Asian Diaspora* 8, no. 2 (2016): 125–46.

Taylor, Jeremy. "'Not a Particularly Happy Expression': 'Malayanization' and the China Threat in Britain's Late-Colonial Southeast Asian Territories." *Journal of Asian Studies* 78, no. 4 (November 2019): 789–808.

Taylor, Jeremy E., and Lanjun Xu, eds. *Chineseness and the Cold War: Contested Cultures and Diaspora in Southeast Asia and Hong Kong.* London: Routledge, 2021.

Taylor, Sandra C. *Vietnamese Women at War: Fighting for Ho Chi Minh and the Revolution.* Lawrence: University Press of Kansas, 1999.

Thompson, Robert. *Defeating Communist Insurgency: Experiences from Malaya and Vietnam.* London: Chatto & Windus, 1966.

Twomey, Christina. *Australia's Forgotten Prisoners: Civilians Interned by the Japanese in World War Two.* Cambridge, UK: Cambridge University Press, 2007.

Viswanathan, Gauri. *Masks of Conquest: Literary Study and British Rule in India.* New York: Columbia University Press, 2014.

Walker, Kristy. "Intimate Interactions: Eurasian Family Histories in Colonial Penang." *Modern Asian Studies* 26, no. 2 (2012).

Webster, Wendy. *Mixing It: Diversity in World War Two Britain.* Oxford: Oxford University Press, 2020.

Wen-Qing, Ngoei. *Arc of Containment: Britain, the United States, and Anticommunism in Southeast Asia.* Ithaca and London: Cornell University Press, 2019.

Wu, Jialin Christina. "'A Life of Make-Believe': Being Boy Scouts and 'Playing Indian' in British Malaya, (1910–42)." *Gender & History* 26, no. 3 (November 2014): 589–619.

Xu, Guoqi. *Asia in the Great War.* Oxford: Oxford University Press, 2017.

Yao, Souchou. *The Malayan Emergency: Essays on a Small, Distant War.* York, PA: Maple Press, 2016.

Yap, Felicia. "Eurasians in British Asia during the Second World War." *Journal of the Royal Asiatic Society* S3, 21, no. 4 (2011).

Yap, Felicia. "Prisoners of War and Civilian Internees of the Japanese in British Asia: The Similarities and Contrasts of Experience." *Journal of Contemporary History* 47, no. 2 (2012).

Yoshimi, Yoshiaki. *Comfort Women: Sexual Slavery in the Japanese Military during World War II.* Cambridge, UK: Cambridge University Press, 2002.

INDEX

Allan, Sheila, 11, 172; experience of
Japanese invasion and British
surrender, 94, 101, 110–14; experience
of Japanese occupation, 118, 124,
128–35, 139
. . . *And the Rain My Drink. See* Han
Suyin
askari, 6, 188–92, 200. *See also* King's
African Rifles

Bahau, 63, 126, 196, 280n103
Baker, Nona, 95, 117
banishment. *See* China: British policy of
banishment to
Bhupalan, Rasammah, 115, 139, 145, 152,
153
Bose, S.C., 149, 151–53
boycotts, 10, 55–56, 61, 64, 65
Briggs, Harold, 6–7, 203, 237, 248
British Indian Army. *See* Indian Army
(British); Indian National Army

Changi, 110, 130, 135; experiences at
Katong and march to, 120–21, 131;
POW experiences of, 106, 144,
148; witnesses to Sook Ching, 103,
104, 106; women's prison camp
experiences, 101, 114, 118, 121–28,

133–34. *See also* internment; Sheila
Allan; Cicely Williams
Chapman, F. Spencer, early war
impressions and recommendations, 81,
94, 102, 105, 155, 182; life in jungle with
guerillas, 156–60, 170–72, 223, 244–45
China, 15, 17, 57, 73; British attitudes
toward people from or connected to,
5, 7, 12, 23, 28, 29, 30, 55, 56, 58, 68,
70, 73, 75, 82, 83, 85, 91, 107, 111, 135,
137, 155–69, 172, 173–76, 189, 203–5,
218–26, 231–41, 246; British policy of
repatriation and banishment to, 56,
58, 59, 60, 63, 178, 213, 218, 223, 242,
301n123; demographics in Singapore
and Malaya of people from, 14,
56–57, 69, 76, 237; Japanese relations
with, 48, 56, 64, 65, 101, 102, 116, 150;
migration to Singapore from, 5, 14,
15, 56–57, 59, 60, 69, 72, 73, 75–76, 77,
101, 173, 174, 196, 237, 238; military
and police contributions of people
connected to, 28, 33, 42, 57–58, 63, 78,
80, 94, 113, 143–44, 155–69, 183, 215,
226–34, 245, 246; nationalism related
to, 48, 56, 58, 59, 60, 61, 64, 65, 155, 161,
162, 174, 175; secret societies and, 55,
56, 57, 67, 68, 174, 175. *See also* boycotts;

167; German subjects and British policies of, 17, 24, 26, 33, 37; Japanese subjects and British policies of, 80, 93, 94, 100, 246. *See also* Changi; New Villages; Prisoners of War (POW)

Japan, 15, 16, 60, 134, 176, 234; British attitudes toward and relations with, 47, 48, 77, 86, 89, 93, 94, 95, 100, 106, 138–39, 140, 141–42, 146, 170, 172, 178, 206; Chinese attitudes toward and relations with, 56, 57, 58, 61, 64, 65, 89, 101, 102, 103–6, 136, 143, 144, 154–58, 160, 161, 162, 163, 165–66, 167, 174–75, 183, 213; Indian attitudes toward and relations with, 88, 89, 90, 143, 146–54; Japanese Empire, 66, 76, 77, 101, 103, 145; Second World War invasion and occupation of Malaya and Singapore by, 1, 2, 10–11, 12, 79, 80, 81, 87, 89, 91, 92, 94, 95, 98, 102–8, 109–23, 125–26, 128, 131, 134, 136, 140, 141–63, 165–66, 171, 177, 183, 189, 192, 202, 205, 212, 222, 223, 234–35, 244–45, 246; Singapore Mutiny and, 10, 13, 24, 29, 36, 37, 47–49. *See also* sex work: coerced; *Sook Ching*; war crimes trials (Asia)

Kathigasu, Sybil, 95, 115–16, 138
Kempeitai, 101, 103, 117
King's African Rifles, 189–92, 199–200, 201, 298n68
Komagata Maru, 17–18, 20, 22, 45
Kuomintang (KMT), 56, 59, 61, 65, 175

labor activism, 14, 18, 56, 60, 61, 64–65, 78, 157, 175, 212, 213
Lai Teck, 160–61, 175
Lim Bo Seng, 160–61

Malay States Guides (MSG), 17, 18–22, 24, 25, 26, 27, 32, 37–38, 39, 40
Malayan Communist Party (MCP), 61, 63, 64, 80, 155, 156, 160, 169, 173, 175,

192, 212, 213, 219, 245, 247. *See also* communism
Malayan People's Anti-Japanese Army (MPAJA), 143, 155, 160, 161–62, 163, 172, 174–75, 216, 287n126
Malayan Emergency, 1–2, 4, 7, 11–12, 172, 173–43; participation of international troops in, 2, 11–12, 176–77, 183, 184–202; women and, 197–201, 203–43; U.S. militarism and influence of, 2, 12, 180, 244, 248, 249. *See also* communism; hearts and minds
Maori, 179, 192–97, 198, 202
martial races, 5–6, 197, 254n28; ANZAC soldiers and, 193, 202; askari and, 188, 191, 192; Indian Army and, 5–6, 14, 32, 38; influence on Malaya and Singapore of, 62, 197, 202; loss of prestige for, 142–44, 149, 154, 171; postwar revitalization of, 176, 180, 206; Nepali "Gurkhas" and, 184, 196; Maori soldiers and, 192–97

Nepalis, recruited as "Gurkhas," Malayan Emergency and, 2, 8, 11–12, 179, 183, 184–88, 189, 190, 191, 196, 198, 200, 201, 202, 207, 238, 241, 249; Second World War and, 91–92, 106, 145, 154, 162, 174. *See also* martial races
New Villages, 7, 176, 183, 205, 234–37; forced resettlement in, 178, 205, 210, 226, 241, 242, 290n34; sexual harassment in, 225, 236–37
New Zealand, race relations and, 3, 201; Malayan Emergency and troops from, 173, 183, 192–97, 219

Percival, Arthur, 94, 164, 165, 167, 169
police, 5, 6, 10, 11, 14, 57–59, 60, 61, 93, 96, 99, 178, 179, 183, 202; communism and, 63–64, 180, 192, 205, 224, 235, 236, 239, 241–42; labor activism and, 64–65; Japanese occupation and, 108, 112, 143, 160, 165, 183; postwar reprisals and,

STANFORD BRITISH HISTORIES

Priya Satia, Series Editor

Stanford British Histories publishes new works of scholarship that expand our understanding of British culture, society, and power from regional to global scales. This series highlights histories of Britain and its empire that attend to the roles of institutions, systemic forces, and global historical forces such as capitalism, imperialism, and globalization, but that also recognize and value individual agency and lived experience. The series aims to bridge the early modern/late modern divide, and is particularly interested in projects that prioritize the voices of historical subjects who have previously been elided, including imperial subjects, the working classes, and other marginalized groups. At the same time, books in the series take seriously the material impact of institutions such as the military and imperial administration. Topics of interest include, but are not limited to, histories of ecology and the environment; military history and the history of war; violence and resistance; infrastructure and resource extraction; foodways and human-animal studies; histories of economic life; education; science, medicine, information, intelligence, technology, and knowledge production; intellectual history and the history of political movements; and the history of gender, race, and class.

Printed in the USA
CPSIA information can be obtained
at www.ICGtesting.com
JSHW080611170524
63176JS00005B/6

9 781503 639850